Twentieth Century Limited

America: World War Two to the Present

Houghton Mifflin Company

Boston

Dallas   Geneva, Illinois   Hopewell, New Jersey

Palo Alto   London

Twentieth Century Limited

Volume II ∾ America: World War Two to the Present

David W. Noble

University of Minnesota

David A. Horowitz

Portland State University

Peter N. Carroll

∾

Art Credits

Dedication

To Maggie Kuhn and the Gray Panthers, whose struggle for the rights and dignity of older Americans is helping to create a vision of the future in which the young can free themselves from traditions of self-interest and competition and come to celebrate traditions of community and cooperation.

Contents

Preface / xi

Acknowledgments / xiii

Chapter 10
World War Two / 273

The Open Door / 274
Isolationism / 275
Neutrality, 1939–1941 / 280
The Road to Pearl Harbor / 282
The Grand Alliance / 285
Mobilization for Victory / 287

The Home Front / 294
Politics in Wartime / 296
Domestic Conflict / 298
Truman and Truce / 303
Suggested Readings / 304
SPOTLIGHT: *The Nuremberg Trials* / 307

Chapter 11
Postwar Society, 1945–1960 / 313

Science and Society / 314
Business Reconversion / 317
Population Mobility / 319

Housing Shortage and Suburban
Development / 320

Residential Segregation / 322

Rootlessness and Rootedness / 323

Corporate Economy / 325

Consumer Spending / 327

Labor Unions and Economic Stability / 329

Poverty and Social Class / 331

Women and the Work Force / 332

Family Relations / 334

Youth Culture / 336

Public Education and Educational
Goals / 336

Educational Segregation / 338

Sports, Entertainment, Sexuality / 339

Alternative Voices / 342

Suggested Readings / 343

Chapter 12
The Truman Administration,
1945–1952 / 345

The Problems of Reconversion / 346

Postwar Foreign Policy / 348

The Cold War / 351

The Truman Doctrine / 354

Mobilizing a Domestic Consensus / 359

Truman and Military Crisis / 360

The Election of 1948 / 363

The Fair Deal / 366

A Bipartisan Foreign Policy / 368

McCarthy and Subversion / 370

The Korean War / 371

Suggested Readings / 377

SPOTLIGHT: The Case of Ethel and Julius
Rosenberg / 379

Chapter 13
The Eisenhower Administration,
1952–1960 / 385

The Election of 1952 / 385

Waging the Cold War / 389

Secret Foreign Policy / 394

Domestic Conservatism / 396

The Anti-Communist Crusade / 397

The Politics of Consensus / 402

Foreign Policy in Asia / 403

European Diplomacy / 407

Crises in the Middle East / 409

The Politics of Moderation / 410

Domestic Debate / 412

Presidential Diplomacy / 415

Suggested Readings / 418

Chapter 14
The Kennedy Years, 1960–1963 / 419

Kennedy versus Nixon / 420

The Kennedy Presidency / 423

New Frontiers / 425

Counter-Insurgency in Southeast Asia / 428

Kennedy and Khrushchev / 432

The Cuban Missile Crisis / 434

Toward Detente / 435

Politics and the Domestic Economy / 437

The Civil Rights Crisis / 442

Radical Politics / 445

Suggested Readings / 447

SPOTLIGHT: *The Kennedy Assassination* / 449

Chapter 15
The Lost Consensus, 1964–1968 / 455

Kennedy Legacy / 455

The Landslide of '64 / 457

Racial Turmoil in the Cities / 461

Corporate Wealth and Empire / 463

Vietnam / 466

The War at Home / 472

The Chaos of '68 / 477

Suggested Readings / 480

Chapter 16
Fragmentation of American Society, 1960–1980 / 483

The Crisis of Adolescence / 483

Woodstock Nation and the New Adolescence / 485

Antiwar Protest and a New Left / 489

Black and White Radicals / 490

Black Power and Afro-American Culture / 498

Chicano Culture and Activism / 499

Native American Culture and Militance / 502

Ecology and the Limited Frontier / 504

Women's Liberation / 506

Gay Liberation / 508

Middle America and Moral Crisis / 510

The New Age / 513

Suggested Readings / 515

Chapter 17
The Search for Authority, 1968–1980 / 517

Nixonian Social Management / 517

The Revival of Social Conservatism / 520

Detente and Escalation / 522

The Failure of National Unity / 525

Watergate and Political Repression / 530

Nixon's Re-Election / 533

The Watergate Coverup and Nixon's
Fall / 537

Ford and Carter / 540

Suggested Readings / 545

SPOTLIGHT: *The Meaning of Watergate* / 547

Index / 553

Preface

The history of the United States in the twentieth century is usually told from the perspective of the government in Washington, D.C. Such a focus leads most history books to stress the role of the nation's political leaders — the politicians and Cabinet members who wield power in Congress, enact legislation, and shape foreign policy. Yet these political leaders constitute a limited segment of American society. For the most part, national politicians have been white males with Anglo-Protestant cultural roots, and often they have been relatively wealthy.

A historical perspective that focuses on Washington politicians, therefore, tends to ignore the existence of social groups that have not participated in — or have been denied access to — political power: racial and ethnic minorities, women, and poor people in general. To correct this imbalance, *Twentieth Century Limited* not only examines the history of the political leaders, but also explores the historical role of non-leadership groups. Many of these political outsiders shared the attitudes and values of the leadership groups. But many did not. This book attempts to explain the differences as well as similarities among various social groups.

In presenting a pluralistic history of the United States, we emphasize the relationships among the nation's leaders and the other social groups, thereby trying to avoid the "tunnel-vision" view that treats minority cultures as exclusive entities. We examine the areas of society in which dominant groups have dramatically influenced the lives of minority Americans. But we are also aware of aspects of minority culture that have been resistant to the influence of the leadership groups. Moreover, we take into account those aspects of society that reflect the influence of cultural minorities on the dominant groups.

By examining the pluralistic history of the American people, we emphasize the importance of human choice in shaping major historical patterns. Many textbooks explain such broad issues as urbanization, industrialization, and overseas expansion as the result of mysterious, impersonal forces. By contrast, we try to explain how specific decisions have created the structure and texture of American society.

This book traces the rise of a corporate bureaucratic culture that supplanted an earlier, more individualistic society based on small businesses and farms. This transformation of American society also involved a broader acceptance of "liberal-rational" values that promised progress, efficiency, and order. As a result, Americans of the twentieth century have placed great confidence in the ability of educated experts to solve social, economic, and political problems. Increasingly, Americans have looked to professionals who frequently have had government backing and have seemed to offer unlimited vistas of prosperity and expansion.

In recent years, however, Americans have become increasingly aware of the limits of corporate society. The failures of American foreign policy since World War Two, the crisis of energy resources, the threat of ecological disaster, the decline of voter participation, the increasing difficulty of social mobility, and the growing disparity of personal wealth — all reinforce a sense of limits. These problems sometimes appear to be new. But *Twentieth Century Limited,* as its title implies, demonstrates that the crises of the sixties, seventies, and eighties have historical roots that both are obvious and offer the possibility of resolution.

Besides the textual material, this book includes in each chapter a biographical sketch of a significant though often ignored American whose life illuminates a specific historical issue and a list of additional reading for students who wish to embark on further research. We have also written four special sections, or spotlights, that feature a particularly significant or controversial issue. These essays are designed to spark student debate and curiosity.

David W. Noble
David A. Horowitz
Peter N. Carroll

Acknowledgments

In preparing this book, we have benefited from a variety of institutional aids, colleagues, friends, and family.

David Noble acknowledges the invaluable assistance of Lois Noble in editing and typing the manuscript.

David Horowitz appreciates the financial and clerical assistance provided by the department of history, the college of social science, and the office of graduate studies and research at Portland State University. Gerry Foote and Joni Ueland provided valuable assistance in assembling research materials. Dorothy Childester did a superb performance under the pressure of typing deadlines. The author is also grateful to Michael Horowitz for galley proofreading and generous moral support, and to Charlene Lowry Horowitz, whose patience and understanding enabled him to survive the completion of this task.

Peter Carroll extends thanks to Lorraine Whittemore of the San Francisco State faculty manuscript service. Leo Ribuffo added wit, criticism, and sturdy advice, though not necessarily in that order. Jeannette Ferrary shared fully in this enterprise, smoothing the rough points, intensifying the satisfactions.

All three authors wish to thank the following reviewers, who contributed to the development of the manuscript: Allen F. Davis, Temple University; J. Carroll Moody, Northern Illinois University; and Robert C. Twombly, City University of New York.

Twentieth Century Limited

America: World War Two to the Present

Chapter 10

WORLD WAR TWO

President Franklin Delano Roosevelt was a master of the media. He thoroughly enjoyed his frequent meetings with the press — by 1945 he had held 998 press conferences — and he relied on his verbal skill and quick wit to win media support for his policies. But Roosevelt's easy style could be deceptive, perhaps deliberately so. After the outbreak of World War Two on September 1, 1939, Roosevelt's public messages increasingly focused on questions of foreign policy. The president repeatedly assured a worried public that the American people were the "best informed" in the world. Yet on December 7, 1941, most Americans were shocked to learn that Japanese aircraft had executed a surprise attack on the United States naval base at Pearl Harbor, Hawaii.

The shock of Pearl Harbor, besides affirming the skill of the Japanese plans, also stemmed

directly from Roosevelt's lack of candor about the changing implications of his foreign policy. Though Roosevelt openly admitted his growing commitment to what he called the "democracies" of the world, he continued to insist that his policies were designed to keep the United States out of war. While campaigning in Boston for an unprecedented third term in 1940, Roosevelt won ringing applause when he announced: "Your boys are not going to be sent into any foreign wars." The president assumed — though he chose not to mention it — that an attack on the United States would not be a "foreign" war.

Such duplicity partly reflected the pressure of electoral politics. In Roosevelt's case, it illuminated the president's pragmatic approach to difficult policy questions, his reluctance to be pinned down to a course of action. This type of leadership also revealed the limitations imposed by the historical position of the United States. Roosevelt's options were limited not only by his personality, but also by the interests and values of the nation that were beyond his control. His approach to foreign affairs depended heavily on the attitudes of Congress and the general public. In a radio broadcast on September 3, 1939, Roosevelt announced that the United States would remain "a neutral nation." But unlike President Wilson during World War One, he added, "I cannot ask that every American remain neutral in thought as well. Even a neutral has a right to take account of facts. Even a neutral cannot be asked to close his mind or his conscience."

THE OPEN DOOR

When he came to office in 1933, Roosevelt inherited a foreign policy based on economic expansion and political isolationism. The defeat of the Versailles Treaty and the League of Nations in 1919–1920 had committed the United States to a policy of independent action. Even Roosevelt, who had supported Wilson's internationalism and had endorsed the league in his vice presidential campaign of 1920, moved away from the principle of international cooperation. But though the State Department preferred the idealized rhetoric of the Kellogg-Briand Pact of 1928, which "outlawed" aggressive warfare, American business interests remained vitally concerned with questions of international markets and foreign trade. In Asia, particularly in China, these economic concerns translated into a continuation of the Open Door policy, by which the United States advocated free trade for all nations in place of spheres of influence.

This commitment to the Open Door brought the United States into conflict with Japan and provided the background for the events that ultimately led to Pearl Harbor. At the Washington Arms Conference of 1921–1922, the United States persuaded Japan to agree to the Nine Power Pact, which formalized the Open Door in China. In this treaty Japan agreed to restore to China sovereignty of the Shantung peninsula and promised to remove Japanese soldiers stationed in southern Siberia since World War One. Japanese troops, however, remained in other parts of China. These agreements failed to consider the interests and sentiments of Chinese nationalists, who continued to oppose any foreign exploitation of their country. In 1929, for example, the Chinese Kuomintang, led by Chiang Kai-shek, seized Russian holdings in northern Manchuria, which led to an undeclared war.

Faced with strong Soviet competition in Manchuria as well as threats from Chinese nationalists, Japanese military leaders stationed in southern Manchuria took matters into their own hands. In September 1931 the Japanese army attacked Manchuria, defeated weak Chinese resistance, and by January 1932 converted the province, renamed Manchuko, into a Japanese protectorate. This assertion of Japanese power threatened American access to Chinese raw materials and markets and consequently violated the principles of the Open Door. But President Hoover, preoccupied by the problems of the Depression and reluctant to seek military confrontation, offered no counter-policy. Hoover also rebuffed suggestions that the United States cooperate with the league in exerting economic pressure on Japan.

Hoover's secretary of state, Henry L. Stimson, advocated a firmer response. With the president's approval, he sent a public letter to China and Japan in 1932 that became known as the Stimson Doctrine. In this letter Stimson reaffirmed the United States's commitment to the Open Door and refused to recognize the puppet government of Manchuko. Great Britain and France, like Hoover, were also reluctant to challenge Japan, and so the league merely adopted the American policy of nonrecognition. The Japanese responded to these rhetorical attacks by withdrawing from the league in February 1933, one month before Roosevelt's inauguration.

ISOLATIONISM

As Roosevelt took office in March 1933, Germany also chose a new leader, Adolf Hitler. Like Roosevelt, Hitler promised to end the Depression. His program of national socialism, however, aggravated differences with the United States. To offset a severe slump in German international trade, the German government subsidized German corporations to make them more competitive. These policies, by discriminating against American business, attacked the principles of the Open Door. The conflict of national economic interest prevented the two nations from signing a new commercial agreement in 1935. At the same time, the United States refused to extend the Open Door to Latin America. When German investors tried to penetrate the Western Hemisphere, the Roosevelt administration responded by offering better terms to preserve the United States's

dominance in its own sphere of influence. In 1938, for example, the United States underbid Germany for training of Latin American armies.

This economic competition was exaggerated by fundamental political differences. Hitler's Nazi party pursued an aggressive anti-Jewish program that offended American public opinion. Hitler also threatened the international order by demanding a revision of the Versailles Treaty to restore Germany as a world power. In 1933 the German leader attended the Geneva World Disarmament Conference and insisted on German military equality. When France refused, Germany withdrew from the conference and then from the league in October 1933. The next year, Hitler announced a program of German rearmament in violation of Versailles. While Hitler defied the league powers, the Italian Fascist leader, Benito Mussolini, sought glory and conquest in Ethiopia, using a clash between Italian and Ethiopian troops at a desert oasis in December 1934 as an excuse to make demands for an indemnity. When Emperor Haile Selassie refused, Mussolini prepared for war. As the arms race exploded in Europe, Japan went to the London Naval Conference of 1935 to demand revision of the Washington agreement in order to acquire naval equality. When Great Britain and the United States rejected the request, Japan withdrew from the session and announced it would increase its navy anyway.

These militaristic rumblings reinforced isolationist feelings in the United States. Since the disillusionment of World War One, Americans were suspicious of involvement in foreign affairs. Most congressmen, as well as their constituents, believed that the United States could preserve its unique institutions only by limiting foreign entanglements. These assumptions were supported by a growing belief that the United States had been tricked into participation in World War One. In 1934 a Senate investigating committee, headed by Gerald P. Nye of North Dakota, held a series of public hearings that revealed huge wartime profiteering by munitions manufacturers and bankers and implied close connections between the armaments industry and American policy making. The idea that American businessmen had lured the country into war was the thesis of a 1935 Book-of-the-Month Club selection, *Road to War: America, 1914–1917* by Walter Millis.

These exposures of the "merchants of death," though greatly exaggerated at the time, had important implications for American foreign policy. As early as 1933 the Senate Foreign Relations Committee, led by staunch isolationists, rejected an administration proposal that would have given the president power to stop the trade of arms with selected aggressor nations. When the committee substituted an amendment requiring an arms embargo against all belligerents in any war, Roosevelt reluctantly killed the entire bill. But because war seemed imminent in Europe and as the Nye committee released its findings, the isolationist Congress became less satisfied with Roosevelt's deliberate vagueness. Besides fearing another war, many conservatives in Congress opposed the increase of executive power by allowing the president to determine embargo policies. Over the objections of Roosevelt, therefore, Congress enacted the Neutrality Act of 1935, which required the president to establish an arms embargo against all belligerents and authorized the notification of American citizens that they sailed on belligerent vessels at their own risk. These provisions attempted to eliminate the issues that

had led to American entry in World War One. But the law left little room for the administration to pursue a creative foreign policy to protect the national interest. In signing the measure, Roosevelt warned that its "inflexible provisions might drag us into war instead of keeping us out."

Five weeks after the passage of the Neutrality Act, Mussolini invaded Ethiopia. Though the league declared Italy the aggressor and voted to impose mild economic sanctions, Britain and France refused to challenge Mussolini and continued their policy of appeasement. Roosevelt, however, used the provisions of the Neutrality Act to call for a "moral embargo" on the shipment of oil to Italy and managed to limit the export of other war materiel. Such gestures, in the absence of collective action, could not prevent the conquest of Ethiopia. Mussolini then withdrew from the league and signed a treaty of alliance with Hitler in October 1936.

As Europe seemed to move closer to war, Congress moved closer to isolation. In February 1936 Roosevelt tried to add a discretionary clause to the Neutrality Act that would have allowed the United States to support certain belligerents. But in the face of stiff opposition, the administration settled for an extension of the old policy. In March German armies moved into the Rhineland in violation of the Versailles Treaty. Britain and France froze in fear. The United States, not even a signer of the treaty, did nothing. The 1936 Democratic party platform reaffirmed the principles of neutrality. Roosevelt, in his only foreign policy speech of the campaign, assured Americans, "We shun political commitments which might entangle us in foreign war; we avoid connection with the political activities of the League of Nations. . . .

We are not isolationists except insofar as we seek to isolate ourselves completely from war."

The decision to remain uninvolved in European political affairs shaped Roosevelt's response to the Spanish civil war. In July 1936 a right-wing coalition led by the Fascist General Francisco Franco rebelled against the republican government. Despite claims of neutrality, Hitler and Mussolini provided crucial military support for Franco, including the air forces responsible for the first major bombing of civilians at Guernica in 1937. Meanwhile, the Soviet Union sent supplies to the republic (Loyalists). Britain and France, fearful that the war might spread and doubly fearful that a Loyalist victory might lead to a socialist government, formed a Nonintervention Committee to halt all arms shipments to Spain. Since Germany, Italy, and the Soviet Union ignored this policy, its main effect was to deny supplies to the legally constituted republic.

In the United States, the Spanish civil war polarized public opinion. Members of the American Left, ranging from New Deal liberals to Communists, saw Spain as a moral battleground between the forces of democracy and the legions of fascism. Besides organizing mass rallies to support the republic, several thousand men formed the Abraham Lincoln Battalion to fight in Spain. Conservatives and Catholics, however, saw Franco as a defender of traditional social order, especially the Catholic church. For them, Franco was a barrier against world revolution and atheism. Though Gallup polls indicated that pro-Loyalist sentiment greatly exceeded pro-Franco support, Roosevelt feared alienating the Catholic electorate or supporting a pro-Communist Spanish regime. Stating that a civil war could be treated

the same as an international war, he imposed a "moral" embargo on the shipment of arms to either side. In 1937 Congress extended the Neutrality Act to Spain. Neither Congress nor Roosevelt viewed the survival of the Spanish Republic as vital to American national interest or security.

Most Americans believed that neutrality legislation would avoid involvement in another European war. But there was still a risk that the United States might also have to surrender its foreign trade in nonmilitary goods to avoid direct conflict. The loss of such trade, however, would undermine economic recovery at home. To solve this problem, presidential adviser Bernard M. Baruch suggested a revision of the Neutrality Act on the principle of "cash and carry." As enacted by Congress in 1937, the cash-and-carry formula permitted the sale of nonmilitary products to nations at war. But belligerents had to pay cash (to avoid the debt entanglements associated with American entry in World War One). The goods also had to be transported in non-American ships (to avoid the problem of neutral rights on the high seas). Cash and carry favored nations with strong navies and large cash reserves. Roosevelt understood that Britain and France, not Germany, would benefit by the law's provisions. The Neutrality Act of 1937 also continued the mandatory embargo on arms sales to all belligerents.

While Congress worked to perfect neutrality legislation, decisions made in other capitals undermined the possibility of implementing strict neutrality. In July 1937 Japan moved to extend its control of the Asian mainland by attacking the northern provinces of China. The Japanese promised to create an East Asia Coprosperity Program that would exclude other nations from Chinese markets and resources. Such a sphere

MAP 10.1   JAPANESE EXPANSION, 1937–1942

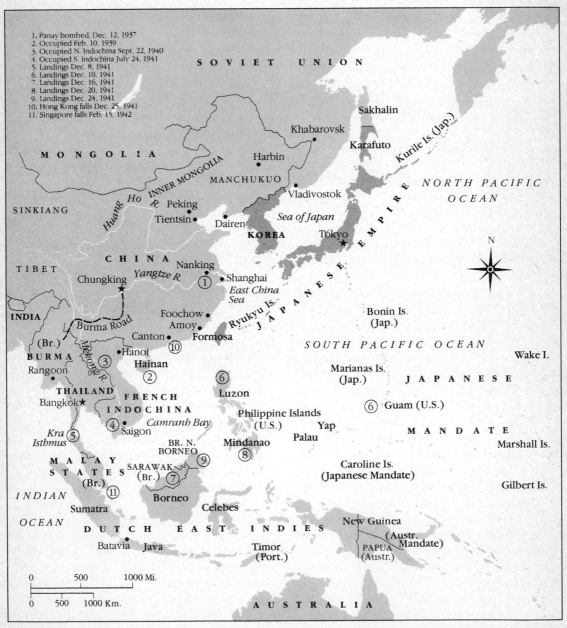

1. Panay bombed, Dec. 12, 1937
2. Occupied Feb. 10, 1939
3. Occupied N. Indochina Sept. 22, 1940
4. Occupied S. Indochina July 24, 1941
5. Landings Dec. 8, 1941
6. Landings Dec. 10, 1941
7. Landings Dec. 16, 1941
8. Landings Dec. 20, 1941
9. Landings Dec. 24, 1941
10. Hong Kong falls Dec. 25, 1941
11. Singapore falls Feb. 15, 1942

From The Growth of American Foreign Policy *by Richard W. Leopold. Copyright © 1962, by Richard W. Leopold, reprinted by permission of Alfred A. Knopf Inc.*

of influence paralleled Nazi expansion in central Europe, Britain's control of her Commonwealth nations, and United States dominance of Latin America and the Philippines. But from the American perspective, Japan's denial of the Open Door threatened not only current business but also American aspirations to develop trade with China as a long-term solution to economic depression. To protect American interests, Roosevelt decided to by-pass the Neutrality Act of 1937 and support China simply by refusing to acknowledge that a state of war existed. Without invoking cash and carry, Roosevelt could allow American ships to continue to trade with China.

Such technicalities did not alleviate Roosevelt's concern about Japanese expansion nor did it remove his fears about the cementing of a Berlin-Rome-Tokyo alliance. To counteract the prevailing isolationism in the United States, Roosevelt spoke out in October 1937 against the "epidemic of world lawlessness." "War is a contagion," he warned. "We are determined to keep out of war, yet we cannot insure ourselves against the disastrous effects of war and the dangers of involvement." Asserting that neutrality would "minimize our involvement," the president admitted "we cannot have complete protection in a world of disorder." Roosevelt offered no solutions to the predicament — he had none to make — except to propose a vaguely defined "quarantine" against aggressor nations. The liberal press greeted Roosevelt's speech with enthusiasm. But the isolationists, scrupulous about any international commitments, even amorphous "quarantines," condemned the address and forced the president to reconsider any alterations of policy.

When Japanese planes attacked the United States gunboat *Panay* on the Yangtze River in December 1937, Roosevelt accepted a Japanese apology and promise of indemnity. Despite mild public indignation, the president dared go no further. The strength of isolationism could be seen in the popularity of a constitutional amendment, sponsored by Representative Louis Ludlow of Indiana, to require a popular referendum before Congress could exercise its power to declare war. Only after intense pressure from the administration did the House of Representatives reject the measure — by a narrow 209–188 vote.

The blandness of American foreign policy paralleled the impotence of Britain and France. In March 1938 the two nations allowed Hitler to take over Austria. Six months later they refused to stand up to Germany when Hitler demanded the Sudeten province of Czechoslovakia, which was inhabited by a minority of Germans. At the Munich Conference of September 1938, Britain and France forced Czechoslovakia to concede German demands. When Prime Minister Neville Chamberlain returned to England bearing "peace in our times," Roosevelt telegraphed his congratulations. After seizing the Sudeten, however, Hitler remained unsatisfied. In March 1939 German soldiers occupied the rest of Czechoslovakia, and in April Hitler began to threaten Poland. Britain and France now realized that appeasement had failed and they pledged to defend Poland from German aggression. The Soviet Union remained suspicious of British and French intentions, fearful that the Western allies would be quite content to see Nazis and Communists engaged in mortal conflict. Hitler was equally afraid of a two-front war and, to protect his eastern flank, he signed a nonaggression pact with Soviet leader Josef Stalin in August 1939. Then, on September 1, Germany moved against Poland. Two days later Britain and France declared war on Germany.

NEUTRALITY, 1939–1941

The outbreak of World War Two intensified the contradictions in Roosevelt's foreign policy —his desire to see Hitler defeated and his commitment to keep the United States out of war. To reconcile these divergent interests, Roosevelt emphasized that support of the Allies, while preserving the letter of American neutrality, would protect the United States from foreign aggression without embroiling the nation in war. Accordingly, Roosevelt called Congress into special session in September 1939 to repeal the arms embargo.

The summons produced a bitter debate between isolationists and internationalists. Charles Lindbergh, the popular aviator, and ex-President Hoover broadcast fervent appeals to the public, urging a continuation of the isolationist policy. In response, interventionists formed a Nonpartisan Committee for Peace Through Revision of the Neutrality Act, headed by the prestigious Republican journalist William Allen White, which sponsored radio addresses and grassroots protests to repeal the embargo. In the end, the issue hinged on congressional votes — and, because of powerful public pressure, the interventionists obtained them. The revised Neutrality Act of 1939 still prohibited American vessels from entering the war zones. But it revised the old law to permit belligerents to purchase military supplies on a cash-and-carry basis. "We are trying to keep out of war," insisted an administration supporter in Congress, "not to get closer into it." But the law clearly placed the United States in the Allied camp.

German threats to American interests became clearer in the spring of 1940 when Hitler launched a military campaign against Scandinavia, the Low Countries, and France. As German troops blitzed toward Paris, Roosevelt warned the public against "the illusion that we are remote and isolated." He now asked Congress for a multibillion dollar defense appropriation and, despite isolationist objections, obtained its passage. To encourage the administration, internationalists, led by William Allen White and Clark Eichelberger, formed the Committee to Defend America by Aiding the Allies, a grassroots pressure group that claimed nearly one million members by October. Meanwhile, Roosevelt moved to undercut Republican opposition in foreign policy matters by appointing two leading Republicans to his cabinet: Stimson as secretary of war and Frank Knox, Landon's running mate, as secretary of the navy. The fall of France in June 1940 further undermined the isolationists. Public opinion polls showed a dramatic decline of isolationist sentiment and a rising commitment to support Britain. But 82 percent of the people polled still drew the line at American intervention in the war. Like Roosevelt, they believed that military assistance would enable Britain to defeat Germany.

During the summer of 1940, however, the British military situation became more perilous as German planes bombed English cities and German submarines sank vital English shipping. Prime Minister Winston Churchill pleaded for American naval assistance. Roosevelt, in an unusual exercise of presidential power, agreed to trade fifty overage destroyers for British bases in the Western Hemisphere and a promise that Britain would never surrender its fleet to Germany. In announcing the deal, Roosevelt stressed its nonintervention features. "This is the most important action in the reinforcement of our national defense that has been taken since the Louisiana Purchase," he claimed. But even that, Roosevelt suggested, might not be enough. In September 1940 Congress increased military appropriations and also enacted the first peacetime conscription law in American history.

Despite considerable opposition to Roosevelt's foreign policy, the president managed to minimize its importance in the 1940 presidential election. The Republican candidate, Wendell Willkie, an acknowledged internationalist, endorsed the destroyers-for-bases agreement and supported conscription. Both nominees made assurances that they opposed American entry into the war. After the election Roosevelt continued to make a distinction between military assistance for Britain and an outright alliance against Germany.

Roosevelt returned to the airwaves in December 1940 for what he considered his most important public address since the early days of the New Deal. Stressing the importance of a British victory for American "national security," Roosevelt declared that the United States must become "the great arsenal of democracy." In his state of the union address of January 1941, the president continued to lead the nation away from a policy of strict neutrality, condemning the "so-called new order of tyranny which the dictators seek to create with the crash of a bomb." Roosevelt now pleaded for the protection and expansion of the "Four Freedoms"—the freedom of speech and expression, the freedom of religion, the freedom from want, and the freedom from fear.

But with Britain running out of capital resources and the United States forbidden under the neutrality laws to extend credit, Britain could not obtain sufficient supplies to stop the Germans. Roosevelt moved, as he put it, to "eliminate the dollar sign." If your neighbor's house was on fire, Roosevelt explained to reporters, it would be prudent to lend him an old garden hose to put out the fire before it spread to your house. Afterward the neighbor would return the hose or, if it had been damaged, replace it. Such was the logic of the Lend-Lease Act of March 1941, by which Congress authorized the expenditure of $7 billion to keep supplies flowing to Britain and its allies.

Lend-Lease finally destroyed the fiction of American neutrality, though most Americans still hoped to keep out of the fighting. But Lend-Lease could be effective only if American goods actually crossed the North Atlantic. By the spring of 1941, German submarines, operating in wolf packs, were sinking 500,000 tons of Allied shipping a month. In the face of negative public opinion, Roosevelt declined to establish naval convoys to escort Lend-Lease materiel. Instead he devised a new fiction, the idea of "hemispheric defense," which extended a neutrality zone halfway across the Atlantic, almost to Iceland, and ordered the navy to patrol this area to report the presence of "aggressor ships or planes" to the British navy. Roosevelt also signed an executive agreement with the Danish government in exile that allowed the United States to establish bases in Greenland.

Roosevelt's willingness to play loosely with the language of neutrality infuriated his opponents. When Hitler invaded the Soviet Union in June 1941, Roosevelt extended Lend-Lease to Britain's new ally. The decision prompted isolationist outrage. Charles Lindbergh announced that he preferred an alliance with Germany "with all her faults" rather than one "with the cruelty, Godlessness, and the barbarism that exist in the Soviet Union." Even Senator Harry S Truman questioned Roosevelt's motives. "If we see that Germany is winning the war we ought to help Russia," he explained; "if Russia is winning we ought to help Germany and that way let them kill as many as possible." Hitler, however, offered no such options. In May 1941 German submarines sank an American ship that carried a cargo of military supplies. In July Roosevelt extended American convoys to Iceland, interfering with the effectiveness of German submarines. But in September the Germans attacked an American destroyer, *Greer*, which had been helping the British track it on radio. Roosevelt used the attack to condemn the German "rattlesnakes of the Atlantic," and he indicated a new policy that allowed American ships to shoot on sight German ships in the so-called neutral zone. But German submarines continued to attack American ships. In November Congress revised the Neutrality Act to permit the arming of merchant vessels and allow them to enter the war zone.

These decisions effectively terminated American neutrality. Though neither Congress nor the administration was prepared to declare war, it was only a matter of time before naval confrontations would create a crisis similar to that of 1917. Equally significant, the arming of merchant ships demonstrated that the United States saw no advantage to traditional peacetime diplomacy. Yet even at this point, Roosevelt backed away from further commitments. While setting the United States on a collision course, the president waited for Hitler to fire the first shot.

Hitler, however, was too involved with the European war and too afraid of American military potential to take up Roosevelt's challenge. But ironically the German invasion of the Soviet Union encouraged Japanese expansion in a direction that led to Pearl Harbor. Hitler did not intend that result; indeed, he opposed Japanese policies that were likely to draw the United States into the war. But Hitler no more controlled Japanese foreign policy than

did Roosevelt. It was the Japanese military leadership that maneuvered the United States into total war against Germany.

THE ROAD TO PEARL HARBOR

While the United States had protested the Japanese invasion of China and had advanced a $25-million loan to the Chinese resisters, private American business continued to sell crucial neutral resources to Japan. In July 1939, however, American policy makers decided to increase pressure on Japan by serving the required six-months' notice that the United States intended to cancel its 1911 commercial agreement. After January 1940, the United States was free to halt shipping to Japan, if it so desired. But Roosevelt and Secretary of State Cordell Hull were reluctant to create a crisis, especially because they viewed Germany as a greater threat to American interests.

The war in Europe nevertheless had important implications for Asia. When Hitler signed the nonaggression pact with Stalin in August 1939, the Japanese realized that the Soviet Union remained an important rival in northern China. But the German victories in western Europe offered tremendous alternative possibilities for Japan in Southeast Asia at the expense of France, the Netherlands, and Britain. Shortly after the fall of France, Japan forced the French to accept Japanese occupation of Indochina and persuaded Churchill to accept the closing of the Burma Road that was providing military assistance to Chiang Kai-shek's Chinese nationalists.

The United States responded to these advances by exercising its power to embargo crucial natural resources. In July 1940 the administration forbade the sale of aviation gasoline and high-grade scrap iron. The decision failed to prevent Japan from moving more troops into northern Indochina. In September the White House decided to tighten the economic screws by embargoing all iron and steel, but it continued to allow the export of certain petroleum products. By such gradual means the administration hoped to persuade Japan to reconsider its imperial expansion. Within a week, however, Japan signed a tripartite military assistance pact with Italy and Germany. Japan was hoping to neutralize American pressure by creating the possibility of a two-front war for the United States. But Roosevelt responded by adding more items to the embargo list.

These economic pressures led the Japanese to open diplomatic negotiations in the spring of 1941. The talks would continue through December. But neither the United States nor Japan was prepared to offer the significant concessions that would have made agreement possible. The conflict was symbolized by the Open Door and the Coprosperity Program. The United States was not prepared to accept the Japanese conquest of China or restore full trade with Japan; the Japanese were not prepared to withdraw from China or accept deprivation of crucial resources. In these terms war became inevitable when the United States first initiated economic sanctions against Japan.

While conversations between the State Department and the Japanese ambassador dragged on, the German invasion of the Soviet Union altered the Asian balance. Though Hitler pleaded with Japan to attack Siberia and expose the Soviet Union to a two-front war, the Japanese preferred to take advantage of the Soviet Union's predicament by avoiding direct conflict and moving southward into Malaya and the Dutch East Indies, both areas rich in

oil and rubber. The Japanese marched into southern Indochina in July 1941. Roosevelt responded by freezing Japanese assets in the United States. By limiting Japan's ability to purchase supplies, this decision assumed massive proportions.

The Japanese now faced a crucial choice. They could either abandon their plans for Asian expansion or attempt to seize vital oil supplies from the British and Dutch colonies. Given the militaristic values of the Japanese regime, the former alternative hardly existed. The Japanese also realized — and Roosevelt confirmed this to the British — that the United States would not tolerate an attack on British possessions in Asia. In other words, further Japanese expansion might mean war with the United States. Even by their own estimates, Japanese military leaders knew they could not defeat the United States at war. Yet faced with the alternative of humiliating surrender in 1941, that is what they chose.

On Sunday, December 7, 1941, the White House announced that Japanese forces had attacked the naval base at Pearl Harbor. Catching the base by complete surprise (it was 8 A.M. local time), the Japanese destroyed or damaged eight battleships, three cruisers, nearly two hundred planes, and vital shore installations and claimed nearly thirty-five hundred casualties, while sustaining minimal losses. The next day Roosevelt told a joint session of Congress that a state of war already existed, and promised to lead the American people to "absolute victory." Congress responded with a thundering ovation and then, with one dissenting vote by pacifist Representative Jeannette Rankin, voted for a formal declaration of war. Three days later Germany and Italy joined the Japanese by declaring war on the United States, and the same day, December 11, Congress responded

MAP 10.2   THE WESTERN EUROPEAN THEATER, 1942–1945

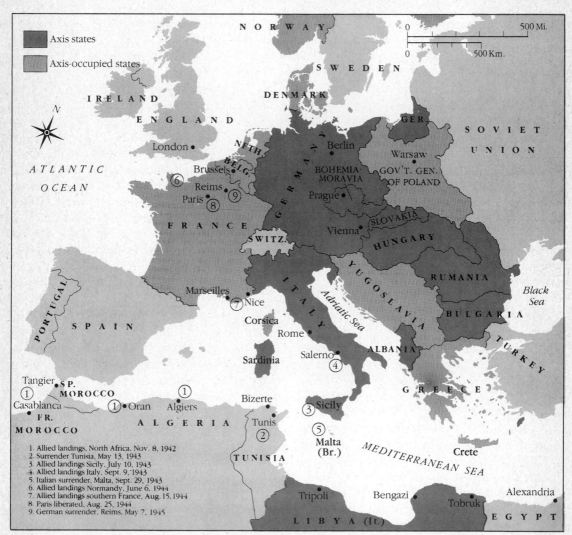

1. Allied landings, North Africa, Nov. 8, 1942
2. Surrender Tunisia, May 13, 1943
3. Allied landings Sicily, July 10, 1943
4. Allied landings Italy, Sept. 9, 1943
5. Italian surrender, Malta, Sept. 29, 1943
6. Allied landings Normandy, June 6, 1944
7. Allied landings southern France, Aug. 15, 1944
8. Paris liberated, Aug. 25, 1944
9. German surrender, Reims, May 7, 1945

From **The Growth of American Foreign Policy** *by Richard W. Leopold. Copyright © 1962, by Richard W. Leopold, reprinted by permission of Alfred A. Knopf Inc.*

in kind. After a decade of diplomatic maneuvering, the United States was again involved in global warfare.

THE GRAND ALLIANCE

The road to Pearl Harbor could be traced back to a fundamental conflict of national interests: the United States's Open Door policy and Japan's desire for a special sphere of influence in east Asia. A similar defense of national interest shaped Roosevelt's policies toward Europe and influenced his decision to wage a "Germany-first" strategy. In August 1941 Roosevelt and Churchill issued a document, known as the Atlantic Charter, that defined America's war goals. Besides disavowing any territorial benefits, the two leaders affirmed the right of all nations "on equal terms to the trade and to the raw materials of the world." In making the statement, Roosevelt attempted to forestall an agreement between Churchill and Stalin to divide Europe into special spheres of influence.

United States entry into the war eliminated some of the mutual distrust among the Allies. But each nation still recognized its own national interest as paramount. The Soviet Union, reeling under the German advance, desperately needed Allied assistance and hoped for the opening of a second front in western Europe. Stalin also wanted a postwar settlement that would protect the Soviet Union from any subsequent invasions from central Europe. Churchill's goals looked toward preserving the colonial empire, particularly Britain's trading advantages with the Commonwealth nations and in the Middle East. As an outspoken anticommunist, Churchill also feared a strong So-

viet presence in central Europe and wished to preserve Britain's status in Europe through postwar alliances with the United States and France. Roosevelt's goal, besides a quick defeat of Germany, was to replace European spheres of influence — whether British or Soviet — with the American Open Door.

These differing approaches had important effects on military strategy. While Stalin pleaded for a second front, Churchill persuaded Roosevelt, against the advice of American generals, to support an invasion of North Africa in 1942. This operation served to eliminate German threats to Middle East oil, protected Britain's Mediterranean shipping, and provided a base for the invasion of Italy. While German and Soviet armies hammered away at each other, Roosevelt and Churchill met at Casablanca in January 1943 and announced a policy of "unconditional surrender." Military advisers criticized the phrase because it might harden enemy opposition and undermine the possibility of a negotiated settlement. But Roosevelt was motivated as much by rhetoric as by a desire to demonstrate his sincerity to Stalin, despite the delay of the second front. The United States still hoped for Soviet intervention in the war against Japan.

With a second front still in question, however, Anglo-American forces invaded Sicily and Italy in the summer of 1943. Soon afterward, Mussolini fell from power and was replaced by Marshal Badoglio, who made a conditional surrender to the Allies in September 1943. In agreeing to negotiate with Badoglio, a conservative militarist, Anglo-American authorities recognized his importance as an anticommunist force in postwar Italy. To make this point clearer, the western Allies excluded the Soviet Union from the Allied Control Commission, answering Stalin's protests by arguing that the Red Army had not participated in the Italian campaign. This decision served as an important precedent for Soviet policy in eastern Europe.

While Soviet armies still bore the brunt of the war, the Big Three — Roosevelt, Churchill, and Stalin — met at Teheran in November 1943. At this meeting Churchill and Roosevelt agreed to open a second front in France in the spring, and Stalin promised to turn Soviet guns against Japan soon after the European war ended. They also agreed on a preliminary division of Germany into zones and accepted the idea of German reparations to compensate for war losses.

As the Allies prepared for the invasion of France, Anglo-American aircraft began "precision" bombing of the Continent, a policy that meant thousands of civilian deaths. Afterward the raids were found to be minimally effective, except insofar as they had the opposite result of strengthening enemy morale. The air war was more successful in destroying the German *luftwaffe*. Air supremacy was also crucial for the successful beachhead landings at Normandy on D Day, June 6, 1944. After tough fighting in northern France, the Allies moved eastward, racing to meet Soviet armies somewhere in Germany. The goal for both sides was Berlin.

As victory appeared imminent, the Big Three met at Yalta in February 1945 to resolve the unsettled questions of the war. Stalin repeated his promise to go to war against Japan after the defeat of Germany. Roosevelt and Churchill agreed to compensate the Soviets with the Kuerile Islands north of Japan as well as economic rights in Manchuria. The Allies also agreed to a temporary partition of Germany, including a three-way zoning of Berlin. But they failed to reach agreement about the amount of

German war reparations or a procedure for collection.

The main problem at Yalta, however, involved Poland — whose invasion had triggered World War Two more than five years before. To protect the Soviet Union's western boundary from future invasion, Stalin demanded recognition of the territory taken from Poland in 1939–1940. In compensation to Poland, Germany would surrender areas of eastern Prussia. Besides the question of boundaries was the problem of Poland's government. Stalin was determined to have a friendly government on his most vulnerable border, an idea that Roosevelt and Churchill accepted in principle. But the Polish government in exile in London was bitterly anticommunist, as apparently was the Polish underground. As an alternative to these two undesirable choices, Stalin established another government of communist Poles at Lublin. At Yalta the western Allies convinced Stalin to broaden the political base of the Lublin government by including some London Poles. They also persuaded Stalin to permit "free and unfettered elections" in Poland as soon as possible. But in Poland, as in Italy, the Allies did not have an equal stake, and Stalin was not yet ready to accept the Open Door in eastern Europe.

Though the Big Three made major international decisions without consulting all the affected nations, the rise of fascist aggression in the thirties convinced Roosevelt of the value of an international organization to oversee the peace. As a disillusioned Wilsonian, Roosevelt believed that collective security was meaningless without the consent of the great powers. Where Wilson had envisioned a league of all nations, Roosevelt suggested that Four Policemen — the United States, the Soviet Union,

Great Britain, and China — would function more effectively. The president also took pains to avoid Wilson's worst mistakes by consulting openly with members of the Senate Foreign Relations Committee. Public opinion strongly supported American leadership in a United Nations, one indication of which was the popularity of the film *Wilson* (1944), which emphasized the mistakes of 1919. Other influential internationalist works were two best sellers, Sumner Welles, *Time for Decision* (1944), and Walter Lippmann, *U.S. War Aims* (1944).

Plans for the United Nations were first drafted at the Dumbarton Oaks Conference in Washington in 1944. Reflecting Roosevelt's distrust of Wilsonian principles, the plan provided for a permanent Security Council that would be responsible for implementing U.N. policy. In the Security Council, the Big Four retained the power of veto. This principle, which differed greatly from the idea behind the League of Nations, helps to explain why even conservative Americans were willing to support the new international body. At Yalta Stalin raised the possibility of using the veto to prevent discussion of controversial matters, but Roosevelt and Churchill persuaded him that the veto should apply only to decision making. Stalin also asked for representation in the General Assembly for the Ukraine and White Russia. The British, with Commonwealth votes in their pocket, readily agreed, but Roosevelt balked — until Stalin pointed out that the United States was sponsoring ten Latin American nations that had not even joined the war.

The Yalta meeting confirmed April 25, 1945, as the opening of the United Nations conference at San Francisco. Roosevelt appointed a bipartisan delegation headed by his new secretary of state, Edward Stettinius. But the presi-

dent's lack of interest in the General Assembly led him to underestimate its importance in public opinion. The American people were shocked to learn that Roosevelt had consented to three votes for the Soviets, and many became convinced that an ailing Roosevelt had sold out American interests at Yalta. Roosevelt did not live to hear these complaints. He died of a cerebral hemorrhage on April 12.

MOBILIZATION FOR VICTORY

Though Roosevelt's declining health had been a matter of public speculation, his death stunned the nation. For twelve years he had provided confidence in government. During the wartime crisis his presence in the White House had helped to reduce the level of tension. News of Pearl Harbor had produced a mixture of fear and relief. No one who lived through the event ever forgot that peculiar feeling of catharsis. "The war came as a great relief, like a reverse earthquake," explained *Time* magazine. "Japanese bombs had finally brought national unity to the U.S." On December 8, 1941, sixty million Americans tuned in their radios to listen to Roosevelt's war message. That night air raid sirens in San Francisco, Los Angeles, and New York wailed false alarms that revealed a fundamental insecurity.

Despite the catastrophe at Pearl Harbor, the Japanese attack barely touched American military capacity. The key to military success rested on the nation's vast industrial potential. War mobilization involved the conversion of civilian industries to war-related activity, the creation of new plants, the harnessing of raw materials, and the organization of a work force to perform

Audie Murphy

1924-1971

The most decorated American soldier of World War Two was Audie Murphy. Not yet twenty-one at the war's end, Murphy was credited with killing 240 Germans and capturing dozens more in Italy and France, for which he earned the Congressional Medal of Honor as well as twenty-three other military decorations. His postwar autobiography, To Hell and Back (1948), graphically described the trauma and the bravery of the men who did the fighting. In 1955 it was made into a Hollywood film in which Murphy played himself.

Though nearly sixteen million men and women served in the armed services, only one in eight saw active combat duty. By comparison to the other belligerents, the United States's casualties were low; but nearly 300,000 died in action, and other casualties approached one million. From the perspective of the "GI"—a popular abbreviation of "general issue"—the war was a mixture of boredom and, in Murphy's words, "an endless series of problems involving blood and guts."

Murphy's popularity after the war reflected not only his outstanding battlefield achievements but also the cultural values he represented. He was one of eleven children of poor Texas sharecroppers. His father, a victim of the Depression Dust Bowl, abandoned the family, and his mother died soon after. For Audie Murphy the war offered an opportunity to escape from poverty and personal frustration. But at nineteen he was too skinny for the marines and paratroopers and he barely persuaded the infantry to accept him for front-line service.

Murphy's rise from small-town poverty to national heroism seemed to vindicate the traditional values of self-help and tough determination. Yet his youthful features evoked a simpler time of innocence and virtue. These *attributes enabled Murphy to forge a movie career in Hollywood. But with limited acting ability, he settled into dreary roles in westerns and war films.*

He died on the Memorial Day weekend in 1971 in an airplane crash. Murphy's obituary ironically appeared at a time when Americans were confronting a different type of war veteran — the "grunt" soldier of Vietnam — who, unlike GI Joe, was challenging the wisdom of the military leadership.

war-related jobs. One year after Pearl Harbor, the United States was producing more war materiel than were all its enemies combined.

Roosevelt had recognized the importance of preparing American industry for war as early as 1938. But, typical of his earlier New Deal strategy, he was reluctant to commit himself to any one plan or to delegate authority to a single commission. In 1939 he appointed a War Resources Board to study the problem of military conversion, but in the face of anti-intervention public opinion, he decided to ignore its report. After the fall of France in May 1940, Roosevelt became more resolute, asking Congress for large military appropriations and establishing an Advisory Commission for National Defense. As new problems emerged, Roosevelt reacted by creating new bureaucracies: the Office of Production Management (OPM) replaced the Advisory Commission; the Office of Price Administration (OPA) supervised price controls; the Supply Priorities and Allocations Board (SPAB) dealt with the problems of conversion. Despite considerable administrative confusion, these agencies started the economy moving toward a wartime basis. During 1941 arms production increased by 225 percent.

After Pearl Harbor Roosevelt stressed the importance of even greater production, calling in 1942 for sixty thousand planes, twenty-five thousand tanks, and eight million tons of shipping, and for higher outputs in 1943. To tighten government control of the war industries, he also created the War Production Board (WPB), headed by Donald Nelson of Sears, Roebuck. But when Nelson proved ineffective, Roosevelt moved again, creating the Office of War Mobilization (OWM) in 1943 under the supervision of former Supreme Court Justice James F. Byrnes. These agencies, besides overseeing the division between civilian and military production, set production goals and established priorities for the allocation of scarce resources. Other crucial administrative decisions involved coordinating supplies for American military needs and those of Lend-Lease. By the war's end, nearly $50 billion worth of Lend-Lease material was shipped to the Allies (60 percent to Britain; 20 percent to the Soviet Union; the rest to other nations).

In developing a war economy, an early problem was convincing private business to make the necessary adjustments. After nearly a decade of Depression, manufacturers were cautious about building new plants and shifting to military production. Many feared that conversion would lead to overproduction and create a postwar depression. Equally important, with the beginning of war production in the summer of 1940, the civilian economy began to boom as workers had more money to spend. Many business leaders preferred the known profits of the consumer economy to the uncertain advantages of war production.

The Roosevelt administration attempted to restore business confidence in government by appointing business leaders such as Nelson, U.S. Steel's Edward Stettinius, and General Motors' William Knudsen to "dollar-a-year" positions. These administrators adopted policies that helped to reduce the economic risks associated with war conversion. In 1940 Congress authorized government financing of new construction. The WPB later offered generous tax advantages and "cost-plus" contracts that guaranteed a fixed profit for war business. The federal government also began to finance the cost of industrial research and development for war-related materials, a practice that became a critical ingredient of the American economy even after the war ended. To further encourage business cooperation, the Roosevelt administration abandoned antitrust actions in war-related fields.

Such policies generally favored big businesses over small, even after competitive bidding had been dropped. Larger corporations had greater access to government bureaucracies and had greater experience in handling huge procurement contracts. From the government's point of view, it was simpler to deal with one contractor instead of many. Though some New Dealers criticized the disproportionate awarding of war contracts to the largest companies, the prevailing opinion was expressed by Secretary Stimson: "If you . . . go to war . . . in a capitalist country, you have to let business make money out of the process or business won't work." During World War Two, industrial production increased by 96 percent and net corporate profits doubled.

The mobilization of the war economy also depended on the recruitment of an adequate labor supply. Unemployment figures in 1939 still totaled eight million (17 percent of the labor force), but these unemployed were steadily absorbed into the expanding economy. By 1942 other previously unemployable workers — teenagers, the elderly, blacks, and women — also began to find jobs. One source of employment was the armed services, which took over fifteen million men and women during the war. Another seven million jobs opened on the home front.

This rapid expansion of the labor force, although clearly ringing the end of the Depression, raised serious problems of another sort. The most compelling need was finding the right workers for critical defense industries. Not only was there a shortage of skilled labor, but workers revealed a remarkable willingness to leave their jobs. To deal with these problems, Roosevelt created a War Manpower Commission. But this agency lacked the power to enforce its policies and it could never win presidential support for the idea of "work or fight." As a result, absenteeism and job mobility remained common. In 1944 the turnover in manufacturing industries was 82 percent, three-quarters of which was voluntary. As in the Depression, however, losses in the labor force were more than offset by the use of time-saving machinery that increased individual worker productivity. The Department of Agriculture estimated that farmer productivity increased 25 percent per work-hour between 1939 and 1945 because of mechanization, land consolidation, and the increased use of chemical fertilizers.

The shortage of labor provided opportunities for people who had previously been underrepresented in the work force. Black Americans, disproportionately unemployed during the Depression, repeated the World War One pattern of migration to the cities. Yet black workers still confronted racial discrimination in employment and vocational training, even in government programs and within the armed forces. In the private sector, discrimination in employment was unconcealed. "While we are in complete sympathy with the Negro," declared the president of North American Aviation, "it is against company policy to employ them as aircraft workers or mechanics ... regardless of their training.... There will be some jobs as janitors for Negroes."

Such discrimination led A. Philip Randolph, president of the Brotherhood of Sleeping Car Porters, to call for a protest march on Washington in the summer of 1941. Deeply embarrassed by the proposal, Roosevelt tried to persuade Randolph to change his plans. But at last the president was forced to take a public stand against discrimination in employment. On June 25, 1941, Roosevelt issued Executive Order 8802, which prohibited job discrimination in defense industries and created a Fair Employment Practices Commission (FEPC) to investigate cases of discrimination. Roosevelt never felt secure enough to order the desegregation of the armed services, however, and the FEPC, despite the intentions of its members, never possessed sufficient power to enforce its policies. Some two million blacks eventually found work in war industries.

More successful in penetrating the labor force were women. Though females comprised 25 percent of the prewar work force, popular opinion disapproved of working women, particularly when they competed with men for jobs. Even as the nation prepared for war, defense contractors preferred not to hire female employees. Pearl Harbor put aside those prejudices. Between 1941 and 1945, 6.5 million women entered the labor force, a 57 percent increase in female employment. By the war's end, 36 percent of all civilian workers were women. Though initially limited to "light" work, women eventually performed a variety of previously "male" tasks, the most publicized female stereotype being Rosie the Riveter.

Despite widespread recognition of women's capabilities, female workers continued to face prejudicial conditions. Although the War Manpower Commission announced that female workers were entitled to the same pay as men for the same work, employers routinely ignored such requirements. Most women earned no more than the minimum wage, and women were usually kept out of high management positions. These practices reflected the generally accepted belief that war work was temporary. Even though a Women's Bureau survey revealed that 75 percent of working women wished to keep their jobs, business policy assumed that women should give way to men.

"Americans may no longer believe that a woman's place is in the home," sociologist Jerome Bruner observed. "But more important, we believe even less that a man's place is on the street without a job." Women nevertheless resisted giving up their jobs at the war's end.

The fear that women workers would supplant men also influenced the attitudes of organized labor. Worried about the possibility of a postwar depression, union leaders discouraged permanent gains for women even though 20 percent of organized workers were female. Such conservative postures partly reflected a growing alienation of union leaders from the rank-and-file membership. As employment boomed, unions demanded double work shifts, but Roosevelt forced them to accept a forty-hour week — later extended to forty-eight hours — and time and a half for overtime. Between 1941 and 1945 union membership increased by nearly 40 percent.

While organized labor made a general "no-strike" pledge shortly after Pearl Harbor, unions continued to press for higher wages. To deal with these disputes, Roosevelt created a National Defense Mediation Board in 1941, composed of representatives of labor, management, and the public. But when CIO members resigned over a dispute involving union jurisdiction, Roosevelt established another bureau, the National War Labor Board, in 1942. As an extension of the president's wartime emergency powers, the NWLB could set wages, hours, and working conditions and had the legal authority to order government seizure of noncomplying plants.

The first major labor dispute involved union membership. Organized labor supported the "union shop," in which all workers must join the union, but management insisted on an "open shop." The NWLB finally persuaded both parties to accept a compromise based on the principle of maintenance of membership. Workers did not have to join a union, but union members had to remain within their union; if membership declined because of turnovers, the union could recruit just enough workers to maintain the initial membership figures. After these grievances were resolved, the unions turned to questions of higher wages to compensate for inflation. Here too the NWLB worked out a compromise formula known as Little Steel. Recognizing a 15 percent inflation between January and July 1942, the board allowed a 15 percent cost-of-living increase for that period. Such wage limits did not apply to overtime, however, and while hourly wages increased 24 percent during the war, weekly earnings went up about 70 percent. Moreover, since Little Steel applied only to disputed cases, employers were often willing to pay higher wages, especially in jobs involving cost-plus contracts.

Despite these economic gains, organized labor still opposed government restraints, and by 1943 union members were complaining about the no-strike pledge. Numerous unauthorized strikes occurred, even in critical war industries. The most serious crisis was John L. Lewis's defiance of the Little Steel formula in seeking higher wages for the United Mine Workers. Protesting that Little Steel offered too little for the impoverished mine workers (annual wages averaged $1,700 in 1942), Lewis led the coal miners in a controversial strike in 1943. Congress responded by passing, over Roosevelt's veto, the Smith-Connally Labor Act, which imposed a thirty-day cooling off period before striking, prohibited strikes in defense industries, and banned union contributions to political parties. Lewis nevertheless continued to agitate for the miners, finally winning additional pay that effectively circumvented the 15 percent ceiling.

With business booming and with full employment, the Roosevelt administration worked to prevent runaway inflation. One solution was to set wage controls, but these, as John L. Lewis demonstrated, frequently could be ignored. Another approach was to establish price controls. In 1942 the Office of Price Administration put a freeze on consumer prices based on the highest prices of March 1942. But despite increased production, food prices continued to skyrocket, upsetting the administration's attempt to balance the economy. Though representatives of the farm states welcomed farm prosperity, Roosevelt persuaded Congress to pass an Anti-Inflation Act in 1942 that enabled him to freeze agricultural prices, wages, and rents. During the last two years of the war, consumer prices increased by less than 2 percent.

Besides price controls, the OPA also instituted a rationing program for scarce materials. These included canned goods (because of tin shortages), rubber, gasoline (because rubber shortages limited tire production), coffee, shoes (because of military needs), sugar, meat, butter, and fuel oil. Rationing produced inadvertent inequities, such as the decline of the quality of merchandise and, more serious, an illegal black market.

Another strategy to decrease consumer purchasing power was the sale of war bonds. Through payroll deduction plans and organized bond drives, bond sales reached $135 billion, of which about $40 billion was purchased by small investors. The deflationary effect of these bond sales was significant, absorbing over 7 percent of net personal incomes in 1944, even though many purchasers redeemed their bonds before the war's end.

More effective in soaking up purchasing power was taxation. Despite vast public expenditures, over 40 percent of the total war bill was financed through taxation. The Revenue

To inspire support on the home front, this 1942 poster exaggerated the danger of enemy attacks on civilian property. (National Archives 179-WP-470)

Act of 1942, besides raising tax rates, broadened the tax base to include lower income workers for the first time. It also increased corporation taxes to 40 percent and raised excess-profits taxes to a whopping 90 percent. Loopholes and generous interpretations of the law frequently lowered these rates in practice. Other provisions promised to rebate the excess-profits taxes to corporations after the war to facilitate reconversion to civilian industries. The law also initiated the policy of payroll withholding, ostensibly to simplify the procedure, but also to take tax dollars out of consumer circulation.

These taxes, even when revised in 1944 to lower revenues, brought $138 billion into the treasury. Business interests often managed to avoid heavy taxes by such devices as nonreporting, expense accounts, and deferred salaries. But the taxes on high personal income and excess profits still produced a significant, though temporary, redistribution of personal income, reversing the old adage that the rich get richer and the poor, poorer. The top 5 percent income bracket declined in relative economic worth as its control of disposable income dropped from 23 percent in 1939 to 17 percent in 1945. At the same time full employment and the expansion of two-income families brought greater purchasing power to poorer people. Yet commodity shortages and rationing, though often ignored, cut across class lines: people with money could not always find what they wanted to buy. Additional incomes thus went into savings, providing the necessary capital for postwar spending.

THE HOME FRONT

If personal savings provided the economic basis for a postwar splurge, other aspects of wartime culture provided the incentive. After a decade of Depression, consumers were anxious to spend their wartime paychecks, but desirable commodities were often unavailable. In 1942, for example, the WPB ordered the automobile industry to stop producing cars and light trucks and to switch to manufacturing tanks and airplanes. When unable to satisfy consumer demands, industry resorted to mass advertising to direct attention from wartime shortage to postwar possibilities. "Ordnance Today," boasted the Easy Washing Machine Company, "Washers Tomorrow." The Cessna Aircraft Company predicted that the "Family Car of the Air" would enable weekend golfers to tee off 500 miles from home "after the war." This involuntary acceptance of the principle of delayed gratification went a long way toward explaining mass consumption in the postwar period.

With a shortage of consumer goods, Americans began spending more money on entertainment. Hollywood was a major beneficiary: movie attendance reached eighty million customers a week in 1942. Hollywood's War Activities Committee donated over forty thousand prints to the armed services, assuring that more than half a million soldiers watched a Hollywood film every night. With an eye on building national morale, Hollywood glorified the exploits of the American soldier, usually described as the boy next door, and defined the war as a crusade for freedom rather than as a defense of national interest. During the war years horror films declined in popularity, perhaps because of the real horrors of war. The war saw the emergence of a new film genre, the nostalgic musical, in which films like *Meet Me in St. Louis* (1944) described a simpler and happier America. Women's films stressed the importance of self-sacrifice while American men were away from home, and even emancipated women like Bette Davis were placed in unrealistically lavish settings to emphasize the fantasy rather than the reality of female independence.

The political content of Hollywood films changed dramatically after Pearl Harbor. During the era of neutrality, the major studios scrupulously censored politically controversial scenes. In *Blockade* (1938), for example, an early film about the Spanish civil war, it was

People of all ages and from diverse ethnic backgrounds supported the war effort by buying United States defense bonds. (Library of Congress)

impossible to tell which side the protagonist supported. In 1942, however, *Mrs. Minniver,* a sentimental story about British resistance to the Nazi blitz, won seven Academy Awards. Public opinion toward the Soviet Union also changed as Communists became military allies. Though most Americans remained suspicious of Soviet intentions, a 1944 poll showed that one-third of the people interviewed had favorable impressions of the Soviet Union and 46 percent believed that the Stalinist government was as good as could be expected for the Russian people. These favorable ideas were reinforced in numerous magazine articles and in two highly acclaimed Hollywood productions, *Mission to Moscow* (1943) and *Song of Russia* (1944). Both films later became severe embarrassments to Hollywood when the Cold War led to the investigation of Communist subversion in the movie industry.

Popular images of the Axis enemies also revealed underlying assumptions that had important wartime ramifications. Italian-Americans, like other Roman Catholic immigrants, had faced traditional discrimination. Within the Catholic church, moreover, Italians resented the dominance of the Irish hierarchy. These negative experiences left many Italian-Americans with ambivalent feelings about the United States. In 1942, 600,000 Italians had not become naturalized citizens. After the outbreak of war, they technically became "enemy aliens." Yet the Roosevelt administration, aware of the ethnic antagonism caused by World War One, attempted to avoid racist hysteria against Europeans. Moreover, Roosevelt appreciated the importance of the Italian vote for the Democratic party in the 1942 congressional elections. On Columbus Day, therefore, Roosevelt revoked the enemy alien status of Italians and facilitated the procedures for naturalization. In a similar electoral situation in 1944, Roosevelt appealed to Italian voters by announcing a loan and relief supplies for the defeated Italian enemy.

The desire to differentiate between the Italian people and the Italian government emerged clearly in Hollywood films. In *Sahara* (1942), for example, which featured Humphrey Bogart as an American desert fighter, an Italian prisoner of war was described contemptuously as a "pot of spaghetti," but the film went on to point out that loyal Italian-Americans probably had helped make the steel for Bogart's tank. "Italians are not like Germans," the film concluded; the Fascist uniform covered only the body, not the soul. Such notions helped prepare the American public for the relatively lenient treatment toward the defeated Italian government in 1943.

While Hollywood portrayed Italians as inadvertent enemies, it depicted Nazis and Japanese as ruthless barbarians. Since the Roosevelt administration played down anti-German feeling at home, Hollywood also distinguished between Nazis and other Germans. The cruel, callous Nazi, however, became a common stereotype on the silver screen. In *Sahara*, the captured German flyer, unlike the Italian, remains intransigent, dedicated to the philosophy of the master race. In another Bogart film, *All Through the Night* (1942), Hollywood revealed another aspect of nazism — its gross stupidity, a recurring screen phenomenon that encouraged audiences to laugh at the world conquerors. Such laughter reduced the Nazis to human proportions. Depictions of the Japanese, however, were utterly humorless. Partly because of the anger created by Pearl Harbor and partly because of anti-Asian racism, Americans were unable to see the Japanese enemy as human. Instead the typical Japanese warrior was a robot-like creature prepared to die for the emperor.

POLITICS IN WARTIME

Though the popular media emphasized the theme of national unity, disagreements between liberals and conservatives undermined Roosevelt's search for consensus, especially after the 1942 elections brought a Republican majority to Congress. Having learned from Wilson's failure the importance of maintaining a working relationship with Congress on matters of foreign policy, Roosevelt decided to abandon the more liberal aspects of the New Deal. At a press conference in December 1943, he announced that "Dr. New Deal" had given way to "Dr. Win the War."

Roosevelt's surrender reflected the realities of congressional power. But it did not weaken the president's hopes for postwar reform. In January 1944 he used his annual state of the union message to propose an economic "bill of rights." "We cannot be content," he declared, "if some fraction of our people — whether it be one-third or one-fifth or one-tenth — is ill-fed, ill-clothed, ill-housed, and insecure." Roosevelt proceeded to throw his weight behind liberal legislation for veterans' benefits. By 1944 about one million veterans had returned from the armed services, many of them injured or otherwise unable to adjust to civilian life. Congress responded to presidential urging as well as a strong American Legion lobby by enacting the GI Bill of Rights, which provided unemployment, social security, and educational benefits to veterans. But a conservative Congress fought back attempts to link this legislation to a broader program of social welfare. In the end, the GI Bill, by providing scholarship, home loans, life insurance, and burial costs, offered traditional middle-class opportunities.

Though Roosevelt envisioned a liberal Democratic program, conservatives continued to grow in strength even in his own party. When the president supported a federal election law to enable soldiers to vote, southern Democrats joined Republicans to defend the principle of states' rights and defeat the measure. In 1944 Roosevelt vetoed an appropriation bill that gave generous depletion allowances to oil and lumber investors and exempted the natural gas industry from excess-profits taxes. Roosevelt's stinging message aroused the hostility of his previously loyal supporters in Congress, and

Democratic votes were essential in overriding the veto.

Roosevelt's problems with conservative Democrats encouraged the Republican party. Wendell Willkie, the Republican candidate in 1940, had returned from a round-the-world goodwill tour as a committed internationalist, enthusiastic about America's responsibilities to the world as well as to social reform at home. The Republican party, more conservative than its titular head, rejected his call and turned instead to Governor Thomas E. Dewey of New York, an energetic but undazzling candidate.

Despite rumors of Roosevelt's ill health, there was never any question of his renomination. The problem for Democrats focused on the vice presidential choice. Henry A. Wallace, the incumbent, had offended regular party bosses as well as conservative southern Democrats by his outspoken liberalism. Wallace's rival, James Byrnes, a southerner, was hated by organized labor. Roosevelt shrewdly picked a compromise candidate, Harry S Truman of Missouri, a loyal New Dealer whose major claim to fame was his chairmanship of the Senate War Investigating Committee, which had assiduously exposed unnecessary government waste and attempted to prevent war profiteering.

Few issues separated the candidates. Dewey readily endorsed a bipartisan foreign policy, including a commitment to postwar internationalism, and also accepted such New Deal policies as social security, unemployment insurance, collective bargaining, and farm price supports. The Democrats benefited greatly by campaign support from the CIO's Political Action Committee (PAC), which brought out the workers' votes. The urban electorate provided Roosevelt's margin of victory: 25.6 million to 22 million popular votes; 432 to 99 electoral votes.

DOMESTIC CONFLICT

While Democrats and Republicans struggled for control of the nation's political institutions, other Americans struggled more simply for survival. Roosevelt's Four Freedoms served as a convenient rallying point for the war effort, and the president's Office of War Information tried to portray the war as a democratic crusade. But members of outgroups — political dissenters, Japanese-Americans, blacks, Jews, Chicanos, young people, and women — discovered basic inconsistencies in the so-called American Creed. Despite Roosevelt's rhetoric, many Americans found themselves excluded from the national identity.

Roosevelt and Attorney General Francis Biddle tried to avoid the rabid hysteria of World War One in dealing with political dissenters. Their task was made easier by the Communist party's unqualified support of a war that put the United States on the same side as the Soviet Union. But the administration remained totally unsympathetic to right wing critics and American Fascists. In 1942 Biddle invoked the Espionage Act of 1917 to prevent the mailing of Father Coughlin's *Social Justice,* an isolationist, Jew-baiting magazine, and when Coughlin protested, the administration persuaded the Catholic hierarchy to silence the priest. Biddle also indicted twenty-six Fascists in a celebrated sedition trial that dragged on for over two years before the administration decided to drop the charges. Under the Hatch Act of 1939, which attempted to eliminate subversives from federal employment, the Civil Service Commission instituted a series of loyalty checks.

The government demonstrated even greater intolerance toward those who refused to comply with the Selective Service Act on grounds of conscience. Though the law allowed for Conscientious Objector status, Selective Service Director Lewis B. Hershey chose a narrow definition, ruling in 1942 that religious conscience implied a belief in divinity. About thirty-five thousand COs were willing to work at alternative government service. But many draft boards refused to recognize CO status, and

Fearing the possibility of subversion, Roosevelt ordered the roundup of all Japanese-Americans, including this girl photographed at Owens Valley, California. These Japanese-Americans, many of them American citizens, were placed in internment camps. (Library of Congress USF-33-13288-M3)

many pacifists refused to compromise with any government service. Over fifty-five hundred men, most of them Jehovah's Witnesses, chose prison over compliance with Selective Service. Jail sentences averaged four to five years. Meanwhile, civilian Jehovah's Witnesses were subject to government harassment and occasionally mob violence.

The most serious attack on civil rights and cultural differences emerged in government policy toward Japanese-Americans. Alarmed by Pearl Harbor and by subsequent Japanese victories in the Pacific, Americans focused their

"Hard hat" workers in defense industries enjoyed unprecedented prosperity as the wartime economy finally brought an end to the Great Depression. (Dorothea Lange/City of Oakland/The Oakland Museum)

fear and then their venom on the Japanese-American population, most of whom lived on the West Coast. In looking for scapegoats, journalists falsely reported that California Japanese had conspired in the attack on Pearl Harbor and were planning further subversion at home. When none occurred, California Attorney General Earl Warren used this demonstrable loyalty as counter-proof. "We are just being lulled into a false sense of security," he told a congressional investigating committee in February 1942, "and the only reason we haven't had disaster in California is because it has been timed for a different date." The commanding general of the area, John DeWitt, analyzed the situation more simply: "A Jap's a Jap.... It makes no difference if he is an American citizen." Even the prestigious liberal journalist Walter Lippmann warned against "the Fifth Column on the Coast."

Roosevelt responded to this public pressure with Executive Order 9066, which ordered the internment and relocation of all Japanese. Of the 110,000 people affected by the decision, two-thirds were American citizens by birth (under the Naturalization Act of 1924, Japanese immigrants were not permitted to become American citizens). Many of these victims, particularly the assimilationists, were anxious to demonstrate their loyalty to the United States and saw compliance as the most convincing proof. Others protested vigorously: "Has the Gestapo come to America? Have we not risen in righteous anger at Hitler's mistreatments of the Jews? Then, is it not incongruous that citizen Americans of Japanese descent should be similarly mistreated and persecuted?"

Forced to sell their private possessions at short notice—usually to unscrupulous white buyers—the Japanese were herded into detention centers and then relocated into ten concentration camps in arid parts of the country. These executive decisions were upheld in a series of Supreme Court rulings in 1944. In the *Korematsu* case, the Court upheld the relocation from the West Coast on grounds of military necessity. But in the *Endo* case, the Court denied that citizens could be detained once their loyalty had been established. By that time the War Relocation Authority already had begun to release loyal Japanese and had announced the termination of the camps on January 2, 1945.

Though surrounded by barbed wire and military guard, the relocation camps were less like Nazi concentration camps than American Indian reservations. Government authorities had relatively little social contact with inmates, who lived in segregated areas. Such straitened circumstances encouraged a revitalization of traditional Japanese culture — similar to the Ghost Dance traditions that emerged when the Plains Indians were forced onto reservations. The internment created severe conflicts between these traditional Japanese and the assimilationists, who wished to break completely with the old culture. Tensions intensified in 1943 when the government attempted to separate the "disloyal" Japanese. The issues were complicated by questions of military service (Japanese volunteers eventually were accepted by the army, fought in segregated units, and proved to be exceptionally tough soldiers), by parental attachment, by fear of reprisal, and by distrust of the government. Those deemed disloyal were moved to the Tule Lake camp, where the renaissance of Japanese culture was seen as a preparation for a return to Japan. During the war nearly six thousand Japanese renounced their United States citizenship and forty-seven hundred Japanese-Americans obtained "repatriation" after the war.

Though wartime necessity rationalized the destruction of Japanese civil rights, the same imperatives of national unity enabled Afro-Americans to challenge traditional race prejudice. Where the theme for blacks in World War One had been W. E. B. DuBois's summons to "close ranks," black leaders in World War Two insisted that "declarations of war do not lessen the obligation to preserve and extend civil liberties" at home. Even after Roosevelt established the FEPC, Randolph's March on Washington movement did not disband but remained as an important all-black, mass-based pressure group. The NAACP also grew during the war, increasing its membership ninefold to 450,000. "Not since Reconstruction," concluded Gunnar Myrdal's massive study of race relations, *An American Dilemma* (1944), "has there been more reason to anticipate fundamental changes in American race relations, changes which will involve a development toward the American ideals."

The changes came slower than Myrdal predicted. In the army, blacks, like Japanese, served in segregated units, while the Red Cross separated "colored" blood from "white." Military policy, as Lewis Hershey explained, "is simply transferring discrimination from everyday life into the Army." Fundamental to that policy was a belief that blacks were too docile to make good fighters. As a result, blacks were initially assigned to labor units, denied opportunity for promotion, and barred from prestigious duties such as flying. Even after proving their battlefield valor, black service remained unrecognized; no blacks were awarded medals of honor in World Wars One and Two. Most humiliating of all to black soldiers was the realization that Nazi prisoners of war could use public eating facilities whereas blacks in American uniforms were denied service. Such treatment did not go unchallenged in the army. Numerous race riots occurred both on and off base, and in one notorious case the black athlete Jackie Robinson was court-martialed for defying Jim Crow policy.

Blacks on the home front continued to face racist policies. The extent of the problem was revealed in a public opinion poll taken at the beginning of the war. As reported by Myrdal, 18 percent of blacks admitted pro-Japanese feelings; in a similar poll, southern white industrialists, when asked to choose between complete racial equality or a German victory, chose the latter by a large majority. Such sentiments were equally strong in the North. In Detroit, white crowds rioted in 1942 to prevent blacks from moving into the federally funded Sojourner Truth housing project. The next year Detroit exploded again as racial tensions produced a two-day race riot that left thirty-five dead and over seven hundred wounded. Major race riots also occurred in Texas; Ohio; Springfield, Massachusetts; and Harlem.

Despite these conflicts, World War Two represented an ideological turning point in American race relations. The repudiation of Nazi racism, reinforced at the war's end by the discovery of the infamous death camps, challenged the validity of America's own racist assumptions. A chapter of Wendell Willkie's best-selling *One World* (1943) criticized "Our Imperialism at Home" and called for an end to "a smug racial superiority, a willingness to exploit an unprotected people." In 1944 the Supreme Court abolished the white primary, which had served to disfranchise black voters in most southern states. The changing attitudes could be seen in popular films, which began to move away from the Sambo stereotypes of the thirties. In the classic *Casablanca* (1943), for example, the black pianist, Sam, portrays a

mature adult capable of deep political conviction, while *Sahara* contrasted the reliability of an African soldier with the brutality of the Nazis. Such changes provided an important bedrock for the civil rights movement of the postwar era.

The experience of blacks was comparable to that of Jews. Though Roosevelt appointed many Jews to important positions in government, it was not uncommon before the war for Jews to face discrimination in business, social life, and education. In Boston young supporters of Father Coughlin roamed the streets to attack Jews and vandalize synagogues. Immigration laws established quotas that discriminated against Jews, even when refugees from Nazi persecution literally faced death as the only alternative. Not until 1944 did Roosevelt move to facilitate the admission of Jewish refugees from Europe. Yet the horror of Nazi anti-Semitism thoroughly discredited American anti-Semitism and, although private prejudices remained, removed the gross forms of discrimination in such areas as education quotas.

While it became relatively easy for Jews to overcome ethnic discrimination, other groups encountered stronger barriers. The Spanish-speaking, brown-skinned Mexican-Americans of the Southwest continued to face overt discrimination. Besides housing segregation, they suffered from unemployment, low wages, and endemic poverty. During the war younger Chicanos formed teenage "pachuco" gangs and dressed in lavish costumes known as "zoot suits." Though zoot suiters hardly differed from other adolescent youths, newspapers exaggerated the threat of gangsterism. In July 1943 rumors that pachucos had beaten a sailor provoked a four-day race riot in Los Angeles. White servicemen raided the barrios, attacked the zoot suiters, and stripped them of their clothing. Though prominent leaders condemned the riot, the situation typified the problems of politically weak ethnic minorities. Like the Japanese, Mexican-Americans lacked the power to protect their communities.

The fear of the zoot suiters revealed not only a persistent problem of ethnic antagonism but also a more general anxiety about youth. "The youngsters of this spontaneous movement are *not* delinquent," insisted psychologist Fritz Redl. "They are normal, growing youngsters." Like other adolescents, zoot suiters adopted a distinctive uniform to reinforce group identity. During the war years there was also a dramatic rise in juvenile delinquency, particularly in sex crimes, and army officials openly worried about a venereal disease epidemic. Contemporaries speculated about the reason for adolescent delinquency, wondering if the war had unleashed some primal antisocial instinct. Yet the "crimes" attributed to the youth culture — premarital sexual relations, drinking, frivolity — were closely related to adult fantasies. "In a society where such strong emphasis is placed upon individual achievements," observed Harvard sociologist Talcott Parsons, "it is not surprising that there should be a certain romantic nostalgia for the time when the fundamental choices were still open." Adults, particularly people whose lives were disrupted by and preoccupied with war, resented the independence and spontaneity of the youth culture. "To label them all delinquents," Redl concluded, "is nothing but self-deception."

Whatever its basis, the concern about youth reflected a growing belief that the American family was disintegrating because mothers were leaving their children to take war work. According to conventional wisdom, marriage was the single most important event in a woman's life. "That determines a woman's fundamental

Two "pachuco" Mexican-Americans display their pegged trousers, slashed by rioting servicemen. (Wide World Photos)

status," explained Talcott Parsons, "and after that her role patterning is...a matter of living up to expectations and finding satisfying interests and activities." Career women were supposed to be unmarried. But during World War Two the largest number of new workers were married. It was this group, particularly those past childbearing years, that desired to remain in the work force after the war. Participation in war work thus legitimated women's employment among middle-class families. But the widespread recognition of women's contribution to the war effort failed in the short run to alter traditional expectations.

The tendency for social values to lag behind wartime changes reflected the inability of Americans to confront the vast implications of World War Two. Despite a sense of crisis, most Americans viewed the war as a temporary detour. Where the "doughboys" of World War One were celebrated as heroic adventurers, the soldiers of World War Two appeared as civilians in uniform. "Home," wrote the front-line journalist Ernie Pyle, "the one really profound goal that obsesses every one of the Americans marching on foreign shores." Even the fictional heroes were different. The outstanding novel of World War Two, Norman Mailer's *The Naked and the Dead* (1948), used the device of flashback to accentuate the temporary nature of soldier status. Such attitudes encouraged the notion that things would revert to prewar status after the defeat of Germany and Japan.

The experiences on the home front, however, destroyed those illusions. Shortly after Pearl Harbor, Jonathan Daniels, a journalist who later joined the White House staff, urged a return to America's frontier heritage. "The forties are here in which Americans stand on a continent as men," he exulted. America was "grown magnificently male again.... We are men again in America." The male warrior, like the nineteenth-century pioneer, would restore the national identity. But Daniels's appeal of 1941 neglected the existence of other Americans — women and racial, ethnic, and religious minorities. World War Two brought these groups into greater prominence. By 1945 few would settle for the invisibility implied in Daniels's statement.

TRUMAN AND TRUCE

Roosevelt's successor, Harry Truman, inherited the delicate diplomatic responsibility for settling the peace. Though he lacked Roosevelt's experience and skill, Truman determined to obtain concessions from the Soviet Union. Where Roosevelt had pragmatically accepted the vague language of Yalta, the new president insisted that the Soviet Union adopt the American interpretation of the meeting. Almost immediately he attacked Stalin's foreign minister, Molotov, over Soviet policy in Poland and threatened to cut off American assistance to the Soviet Union. At San Francisco American delegates reluctantly accepted the three Soviet votes that Roosevelt already had conceded at Yalta, but not without forcing other compromises from the Soviets. After the formal German surrender on May 8, 1945 (V-E Day), the United States abruptly halted Lend-Lease, ordering ships in mid-Atlantic to turn around. After British and Soviet protests, however, Truman denied responsibility and reversed the order. Worried about the deterioration of American-Soviet relations, Truman decided to call another summit conference.

Truman's desire to meet with Stalin reflected an important change in the balance of power. Shortly after succeeding Roosevelt, Truman learned about a top-secret military project to build a nuclear bomb. Truman speculated that the bomb might give the United States greater leverage in winning concessions from the Soviets. He accordingly timed the summit meeting at Potsdam for mid-July 1945, the same week the first atom bomb would be tested in New Mexico.

The atom bomb had emerged as a logical outgrowth of modern physics. Its fundamental principles were brought to the United States by scientists fleeing from Nazi Germany. In 1939, at the urging of the physicist Leo Szilard, Albert Einstein wrote to Roosevelt suggesting the possibility of nuclear weapons and warning that German scientists might already be developing them. After initial caution, Roosevelt created a National Defense Research Committee to encourage nuclear research. Because refugee scientists were considered security risks, they were not allowed to work on such top-secret projects as radar; ironically, many turned to the atom bomb instead.

As the atom bomb developed, Roosevelt decided to share its secrets with the British (who had made important early contributions). At Churchill's urging, he refused to divulge the secret Manhattan Project to Stalin, even though he knew that spies already had informed the Soviets of the project. In reaching this crucial decision, Roosevelt assumed that Britain would be a vital postwar ally, especially if isolationism again became a dominant force. But he believed that the Soviets could not be trusted. Since Stalin already knew about the bomb project, however, the decision created mutual distrust. Within the administration there was never any doubt that the atom bomb would be used against the enemy. Fire bombings of Dresden and Tokyo had claimed more victims than would die in atomic bombings. In May 1945 a committee of administrators and scientists agreed that the bomb should be dropped against Japan. The major reason for this decision was the belief that the new weapon would forestall an invasion of Japan and thus save one million American lives. The bomb would also demonstrate — to friend and foe alike — the superiority of American military strength in the postwar world.

The Potsdam conference failed to resolve Soviet-American conflicts. With news of the successful atom bomb test, Truman tried to force Stalin to alter the political arrangements in eastern Europe, where leftist parties prevailed. Stalin refused to change these governments, viewing Truman's request as a betrayal of the principle of spheres of influence reached at Yalta. Those principles had permitted Soviet dominance in eastern Europe, but also had allowed the suppression of Greek Communists and the creation of a pro-Western government in Italy. At Potsdam the Big Three did agree to partition Germany, but again failed to resolve the question of reparations. Final peace treaties were delegated to a subsequent Council of Foreign Ministers.

By the summer of 1945, the Japanese cause seemed hopeless. In July the Japanese premier made overtures through the Soviet Union, indicating a willingness to sue for peace. The Truman administration responded with demands for unconditional surrender and warned that Japan faced imminent destruction. When the Japanese failed to reply, Truman allowed military decisions to proceed. On August 6, 1945, a B-29 dropped a single atom bomb on the city of Hiroshima, killing 80,000–100,000 inhabitants. On August 9 the Soviet Union entered the war. The same day, another atom bomb fell on the city of Nagasaki. The Japanese now sought immediate peace, agreeing on August 14 to surrender, provided only that the emperor be retained. When Truman agreed, World War Two was over.

SUGGESTED READINGS

The most comprehensive treatment of Roosevelt's foreign policy is Robert Dallek, *Franklin*

D. *Roosevelt and American Foreign Policy, 1932–1945* (1979). A brief but thorough introduction to the major issues of foreign policy on the eve of World War Two is Robert A. Divine, *The Reluctant Belligerent: American Entry into World War II* (1965). More detailed is a two-volume study by William L. Langer and S. Everett Gleason, *Challenge to Isolation, 1937–1940* (1952) and *The Undeclared War, 1940–1941* (1953). These surveys may be supplemented by John E. Wiltz, *From Isolation to War, 1931–1941* (1968).

The ideological context of United States foreign policy is explained in the relevant chapters of William Appleman Williams, *The Tragedy of American Diplomacy* (1962). These themes emerge in greater detail in Lloyd C. Gardner, *Economic Aspects of New Deal Diplomacy* (1964). Also helpful in understanding the relationship between economic interest and ideology is a brief essay, Thomas H. Etzold, "Why America Fought Germany in World War II" (1973). For studies of isolationism, see John E. Wiltz, *In Search of Peace: The Senate Munitions Inquiry, 1934–1936* (1963), and Manfred Jonas, *Isolationism in America: 1935–1941* (1966). The diplomatic implications of isolationism emerge in two studies of the United States's response to the Spanish civil war: Allen Guttmann, *The Wound in the Heart* (1962), and Richard P. Traina, *American Diplomacy and the Spanish Civil War* (1968). Roosevelt's perception of the national interest is examined in Robert A. Divine, *Roosevelt and World War II* (1969).

A thorough study of the United States's relations with Japan is Dorothy Borg, *The United States and Far Eastern Crises of 1933–1938* (1964), which should be supplemented by Herbert Feis, *Road to Pearl Harbor* (1950). For the Japanese context, see Robert J. Butow,

Tojo and the Coming of the War (1961). The attack on Pearl Harbor is examined in Roberta Wohlstetter, *Pearl Harbor: Warning and Decision* (1962).

The issues of wartime diplomacy are described in Gaddis Smith, *American Diplomacy During the Second World War, 1941–1945* (1965), and John Snell, *Illusion and Necessity: The Diplomacy of World War II* (1963). The relationship between military and diplomatic affairs is emphasized in A. Russell Buchanan, *The United States and World War II*, 2 vols. (1964). More specific is Raymond G. O'Connor, *Diplomacy for Victory: FDR and Unconditional Surrender* (1971). Gabriel Kolko's *The Politics of War: The World and United States Foreign Policy, 1943–1945* (1968) stresses the inherent contradictions of national interest within the Grand Alliance. The origins of the United Nations is well treated in Robert A. Divine, *Second Chance: The Triumph of Internationalism in America During World War II* (1967). For a brilliant analysis of the diplomatic implications of the atom bomb, see Martin J. Sherwin, *A World Destroyed: The Atomic Bomb and the Grand Alliance* (1975).

Domestic issues during World War Two are best described in Richard Polenberg, *War and Society: The United States, 1941–1945* (1972). For Roosevelt's presidential role, see James MacGregor Burns, *Roosevelt: The Soldier of Freedom* (1970). John Morton Blum's *V Was for Victory: Politics and American Culture During World War II* (1976) explores the cultural context of wartime decision making. It may be supplemented by Geoffrey Perrett, *Days of Sadness, Years of Triumph* (1973), Richard Lingeman, *Don't You Know There's a War On?* (1970), and a compilation of "oral" histories, Roy Hoopes, *Americans Remember the*

Home Front (1977). For the movie industry, see Charles Higham and Joel Greenberg, *Hollywood in the Forties* (1968).

The impact of the war on Japanese-Americans is examined by Roger Daniels, *Concentration Camps USA: Japanese-Americans and World War II* (1971), as well as by Edward Spicer et al., *Impounded People: Japanese-Americans in the Relocation Centers* (1969), a report originally written in 1946 for the War Relocation Authority. The experience of blacks emerges in Richard Dalfiume, *Desegregation of the Armed Forces, 1939–1953* (1969). Also illuminating are the memoirs of black soldiers compiled in Mary Penick Motley, *The Invisible Soldier* (1975). The best sources for the impact of the war on women are the relevant chapters of William H. Chafe, *The American Woman* (1972). An excellent comparative study is Leila Rupp, *Mobilizing Women for War: German and American Propaganda, 1939–1945* (1978). For the pacifist movement, see Lawrence S. Wittner, *Rebels Against War: The American Peace Movement, 1941–1960* (1969).

For the Nuremberg trials, see Bradley F. Smith, *Reaching Judgment at Nuremberg* (1977), and Telford Taylor, *Nuremberg and Vietnam: An American Tragedy* (1970).

Spotlight: The Nuremberg Trials

The difficulty in reaching international agreements at Yalta and Potsdam contrasted with the unanimity felt by the Allies about punishing German war criminals. Over the centuries of warfare, an international "common law" had emerged, which prohibited certain wartime behavior, such as the indiscriminate murder of prisoners of war and civilians. These precedents included articles of the Treaty of Versailles that attributed war guilt to Germany after World War One and obligated that defeated country to pay war "reparations" to the victors. During the interwar period, however, many Americans criticized these provisions on the grounds that the victorious nations often had been guilty of similar activities and yet had gone unpunished. Moreover, many of the so-called German atrocities during World War One had subsequently been found to be figments of Allied propaganda.

Such ambiguities were at great remove from obvious German war crimes in World War Two. Besides invading other countries, Nazi Germany had wantonly violated rules of warfare regarding civilian populations. In defeated countries, German armies instituted reigns of terror — robbing, raping, and murdering innocent people. The Germans also implemented Nazi racial policies designed to exterminate "inferior" peoples such as gypsies and Jews. At the war's end, the Allied armies liberated barbaric concentration camps, such as Auschwitz and Dachau, in which millions of civilian captives had been enslaved, tortured, and starved before they were sent to mass deaths in gas chambers and their bodies plundered of hair, artificial teeth, and tattooed skin.

The enormity of German war crimes led Allied leaders to seek an unambiguous criminal judgment. At the Moscow foreign ministers' conference of 1943, the Big Three warned that war criminals would be punished "by joint decision." As victory appeared imminent in 1944, exiled leaders of occupied countries and Jewish refugees called for a more explicit statement to avert last-ditch Nazi atrocities. But Great Britain and the United States feared jeopardizing the lives of Allied prisoners of war and remained doubtful of the atrocity descriptions. But the murder of captured American soldiers at Malmedy during the Battle of the Bulge in December 1944 stiffened the Allied position.

Allied leaders, including such prominent members of the Roosevelt administration as Secretary of the Treasury Henry Morgenthau, proposed the summary execution of Nazi war criminals. But other administration officials, such as Secretaries Stimson and Hull, recognized the importance of establishing legal precedents to discourage future wartime behavior. With Roosevelt's approval, the War Department made elaborate preparations for the creation of a postwar international tribunal to try Germans accused of war crimes. Such a trial would avoid the possibility of making martyrs of German war leaders, establish a clear record of German war guilt, and reaffirm the nature of wartime criminal activities.

The major powers, which after the defeat of Germany included France, agreed to an international tribunal on war crimes at the San Francisco conference of April 1945. Negotiations about the nature of the trial, the definitions of "war crimes," and the list of defendants continued in London through the summer. These prolonged discussions revealed inherent problems within the Grand Alliance, ranging from Soviet demands for mass retribution (German criminality had been particularly severe on the Russian front) to American insistence on prosecution for "conspiracy" to commit crimes (a concept that was alien to continental law) and the inclusion of prewar policies in the indictment. But the Allied leaders at Potsdam, in one of their last demonstrations of wartime unity, recognized the importance of an international trial and broke the deadlock.

The Big Four announced agreement on the International Military Tribunal on German war crimes in August 1945. Each of the Allies would appoint a judge and an alternate; each would prosecute separate aspects of the united case. The defendants would be given rights of counsel and due process to assure a fair trial. The sessions would be held in the Bavarian city of Nuremberg. Its medieval fortress and prison provided one of the few undestroyed facilities in Germany capable of holding the defendants. Moreover, Nuremberg symbolized the former strength of Nazi ideology. It had supported torchlight parades and mass rallies. And a series of laws promulgated at Nuremberg in 1935 stripped the Jews of their political rights, leaving them defenseless for Nazi atrocities.

In drawing up the indictment, Allied prosecutors established four major categories of criminality — conspiracy to commit war crimes, violations of traditional laws of war (mistreatment of prisoners, murder not justified by military "necessity"), crimes against peace (aggressive warfare, violating treaties), and crimes against humanity (racial, religious, and political persecution, extermination). These legal divisions were designed to cast a wide basis for establishing complicity, embracing leaders and followers, and members of both the military and civil government. Since Hitler and other prominent Nazis already were dead, the Allies selected defendants who were most representative of Nazi institutions, though not necessarily the most abominable criminals. Within these guidelines, twenty-two representatives of Nazi Germany were accused of various war crimes. The Allies also charged that certain Nazi organizations, such as the Gestapo (secret police), the SS (paramilitary elite), and the Nazi party leadership, were criminal. A judgment against criminal organizations would extend guilt to members of those groups. This aspect of the charge emphasized the principle of individual responsibility for criminal actions and undercut the defense that a criminal could be excused merely for obeying the orders of superiors.

In presenting its case, the prosecution stressed the universal implications of punishing war crimes. "While this law is first applied against German aggressors," explained Supreme Court Justice Robert H. Jackson, who served as chief American prosecutor, "if it is to serve any useful purpose it must condemn other nations, including those which sit here now in judgment." By establishing a strict rule of international law, the Nuremberg proceedings promised to limit the devastating effects of modern warfare.

Despite such claims, the Nuremberg trials reflected the realities of political power in postwar Europe. Although the London Charter that authorized the proceedings made no distinctions among the Axis enemies, no Italians were charged with war crimes. This omission reflected a general satisfaction that the lynching of Mussolini in 1943 served as sufficient retribution. Equally important, the western Allies who fought against Italy were more concerned with bringing that nation into a Western anticommunist coalition. Similarly, in examining the question of conspiracy to plan aggressive warfare, the Nuremberg Tribunal skirted the sensitive question of the Nazi-Soviet pact of 1939. Though publication of the secret passages of that alliance indicated that Stalin knew about Hitler's plans to attack Poland and had continued to "cooperate" with Nazi aggression, the Soviet representatives forced a rewording of the final judgment to avoid implicating the Soviet leadership.

The defense of national interests by the Allies also led them to apply separate standards in judging German war policies. Evidence used by the prosecution came almost exclusively from captured German documents, material that most governments manage to keep secret for a specified time. Thus the German defendants did not have access to material in the Allied archives that might have demonstrated similar policies executed by the prosecuting countries. In any case, the tribunal ruled that a defense argument based on the Allies having committed similar acts was inadmissible.

These principles enabled the Allies to avoid several embarrassing contradictions in their judgment. One of the grounds for accusing the Germans of waging aggressive warfare was the invasion of neutral Norway in 1940. At that time, however, the Germans captured Allied documents that revealed that Great Britain had been planning a similar invasion. The German defendants thus adopted the defense that the invasion of Norway was designed to forestall British plans. At Nuremberg, the British judges knew that the German evidence was correct, but the British government suppressed such confirmation from other judges. Though the United States and France were prepared to ignore the German allegations, the Soviet judge argued that British invasion plans did exist, but differed qualitatively from the German attack because of military "necessity." This Soviet position indirectly supported the Soviet invasion of Finland in 1939. In the end, the Nuremberg Tribunal dismissed the argument that British strategy justified the German attack. It took no position on similar British attack plans.

A contradictory decision also emerged in the judgment against Admiral Karl Doenitz, commander of the German submarine program, later head of the German navy, and after Hitler's suicide, leader of the Third Reich for twenty days. According to the indictment, Doenitz had authorized violations of international law, such as sinking neutral merchant vessels, establishing naval war zones, and failing to rescue passengers and crews from ships sunk by German submarines. Yet considerable trial evidence, including the testimony of the American naval commander of the Pacific, Admiral Chester Nimitz, demonstrated that the Allied navies had pursued policies nearly identical to those of the Germans. After considerable disagreement within the tribunal (the American judge, Francis Biddle, argued for complete acquittal), Doenitz was nevertheless convicted.

Despite the judgment against Doenitz, the similarities between German and Allied warfare prevented a clear resolution of the legal questions regarding weapons, not only involving submarines, but also aerial bombardment of civilians. The German air forces had initiated programs of terror bombings as early as the Spanish civil war and had blatantly attacked such civilian centers as London and Coventry. But the Allied air forces had retaliated in kind, destroying most German cities, unleashing incredible fire storms in Dresden, and ultimately concluding the war with atomic bombings of Japan. Such a record kept the Nuremberg Tribunal from examining the legality of total warfare tactics.

The Allies nevertheless recognized the importance of mass communications in modern warfare by indicting the Jew-baiting propagandist Julius Streicher. As editor of a German newspaper, Streicher personified the most egregious forms of anti-Semitism, freely advocating the annihilation of all Jews. Yet despite his inflammatory rhetoric, the journalist held no civil or military positions that related to war crimes. He was convicted instead for contributing to a political climate that enabled "crimes against humanity" to flourish. Streicher's case symbolized a widespread repudiation of public racism in the United States. Though race prejudice might remain within people's minds, the Nazi experience undermined its social acceptability.

Despite the attempt to prosecute representatives of all aspects of Nazi society, the Nuremberg proceedings failed to include leading industrialists. The original indictment had listed the patriarch of the Krupp family, whose factories had employed slave labor and had profited by the rearmament of the Third Reich. Yet because of a prosecution error, the named Krupp was not in charge of the family business, but was a senile, incontinent old man who was incapable of standing trial. This prosecution oversight had important implications. First, it left the legal questions of industrial complicity in war crimes unexamined. Second, it assured that the role of multinational affiliates of the Krupp combine, including American corporations, would go unchallenged (some of these corporations later obtained benefits from the United States government as a result of damage caused to their European holdings by Allied attacks). Finally, by leaving the Krupp empire intact, the Nuremberg proceedings indirectly facilitated the rebuilding of the German economy with its heavy industry closely wedded to the anticommunist nations.

Though political power influenced certain aspects of the Nuremberg trials, the judges strove to follow recognized legal precedents regarding evidence and due process. The final verdicts thus reflected the judges' determination of individual cases. Of the twenty-two defendants, twelve were sentenced to hanging, seven received prison terms ranging from ten years to life, and three were acquitted. Three of the six Nazi organizations charged with criminality were so declared. In reaching these diverse verdicts, the Nuremberg Tribunal managed to balance demands for severe retribution with complaints that the proceedings involved laws that were created after the crimes were committed (ex post facto laws). Whatever their political prejudices, the judges emphasized their roles in further defining the nature of international rules of war.

The Nuremberg proceedings provided guidelines for the trial of lesser war criminals in Japan and Germany. These subsequent trials, conducted by military tribunals of the individual victors and by the reconstituted German governments, eventually dealt with several thousand accused war criminals and resulted in hundreds of death sentences and prison terms. In sum, these various proceedings reaffirmed the basic principles of Nuremberg: aggressive warfare, violations of traditional warfare, and inhuman acts constituted crimes; individuals remained accountable for their criminal actions despite superior orders; and individuals accused of war crimes were entitled to judicial trials.

The legal precedents served to institutionalize the moral outrage caused by Nazi war crimes. "The time was ripe to step across the line from conscience to a legal order," explained the philosopher Ralph Barton Perry, "and to create a legal precedent for future times." The past three decades, however, have revealed the limitations of the Nuremberg precedent. During the Vietnam War, for example, proponents of American foreign policy and their critics both cited the Nuremberg conclusions to justify their mutually exclusive policies. Despite the high idealism of the participants, the Nuremberg Tribunal remained a political creature of the Grand Alliance.

Chapter 11

POSTWAR SOCIETY, 1945-1960

The atomic bombing of Hiroshima and Nagasaki ended World War Two much earlier than most Americans had anticipated. The mass jubilation of V-J Day was soon followed by a demand for rapid demobilization of the armed forces. More than one million servicemen had been discharged before the war's end, but nearly fourteen million remained under arms. These veterans viewed themselves as civilians-in-uniform. After an average of three years of military service, they were anxious to go home. But few were nostalgic for the prewar era, a time of general economic hardship. Their prevailing sentiment was expressed in a popular song of 1945: "Gotta Make Up for Lost Time."

Public attention focused on the problems and difficulties of readjustment. In 1945 the nation's divorces leaped to over half a million, twice as high as prewar figures. Such statistics reflected the haste of wartime marriages, the problems of long separations, and a growing sense of economic independence among women who had entered the labor force during the war. Veterans also faced serious economic problems. Most veterans wanted a job "with a future," but many found their wartime skills of little help in finding any employment. Government benefits under the GI Bill provided one year's unemployment insurance (at $20 per week) to ease the transition. Also vital for the ex-soldiers were their large wartime savings.

Readjustment was especially difficult for certain minority groups. Japanese-Americans, released from concentration camps in 1945, faced pervasive hostility and discrimination on the West Coast. White farmers who had confiscated Japanese agricultural property sometimes refused to surrender it and resorted to arson and violence to intimidate the rightful owners. In the southern states black veterans were reminded of their second-class status by a series of brutal lynchings that captured national attention. And poor veterans, of every nationality, returned to living conditions that reflected fifteen years of economic shortage.

The availability of government-financed scholarships under the GI Bill, however, offered veterans the possibility of attaining better-paying jobs. Between 1945 and 1950 over two million veterans took advantage of these appropriations to enroll in colleges and universities; millions more returned to high schools and vocational training programs. A postwar survey indicated that as many as one-fifth of the college-bound veterans would not otherwise have gone back to school. The heavy influx of students forced colleges to expand their facilities by opening branch campuses and offering evening instruction. Federal funds, by underwriting tuition bills, indirectly served as a catalyst for this expansion.

SCIENCE AND SOCIETY

The growing interest in higher education was stimulated by the achievement of American science during World War Two. The secret development of radar, the use of the pesticide DDT to kill malaria-carrying mosquitoes, the effectiveness of "miracle drugs" like penicillin in treating infection, the emergence of synthetic compounds to substitute for scarce resources like rubber—all testified to the importance of scientific research. In popular imagery, the scientist and the engineer became heroic figures.

These accomplishments were dwarfed at the war's end by the development of atomic bombs. During the war, atomic energy research had been classified top secret for reasons of military security. But the theoretical basis of the bomb had been established by physicists throughout the world. What was secret about the atom bomb was whether it would work. Once the bomb had been dropped over Japan, the secret was revealed. It was only a matter of time before other scientists could develop similar weapons. For this reason, Secretary of War Henry L. Stimson urged President Truman to allow the Soviet Union to share the atomic secrets along with Great Britain. Stimson was overruled, however, and the Truman administration chose to keep the bomb a secret—a symbol of American superiority.

Congress endorsed the policy of secrecy in the Atomic Energy Act of 1946. The law established an Atomic Energy Commission (AEC) and placed control of nuclear research and development in civilian hands. Though the United States held a monopoly of atomic weapons, official policy claimed to be seeking the abolition, or at least the limitation, of further nuclear production. Even proponents of secrecy shared Stimson's fear that modern civilization might be completely destroyed. The decision to keep the bomb secret also represented an attempt to remove atomic weapons from public discussion, where its feasibility might become a subject of political or military pressure.

Though a politically unmentionable subject, the bomb nevertheless unleashed profound fears about the future of scientific investigation. J. Robert Oppenheimer, head of the Los Alamos research team that developed the atom bomb, warned his colleagues in October 1945 that "if atomic bombs are to be added...to the arsenals of a warring world,...the time will come when mankind will curse the names of Los Alamos and of Hiroshima." Oppenheimer's concerns were mirrored on a popular level in postwar science fiction. Flourishing as never before, new science fiction writers like Isaac Asimov developed futuristic themes of human beings seeking to avert ultimate catastrophe. In Hollywood films the serious scientist became an ambivalent character, simultaneously capable of bringing salvation or annihilation.

These ambiguities began to disappear after 1949 when the Soviet Union tested its own atomic weapons, and the United States decided in 1950 to develop a hydrogen bomb of even greater destructive capability. Congress appropriated larger budgets to the AEC, which thereby attracted the best academic scientists. Cloaked in secrecy, American scientists no longer appeared as a demonic force, but as technicians in the service of their country. Despite civilian control of atomic energy, nearly all nuclear research and development involved military weapons. Scientists, instead of representing the independent search for truth, became subordinate to the military. These themes dominated the science fiction films of the fifties; invariably military personnel, portrayed as individualistic heroes, saved the scientist from his own confusion.

The popular distrust of atomic research reflected an underlying ambivalence about the alienation of modern society from nature and the physical environment. In glorifying the concept of scientific objectivity, natural and social scientists defined the universe as matter, a material entity that could be manipulated to serve human ends. Instead of seeing the universe as a home for all forms of life, the scientific mind stressed the importance of subduing and conquering nature. "Any addition to our store of adequately established knowledge," ar-

gued sex researcher Alfred C. Kinsey in 1953, "may ultimately contribute to man's mastery of the material universe." Such attitudes justified the scientists' "right to investigate," whatever the opinion of the larger society or the consequences of scientific research.

In advocating mastery of the material universe, however, scientists merely expressed the beliefs of most Americans. The sense of alienation from the environment appeared in such basic areas of life as food, clothing, and housing. "To change every contour of a site is not only to strip it of every root, tree and flower," complained the architect Robert Woods Kennedy. "It is to make an enemy of it." Throughout the postwar period, consumers welcomed inventions in chemistry that accelerated the production of synthetic goods. Fibers made of rayon, nylon, and Dacron were used in place of cotton and wool. In home furnishings, wood and leather increasingly gave way to plastic substitutes. Artificial flavors and food preservatives became staples in the American diet.

The widespread use of synthetic products, besides changing the quality standards of ordinary consumption, had serious side effects on the natural environment. Most synthetics were derivatives of petroleum products. Thus the use of artificial fibers in clothing or vinyl interiors in automobiles drained irreplaceable fossil resources. Yet postwar Americans seldom questioned the corporate or government decisions that irrevocably altered the face of the land. In 1957, for example, to avoid the possibility of a Japanese trade treaty with Communist nations, the Eisenhower administration authorized Japanese lumber companies to cut huge forests in the Tongass National Forest in Alaska. Equally serious, artificial waste products did not readily disintegrate into a natural organic state. Chemical waste products remained in the environ-

Ground zero, Hiroshima, symbolized the awesome power of atomic bombs. (U.S. Strategic Bombing Survey, National Archives 243-H-269)

ment to contaminate and even destroy the ecological balance. Only exceptional cases aroused public attention — such as the belated discovery that radioactive strontium 90, a "fallout" of atomic bomb testing, might be poisoning milk.

The lack of interest in ecological questions reflected a belief in unlimited growth. "The people of America need to be electrified by our limitless possibilities, not frightened into action by prophets of disaster," declared Truman's chief economic adviser, Leon Keyserling. Such optimistic assumptions encouraged needless use of natural resources. Thus when the

automobile industry began developing high horsepower engines, it easily persuaded the petroleum industry to develop appropriate high-octane gasoline. Similar waste appeared in the "planned obsolescence" of supposedly durable products such as automobiles. Two books of 1948, William Vogt's *Road to Survival* and Fairfield Osborn's *Our Plundered Planet*, warned about the limits of resources. "Man must recognize the necessity of cooperating with nature," Osborn declared. "The time for defiance is at an end." But most scientists simply denied the accuracy of such arguments.

The atomic age comes home — the predawn sky is lit by a test explosion 90 miles away, 1952. (UPI Photos)

And less articulate Americans preferred to accept business assurances that technology could solve all technological problems.

The reckless destruction of natural resources could be attributed not only to popular ignorance about the implications of technology but also to the culture's separation from the natural environment. Lacking any attachment to nature, postwar Americans glorified mobility, the use of synthetics, and the indiscriminate consumption of resources. These values encouraged the emergence of a rootless society that

was unconnected to nature. The lack of rootedness had profound effects on social and economic relationships.

BUSINESS RECONVERSION

The triumph of rootless social values was facilitated by a new alliance between government and big business. In accepting the scientific values of objectivity and detachment, postwar Americans also acknowledged the importance of expertise in decision making. They assumed that professional experts would render impartial decisions for the betterment of the entire society. Those with such expectations, however, failed to realize that government decisions increasingly reflected the interests of the business community.

During World War Two, the Roosevelt administration had depended heavily on the expertise of business leaders. These dollar-a-year men remained on the payrolls of their private corporations while making crucial economic decisions for the government. Their primary commitment to big business triggered a bitter debate about the reconversion to a civilian economy that began in 1944. As the demand for war production declined, Donald Nelson, chairman of the War Production Board, recommended that small businesses that were losing war contracts be allowed to reconvert to peacetime production. The larger corporations, he maintained, could continue to meet the military demands. This proposal was resisted vigorously within the WPB by big business leaders like Charles E. Wilson of General Electric. Fearing that small businesses would gain an advantage in the transition to civilian production and thereby threaten the prewar patterns of corporate competition, Wilson convinced military leaders to pressure the WPB to defeat Nelson's plan. Claiming wartime necessity, military and big business leaders combined to delay reconversion until 1945. Their resistance effectively protected the wartime expansion of big business; but it resulted in a continued shortage of civilian goods when the war ended.

Government also cooperated with big business in administering veterans' benefits. When only one-fifteenth of the first 1.5 million veterans chose to continue their GI life insurance policies, the military joined with commercial life insurance companies to launch an advertising campaign to reverse the trend. By early 1946 one-third of the veterans opted to continue their policies. The administration of GI mortgages also benefited private business. Though over one million veterans had taken out home loans by 1947, the mortgages were administered by the Veterans' Administration rather than the Federal Housing Authority. Veterans as a result had to satisfy the requirements of private bankers and pay higher interest rates. Moreover, while the VA would guarantee loans for private investors, it was notoriously lax in protecting veterans from unscrupulous builders and real estate agents.

The alliance between government and big business had important repercussions in the postwar economy. As World War Two ended, Chester Bowles, chairman of the Office of Price Administration (OPA), recommended the continuation of wartime economic controls to ease the transition to a civilian economy. Rapid decontrol, he warned, would benefit big businesses that controlled the lion's share of scarce resources; it would seriously undermine small businesses and would cause a severe inflation of prices. But the WPB instead responded to big business pressure and quickly lifted most of its wartime controls. Bowles's prediction proved remarkably accurate. Unable to obtain scarce material, small businesses folded or sold out to larger corporations. Big business also took advantage of the government's generous reconversion sales and purchased government-built wartime plants at a fraction of their costs. The government also offered liberal tax concessions and dropped the wartime excess-profits tax. Such subsidies facilitated business reconversion. They also assured that the biggest corporations would maintain their dominance of the postwar economy.

The abandonment of government controls created serious problems for consumers. Since businesses could obtain greater profits from expensive goods than from cheaper lines, manufacturers mainly produced high-priced goods. The resulting shortage of such necessities as clothing led to skyrocketing prices and an illegal black market. The abrupt lifting of WPB controls of building materials produced a similar crisis in the housing industry. Despite OPA protests, the WPB's reconversion policies encouraged the construction of higher-priced industrial plants without alleviating residential housing shortages. Builders and real estate brokers profited immensely as house prices soared overnight, in some cases even doubling.

Such economic problems forced President Truman to re-establish some of the wartime controls. But the larger businesses continued to monopolize scarce materials, keeping prices high. With the authority of OPA scheduled to end in June 1946, Truman appealed to Congress to extend its life. But when a conservative Congress reacted to business pressure and passed a weak bill, Truman vetoed it. The inflation only became worse, jumping as much as 35 percent in one month. Congress then passed another weak bill that Truman reluctantly approved. The new law extended price controls for one year. But ceilings on meat prices led farmers to withhold their products, creating shortages and a black market. Scarcity and inflation became important political issues in the 1946 elections.

The problems of reconversion were particularly acute for young adults. Many believed that the war had taken, in the words of the Hollywood Academy Award–winning film of 1946, "The Best Years of Our Lives." Two-thirds of the veterans had been unmarried while in uniform and most were anxious to settle down and start families. Such factors stimulated the largest baby boom in modern American history. Despite low levels of foreign immigration, the nation's population leaped from 140 million in 1945 to 152 million in 1950 and exceeded 179 million by 1960. This increase came largely from a high birthrate that grew steadily from 1940 until 1957, when it began to drop. These fertility patterns are particularly noteworthy, since the rate of marriage declined throughout the postwar period. Such statistics indicate that family size was increasing, particularly in the middle- and upper-income brackets.

The growth of population also depended on a declining death rate. Antibiotics such as streptomycin and Aureomycin helped control infectious diseases. The most dramatic breakthrough was the introduction of the Salk vaccine in 1955 to prevent the childhood killer poliomyelitis. As childhood mortality declined, life expectancy rose considerably between 1950 and 1959: for whites, from 69.1 to 70.5; for non-whites, from 60.8 to 63.5.

POPULATION MOBILITY

The expansion of population accelerated long-term patterns of mobility. Attracted initially by war-related industry, people flocked to the southwestern and western states. In Texas the growth of the petrochemical industry, stimulated by the increased use of fossil fuels, encouraged a population increase of one-third. In Arizona, Tucson and Phoenix mushroomed into sizable cities. The biggest growth came in California, which attracted over five million people between 1940 and 1960. California more than doubled its population in this period and surpassed New York as the most populous state in 1963. This burgeoning population was supported by the expansion of defense-related industries, particularly aircraft, electronics, and machinery. The admission of Alaska and Hawaii into the Union in 1959—the first new states since 1912—symbolized the westward movement of population.

While the national population increased and the center of population shifted toward the west, urban populations grew at an even faster rate. Between 1940 and 1960, 22 million people migrated from rural areas to cities, causing the rural population to decline from 11 million in 1940 to 7.4 million in 1960. This trend, part of a long historical process, reflected the reduced need for farm labor due to an increased mechanization of agriculture. Cities throughout the nation also attracted rural southern blacks who were escaping not only impoverished conditions but also more blatant forms of racial discrimination.

HOUSING SHORTAGE AND SUBURBAN DEVELOPMENT

The most immediate effect of this expanding population was a shortage of housing. During the Depression and World War Two, new residential construction had virtually disappeared. By 1945 the total value of American housing was worth 7 percent less than in 1929. The return of war veterans together with the surge of population put great pressure on existing facilities. The problem was aggravated by postwar shortages of building materials and by a related inflation of real estate costs. To solve these problems and cut housing costs, builders began to construct new residential structures on the fringes of cities, an area that soon became known as suburbia. With apartments unavailable, young families discovered that it was easier to purchase houses by obtaining a home mortgage. Such loans were frequently backed by the federal government under the FHA or VA. New construction soared in the decade after World War Two, stimulating the economy by its consumption of building materials and by creating new employment.

The most dramatic building success of the postwar period was made by Arthur Levitt, who popularized the construction of standardized housing. Using specialized work crews, interchangeable designs and materials, and package deals that included interior appliances, landscaping, and legal fees, Levitt brought single-unit dwellings to lower-middle-class families. To keep prices down, Levitt eliminated dining rooms, basements, and attics as well as unnecessary trim. When critics complained that Levitt's houses were monotonously repetitious, he offered customers different exterior paints, curved streets, and structures placed at slightly different angles. Levitt's mass-produced houses, which were imitated by builders throughout the nation, benefited from a new standardization within the appliance industry. Because postwar houses scrimped on such "extras" as closet space, built-in cabinets with standardized and interchangeable parts became a feature of kitchens and bathrooms.

The creation of suburban neighborhoods accentuated the rootlessness of American society. Remote from city centers, suburban workers had to commute to their jobs. The new housing developments, built in sparsely populated areas, also lacked such community institutions as libraries, schools, hospitals, mass transportation, and shopping facilities. Also absent from many of these neighborhoods were old people, who might have provided a sense of continuity. Even the landscape lacked roots. "The trees are so small," complained one midwesterner.

Suburbanites compensated for the lack of institutions by relying more on the automobile. Registered cars and trucks increased from thirty-one million in 1940 to sixty-one million in 1955. Where housewives were left behind, second cars became necessary to reach the new shopping centers, schools, or medical facilities. Besides consuming vast amounts of gasoline, automobiles produced noxious fumes that polluted the air. In 1947 the journalist John Gunther boasted that Los Angeles, by relying on electricity, would enjoy "clean industry... which in turn means clean towns." Yet within one decade the Los Angeles smog, caused by automobile exhausts, had become a serious health hazard.

The sense of suburban rootlessness was aggravated by a lack of attachment to the new houses. Since home buyers had little choice but to accept the limitations of postwar building design, they were prepared to sell their houses when economic conditions improved. As families grew in size, suburbanites readily moved to larger accommodations. The interchangeableness of residence was closely related to the interchangeableness of jobs. As chain stores proliferated in the new shopping centers, employees were "relocated" at the convenience of management. Store managers, Gunther complained, never became "a real ingredient in the life of a community." Gone too was the intimacy between small businesspeople and their customers. "Ever since the war," complained TV's Alice Kramden, "the butchers don't treat a woman with respect."

Though the withdrawal to the suburbs relieved some of the housing pressure, metropolitan centers remained desperately overcrowded.

Social critics blamed urban slums for encouraging crime, particularly juvenile delinquency. The idea gained popularity from such Hollywood films as *Knock on Any Door* (1949) and *Blackboard Jungle* (1955). When local government seemed unable to solve the urban housing problem, President Truman joined with conservative Senator Robert Taft to persuade Congress to pass the Housing Act of 1949. This legislation, asserting the importance of "decent" housing for all Americans, authorized slum clearance and the construction of 810,000 units of low-rent housing. Despite imaginative plans, however, the federal housing program was sidetracked by Korean War expenditures and further undermined by real estate interests and the unsympathetic Eisenhower administration.

The departure of middle-class taxpayers to the suburbs narrowed the urban tax base at a time when more people needed municipal services than ever before. With increased use of automobiles, mass transit deteriorated for want of funds. In some cities urban officials accepted bribes from bus companies to replace inexpensive electric trolley cars with gas-consuming buses. The resulting traffic congestion, together with air pollution, could not be eased even by the construction of new freeways that surrounded most major cities.

While city dwellers watched the quality of urban life decline, city planners discovered loopholes in the Housing Act that permitted them to destroy old buildings without constructing low-cost housing. Encouraged by the Eisenhower administration, urban renewal saw old neighborhoods, often with homogeneous ethnic populations, uprooted to make way for convention centers, office buildings, parking lots, and other nonresidential units. Such reconstruction brought profits to real estate interests, who accepted the values of rootlessness.

Lost, however, was the sense of urban communities that rooted people to local churches, playgrounds, and small businesses.

RESIDENTIAL SEGREGATION

The problems of urban congestion and housing shortage fell most heavily on racial minorities. Besides the problems of poverty, nonwhites also faced a pattern of organized discrimination that prevented them from finding adequate housing. Through "restrictive covenants," white property owners, with support from real estate brokers, frequently signed legally valid contracts agreeing not to sell or rent their dwellings to minorities. Such practices enjoyed the support of the federal government. "If a neighborhood is to retain stability," advised an FHA underwriting manual, "it is necessary that properties shall continue to be occupied by the same social and racial classes." And the FHA enforced its guidelines by refusing to insure any nonsegregated projects. For minority groups such practices meant overcrowding and high rents.

Patterns of residential segregation could be justified under the principle of "separate, but equal" that the Supreme Court had articulated in *Plessy* v. *Ferguson* in 1896. After World War Two, however, these assumptions increasingly came under attack. In 1947 Truman's Civil Rights Commission condemned the use of restrictive covenants. Black protesters described a federal plan for land clearance in Washington, D.C., as "a concerted drive...to establish a Hitler-like ghetto" and persuaded Congress to reject the plan. In his 1948 book, *The Negro Ghetto,* Robert C. Weaver charged that residential segregation was the major impediment to northern blacks' full participation in American life.

In protesting residential segregation, Weaver not only questioned the legality of restrictive covenants but also suggested that the principle of separate, but equal had inherent limitations. "As long as colored groups are relegated to separate parts of the city," he wrote, "as long as they live in a world apart..., colored Americans are stigmatized in the eyes of the rest of the population." Such stigmas created profound problems for blacks. Some blacks took pride in their blackness and accepted its social inconveniences. But others, who had partially absorbed the values of whites, tried to overcome their racial identity by bleaching their skin, straightening their hair, or, in the case of lighter-skinned people, "passing." These strategies created a hierarchy within the black community: "If you're white, you're all right/if you're brown, stick around/if you're black, keep back." The solution to such problems, most black leaders believed, was to eliminate the institutions that caused racial injustice.

Protests against segregated housing culminated in an NAACP-sponsored lawsuit, *Shelley* v. *Kraemer*. To support the case, the Justice Department argued that restrictive covenants undermined "respect for the dignity and rights of the individual." In 1948 the Supreme Court ruled that government support of such covenants was illegal. In accepting social science testimony that depicted the psychological and sociological damage caused by segregation, the Court laid the basis for a revision of the *Plessy* doctrine. But the *Shelley* case did not overturn the principle of separate, but equal. In throwing out restrictive covenants, however, it enabled blacks in northern cities to move into some previously exclusive neighborhoods.

Despite these advances, residential segregation persisted in most areas, affecting not only blacks but also Spanish-speaking and other minorities. Of the nearly one million Puerto Ricans who lived in New York in 1960, 40 percent were forced to live in inadequate dwellings. Yet their monthly rentals remained high, absorbing as much as one-third of their incomes. Spanish-speaking people in the western states suffered from similar disadvantages. In higher-income brackets, residential segregation affected such groups as Chinese, Japanese, and Jews, who tended to cluster in homogeneous communities. The existence of ethnic neighborhoods in cities, however, frequently reflected a positive assertion of cultural identity. Not all minorities wished to be assimilated in the American melting pot.

ROOTLESSNESS AND ROOTEDNESS

The tension between assimilation and cultural identity appeared most clearly in the case of Native Americans. Prior to World War Two, federal policy toward reservation tribes had wavered between detribalization and protection of Native American rights. In 1946 the Indian Claims Commission Act allowed the tribes to bring legal action against the federal government for violations of previous treaties. But though the law seemed to be protecting Native American culture, it was administered by the Bureau of Indian Affairs to hasten the removal of government services. This policy was made explicit in 1954 when Congress approved a series of termination bills. These laws called for the dissolution of tribal structures, the disbursement of tribal assets, and the ending of federal assistance. Implemented against the Meno-

menie of Wisconsin and the Klamath of Oregon, the policy created severe economic and social problems.

Within the Native American communities, two antithetical processes emerged after World War Two. Native American veterans frequently had trouble readjusting to traditional tribal life. In addition, many tribes were affected by the white technological culture, such as electricity and the mass media it introduced. As a consequence, traditional tribal rituals became less important and the number of Native American languages declined. In the face of this assimilation, Native Americans who were more traditional chose to resist the absorption of white culture. Thus the postwar period also saw a revitalization of Native American religions and a self-conscious attempt to preserve Native American identity. The reassertion of traditional cultures enabled Native Americans to oppose the termination program. In its place they proposed self-determination for each community. Yet the status of reservation tribes remained unresolved in the sixties.

The clash between a rooted society and a rootless one could also be seen in the status of American farmers. Though agriculture flourished through most of the postwar period, the farm population itself continued its historic decline. The application of technology to farming dramatically increased agricultural output by 6 percent per year between 1949 and 1959. But farm production rose chiefly because machines replaced workers. Equally significant, the total number of farms continued to decrease. These trends revealed the impact of technological values on rural America. Benefiting from research and development programs at state agricultural colleges, farmers invested in new equipment and new hybrid crops that could be handled safely by machines. In the Southwest, irriga-

Many elderly Americans found modest housing in trailer camps that sprang up in warm-weather states, such as this one in Florida. (Wide World Photos)

tion brought additional acreage under cultivation. Farmers also greatly increased the use of chemical fertilizers to stimulate growth; chemical pesticides to kill weeds, plant diseases, and insects; and chemical additives to fatten livestock and to assure that fields would ripen uniformly. Such practices involved vast inputs of fossil energy to fuel machinery and to stimulate crop growth. Many of the commonly used pesticides, such as DDT, were later found to be harmful to the ecological balance.

Technological agriculture proved to be extremely profitable. But mechanization and mass production required large capital outlays that small farmers could not afford. Moreover, mechanized agriculture was most efficient on large acreage. These factors encouraged the consolidation of farmlands in gigantic holdings and the shifting of ownership to large corporations. As conglomerates moved into farming, they formed monopolistic agribusinesses that controlled the food industry from seeding the fields to distributing the processed products.

The profitability of corporate agriculture depended heavily on federal government expenditures. Postwar food shortages in Europe provided large markets for American farm surpluses. As those outlets diminished, Congress approved the Agricultural Acts of 1948 and 1949, which provided government price supports for basic crops. Truman's secretary of agriculture, Charles Brannon, also pressed for a program of direct subsidies to farmers to compensate for overproduction. Though the Brannon Plan would have protected farmers from unprofitable markets, it rewarded the largest producers who grew the most crops. Even so, critics denounced the scheme as socialistic and a conservative Congress refused to pass it.

During the fifties, farmers producing agricultural surpluses continued to benefit from government price supports. This program was augmented in 1956 by an Agricultural Act that rewarded farmers for not planting certain crops. The Soil Bank Act of 1956 also reimbursed farmers for converting crop land into noncommercial conservation acreage. Despite such measures farmers continued to produce large surpluses. Moreover, the price support program offered disproportionate subsidies to the biggest farms. "The majority of farm people derive little or no benefit from our agricultural price support legislation," admitted the *Economic Report of the President* in 1959; "those with the higher incomes are the main beneficiaries."

The rise of technological agriculture not only destroyed community patterns of rural society but also imposed mass-produced food on the rest of the nation. Between 1950 and 1959 average per capita consumption of dairy products declined from 29.4 to 25.6 pounds per year, fresh fruits from 107.4 pounds to 101.5 pounds, and fresh vegetables from 139.5 to 125.2 pounds. Consumers made up for these losses by eating greater quantities of processed and frozen foods. Such products relied on nutritional additives, artificial flavoring and coloring, and preservatives to maintain a modicum of food value. These processes added as much as 30 percent to the cost of each edible pound of food.

The proliferation of chain supermarkets offered consumers few alternatives to this mass-produced fare. The inaccessibility of suburban shopping centers discouraged daily food purchases. And the availability of larger refrigerators and freezers, together with the growing use of preservatives, enabled families to store packaged foods for later consumption. Such eating habits also encouraged the expansion of drive-in restaurants and snack shops that offered standardized food throughout the country. Eating in restaurants, however, also introduced middle-class people to new varieties of cuisine. In reaction to mass food, a new interest in gourmet cooking appeared, and the sensuality of eating became an acceptable form of middle-class recreation.

CORPORATE ECONOMY

Government support of corporate agriculture reflected a general pattern of economic relations. During World War Two, business and political leaders expressed concern that reconversion and demobilization would bring another Depression. "We cannot have full employment and prosperity in the United States without foreign markets," Assistant Secretary of State Dean Acheson told a congressional committee in 1944. To obtain such markets, business needed adequate credit. But Acheson admitted that private capital was insufficient for the task. In the postwar years, therefore, government subsidies directly and indirectly bolstered business prosperity.

The likelihood of a postwar depression was initially offset by large wartime savings amounting to $140 billion and a strong desire of consumers to acquire scarce durable goods. This unusual demand, in the face of industrial shortages, produced a serious inflation that lasted through 1947. Business also benefited from huge government-sponsored exports to war-torn Europe. Encouraged by the Marshall Plan of 1947, merchandise exports exceeded imports by $25 billion in the first four years of peace.

By 1949, however, the demand for consumer durables declined and the economy entered a period of recession. Some economists saw this downturn as the end of the postwar honeymoon. But the recession was cushioned by growing expenditures for residential housing. These investments were supported by federal government policies that protected home loans and kept interest rates low while requiring minimal down payments and long-term mortgages. In this manner, government intervention in the economy helped to prevent a serious depression. The recessions of 1954 and 1958 evoked similar government responses. In both cases, federally supported private housing and new public construction increased to ease the problem.

Government intervention in the economy was even more important in the area of deficit spending for military purposes. In 1946 the Pentagon began an elaborate public relations campaign to persuade Congress to maintain American military strength. But a conservative Congress preferred to cut government expenditures and rejected the program. Despite such failures, military leaders joined business groups in advocating larger defense budgets. By 1947 the official acknowledgment of a "Cold War" with the Soviet Union reinforced these appeals. By that time Congress was prepared to increase military appropriations.

Such expenditures were crucial for stimulating economic growth. "Pressure for more government spending is mounting," reported *Business Week* in early 1950. "The reason is a combination of concern over tense Russian relations and a growing fear of a rising unemployment here at home." The outbreak of the Korean War in June 1950 ended any further debate. In the first year of the war, the military budget leaped from $14 billion to $34 billion, and exceeded $50 billion in 1953, the last year of the war. By then military expenditures represented 13.5 percent of the gross national product, while other defense-related federal government expenditures raised that number to 21 percent. It was no coincidence that unemployment in October 1953 reached a postwar low point of 1.8 percent, with slightly more than one million people out of work.

The continuation of the Cold War after the Korean cease-fire assured that high military budgets would be an integral part of the American economy. During the Eisenhower administration more than $350 billion was spent on defense, and 77 percent of every budget dollar was spent on military-related appropriations. The annual military budgets often meant the difference between corporate profits and losses. These vast expenditures included a program to stockpile strategic material that might be unavailable in time of future war. The program became a bounty for numerous industries.

Such supports to private industry illuminated an inseparable tie between military preparedness and business prosperity. Talk of a thaw in the Cold War invariably brought falling prices on Wall Street. A growing concern about these tendencies led President Eisenhower to devote his farewell address of 1961 to warning against the "military-industrial complex." "We have been compelled to create a permanent armaments industry of vast proportions," the outgoing president observed. "We annually spend on military security alone more than the net income of all United States corporations." Yet Eisenhower offered no solution to the situation, and John F. Kennedy campaigned in 1960 on the false assertion that the Republican administration had been lax enough to create a "missile gap."

The relationship between government and business involved more than the amassing of armaments. Central to the expansion of the economy was government support of research and development. Between 1950 and 1959, expenditures for "R and D" increased about threefold to an estimated $12 billion. Besides helping the defense industry, such appropriations supported university research programs at a rate of $300 million per year. With such incentives academic science readily worked to fight the Cold War. Most of the funding for these projects came from the federal government under the category of defense. For example, aircraft manufacturing, which was one of the largest growth industries of the postwar period, drew 80 percent of its business from military agencies. Employing 1.25 million workers in 1959, the aircraft industry was a major factor in the burgeoning West Coast economy. So too was the electronics industry, which grew 15 percent

a year, becoming the fifth largest industry in 1960. Most electronics sales went to the federal government, primarily for missiles and other military equipment.

Government agencies continued the World War Two pattern of relying on the largest corporations in awarding contracts to private business. Despite efforts of the Small Business Administration to encourage government procurement from smaller businesses, Defense Department awards to small firms steadily declined. The amount of R and D funds that reached small businesses was 4 percent, a figure unlikely to stimulate new corporate growth. Though convenient for government administrators, the support of big business did not bring reduced costs. Most contracts were awarded without competitive bidding, and business "overruns" were readily absorbed by federal budgets. There was little irony, therefore, when Eisenhower's secretary of defense, Charles E. Wilson, remarked, "For years I thought what was good for the country was good for General Motors, and vice versa."

CONSUMER SPENDING

Corporate prosperity reinforced a belief in unlimited growth that in turn stimulated unprecedented consumer spending. "Not only do the younger people accept the beneficent society as normal," reported sociologist William H. Whyte, Jr.; "they accept *improvement,* considerable and constant, as normal too." Despite significant economic recessions in 1948–1949, 1953–1954, and 1957–1958, private consumption steadily increased each year. Even though real wages did not return to World War Two levels until 1955, consumers drew upon savings in the immediate postwar years to acquire such durable goods as appliances, automobiles, furniture, and television sets. This mass consumption was a reaction to the commodity shortages that dated from the Depression. By 1949, however, the demand for durables dwindled and contributed to the recession.

As consumers satisfied their demand for durables, they shifted their interest to other types of commodities. Attracted by seemingly liberal credit policies, purchasers went into debt beyond the prewar highs of the twenties. Consumer installment indebtedness reached $34 billion in 1957, or nearly 10 percent of personal income. Such "conspicuous consumption" may have been an attempt to assert individuality. Though American culture traditionally valued personal uniqueness, the nationalization of the marketplace, together with the mass media, seemed to be homogenizing social differences. By purchasing new innovative products (such as "hi-fidelity" or stereophonic record players), middle-class consumers could reassert their unique personalities. Similarly, larger cars, with exaggerated "fins" on the rear fenders, allowed drivers to appear particularly bigger and bolder. Men's clothing styles began imitating women's fashions by undergoing annual changes that made serviceable wardrobes outmoded overnight. The attempt to live one step ahead of the Joneses, moreover, created an endless cycle of buying.

These consumption patterns closely followed one of the major growth industries of the postwar period: advertising. Though popular exposés like Vance Packard's *The Hidden Persuaders* (1957) explained the underlying techniques of advertising, market research showed that the consuming public remained more responsive to emotional appeals than to product substance. Annual advertising expenditures

soared over the $10-billion mark by 1960. The largest expenditures were in consumer softwares and luxuries such as tobacco, beverages, drugs, amusements, and home furnishings. A significant factor in postwar advertising was its emphasis on national media rather than local outlets. The trend facilitated product identification for a rootless population that migrated at an increasing pace. The importance of advertising was attested by the highly effective TV commercials developed by Batten, Barton, Dursten, and Osborn for Eisenhower's 1952 presidential campaign.

The growth of the advertising industry was part of a larger expansion of all service industries in the postwar economy. Once consumers had purchased their durable commodities, they steadily spent larger sums for such services as rent, insurance, automobile repairs, and medical care as well as for utilities and public transportation. This heavy demand for services, though unable by itself to support a high growth rate in the economy, was a crucial factor in avoiding a downturn. Yet when the rate of military expenditures dropped in 1957, the result was a severe recession.

The expansion of service industries indicated a new dimension of the American labor force. As part of a long historic tradition, technological innovation had increased individual worker productivity. This process in turn diminished the number of blue-collar jobs. Yet technology also created new occupations in white-collar services. Equally important, the growth of corporations led to the expansion of a managerial corps of employees who administered the bureaucracies rather than produced commodities. In 1956 the number of workers in service industries exceeded the number of producers for the first time, thus heralding the postindustrial society.

Indicative of this pattern was the growth of government bureaucracy. Employment in state and local government rose two million between 1950 and 1960, an increase of 52 percent. The federal bureaucracy also expanded in both civilian and military spheres. By 1960 nearly 8.5 million employees were drawing government paychecks, largely for white-collar employment.

LABOR UNIONS AND
ECONOMIC STABILITY

Despite the remarkable economic growth of the postwar period, unemployment remained an endemic problem. Worried about the possibility of another Depression, Congress approved the Employment Act of 1946. The law committed the federal government to maximize employment by direct intervention in the economy. It also created a Council of Economic Advisers to help the president formulate policy. Though the act only made explicit what the government had done during the Depression and World War Two, neither Truman nor Eisenhower wholly endorsed its implications of a government-regulated economy.

The feared levels of mass unemployment never materialized. But the sudden termination of war contracts resulted in temporary layoffs and a cut in overtime work. Worker take-home pay dropped just as the lifting of wartime controls stimulated an inflation of prices. Workers responded with a series of prolonged strikes that threatened the entire economy. Though the Truman administration condemned the strikes, workers managed to win substantial wage increases as well as "cost-of-living" adjustments to offset inflation. Businesses passed these raises on to consumers, however, thereby

feeding the inflationary cycle. Though the 1946 strikes aroused bitter verbal controversy, John Gunther pointed out that during the large automobile walkout, "there was not one bloody nose." Labor unions continued to seek higher wages, better working conditions, and job security packages. But labor radicalism waned as unions recognized the importance of cooperating with business and government in stimulating the economy. Fundamental to this growing conservatism was the purging of Communists from AFL and CIO unions and the passing of leadership to staunch defenders of capitalism.

The legal guidelines for cooperation between labor and business were established in the Taft-Hartley Act of 1947. To protect the public interest from harmful labor-management disputes, the law allowed the government to seek an injunction against strike action and provided for a sixty-day "cooling-off" period during which federal mediators would try to settle the issues. If disputes remained unsettled, the president could ask Congress for additional legislation. Truman and Eisenhower called for strike injunctions seventeen times between 1947 and 1959.

Taft-Hartley also prohibited "closed" shops (which forced employers to hire only union members) but permitted "union" shops (in which all employees had to join a union after being employed). It prohibited secondary boycotts, jurisdictional strikes, and certain "unfair labor practices." As an additional conservative measure, the law required union leaders to certify that they were not members of the Communist party or other subversive groups. On the level of state government, Taft-Hartley was followed by "right-to-work" laws that permitted "open" shops, in which workers did not have to join a union.

Organized labor viewed Taft-Hartley as an attack on basic workers' rights and vowed to see the law repealed. Yet union membership, which had increased dramatically during the Depression and World War Two, stabilized near the wartime highs. White-collar workers, more numerous than ever before, remained nonunion. Even before Taft-Hartley restricted organizing activities, many unions were ignoring the unorganized segments of the labor force. During World War Two the NAACP battled with racist unions to win admission for blacks, but often failed to persuade all-white locals to change their policies. Many unions also neglected to organize women workers, believing that females were a threat to male union-members' jobs. Instead, rival AFL and CIO unions debated jurisdictional issues and raided each other's membership.

The threat of Taft-Hartley forced organized labor to re-evaluate its goals. In 1951 the CIO expelled eleven member unions for communist leanings, a decision that not only emphasized labor's support of the Cold War but also indicated the similarities between the CIO and the AFL. By the fifties the AFL had accepted the idea of industrial unionism, while the CIO had endorsed labor stability. Such agreement of purposes led to the merger of the AFL-CIO in December 1955.

The resolution of interunion rivalry enabled organized labor to present a united front on political and economic issues. But the AFL-CIO, under the leadership of George Meany, supported the existing pattern of government-subsidized business prosperity and simply tried to obtain its share of the wealth. Union negotiators accepted the importance of cooperating with business by accepting cost-of-living increases, clauses that permitted reopening contracts if economic conditions changed, and

long-term settlements. More concerned with economic security than with altering the structure of society, unions increasingly sought such fringe benefits as pensions, paid vacations, paid sick leaves, and medical and hospitalization plans. Even without these extras, the annual real income of wage earners increased about 25 percent between 1946 and 1959.

With priorities on economic stability, however, unions preferred industry-wide agreements that tended to eliminate competition between separate businesses. Such broad settlements also reduced the autonomy of individual unions. In effect, organized labor used its strength to assure worker compliance with agreed-upon business decisions. "We need the union to insure enforcement of the contract we have signed, to settle grievances, to counsel employees in giving a fair day's work for a fair day's pay," acknowledged a business leader, "to help increase productivity." Unauthorized "wildcat" strikes were aimed not only at employers but also at unresponsive union bureaucrats.

The separation of union leadership from rank-and-file workers often encouraged the alliance between labor and business. The amount of worker participation in union elections declined from 82 percent in the prewar period to 58 percent in 1958, a trend that continued through the next two decades. Such patterns enabled the existing leadership to maintain its control of union policy and to suppress dissident rank-and-file movements. Union leaders often drew large salaries and enjoyed executive privileges such as nontaxable expense accounts that put them in the same class as business leaders.

While critics complained about the union leadership's "passion for respectability," congressional investigation unearthed widespread corruption in the management of union funds.

In 1954 a Senate investigating committee, chaired by James L. McClellan of Arkansas, exposed financial abuses and racketeering, particularly in the Teamsters Union. Such revelations led the AFL-CIO leadership to expel the Teamsters as well as other suspected unions. This belated housecleaning failed to prevent further government action. In 1959 the Landrum-Griffin Act required unions to file economic statements with the Department of Labor, a measure the Executive Council of the AFL-CIO viewed as a "severe setback."

POVERTY AND SOCIAL CLASS

Steady increases in annual average wages and the expansion of white-collar employment seemed to justify John Kenneth Galbraith's vision of *The Affluent Society* (1958). But Galbraith's title was unduly optimistic. Despite the appearance of affluence and prosperity, certain groups remained deeply impoverished, even by the government's conservative definitions. As workers lost their jobs to automation, unemployment became a pervasive problem. Rates of unemployment ranged between a low of 3 percent during the Korean War to nearly 8 percent during the recessions of 1948–1949 and 1957–1958. Even in the recovery years of 1956 and 1959, they averaged 4.2 percent and 5.3 percent respectively. These wage losses were not offset by government welfare programs. Unemployment insurance reimbursed only 20 percent of lost worker incomes. Not only were payments low, but many workers were not protected by insurance programs or had exhausted their benefits.

Another class of impoverished people were the elderly, people over the age of sixty-five. A 1960 Senate report admitted that "at least one-half of the aged — approximately eight million people — cannot afford today decent housing, proper nutrition, adequate medical care, preventive or acute, or necessary recreation." Unable to work for reasons of health or mandatory retirement policies, they derived most of their incomes from social security payments, private pensions, or welfare. During the fifties the number of people entitled to social security benefits increased nearly fivefold, to 9.6 million. Yet government assistance provided only a small fraction of their incomes. As a result, more than half of the households headed by people over sixty-five had an income level of less than $3,000 a year in 1960. Even elderly property owners found their standards of living declining as inflation and higher property taxes cut into their fixed incomes. One symptom of this problem was the proliferation of old-people's trailer camp settlements in warm-weather states like Florida.

Nonwhites also suffered disproportionately. As victims of racial as well as economic discrimination, nonwhites earned substantially less than whites in all parts of the nation. Moreover, in the period from 1949 to 1959, the gap between black and white incomes increased. The major problem for nonwhites was obtaining entry into occupations that paid better wages. Consigned by custom and prejudice to menial jobs, blacks experienced upward occupational mobility at a rate far below that of immigrant ethnic groups. A study of occupational patterns in Boston demonstrated that this gap was a function not of education, but of racial discrimination. Black women, for example, concentrated in low-paying jobs such as housekeeping, waitressing, and practical nursing. On these levels their paltry incomes were not significantly different from those of white women. But in factory work, which still paid only poverty-level wages, black women earned substantially less than whites.

Other minority groups, such as Puerto Ricans, Mexican-Americans, Native Americans, Asian-Americans, and rural whites, also obtained extremely low incomes. Most worked in occupations that were not protected by minimum-wage laws. In New York City 80 percent of the Puerto Rican families earned less than the Department of Labor's estimated minimum levels for "modest but adequate" standards of living. Such figures placed Puerto Ricans below blacks in the city's hierarchy. In the western states the income of Spanish-speaking workers ranked higher than that of blacks but substantially below that of whites. In California the average income of Japanese and Chinese families in 1959 was a lowly $3,000, but even that was higher than the income of Spanish-speaking Americans. Poorest of all nonwhites were Native Americans, who lived in such severe squalor on reservations that their death rate was three times the national average.

Rural whites also earned less than the national average. In 1959, 1.5 million farmers, five-sixths of them white, earned less than $3,000. Most of them lived in the South in dilapidated housing that lacked electricity and plumbing. Government studies indicated that 56 percent of these low-income farm families suffered from serious dietary deficiencies. During the fifties 1.5 million whites were forced to leave Appalachia, perhaps the most rooted white culture in the nation, to find jobs in the cities. These migrants settled in poor urban neighborhoods, estranged from their rural roots. But they retained their traditional culture and helped to popularize country and western music among urban dwellers much as blacks had carried the blues to the cities in the twenties.

A black schoolhouse in rural Alabama, 1945. The war bond poster contrasts with an otherwise stark interior. (Amistad Research Center)

WOMEN AND THE WORK FORCE

Among the poorest households were those headed by women. Widows, unmarried mothers, and women who were divorced, separated, or deserted headed one-twelfth of American households in 1956. Most worked as secretaries, sales help, or in semiskilled trades — occupations that were generally unorganized by unions. Lacking union support, women were forced to accept lower salaries than men for similar work tasks. Such discriminatory patterns reflected a larger ambivalence about the status and role of women in postwar society.

Many Native Americans, like this woman on an Apache reservation in Arizona, still obtain water from unsafe or contaminated sources. (Office of Information Services, Division of Indian Health, U.S. Public Health Service)

Women's participation in the wartime work force set an important precedent for female employment. Though many women were subsequently replaced by returning veterans, female employment increased sharply in 1947 and returned to the World War Two levels by 1950. This trend continued in the next decade. Between 1940 and 1960 the number of female employees doubled. By 1960, 40 percent of the adult female population was at work, a striking increase from the prewar 25 percent rate.

The persistence of economic discrimination against women workers, however, revealed a new aspect of this burgeoning female employment. The average age of women employees in 1960 was forty-one; and 60 percent of women workers were married. Households in which both husband and wife worked reached

333

the ten-million mark by 1960. These two-income families included a growing number of mothers with young children. Prior to World War Two, working wives and mothers usually came from the poorest classes of society. But in the postwar period, an increasing number of middle-class women found jobs even when their husbands earned substantial incomes.

In explaining their entry into the labor force, most working women emphasized financial necessity as a motive. Yet that response took on a new meaning in the fifties. Since real wages remained lower than wartime earnings until 1955, families needed additional incomes to acquire goods and services they desired to compensate for prewar and wartime deprivation. The soaring birthrate reinforced these felt needs. Moreover, as consumption became an integral part of middle-class culture, the demand for luxury items encouraged two-income families. Finally, at the end of the fifties, an inflation of prices exceeded wage increases, again causing a decline of real income and providing an impetus for wives to work. Yet such economic motives, pervasive though they were, did not persuade employers to offer equal pay for equal work. Working women, it was commonly believed, did not need as much income as working men.

The middle-class status of postwar working women indicated that more than economic necessity was a reason for employment. The desire to purchase luxury items and other consumables satisfied psychological desires that women shared with men. Working wives, like their husbands, also stressed the relationship between work and a sense of personal fulfillment. The higher the level of female education, the more likely it was that women would enter the labor force. Finding satisfaction in occupational roles rather than in traditional domestic situations provided the background for a growing sense of female independence.

The rise of female employment challenged the traditional view that a woman's proper place was in the home. According to accepted psychological theory, women were naturally passive, unassertive, and therefore ill equipped to cope with the problems of business. Women who were competitive or who ventured into public life were by definition unnatural. "I Denied My Sex," a popular-magazine story about a woman's career in police work, typified a pulp literature that advocated domesticity. The most popular television comedy of the fifties, "I Love Lucy," consistently parodied the housewife's craving to become a success outside the home. Middle-class magazines like *Good Housekeeping* and *Mademoiselle* urged women to accept the satisfaction of raising children and supporting their male breadwinners. "A family is like a corporation," declared a journalist. "We all have to work for it."

FAMILY RELATIONS

This celebration of domestic tranquillity nevertheless concealed a basic tension in American family relations. Many housewives, frustrated by domesticity but afraid to challenge traditional values, turned to alcohol, tranquilizers, or psychiatrists for solace. The desire to make some "contribution" to the family income impelled some well-to-do housewives to become shoplifters, even though they had sufficient money to purchase the goods they stole. TV programs with titles like "The Honeymooners," "Make Room for Daddy," and "Father Knows Best" ostensibly portrayed marital bliss. But the plot structures emphasized intense family conflicts, often characterized by verbal aggression. TV commercials also appealed to an unceasing battle of the sexes. Such evidence helps to explain why, despite all the propaganda for domesticity, marriage rates steadily declined while divorces increased.

The disintegration of traditional marriages also reflected a conflict between sexual values and sexual behavior. In 1948 Alfred Kinsey and a group of researchers at Indiana University published *Sexual Behavior in the Human Male*, followed five years later by a similar study of females — both of which became best sellers despite an esoteric format and a mass of statistical charts. At a time when popular magazines advocated premarital virginity, the Kinsey report revealed that most men and nearly 50 percent of women had experienced premarital intercourse. Kinsey also discerned that many people were reluctant to discuss sexual immorality, considering it "a religious obligation to impose their codes upon all other segments of the population." Yet half the men and 26 percent of the women interviewed had experienced extramarital sexual relations. In addition, 37 percent of the men and 28 percent of the women had some overt homosexual contacts. Kinsey concluded that two-thirds of the marriages studied had serious sexual disagreements and he speculated that 75 percent of the divorces were caused by sexual incompatibility.

The erosion of the traditional family was seen by conservatives as the cause of a new national malaise — juvenile delinquency. President Truman joined a chorus of politicians who saw the cure for juvenile crime in women staying at home. But statistical surveys in Detroit indicated that the children of working mothers had a lower-than-average rate of delinquency. Social workers and economists pointed to the relationship between poverty and juve-nile crime, suggesting that slum clearance and social welfare programs would solve the problem. Newspapers were particularly interested in juvenile sex crimes, luridly describing teenage sex clubs, prostitution, and rape. This emphasis on adolescent sexuality fit a statistical pattern described by the Kinsey report. According to Kinsey, males reached a peak of sexuality in their late teens (women, Kinsey found, peaked in their thirties), but the existing values denied them a legitimate sexual outlet. Kinsey suggested that teenage sexuality was normal and healthy, and he urged parents and law enforcement authorities to be more understanding and more tolerant.

Kinsey's advice reinforced the messages that adults were receiving from the most popular pediatrician of the postwar era, Dr. Benjamin Spock. His *Baby and Child Care*, published in 1946, sold over twenty-two million copies. The book's popularity indicated that postwar adults, having migrated away from their own parents, felt a need for expert counsel on so fundamental a matter as child rearing. "Trust yourself," Spock told these anxious parents. "Don't take too seriously all that the neighbors say. Don't be overawed by what the experts say. Don't be afraid to trust your common sense." Where earlier government child-rearing pamphlets had emphasized a strict regimen in nurturing, Spock called for flexibility. His respect for children led critics to denounce his "permissiveness." Yet Spock advocated firm parental control based on a spirit of love and understanding.

The reliance on child-rearing expertise and the general concern about juvenile crime shared a common basis: adults lacked confidence in their ability to understand and to guide the young. Hollywood films like *The Wild One* (1953) and *Rebel Without a Cause* (1954) portrayed a youth culture that rejected the materialistic values of their parents. "I love people with kids," scoffed a gangster in *Desperate Hours* (1955). "They don't take no chances." The caution of adults toward their children led to an emphasis on "social adjustment" and "conformity," a trend symbolized by the growth of Little Leagues that replaced the spontaneous play of childhood with adultlike uniforms, schedules, and scorecards. "No longer is it thought to be the child's job to understand the adult world as the adult sees it," complained David Riesman in his classic study, *The Lonely Crowd* (1950). Instead, children reacted to a media-built world that depicted appropriate childhood models.

YOUTH CULTURE

The separation between adults and children culminated in the emergence of a unique youth culture. More concerned about peer approval, adolescents formed clubs, cliques, and gangs that experimented with cigarettes, alcohol, and sex. From the mid-fifties, their music was rock and roll. The language of their songs complained about parents who pried into their private lives, warned people not to step on their territory, and boasted that rock and roll was here to stay. Their hero was Elvis Presley, who mixed pelvic thrusts with knowing grins. And they swayed romantically to songs like "Love Me Tender" and "Earth Angel." Though the rate of premarital sexual intercourse increased during the fifties, teenagers avoided public sexuality lest they acquire a "reputation." The introduction of a new dance, "The Twist," by Chubby Checker in 1959, however, turned suggestive dancing into a national fad. But it was

not until the next decade that adolescents discarded all conventional dance steps and found communal rhythms by dancing en masse.

Adults claimed to be shocked by the rock-and-roll generation and its flaunting of convention. But to a remarkable degree, the youth culture simply imitated middle-class adult models. Though delinquents might dress in black leather jackets and motorcycle boots, most teenagers aspired to "dress up" like their parents. Teenagers also borrowed their parents' attitudes toward consumption, forming a multibillion dollar adolescent market for records, clothing, jewelry, automobiles, and entertainment. Marriage also remained a major goal for most, so much so that teenage girls were known to sacrifice academic grades to avoid appearing exceptional and therefore unpopular. So pervasive were these values that truly exceptional youth, such as the poet Sylvia Plath, felt they were suffocating inside a "bell jar" of conformity. This mood of acceptance dominated college campuses, where a "silent generation" expressed a distinct preference for courses in business administration and education.

PUBLIC EDUCATION AND EDUCATIONAL GOALS

Despite this youthful conservatism, parents worried about the next generation and hoped that public schools could compensate for the deficiencies of home. School buildings were strained beyond capacity, however, as the arrival of the first baby-boom students forced school districts to open makeshift quarters and adopt "split-session" instruction. As more parents became concerned about the quality of education, school budgets increased, making teaching an attractive occupation for college graduates. The academic content of the curricula largely reflected the pedagogical philosophy of John Dewey and progressive education. Education, according to progressive theories, should discard rote learning and instead emphasize the individuality and life experiences of the students. Progressive educators went further to suggest that vocational training, social guidance, and "hygiene" were appropriate subjects of instruction.

Such goals were not always implemented. "The best thing about contemporary education," wrote psychologist Paul Woodring in 1952, "is that a great many classroom teachers ignore the gobbledygook and the pedagoguese and go right ahead and do a sensible job of teaching." These sentiments reflected a growing belief that American public schools, by emphasizing such amorphous goals as a student's social adjustment, were failing to provide basic education. Right wing anticommunists claimed that certain textbooks were "un-American" and, in many cases, succeeded in purging so-called subversive material. Educators like the historian Arthur E. Bestor challenged the lack of intellectual development in the public schools and suggested taking education out of the hands of academic professionals. Such comments had little effect on the public school system.

The optimistic belief that Americans had created a superior educational program, however, was rudely destroyed in 1957 when the Soviet Union launched Sputnik, the first artificial satellite. Shocked by this Cold War defeat, educational reformers scurried to make amends. As Admiral Hyman Rickover stated, the proper sphere of education was *the intellect alone.* For most people this philosophy meant rejuvenating mathematics and the sciences and de-emphasizing "softer" subjects in the humanities. Spurred by the crisis, President

For white middle-class youth, the 1950s were a time of affluence, with more people attending high schools and colleges than ever before. (Elliott Erwitt/Magnum)

Eisenhower persuaded Congress to pass the National Defense Educational Act in 1958. The law, which provided the first major federal aid to education, offered funds to encourage the study of science, mathematics, and foreign languages. This government support, which later was extended to include such subjects vital to the "national defense" as history, stimulated the vast expansion of higher education in the next decade.

EDUCATIONAL SEGREGATION

The extraordinary faith that Americans placed in public education vividly contrasted with the social caste system that excluded minority groups from equal educational opportunities. Under the doctrine of separate, but equal, seventeen states required segregated public schools in 1951. But the problem involved more than separate facilities. In 1945 the southern states spent twice as much to educate white children as blacks; in 1947 four times as many whites as blacks finished high school. Such statistics belied the fiction of separate, but equal.

Determined to challenge these policies, the NAACP, under the direction of lawyer Thurgood Marshall, initiated a series of legal suits to end discrimination in education. Benefiting by postwar antipathy to racism, Marshall won significant victories against segregated law schools and graduate schools by arguing that the alternative black institutions were unequal in quality to white schools. Such arguments failed to confront the negative effects of segregation itself.

In a bold departure, Marshall decided to attack public school segregation by denying the concept of separate, but equal. Using psychological evidence demonstrating that "prejudice and segregation have definitely detrimental effects on the personality development of the Negro child," Marshall persuaded the Supreme Court to reconsider the *Plessy* doctrine. In a historic ruling, *Brown* v. *Board of Education of Topeka,* delivered May 17, 1954, the Su-

preme Court acknowledged that to segregate children "because of their race generates a feeling of inferiority ... that may affect their hearts and minds in a way unlikely ever to be undone." In public education, the Court concluded, " 'separate but equal' has no place. Separate educational facilities are inherently unequal."

The *Brown* decision, which was written by Eisenhower's first appointee to the Supreme Court, Chief Justice Earl Warren, heralded a new era in race relations. Most liberals, including the NAACP attorneys, believed that institutional segregation was the cause of racial prejudice. They therefore believed that the new legal principle would establish a society based on racial equality. In 1955 the Supreme Court reaffirmed that idea by ordering immediate compliance with the *Brown* ruling. Other segregated institutions, such as restaurants, movie theaters, toilets, and transportation, seemed likely to fall.

The southern states, however, refused to accept the Court's decision. Some opposed any alteration of traditional race relations; others bitterly resented this new expansion of federal power over states' rights. Southerners then launched a determined and bitter program of "massive resistance" to public school integration. Inspired by White Citizens' Councils, some areas, such as Prince Edward County in Virginia, closed all the public schools rather than integrate. Mobs attacked black schoolchildren and physically blocked their attendance at white schools. In 1957 Eisenhower federalized the National Guard and sent paratroopers to Little Rock, Arkansas, to protect black students at Central High School. Even with such dramatic efforts, public school integration proceeded at a snail's pace. In 1960 less than 1 percent of black children attended integrated schools in the southern states. In the North, a pattern of de facto segregation remained unaffected by the Supreme Court's decision.

SPORTS, ENTERTAINMENT, AND SEXUALITY

The antipathy to integration, besides reflecting traditional racist feelings, had a psychological basis in a fear of physical contact between the races. Throughout American history, blacks had symbolized body activity in work, in dance, in sex. Proximity to blacks threatened to expose whites to their own elemental passions. One stereotyped answer to proposed integration — "Would you want your daughter to marry one?" — reflected this underlying fear. The destruction of the principle of separate, but equal eliminated what white racists considered the only alternative to racial and sexual chaos.

The fear of body contact was first attacked in the area of sports. Joe Louis, heavyweight boxing champion during World War Two, carefully avoided challenging the principles of white supremacy. But in some southern states it was illegal for white boxers to meet blacks in the ring. Blacks were permitted to play football on northern college campuses, but were conveniently left behind when their teams played against southern colleges. Blacks were excluded from playing basketball on Big Ten teams. "This is an indoor sport," John Gunther explained, "and taboos are strong...against any contact between half-clad, perspiring bodies, even on the floor of a gym." Major league baseball was not integrated until Jackie Robinson broke the color line with the Brooklyn Dodgers in 1947. But even then, Robinson was forbidden by his managers to argue with umpires or

express any aggression toward whites. By 1960 baseball, basketball, and football were racially integrated industries, though it was observable that nonstarring players were usually white.

The acceptance of black athletes was facilitated by the emergence of mass spectator sports in the postwar period. As personal consumption grew, so too did expenditures for recreation, which increased from $11.3 billion in 1950 to $18.3 billion in 1959 to $21.6 billion in 1962. This pattern was dramatized by the expansion of major league baseball to the West Coast in 1957, a process that helped to nationalize professional sports while destroying local minor league teams. TV revenues became increasingly important as a source of capital, and these monies depended on high viewer ratings. Black athletes helped to expand the size of this spectator base.

A major consumer of sporting equipment, however, was not teams, colleges, or athletes, but rather big business. Concerned about worker morale, large corporations bought recreational facilities for their employees and encouraged the formation of company teams. Such expenditures helped establish corporate loyalty and supported the fiction that corporations were happy families. From the employers' point of view, such benefits linked higher productivity to social reward. Yet organized sports, particularly company-sponsored programs, did not increase free time. By planning recreation, these programs eliminated spontaneous leisure. Such organized entertainment became more common in the postwar decades, culminating in the TV sports spectator culture.

The emergence of television represented a major innovation in mass entertainment. In 1947 there were ten TV broadcasting stations in operation; TV sets numbered about 20,000, and manufacturers were producing about 7,000

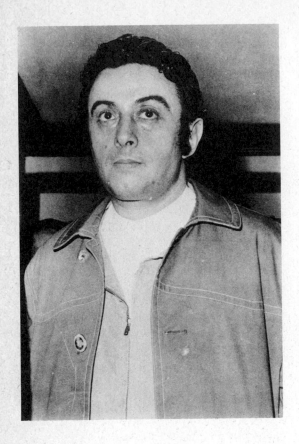

Lenny Bruce

1926-1966

The most controversial comedian of the post-war era was a stand-up nightclub performer named Lenny Bruce. Using a jazz soloist's style, Bruce blended plain street talk with Yiddish idiom to satirize and demystify social convention. His favorite subjects were religious hypocrisy, the artificiality of traditional sexual relationships, and racial chauvinism. He dedicated his autobiography, How To Talk Dirty and Influence People (1972), to "all the followers of Christ and his teachings; in particular to a true Christian—Jimmy Hoffa—because he hired ex-convicts as, I assume, Christ would have."

Born Leonard Schneider in New York, he joined the Navy at the age of sixteen and saw active service in the Mediterranean. After the war Bruce hustled as a con-artist for mock charities before drifting into comedy work in sleazy nightclubs. By the mid-fifties Bruce's type of humor won national attention. He appeared on national television, made popular records, and captivated audiences at top nightclubs across the country.

Bruce's comic routines illuminated the unspoken anxieties of fifties culture. While middle-class ethnic groups embraced homogenized suburban values (including, as in Bruce's case, the changing of ethnic names), the comedian's sketches reaffirmed the vitality of ethnic, religious, and racial identity. As middle-class Americans celebrated traditional monogamous marriages, despite a soaring divorce rate, Bruce spoke about alternative premarital, extramarital, and homosexual relationships. He attacked middle-class consumption patterns, raged against bureaucracy, and pointed to the absurdity of a Christian country waging endless war.

Bruce's insistence on artistic sincerity led him to attack legal censorship of free speech. His use of explicit language brought police repri-

sals, and he faced a series of arrests and court trials in several cities on charges of obscenity. The endless litigation drained his energy, and the subject of legal harassment came to dominate his nightclub act.

As police departments worked with municipal courts to silence the "sick" comedian, Bruce died of an overdose of heroin. His obscenity conviction, however, was overturned posthumously. Bruce's quarrel with the censorship of language provided an important basis for the free speech movements that later spread over many college campuses.

sets each year. In 1948 sales suddenly skyrocketed as consumers discovered a durable household means of entertainment. Set ownership became a status symbol. Each year, the number of TV sales rose as households clamored to buy not only one set, but often two. By 1957 Americans owned forty million TV sets and could select programs from as many as seven broadcasting channels at a time.

TV, as a new industry, was controlled by the same corporations that dominated radio. Programming was determined not by the content of the shows but, as in radio, by the ability of a broadcast to attract commercial sponsors. In the early years of TV broadcasting, when its commercial abilities remained unproved, networks often bought packaged programs manufactured by advertising agencies. In 1951, however, TV advertising sales exceeded those of radio for the first time. With sponsors convinced of the profitability of TV advertising, the problem was only to create programs that attracted wide audiences. Searching for the common denominator that would boost ratings, TV turned to variety programs, situation comedies, and quiz shows. Missing from these audiences, however, were adult men. TV solved that problem by increasing coverage of sports. With a captive audience, the three major networks offered nearly identical fare.

The rise of television severely damaged the other popular media — radio, magazines, and motion pictures. During the immediate postwar years, Hollywood had examined such controversial subjects as racism (*Home of the Brave*, 1948); anti-Semitism (*Crossfire*, 1947; *Gentleman's Agreement*, 1947); alcoholism (*The Lost Weekend*, 1945); and mental illness (*The Snake Pit*, 1949). The investigation of Hollywood for Communist subversion in 1947, however, sent a chill through the industry that discouraged social protest. As TV challenged the motion picture industry, Hollywood also sought bland subjects to win back its audiences, relying on technological innovations that were unavailable on TV screens — 3D, wide screens, and color.

Sex, moreover, was one subject banned from the airwaves. Though still bound by its own industry code that prohibited nudity or overt sexuality, Hollywood exploited the pseudosexuality of symbols like Marilyn Monroe. Women in fifties films were remarkably sexless, despite big bosoms and deep cleavages. This fascination with imaginary sexuality had important social implications. In his study of male sexuality, Kinsey observed that better educated men were more stimulated by erotic objects and stories than the lesser educated. In addition, they were less embarrassed by nudity. Kinsey also discerned that socially mobile males adopted the standards of the group into which they moved. The rise of white-collar employees in the fifties may explain the sexual revolution that began in that decade.

Erotic literature had flourished underground for centuries. But in the fifties it began to surface in such "soft-core" magazines as *Playboy.* Explicit language, still "bleeped" on TV, could occasionally be heard in motion pictures. The best seller of 1957 was a racy suburban novel, *Peyton Place,* by Grace Metallious. In 1948 Norman Mailer's *The Naked and the Dead* had to use the nonword "fug" to get past the censors. But in 1959 the Supreme Court denied the censorship of D. H. Lawrence's *Lady Chatterly's Lover* on grounds of free speech. The decision, though ambiguously enforced, opened the door to other nonconventional sexual literature.

The growing acceptance of eroticism indicated a general reconciliation to the human body, a trend that would later change American attitudes toward sex, food, dance, illness, and death. But in the fifties such possibilities were subsumed by corporate-consumer values. Sexual expression, as defined by Hollywood, *Playboy,* and their imitators, was a reward for the affluent. For example, airline stewardesses who served businessmen their meals and drinks were hired by criteria of beauty and sex appeal. In other words, sexual women, as opposed to stereotyped housewives, were expensive. Such attitudes linked the new sexuality not with social liberation, but with institutional conformity. Women's liberation would require a different constituency.

ALTERNATIVE VOICES

The relaxing of sexual standards of the wealthier classes contrasted with the moral conservatism of most Americans. The postwar era witnessed a resurgence of church membership in all denominations. This interest in spiritual security reflected the underlying anxieties of rootlessness and a pervasive fear of nuclear annihilation. Responding to these secular insecurities, religious leaders offered less a promise of salvation hereafter than a sense of identity and solace on earth.

The titles of best-selling religious books reflected these limited concerns: Rabbi Joshua Loth Liebman's *Peace of Mind* (1946), Bishop Fulton J. Sheen's *Peace of Soul* (1949), and the Reverend Norman Vincent Peale's *The Power of Positive Thinking* (1952). "Believe in yourself!" Peale proclaimed. "Have faith in your abilities! Without a humble but reasonable confidence in your own powers you cannot succeed." Evangelicals, like the Baptist

Billy Graham, also flourished in this religious renaissance.

These conservative tendencies troubled social critics who warned about the stultifying effects of conformity. "By and large," observed Will Herberg, author of *Protestant Catholic Jew* (1956), "the religion that actually prevails among Americans today has lost much of its authentic...content." These patterns accentuated a larger problem of alienation. "When white-collar people get jobs," cautioned C. Wright Mills in *White Collar* (1951), "they sell not only their time and energy but their personalities as well." Similar warnings came from such works as David Riesman's *The Lonely Crowd* (1950), Herbert Marcuse's *Eros and Civilization* (1955), William H. Whyte's *The Organization Man* (1957), and John Keats's *The Crack in the Picture Window* (1957). The publication of these works, however, belies the image of the silent fifties as a time of mass amnesia.

Alternative voices emerged in art, music, and poetry. Though most Americans preferred the representational painting of Thomas Hart Benton, Grant Wood, or Grandma Moses, a new group of "abstract expressionists" turned New York into an international center of non-representational Action Painting. Jackson Pollock, Willem de Kooning, and Mark Rothko painted with vigorous line and color that compelled viewers to seek their own meaning in the work. In music teenagers might shuffle to the refrains of rock and roll while their parents worked and shopped to the tune of Musak. But the "bebop" sound of Charlie Parker and Dizzy Gillespie brought new vitality to jazz. Nightclubs like New York's Birdland and San Francisco's Hungry i mushroomed around the country, offering hard-driving rhythms that shook the walls.

These alternative voices required a consciousness that leaped beyond the dominant values of society. "Once science has to serve, not truth, but the interests of a class, a community, or a state," warned the refugee economist Friedrich A. Hayek in *The Road to Serfdom* (1944), "the sole task of argument and discussion is to vindicate and to spread still further the beliefs by which the whole life of the community is directed." After the development of the atom bomb, American science could only reinforce humanity's separation from nature. Technology was destroying the earth itself, forcing people to abandon traditional communities, to become strangers to each other and to themselves.

The strongest voice of protest came from a group of "Beat" poets and writers who congregated in San Francisco in the fifties. Jack Kerouac, Alan Watts, Gary Snyder, and Gregory Corso decried the alienating effects of American culture and called for a new spiritualism that merged the spirit and the flesh. Most eloquent was the poet Allen Ginsberg. In *Howl*, published in 1956, he indicted a society that watched "the best minds of my generation destroyed by madness." Strong, rolling cadences condemned "the scholars of war" with their "demonic industries" and "monstrous bombs." His vision in the poem "America" reached to the core of the postwar identity:

America when will we end the human war?
Go fuck yourself with your atom bomb.

SUGGESTED READINGS

A thorough social history of the postwar period is Geoffrey Perrett, *A Dream of Greatness: The American People, 1945–1963* (1979). Also useful are Joseph C. Goulden, *The Best Years: 1945–1950* (1976), and Douglas T. Miller and Marion Nowak, *The Fifties: The Way We Really Were* (1977).

The relationship between government and the economy is illuminated in the relevant chapters of Gabriel Kolko's *Main Currents in Modern American History* (1976). For the immediate postwar years, see two articles by Barton J. Bernstein: "The Debate on Industrial Reconversion," *American Journal of Economics and Sociology*, 26 (1967); and "The Removal of War Production Controls on Business, 1944–1946," *Business History Review*, 39 (1965). Also enlightening are Fred J. Cook, *The Warfare State* (1962), and the final chapters of Walter Millis's *Arms and Men: A Study in American Military History* (1956).

A thorough examination of economic trends is provided by Harold G. Vatter, *The U.S. Economy in the 1950's* (1963). For a study of the disparities of wealth, see Herman P. Miller, *Rich Man, Poor Man* (1964). A valuable study of poverty is Michael Harrington's *The Other America* (1962).

For the housing problem in the postwar years, see Richard O. Davies, *Housing Reform During the Truman Administration* (1966). There is a vast literature on suburbia. A good starting point is Robert C. Wood, *Suburbia: Its People and Their Politics* (1959), but it should be supplemented with Scott Donaldson, *The Suburban Myth* (1969).

The status of women is explored in the appropriate chapters of William H. Chafe, *The American Woman* (1972). For popular images of women in film, see Molly Haskell, *From Reverence to Rape* (1974), and Brandon French, *On the Verge of Revolt* (1978).

The struggle to end racial discrimination is brilliantly described in Richard Kluger, *Simple Justice: The History of Brown v. Board of Education and Black America's Struggle for Equality* (1976). It should be supplemented by Donald R. McCoy and Richard T. Ruetten, *Quest and Response: Minority Rights and the Truman Administration* (1973), and Anthony Lewis and the *New York Times's Portrait of a Decade: The Second American Revolution* (1964).

Popular culture may be explored through Erik Barnouw, *The Image Empire* (1970), which examines television; Gordon Gow, *Hollywood in the Fifties* (1971); and James Gunn, *Alternative Worlds: The Illustrated History of Science Fiction* (1975). For the Beat writers, see Lawrence Lipton, *The Holy Barbarians* (1959).

Chapter 12

THE TRUMAN ADMINISTRATION, 1945–1952

The expansion of the American economy after World War Two exceeded the most optimistic expectations of wartime leaders. In 1945 the Truman administration had been more concerned that reconversion would produce mass unemployment and Depression conditions. These fears reflected the failure of the New Deal to eliminate unemployment until the nation began preparing for war in 1940. It was from this perspective that President Truman formulated not only a domestic program, but a foreign policy as well.

Truman's sole distinction prior to obtaining the vice presidential nomination in 1944 had been his support of New Deal legislation. In September 1945 he reaffirmed that commit-ment, telling Congress that "the ultimate duty of Government" was "to prevent prolonged unemployment." The president called for "full-employment" legislation, as well as such reform measures as a permanent Fair Employment Practices Commission (FEPC), public housing, higher minimum wages, and urban redevelopment. This ambitious program soon collided with a conservative Congress that disagreed with the president about the importance of government intervention in the economy. Though Congress acknowledged government responsibility for avoiding a depression in the Employment Act of 1946, it refused to allow automatic government expenditures to assure economic stability.

THE PROBLEMS
OF RECONVERSION

Truman's immediate domestic problems, however, related less to unemployment than to inflation. Within one week of V-J Day, the administration began lifting wartime controls on civilian production, triggering a sudden increase in consumer demand and soaring prices. In this crisis Truman failed to exert adequate leadership. Consumers attacked the administration's unwillingness to establish workable controls, while conservatives denounced Truman's half-hearted efforts as "creeping socialism." In the absence of a coherent government program, prices continued to climb until mid-1948, when consumer demand for durable goods finally began to slacken.

The postwar inflation created serious problems for workers who suffered a real loss of wages at the end of the war. To offset such economic imbalances, organized labor initiated a series of strikes for higher wages in such industries as automobiles, steel, meatpacking, coal, and transportation. In the first year after V-J Day, nearly five million workers were involved in over forty-five hundred work stoppages that resulted in the loss of nearly 120 million workers' days of labor. Truman feared that an increase of wages would lead to a rise in prices, feeding the inflationary spiral and resulting in economic collapse. He therefore urged industry leaders to grant wage increases while maintaining price lines. When they refused, the president could only acquiesce to continued inflation.

Truman, frustrated by the numerous strikes, was convinced that organized labor was threatening the economic structure of the nation. In May 1946 the railroad workers went on strike,

despite the president's seizure of the railroads. Facing a major transportation crisis, Truman presented a dramatic appeal to Congress in which he requested legislative authority to allow the army to operate the trains, to authorize court injunctions to keep workers on the job and punish uncooperative union leaders, and finally to permit the president to draft striking workers into the military services to force them to work. Though labor leaders settled the strike before Congress could act on the president's request, Truman's proposal provoked bitter attacks from organized labor. Conservative Senator Robert A. Taft, a Republican presidential contender, condemned Truman for challenging basic civil liberties. Despite such rhetoric, Congress approved the use of court injunctions to stop certain strikes.

Truman soon used these powers to end a coal strike that threatened to disrupt the economy. In April 1946 John L. Lewis led a strike by the United Mine Workers — which previously had violated labor's "no strike" pledge during World War Two. When contract negotiations failed, Truman seized the mines and ended the strike by accepting an inflationary settlement. In November, however, Lewis again called a strike in defiance of the government. Unlike Roosevelt, who in wartime had met Lewis's demands, Truman obtained an injunction and a $3.5 million fine against the UMW, which forced the union to surrender.

Truman's failure to maintain price controls and his brusque treatment of labor unions alienated liberal support. Republicans, on the other hand, attacked Truman's commitment to the New Deal. With a simple campaign slogan, "Had Enough?" Republicans won a landslide victory in the congressional elections of 1946, obtaining a legislative majority for the first time since 1928. Among the victors were freshman congressmen John F. Kennedy, Richard M. Nixon, and Joseph R. McCarthy. The latter two candidates added an ominous note to the campaign by accusing their Democratic opponents of serving as Communist agents in government.

Once in control of the Eightieth Congress, Republicans established a working alliance with southern Democrats by agreeing to thwart civil rights legislation. This conservative coalition then proceeded to block other liberal measures, such as public housing, federal aid to education, higher social security payments, and certain farm legislation. Reflecting their opposition to organized labor, the conservatives joined in passing the Taft-Hartley Act of 1947, which limited the right to strike. Truman, hoping to win back his labor supporters, denounced the bill as "a clear threat to the successful working of our democratic society." Congress nevertheless overrode the president's veto. But Truman's defense of unions helped return organized labor to the Democratic camp.

The success of conservative Republicans in 1946 persuaded Truman to reassess his domestic program. Within a week of the election, he ended all wage controls and retained only a few price controls, thus acknowledging government's inability to control inflation. Truman also began to move in a liberal direction on civil rights. Though he had advocated a permanent FEPC in his first message to Congress, Truman had subsequently backtracked in supporting equal rights for blacks. Prior to the election, civil rights leaders pressed the president to take a public stand against an epidemic of lynching. But Truman feared antagonizing the South. Instead he decided to pursue a cautious policy by creating a special commission on civil rights, which he staffed with liberals. Yet he waited until after the election before announcing the commission, which was charged with recommending policies to protect civil rights.

While Truman bowed to liberal pressure for civil rights for blacks, his administration was taking the first steps toward curtailing the rights of political minorities considered disloyal or subversive. On the eve of World War Two, President Roosevelt had initiated an internal security program designed to protect government from subversive employees. Although wartime conditions existed, Roosevelt's program attempted to protect the civil rights of government personnel by limiting the investigatory powers of the FBI and by requiring adequate proof of subversion. Despite these restraints, the FBI exceeded constitutional safeguards by wiretapping and by burglarizing private offices and homes of suspected employees. Such violations prevented the government from prosecuting the editors of *Amerasia*, a monthly magazine, for possessing documents stolen from the Office of Strategic Services (OSS). Evidence of subversion was reinforced in 1946 by exposure of Soviet espionage in Canada.

These revelations provided ammunition for Republicans to attack the Truman administration for failing to identify and punish suspected subversives. Such allegations were doubly impressive to people who believed that the New Deal was another form of state socialism. In the aftermath of the Republican electoral victory, therefore, Truman created a Temporary Commission on Employee Loyalty to recommend revisions of the government's loyalty program. The announcement of a new program in the spring of 1947 coincided with a new approach to foreign policy.

POSTWAR FOREIGN POLICY

The fear of depression that motivated Truman's domestic policies was also an essential ingredient in the emergence of his postwar foreign policy. "Our international policies and our domestic policies are inseparable," declared Secretary of State James F. Byrnes in August 1945. "Our foreign relations inevitably affect employment in the United States. Prosperity and depression in the United States just as inevitably affect our relations with the other nations of the world." More specifically, the State Department argued that economic prosperity at home and abroad offered the surest protection against another war.

This economic interpretation of international relations partially reflected the social composition of the policy-making elite throughout the postwar period. Leaders of the State Department invariably had deep personal connections with the nation's largest corporations and held powerful positions as corporate lawyers, financiers, or big-business executives. Such personnel, appointed by both Democratic and Republican presidents, imposed their own values with respect to international order on American policy. Defining the "national interest" in capitalist terms, they endeavored to increase American trade and defend private property at the expense of friend and foe alike.

Such assumptions had a long history in the concept of the Open Door. As expressed by State Department officials, American capitalism required an expanding marketplace to sell the products of industry and so assure domestic prosperity. The immense expenditure of natural resources during the war also indicated that the United States required ready access to raw materials. These twin goals, it was commonly believed, could be achieved only by a world system of free trade. A multilateral economic system, in which all nations had equal access to markets and resources, would prevent the emergence of economic blocs that encouraged international rivalry. "Nations which act as enemies in the marketplace," explained one State Department adviser, "cannot long be friends at the council table."

American diplomacy in World War Two attempted to protect the principles of the Open Door in the postwar period. Such programs as the International Monetary Fund and the World Bank, both created by international agreement in 1944, endeavored to stabilize international currency and trade. Since both institutions were financed by American dollars, their policies protected American interests. A related proposal, which was never implemented, called for a general reduction of world tariffs to avoid the catastrophic competition among nations that occurred during the Depression.

The goal of free international trade promised distinct advantages for the United States. Recognizing that Europe would require extensive American investment to recover from the damage of the war, State Department planners hoped to use American economic power to force Great Britain, France, and the Soviet Union to open their trading blocs to American business. In 1945 these nations applied for American loans to replace aid lost at the expected termination of Lend-Lease. But American negotiators deliberately delayed action, hoping to use this economic leverage to obtain trading concessions. This policy was reiterated by Truman in a "Navy Day" speech in October 1945. "We believe that full economic collaboration between all nations, great and small, is essential to the improvement of living conditions all over the world," he declared.

Truman's position conflicted with both the British policy of preferential treatment for Commonwealth nations and Soviet opposition to capitalist penetration. Moreover, the United States did not always implement its own proposals. Congress failed to approve tariff reductions, fearing that foreign manufacturers would threaten the domestic economy. Nor did the administration advocate opening Latin America to European business. Truman expected the nations of the Western Hemisphere to "work together as good neighbors" and he explicitly repudiated "interference from outside."

Despite such contradictions between American free trade policy and practice, the United States agreed to loan Britain $3.75 billion only on condition that the British open their empire to American trade. The war-ravished ally had no choice but to accept. American negotiators also forced France to accept multilateralism before lending nearly $1 billion to rebuild the economy. But the Soviet Union, though desperate after four years of war, refused to capitulate to American demands. The resulting deadlock increased a tension between the two powers that culminated by 1947 in an undeclared "Cold War."

American conflict with the Soviet Union reflected basic ideological differences on the nature of world order. Stated simply, it was a conflict between a capitalist society dedicated to the Open Door in international relations and a socialist society committed to a regulated economy within spheres of influence. Moreover, each system saw the other as inevitably expansive, inevitably a threat to its own integrity. This image of global rivalry had historical roots that extended back to the Bolshevik Revolution of 1917. In the subsequent three decades, such antithetical values affected relations between the two nations. But ideology was not the only factor in creating Soviet-American hostility after World War Two.

The Soviet position, as expressed by Marx and Lenin, insisted that capitalism was doomed to collapse because of its internal contradictions; a socialist society, it was believed, would inevitably replace this outmoded system. Meanwhile, the Soviet Union must strengthen its own society and lend assistance to socialist revolutionaries elsewhere to accelerate the historical process. These principles were modified by Josef Stalin, who seized power in the Soviet Union in the twenties. Though Stalin continued to advocate world revolution, his foreign policy aimed more at protecting the Soviet Union from its capitalist enemies. When Nazi Germany threatened Soviet interests, Stalin sought an alliance with Britain and France; when they rebuffed him, he signed a nonaggression pact with Hitler. The German invasion of 1941, however, brought the Soviet Union into the Grand Alliance. Stalin's major postwar goal, therefore, was to protect his country from invasion through Poland and to rebuild his war-torn land.

American policy makers, however, saw the existence of a Communist state as a threat to capitalist-democratic institutions. Taking Marxist-Leninist rhetoric at face value, they envisioned an aggressive Soviet Union seeking to conquer the world. This image of the Soviet Union as a revolutionary state dominated the thinking of State Department bureaucrats who advised the president on foreign policy. The necessities of a wartime alliance, however, diminished the influence of these ideas. Though suspicious of Stalin, President Roosevelt was willing to treat the Soviet Union as a "normal" state protecting its national interests. Moreover, he preferred to handle international relations outside the bureaucratic structure of the diplomatic corps. Roosevelt's policies consequently lacked an institutional base to survive him.

Roosevelt also failed to develop public support for his foreign policy. Fearful of a resurgence of isolationism, he hesitated to move too far ahead of public opinion. Though mid-war polls indicated that three-fourths of the population favored American participation in a post-war international organization, Americans continued to express suspicion of power diplomacy. Roosevelt therefore did not challenge the popular view that the United Nations, like the League of Nations, would be based on Wilsonian principles of multinational representation. These ideals would be institutionalized in the General Assembly. But Roosevelt believed that the U. N. could succeed where the league had failed only if international order were based on Big Power diplomacy. And in his diplomatic negotiations, Roosevelt assumed that the Big Four, with veto power in the Security Council, would interact on a basis of power relationships.

Roosevelt's public ambiguity produced serious misunderstandings after his death. At Yalta, for example, Roosevelt and Churchill implicitly accepted Soviet predominance in Eastern Europe, while Britain claimed special privileges in the Mediterranean, and the United States controlled Latin America. Such spheres of influence contradicted a Wilsonian world order as well as the economic principles of the Open Door. Roosevelt accepted these limitations because of the realities of Soviet power in Eastern Europe and his recognition of Stalin's desire to prevent another invasion from central Europe.

At Roosevelt's death, however, Truman knew nothing of his predecessor's foreign policy assumptions. Instead the new president viewed the Soviet presence in Eastern Europe merely as a challenge to the Wilsonian order. More-over, where Roosevelt often ignored the State Department's assessment of the Soviet threat, Truman turned to the cabinet bureaucracies for advice. These altered circumstances precipitated Truman's early clashes with the Soviet Union over U.N. representation, the settlement of Eastern Europe, and the question of German reparations.

The change of administrations also affected American policy toward the European colonies, most significantly the French colony of Indo-china. After the Japanese occupied the territory, the American OSS provided military support for a national liberation movement led by Ho Chi Minh. Such assistance, besides reflecting the wartime crisis, revealed Roosevelt's belief that the French colony should be placed under an international trusteeship until Indochina achieved full independence. Roosevelt did not intend to restore the colony to France; he did not even envision France, a defeated nation, as one of the trustees. In 1945 Ho Chi Minh drafted a formal declaration of independence based on the principles of Thomas Jefferson's statement of 1776.

The Truman administration soon reversed Roosevelt's policy. Pressured by Churchill, who feared that the breakup of the French empire might lead to the disruption of Britain's, Truman agreed to the restoration of Indochina to France. This decision was closely related to Truman's perception of a world Communist menace. Ho's sympathy to communism alarmed State Department officials who hoped to preserve an Open Door in Southeast Asia, the very area that Roosevelt had refused to surrender to Japan in 1941. Equally important, Truman wished to retain French loyalty in Europe, where France would join Britain as allies against the Soviet Union. The United States implemented its new policy by providing ships and military assistance to transport a French expeditionary force to Indochina in 1945. Ho Chi Minh's repeated appeals for American support were ignored by the State Department.

THE COLD WAR

The Big Three met at Potsdam in July 1945 but failed to resolve their differences. Truman, emboldened by the successful testing of the atomic bomb, rejected Stalin's interpretation of the Yalta agreements. He refused to accept a Soviet sphere of influence in Eastern Europe, and he narrowly defined the promised reparations from Germany, so that the Soviet Union would remain vulnerable to American economic pressure. These questions were postponed to a Foreign Ministers Conference in London in September 1945. Truman also decided to exclude the Soviet Union from participation in the occupation of Japan.

The effectiveness of the atom bomb in defeating Japan encouraged Truman and Secretary Byrnes to remain uncompromising with the Soviet Union. Stalin, fearful about the implications of this new atomic diplomacy, offered the minor concession of postponing elections in Bulgaria and Hungary. But Byrnes's continuing hard line could not produce additional concessions at the London meeting. This failure to reach agreement demonstrated the fallacy of Big Bomb diplomacy; the Soviet Union would not be coerced by threat of attack to accept American foreign policy. Secretary of War Stimson, who had once viewed the bomb as a diplomatic lever, now saw an opportunity to ease international tensions by sharing nuclear secrets with the Soviet Union. "If we fail to approach them now and merely continue to negotiate with them, having this weapon rather ostentatiously on our hip," he warned, "their suspicions and their distrust . . . will increase." But after a high-level policy debate, Truman rejected Stimson's suggestion. "The atomic bomb does not alter the basic foreign policy of the United States," he remarked in October 1945.

Despite his doubts about further negotiations, Truman permitted Byrnes to meet with Stalin in Moscow in December 1945. The sessions proved remarkably successful, producing agreements that allowed greater Western representation in Bulgaria and Rumania, established a joint commission to form a government in Korea, and made preliminary plans for a U. N. Atomic Energy Commission. A gleeful Byrnes returned to Washington. But instead of praise, he was met by an angry president who criticized his concessions. "Unless Russia is faced with an iron fist and strong language another war is in the making," Truman declared. "I'm tired of babying the Soviets."

Truman's belligerent position won reinforcement within the State Department from George Kennan, a prestigious student of Soviet affairs. "We have here," he cabled from Moscow in February 1946, "a political force committed fanatically to the belief that with [the] U.S. there can be no permanent *modus vivendi,* that it is desirable and necessary that the internal harmony of our society be disrupted, our traditional way of life destroyed, the international authority of our state be broken if Soviet power is to be secure." Kennan's "Long Telegram" was enthusiastically endorsed in the administration because it confirmed the president's belief that there could be no compromise with Communist nations.

Though highly influential within the government, Kennan's message did not reflect American public opinion. In March 1946 Truman accompanied Winston Churchill to Fulton, Missouri, where the former prime minister presented a bitter attack on the Soviet Union for drawing an "Iron Curtain" around Eastern Europe. Churchill's position, like Kennan's, suggested that the Soviet Union could not be treated like an ordinary nation within the context of international power. Rather, the Soviet Union represented "a growing challenge and peril to Christian civilization." He therefore called for a "special relationship" between the United States and Great Britain, including maintenance of the atomic monopoly. Churchill's rhetoric, though gratifying to Truman, brought storms of protest from the general public. It nevertheless served the administration's purpose of publicizing a shift in foreign policy assumptions. Other well-placed news "leaks" endeavored to mold public opinion according to State Department perceptions. Such publicity was credited in Congress for obtaining approval of the British loan in the summer of 1946.

As part of its attempt to mobilize domestic support, the Truman administration relied increasingly on public forums to express its antipathy to the Soviet Union. The most prestigious — and the most politically secure — of these vehicles was the U. N. With American dominance in the General Assembly, the United States could wage the Cold War while appearing to be idealistic. But when the U.N. did not serve American purposes, the administration conveniently by-passed that body. Since the United States could not prevent shipment of essential U.N. food relief to Communist countries, the Truman administration decided to withdraw support from the U.N. Relief and Rehabilitation Administration, which theoreti-

cally had been a nonpolitical humanitarian agency.

The first major case before the U.N. involved Soviet occupation of Iran in 1946. Though defined by the United States as a question of territorial integrity, the main problem focused on oil. During World War Two, the Big Three had occupied Iran jointly, promising to withdraw after the war. But the Soviet Union hesitated to leave and demanded oil concessions similar to those won by the British. Stalin also supported a revolt in the northern provinces of Azerbaijan. The Truman administration, fearing a Soviet attempt to control vital oil resources, leaped to Iran's support in the Security Council, where the United States held a preponderance of votes. The State Department also sent a strong protest to the Soviet Union. Such diplomatic pressure forced Iran and the Soviet Union to reach a compromise, providing for oil concessions and Soviet withdrawal. The Iranian government then suppressed the northern revolt and soon thereafter repudiated the oil agreement. The United States, using U.N. institutions, had thwarted Soviet policy.

The U.N. also served to justify the United States's monopoly of atomic weapons. In March 1946 the administration announced the Acheson-Lilienthal plan, providing for the internationalization of atomic energy. According to the proposals, the United States would relinquish its control of atomic weapons in a series of transitional stages. During this time the United States would maintain its monopoly, while other countries would remain open to international inspection. Truman appointed the financier Bernard Baruch to present this program to the U.N. The final Baruch plan added other qualifications, including the surrender of the veto on atomic energy issues and the imposition of "condign punishments" by a majority vote (controlled by the United States) for violations. Unwilling to open its resources to outside inspection and fearful of continued American monopoly, the Soviet Union rejected Baruch's proposal. In its place the Soviets suggested immediate nuclear disarmament and sharing of atomic secrets, while postponing specific controls. The Truman administration scoffed at this solution, considering it a sign of Soviet duplicity.

Truman's inability to see the logic of Soviet objections reflected a moral absolutism that dominated the postwar era. Having defined World War Two as a crusade for "liberty" (rather than national interest), the Democratic administration could contrast America's virtuous commitments with the cynical power politics of its opponents. The Soviet Union's attempt to protect its borders and to rebuild its economy could be seen as Machiavellian and evil. These attitudes were strengthened by the memory of Nazi aggression. Asserting that all totalitarian states sought world conquest, members of the Truman administration disavowed any compromise that might appear to be "appeasement." Standing up to the Soviets, they believed, was the best way to avoid World War Three. "The language of military power is the only language which disciples of power politics understand," Clark Clifford assured the president in the summer of 1946.

The assertion that the United States represented the cause of freedom while the Soviet Union symbolized "red fascism" had important implications for domestic attitudes. Primarily it served to silence criticism of the administration. During World War Two most isolationists had come to accept the importance of American leadership in the postwar world. But some Republicans, like Senator Taft, remained skeptical about certain administration programs such as the British loan. Once Truman defined American policy as the antithesis of evil, however, such opposition vaporized. Instead, Republicans, led by Senator Arthur Vandenberg and foreign policy expert John Foster Dulles, supported the administration under the principle of "bipartisanship."

As the Cold War consensus crystalized in 1946, a major voice of opposition was that of Henry Wallace. Secretary of agriculture in the New Deal, Roosevelt's third-term vice president, and now secretary of commerce, Wallace questioned Truman's rigid policy toward the Soviet Union. Truman simply ignored Wallace's private protests. But in September 1946, with Truman's approval, Wallace presented a public address at Madison Square Garden that called for a reorientation of American foreign policy. Though Wallace reaffirmed the importance of "an open door for trade throughout the world," he nevertheless argued that the United States had "no more business in the *political* affairs of Eastern Europe than Russia had in the *political* affairs of Latin America, Western Europe, and the United States." The statement undermined the position of Byrnes, who was then trying to persuade the Soviets to reorganize the governments of Eastern Europe. When Byrnes threatened to resign, Truman withdrew his approval of the speech and fired Wallace. "The Reds, phonies, and the 'parlor pinks,'" Truman wrote, "seem to be banded together and are becoming a national danger."

The dismissal of Wallace reflected the administration's growing intolerance of positions that had seemed thoroughly orthodox only one year before. After the conservative victories in the 1946 elections, liberals continued to desert Truman's leadership. In December influential liberal groups coalesced as the Progressive Citizens of America (PCA). Complaining that the Democratic party had departed from the tradition of Roosevelt, they urged the Democrats to reaffirm their liberal principles or face competition from a new third party. Wallace, it was suggested, would revitalize the New Deal. The PCA significantly prohibited internal discrimination for political beliefs, including communism.

This question of Communist affiliation soon split the liberal movement. Many liberals not only opposed communism but especially resented the conservatives' accusations that liberals were merely an instrument of Soviet foreign policy. In January 1947 these non-Communist liberals formed the Americans for Democratic Action (ADA). Like the PCA, the ADA endorsed expansion of the New Deal, the U.N., and civil rights. But the ADA explicitly rejected "any association with Communists or sympathizers with communism in the United States as completely as we reject any association with Fascists or their sympathizers."

The logic of the ADA was best expressed by one of its founders, the theologian Reinhold Niebuhr. As an orthodox Protestant, Niebuhr saw the human condition as enmeshed in sin; no human achievement could attain perfection. Yet the Soviet Union, like its Fascist antagonists, believed that science and human reason could transcend sin and create perfection on earth. Such optimism was prideful, Niebuhr suggested, and made communism a particularly dangerous enemy. Niebuhr therefore advocated strenuous opposition to the Soviet Union. "Russian truculence cannot be mitigated by further concessions," he declared, dismissing Wallace's optimism about negotiating with Communists.

Niebuhr thus became a firm supporter of Truman's foreign policy.

THE TRUMAN DOCTRINE

During the winter of 1947, American intelligence detected a relaxation in Soviet policy, ranging from demobilization of its armies to a willingness to negotiate a peace treaty with Germany. The State Department nevertheless believed that such changes were deliberately deceptive, merely another tactic in a larger strategy of world domination. Reinforcing this distrust was a growing concern about the slow pace of economic recovery in Europe. Plagued by food shortages and industrial chaos, the European nations seemed incapable of reconstructing their economies. Impoverished economic conditions, the State Department feared, would provide fertile ground for Communist expansion. Already the Communist parties of Italy and France had achieved significant electoral success. Unsettled economic conditions in Europe also threatened to affect the American economy, which required a flourishing export market. "Peace, freedom and world trade are indivisible," Truman declared. "We must not go through the thirties again."

The problem climaxed in February 1947 when Great Britain notified the State Department that it could no longer provide economic and military support for Greece. Since World War Two, a Greek Communist party supported by Yugoslavia (but *not* by the Soviet Union) had been waging guerrilla warfare against a corrupt, undemocratic, British-backed regime. The United States had supported Britain's policy and had even sent economic aid to the Greek government. Britain's inability to finance her commitments now offered the United States an opportunity to become dominant in the area.

American intervention in Greece required congressional approval. Yet a conservative Congress was eager to reduce taxes and cut government expenditures; and the American public remained uninterested in the Balkan civil war. To overcome this resistance, Truman adopted the advice of Senator Vandenberg: he would "scare hell out of the American people." In March 1947 Truman presented Congress with what became known as the Truman Doctrine, in which he requested $400 million of economic and military assistance for Greece and Turkey. Concealing the economic basis of his policy, Truman instead depicted an emergency crisis that pitted the American way of life against that of the Soviet Union. The United States, he declared, must "support free peoples who are resisting attempted subjugation by armed minorities or by outside pressures."

The Truman Doctrine represented a major turning point in American foreign policy. First, it suggested that the United States must initiate unilateral action without consultation with either the U.N. or the Soviet Union. Though a conference of foreign ministers was simultaneously held in Moscow in March 1947, Dean Acheson, later to become Truman's secretary of state, testified in the Senate that it was impossible to "sit down with the Russians and solve questions." Second, the Truman Doctrine abandoned the idea of effecting changes within the Soviet sphere of influence and instead stressed the importance of containing further Soviet expansion. This decision institutionalized the division of the globe into areas of "freedom" and zones of "terror and oppression." Such dichotomies allowed no room for compromise or for degrees of commitment; all Communists were evil, all Communist threats were equally critical. This idea of containment was elaborated by George Kennan in an anonymously published article, "The Sources of Soviet Conduct," in July 1947. Though sharing Truman's view of a pervasive Soviet menace, Kennan put less emphasis on military strategy and stressed the value of economic pressure in weakening the Communist appeal.

Truman's belief that communism was a monolithic threat placed the United States on the side of authoritarian governments. Viewing the Greek Communists as minions of Moscow, Truman preferred to support the undemocratic status quo. In Turkey the United States readily backed a reactionary regime that not only suppressed internal dissent but also had cooperated with the Germans during World War Two. In justifying these questionable alliances, the Truman administration articulated what later became known as a domino theory. "If Greece and then Turkey succumb, the whole Middle East will be lost," advised one State Department official. "France may then capitulate to the Communists. As France goes, all Western Europe and North Africa will go."

Such logic alarmed conservatives and liberals alike. Senator Taft protested that the president's bold initiative had presented Congress with a virtual fait accompli. Though he eventually agreed to support the Truman Doctrine, Taft emphasized that it was not "a commitment to any similar policy in any other section of the world." At the other end of the political spectrum, Wallace broadcast a scathing critique of Truman's proposal. "There is no regime too reactionary" to receive American aid, he cried, "provided it stands in Russia's expansionist path." A Gallup poll indicated that a majority of Americans favored economic aid to Greece but opposed military assistance.

Arthur H. Vandenberg

1884-1951

"The Old Guard dies but never surrenders," wrote Milton S. Mayer in 1940. "Vandenberg surrenders, but never dies." Senator Arthur H. Vandenberg of Michigan personified the transition among many Americans from prewar isolationism to postwar internationalism. Though Old Guard Republicans, like Senator Robert A. Taft of Ohio, refused to compromise an anti–New Deal, "America first" ideology, Vandenberg easily drifted with the changing assumptions of American voters.

Born in Michigan in 1884, Vandenberg embraced the conservative middle-class midwestern values of his surroundings. As editor of the Grand Rapids Herald, he supported progressive reform, backed Woodrow Wilson's decision to seek intervention in World War One, but opposed portions of the League of Nations charter that seemed to impinge on the constitutional limits of foreign policy. Appointed to the Senate in 1928, Vandenberg supported the Hoover administration's efforts to end the Depression. After the election of Franklin D. Roosevelt, however, Vandenberg backed the Democrats' early New Deal program in the interests of bipartisanship. By 1935, however, he rejected Roosevelt's leadership and became an outspoken critic of the administration.

Vandenberg also dissented from Roosevelt's foreign policy. An opponent of international alliances, he favored strict neutrality legislation, was even willing to sacrifice traditional neutral rights, and worked unsuccessfully to prevent the repeal of an arms embargo in 1939. He also attacked the Lend-Lease plan, arguing that it would hasten American entry into World War Two.

Vandenberg's position changed dramatically after Pearl Harbor. He appealed — unsuccessfully — to Roosevelt to support a bipartisan congressional-executive committee to create a united foreign policy. In January 1945 he presented a widely hailed speech in which he endorsed a postwar international organization. He served as a representative to the United Nations conference in San Francisco and was largely responsible for the adoption of Article 51, which provided for regional alliances. Intended to protect United States influence in Latin America, this article later provided the basis for NATO and other regional pacts.

Vandenberg remained suspicious of the Soviet Union. He was one of two senators to oppose recognition of the Soviet Union, and he distrusted Soviet foreign policy throughout World War Two. Vandenberg was personally vain and easily subject to administration pressure and flattery. Though the leading Republican in the area of foreign policy, he uncritically embraced Truman's anti-Soviet policy, working for Senate endorsement of atomic secrecy, the Truman Doctrine, Marshall Plan, and NATO.

His endorsement of a bipartisan foreign policy contrasted with the Old Guard's suspicion of internationalism. Taft's opposition to Truman's intervention prevented the Ohio senator from capturing the Republican nomination in 1948 and 1952. Yet Vandenberg, whose foreign policy position was more popular, failed to win the personal respect of his colleagues and never became a party leader. He died of cancer in 1951.

Despite such opposition, Truman's shrill presentation had correctly gauged congressional opinion. By May 1947 the president signed the Truman Doctrine into law. Yet American aid neither suppressed the Greek rebellion nor made the government less oppressive. Only the cessation of Yugoslavian aid in 1948 permitted the defeat of the Greek insurgents. The limitations of the Truman Doctrine were well understood. "There is no use in pretending . . . that for $400 million we have bought peace," admitted Vandenberg. "It is merely a down payment."

The Truman Doctrine, by emphasizing the military threat of communism, diverted attention from the main purposes of Truman's foreign policy. Despite the president's rhetoric, the administration primarily desired to stabilize the European economy to prevent the spread of communism and to protect the flow of American trade. Military assistance comprised only one part of that program. Yet the administration believed that was the only language Congress and the public would understand.

The second aspect of the program was revealed by Secretary of State George Marshall in June 1947. Using the Harvard University commencement as a forum, Marshall described the severe economic problems that afflicted Europe and called for a program of economic assistance that would provide for the permanent reconstruction of European stability. To accentuate the humanitarian dimension of his proposal, the secretary suggested that the European nations initiate a formal request. He also claimed to offer American assistance to all nations, including Communist. "Our policy is described not against any country or doctrine," he maintained, "but against hunger, poverty, desperation, and chaos."

In inviting Soviet participation, however, Marshall was less than candid. Though Molotov attended a European conference in June 1947 to formulate a response to Marshall's address, he soon discovered that the American-controlled plan would threaten the independence of each nation's economy. Moreover, the program seemed to envision a return to a prewar economy that left Eastern Europe far less industrialized than Western Europe. To satisfy American requirements, the Soviet Union, instead of receiving reparations to rebuild its economy, might actually have to contribute food to other nations. Finally, as Molotov complained, the plan would revitalize Germany and lead to German integration in the Western economy.

The State Department correctly predicted the effects of these objections: the Soviet Union refused to participate in the Marshall Plan. Molotov then offered alternative economic assistance to Eastern Europe and effectively prevented those nations from participating in the Marshall Plan. Besides tightening its economic grip on Eastern Europe, the Soviet Union also eliminated anti-Communist groups from the government of Hungary. By the autumn of 1947, the Soviet Union announced the creation of Cominform, the successor of the prewar Comintern, to assure the ideological unity of Communist parties throughout the world. Such action, though viewed by American leaders as proof of a global Communist conspiracy, could also be seen as a response to American attempts to create an anti-Communist bloc in Europe. Fearing "capitalist encirclement," the Soviet Union sought to solidify its own position. Yet by having to reject what ostensibly was an innocent American gesture of assistance, the Soviet Union acquired the onus of dividing postwar Europe into armed camps.

The Soviet response merely facilitated the implementation of the Marshall Plan. The remaining sixteen nations drafted a four-year program based on increased production, stability of currency, lowered tariffs, and economic cooperation. They also requested over $20 billion of American aid to pay for imports from the United States; but the Truman administration cut that figure to $17 billion. While negotiations continued, the United States began to rebuild German industry as a precondition for European recovery. These measures alarmed the French, who had industrial hopes of their own. But the United States effectively used its economic power to overcome French resistance. Earlier, that same power had been used to persuade the French and Italian governments to drop the Communist party from their coalitions.

The anti-Communist aspects of the Marshall Plan helped create a more favorable reception in Congress. But the conservative majority remained suspicious of executive power and questioned the necessity of economic aid. These problems reinforced a general apathy. In November 1947, 40 percent of the American people had never heard of the Marshall Plan. To overcome this inertia, the Truman administration launched a systematic drive to mold public opinion. The State Department joined with corporate lawyers and big-business leaders as well as organized labor, ADA, and the Farm Bureau to lobby for congressional approval. This issue crystalized when the Truman administration realized that interim assistance was necessary before Congress could act on the full program. Summoning a special session of Congress in October 1947, the president played down the economic basis of his foreign policy and instead returned to the militant anti-Communist rhetoric of the Truman Doctrine.

The strategy worked. By November Truman signed an interim assistance bill into law.

MOBILIZING A DOMESTIC CONSENSUS

The American anti-Communist foreign policy paralleled an anti-Communist crusade at home. Nine days after enunciating the Truman Doctrine, the president created a Federal Employee Loyalty program to eliminate subversive employees from government. Truman's announcement reflected the political pressures of the conservative Eightieth Congress as well as anti-Communist feelings within the administration. In January 1947 the House Un-American Activities Committee (HUAC) had resumed its investigation of Communist infiltration of government, the Hollywood motion picture industry, education, and labor unions. Meanwhile, Truman's temporary commission heard testimony from such experts as FBI Director J. Edgar Hoover and Attorney General Tom Clark, who advocated strong safeguards against disloyal employees and warned of dire consequences for the national security.

Responding to these pressures, Truman's executive order established loyalty investigations of all government employees and of all people seeking government jobs. In attempting to preempt congressional action, Truman ordered the dismissal of any worker for whom there were "reasonable grounds" for suspicion of disloyalty. Though permitting a loose definition of *loyalty,* Truman nevertheless attempted to protect the rights of individuals by requiring proof (not just suspicion) of disloyalty and by limiting the investigating powers of the FBI and the Loyalty Review Board. Such safeguards, however,

were later sacrificed in the interests of administrative efficiency.

The attack on the American Communist party reflected an attempt to assure ideological conformity. The Communist party, though politically vocal, had steadily declined in numbers since 1939. And despite the headline revelations of Communist espionage, no one was convicted of espionage under Truman's loyalty program. Communism represented less a political threat than an unacceptable cultural alternative. Eastern European ethnics within the United States, for example, resented the loss of nationality of their homelands as well as Soviet attacks on their traditional churches. These groups supported a strong domestic anti-Communist program. In 1947 J. Edgar Hoover published a widely circulated article, "Red Fascism in the United States Today," which articulated a fear of totalitarianism in America. The next year, Hollywood produced *The Iron Curtain,* the first of many movies that depicted Communists as puppets of Moscow. In 1949 George Orwell's *1984* was condensed in *Reader's Digest,* while *Life* magazine compared the futurist tyranny with Soviet Russia. Such popular media described communism as a threat to individual liberty, as a pervasive Big Brother stifling all emotional relationships in the name of scientific socialism. The image of the cold-hearted bureaucracy, which in many ways mirrored Americans' fears about their own society, fueled the anti-Communist crusade.

Besides implementing loyalty checks of government employees, Truman also ordered Attorney General Clark to publicize a list of "subversive" organizations. This list, which in 1947 comprised ninety-one groups that Clark considered dangerous, served to stigmatize opponents of government policy. Other branches of government, defense industries, and private organizations accepted the list at face value and used it to discriminate against members. Clark also began a campaign to deport aliens accused of subversion. In a series of headline-grabbing arrests, Clark violated individual civil rights on flimsy charges of subversive activity. Clark's fervor resulted in unprecedented cooperation between the Justice Department and HUAC in the investigation of Hollywood screenwriters who refused to testify about their political affiliations.

The concept of "national security," which Truman used to justify the attack on communism, also stimulated a reorganization of the military elite. In July 1947 Congress passed the National Security Act, which placed the armed services within the Department of Defense, legalized the Joint Chiefs of Staff, created the National Security Council, and established the Central Intelligence Agency. Intended to coordinate military strategy and eliminate interservice competition, the new administrative machinery only intensified rivalry between the military branches for appropriations. The main issue focused on whether the navy or the air force would be the primary line of defense. In January 1948 a presidential commission, headed by Thomas Finletter, concluded that air power and polar route defense should be the basis of American military policy.

The decision to rely on air power had been supported by a massive public relations campaign by the faltering aircraft industry. "Since we are living in a world of peril," editorialized the sympathetic *Fortune* magazine, "it is not too much to say that the present state of the aircraft industry represents as grave an industrio-economic problem as exists in the U.S. today." Such promotional devices were not limited to private industry. In 1946 Truman

had called for Universal Military Training (UMT) as a way of maintaining American defense and to inculcate patriotism in young Americans. The Pentagon promptly initiated a massive public relations effort to win congressional approval; in that year, the army became the third largest advertiser in the United States. Despite such pressure, Congress rejected UMT in 1947. A congressional investigation then attacked the army for seeking to manipulate public opinion. "Government propaganda distorts facts with such authority that the person becomes prejudiced or biased in the direction which the Government propagandists wish to lead national thinking." This criticism failed to deter the military lobby, however, and the Pentagon public relations budget continued to grow, approaching $10 million by 1950.

TRUMAN AND MILITARY CRISIS

The attempt of the military to create a sense of crisis served to inflate not only Pentagon budgets but also the presidential ambitions of Harry Truman. In November 1947 Clark Clifford, the president's counsel, drafted a memorandum that assessed Truman's chances in the next election. In this paper Clifford argued that the president could successfully rebuild the New Deal coalition by appealing to the big-city labor vote and to minorities. To accomplish that task, Truman would have to undermine Wallace's support among liberals. Clifford therefore recommended that Truman "identify him and isolate him in the public mind with the Communists." As for foreign policy, the memorandum emphasized the importance of presidential leadership. "There is considerable political advantage to the Administration in its battle with the Kremlin." The creation of "a sense of crisis," stopping short of real war, Clifford suggested, would rally public support.

Clifford's strategy provided the background for presidential decision making. Despite its approval of the Truman Doctrine and the interim aid to Europe, Congress continued to debate the funding of the Marshall Plan. Taft, hoping to secure the Republican nomination, criticized the program as a "European TVA" and spoke about budget cutting. Wallace, who announced his candidacy in the Progressive party in December 1947, chastised the president for by-passing the U.N. and for provoking the Soviet Union. In January 1948 Truman requested a larger budget to underwrite American air power, but Congress seemed uninterested.

Soviet action suddenly disrupted the domestic scene in February 1948. The crisis began in Czechoslovakia, the nation that symbolized the futility of prewar appeasement. Though the Soviet Union had been willing to accept a coalition government that included non-Communists, it had forced the Czechs to reject participation in the Marshall Plan. The United States then assumed that Czechoslovakia, as a Soviet satellite, could not obtain American assistance without first adopting political changes. The Czechs therefore had to seek economic aid from the Soviet Union. The American decision to rebuild Germany also alarmed the Czechs, who had been early victims of Nazi expansion. These policies weakened the position of non-Communist Czechs. When an internal power struggle began in February 1948, the Communists managed to seize power. Americans reacted to this change with horror, viewing the episode as proof of Soviet aggression. Though newspapers spoke about the "fall" of Czechoslovakia, high administration officials had already assumed that Czechoslovakia was part of the Soviet bloc the previous year.

Truman nevertheless responded to the crisis with a determination not to repeat the 1938 sellout at Munich. When General Lucius Clay, the American military leader in Germany, reported "a subtle change in Soviet attitude," Truman sensed the imminence of war. On March 17, 1948, Truman addressed a joint session of Congress on the perilous situation. "Since the close of hostilities, the Soviet Union and its agents have destroyed the independence and democratic character of a whole series of nations in Eastern and Central Europe," he declared. "It is this ruthless course of action, and the clear design to extend it to the remaining free nations of Europe, that have brought about the critical situation in Europe today." Truman then requested passage of the Marshall Plan, enactment of UMT, and the resumption of selective service.

The president's somber appeal proved effective. Within one month, Congress voted to approve the Marshall Plan and passed a new selective service act. Conservatives once again managed to defeat UMT. But the legislature proved more than generous in allocating $3.5 billion for military purposes (25 percent more than the administration requested). Such funds revitalized the aircraft industry and reinforced the coalition between business and the military. The emphasis on military preparations also represented a rejection of the principles of the Marshall Plan, which had seen economic coercion as the key to victory in the Cold War.

The shift toward military confrontation in 1948 was dramatized by the Berlin blockade. Since the end of World War Two, the United States and the Soviet Union had been unable to agree on a final peace settlement. The disagreement initially had reflected different attitudes toward German reparations. The Soviet Union, devastated by war, had wished immediate payments from current production. But the United States, hoping to use economic pressure to create an Open Door in Eastern Europe and fearing Soviet strength, was reluctant to meet that demand. The State Department countered the Soviet argument by stressing the importance of economic stability in Germany and by suggesting that reparations be paid only after Germany had financed its imports from the United States.

The controversy over Germany in 1948 was complicated by a mutual fear that a rearmed Germany would support one of its former enemies against the other. Committed to containing Soviet communism, the United States could not tolerate a Soviet ally in central Europe. Similarly, the Soviet Union feared a renewed "capitalist encirclement." As the United States and Great Britain began to plan for the economic integration of their zones, the Soviet Union became more conciliatory, offering to negotiate on Lend-Lease, Austrian currency reform, and reparations. But the Western powers ignored these gestures and continued on a program of German currency reform.

Stalin correctly perceived that the currency question was but a preliminary to the creation of an independent German state, firmly wedded to the Western camp. One day after the West announced a new currency, the Soviet Union closed overland routes into Berlin, a city that was jointly occupied by the wartime allies. The United States military immediately prepared for war. Truman, fearful of capitulating to the Soviets, decided to support Berlin. The decision precipitated a gigantic airlift of food and supplies that lasted for nearly eleven months. Unwilling to go to war, Stalin was forced to accept the Western fait accompli in Germany.

The Berlin blockade emphasized the importance of military preparations. "We are playing with fire while we have nothing with which to put it out," declared Secretary of State Marshall. In July 1948 Truman ordered B-29 bombers to England. These were the only American planes capable of dropping atom bombs in Europe, though they were not modified for such work until 1949. The Soviet Union had not yet developed nuclear weapons. But for the first time, atomic weapons had become an instrument of American foreign policy. Truman, who had ordered the atomic bombing of Japan, was prepared to act again.

The repetition of Truman Doctrine rhetoric in the spring of 1948 enabled Congress to reverse administration policy in Asia. The corruption of the regime of Chiang Kai-shek, together with the growing success of the Communist Mao Tse-tung, had persuaded the State Department to allow the Chinese civil war to run its course. But the Truman Doctrine had suggested that *any* Communist expansion threatened American interests. Though the administration was prepared to overlook that inconsistency, conservatives in Congress, known as the China Lobby, insisted on a literal application of the Truman Doctrine. In approving the Marshall Plan, therefore, Congress appropriated funds for the Chiang regime. Thus the United States became committed to a reactionary, but non-Communist, Chinese government in a manner that influenced Asian foreign policy for three decades.

The original decision to abandon Chiang also shaped American policy toward Japan. Recognizing the advantage of Japan as an ally, the United States moved to establish a "democratic," non-Communist government for its former enemy. In 1947 the United States extended economic assistance to bolster Japanese industry and trade. These economic measures were matched by a strengthening of American military bases in Japan. Such policies would protect American interests in Asia, even after Mao had defeated Chiang.

Shifting to a military strategy, the United States moved to solidify its own sphere of influence in Latin America. Though the Truman administration condemned Soviet power in Eastern Europe, the United States had assumed that it would control Latin America. In 1945 the State Department had promoted Articles 51 and 52 of the U.N. Charter, which allowed regional defense pacts. It also had supported U. N. membership for such overtly Fascist countries as Argentina. In 1947 the United States endorsed the Rio Pact, which provided for collective self-defense of the Western Hemisphere. The following year, the Bogotá Treaty created the Organization of American States, which facilitated hemispheric consultations through a regional defense committee. The United States also accepted a clause disavowing intervention in the internal or external affairs of another state.

In creating this hemispheric alliance, the United States avoided any economic commitments to this impoverished portion of the world. Unlike its policy toward Europe, the State Department pressed for private economic development rather than government programs. Yet in a series of bilateral agreements, the United States agreed to provide Latin America with military assistance, including the training of military officers. Such military support served to protect the reactionary status quo throughout Latin America. The United States readily accepted the fiction that social protest in Latin America was Communist inspired.

THE ELECTION OF 1948

Truman's militant foreign policy in 1948 worked, as Clifford had predicted, to increase the president's popularity. Truman also used the Czech crisis to read Henry Wallace out of the Democratic party. The former vice president had scored well in early public opinion polls, indicating that he might drain enough liberal support from Truman to assure a Republican victory. In a St. Patrick's Day speech, however, Truman followed Clifford's advice about isolating Wallace from non-Communist liberals. "I do not want and I will not accept the political support of Henry Wallace and his Communists," he declared. By identifying Wallace with the Soviet threat, Truman kept many liberals from supporting the third-party candidate.

The split between liberals seemed to ensure a Republican victory. To assure that success, the Republicans passed over Taft, whose midwestern conservatism might alienate the eastern vote, and nominated the 1944 standard-bearer, Thomas E. Dewey of New York. The party platform was moderate, if not liberal. The Republicans criticized the postwar inflation, for which they blamed high government expenditures. The party also called for federal support of housing, farm payments, the abolition of the poll tax, a permanent FEPC, and increases in social security allotments. On matters of foreign policy, Republicans shared Truman's Cold War outlook. Endorsing the spirit of a bipartisan foreign policy, the platform advocated "stopping partisan politics at the water's edge." This bipartisan strategy, designed to allow Republicans to share responsibility and glory in the Cold War effort, freed the incumbent party from having to explain the origins of the controversy with the Soviet Union.

The Democratic party approached the election with considerably less confidence. The ADA, skeptical of Truman's liberal credentials, attempted to persuade General Dwight D. Eisenhower to run for president, but he refused the invitation. With Truman controlling the party machinery at the national convention in July 1948, his nomination was assured. In accepting the candidacy, the president revealed an ingenious campaign strategy. He would call the Republican-dominated Eightieth Congress into a special session to allow his opponents to enact their party platform. Then the public could ascertain the sincerity of the Republican candidates.

Though Truman dominated the party convention, he could not prevent a major split over the party platform. The president had joined a southern coalition in supporting a weak position on civil rights. But the ADA, having lost in its attempt to obtain a liberal candidate, now determined to win a liberal platform on civil rights. Led by Minneapolis Mayor Hubert H. Humphrey, the liberals carried the platform fight to the floor of the convention. "The time has arrived for the Democratic party to get out of the shadow of states' rights," Humphrey declared, "and walk forthrightly into the bright sunshine of human rights." The speech galvanized liberal support, and a strong civil rights plank was voted part of the Democratic platform.

The Democrats' stand on civil rights alarmed southern delegates, who bolted from the convention. Three days later, dissidents from thirteen southern states convened in Birmingham, Alabama, to form a States' Rights party and nominate Governor Strom Thurmond of South Carolina for president. The Dixiecrats, as they were called, opposed such civil rights measures as eliminating the poll tax, a permanent FEPC,

and a federal antilynching law. This position reflected more than a refusal to extend civil rights to blacks. It also attacked the growth of the federal government bureaucracy, seeing federal legislation as a threat to local government on such basic matters as voting and law enforcement. The Dixiecrats never expected an electoral victory. They failed to attract such prominent southern leaders as Harry Byrd of Virginia and Richard Russell of Georgia, who remained within the Democratic party. But the Dixiecrats did hope to weaken the Democratic slate to emphasize their importance to the national party.

The supporters of Henry Wallace met in late July to organize the Progressive party and to nominate Wallace and Senator Glen Taylor of Idaho as running mates. Though Communists held important positions within the party, the Progressive platform represented a commitment to liberal principles. Offering a genuine alternative to Truman's Cold War and Dewey's bipartisanship, the Progressives insisted that "responsibility for ending the tragic prospect of war is a joint responsibility of the Soviet Union and the United States." Quoting Wallace's statement that "there is no difference which cannot be settled by peaceful, hopeful negotiation," the Progressives denounced "anti-Soviet hysteria as a mask for monopoly, militarism, and reaction."

On domestic issues the party endorsed a strong civil rights position, and Wallace refused to speak to any segregated assembly. In internal matters the Progressives adopted party rules that based representation on population rather than as a reward for party power. Yet the Progressives could never overcome their association with communism. "Politicians of both major parties have tried to pin the Communist tag on the followers of Henry A. Wallace," acknowledged pollster George Gallup in July 1948. "Apparently their efforts have succeeded." The Wallace campaign was hampered by systematic harassment, which included mob violence and the denial of public meeting places.

While Dixiecrats and Progressives sniped at Truman, the special session of the Eightieth Congress convened. Republican party leaders resented Truman's election strategy. If they enacted their platform promises, the president would get credit for forcing their hands; if not, they would appear hypocritical. Amid much futile discussion, they chose the latter path and adjourned without enacting significant legislation. This decision provided Truman with plenty of campaign ammunition. Not only was the Eightieth Congress reactionary, the president charged, but it was a "do-nothing" bunch. Truman carried this message in a strenuous "whistle-stop" campaign in which he delivered hundreds of speeches throughout the land.

Truman's intent was to recapture the New Deal supporters. His stinging veto of the Taft-Hartley law in 1947 had won him the endorsement of organized labor. This support was reinforced by the purging of Communists from the CIO leadership. As the big unions worked to prove their non-Communist orthodoxy, Truman appeared as their only logical choice. Wallace, whose New Deal credentials were as sound as Truman's, could not overcome the Communist taint. Meanwhile, Truman appealed to the farm vote by blaming Republicans for weakening the support program at a time when food prices had begun to slip.

Truman also benefited from the departure of the Dixiecrats. Though he had accepted the report of his civil rights commission in 1947, Truman had been slow to implement its proposals. Wallace's attack on racism forced the president to act. With southern Democrats nominally out of the party, Truman had less to lose by taking a bold stand on civil rights. In July 1948 he prohibited discrimination in federal employment and ordered the end of segregation in the armed services. Truman also campaigned in Harlem, where he promised support of civil rights legislation. Unlike Wallace, Truman never launched a full-scale attack on Jim Crow laws. Yet black voters remained faithful to the Democratic party.

While Truman castigated Republican conservatism, Dewey coasted toward what appeared an easy victory. He failed to challenge Truman's foreign policy, despite the crisis of the Berlin blockade. He also ignored the startling testimony of Whittaker Chambers, a former editor of *Time* magazine, who told HUAC that a State Department official, Alger Hiss, had been a member of the Communist party. Dewey's self-confidence was based on pre-election public opinion polls that forecast a Republican victory.

These prophecies were overturned in November when Truman defeated Dewey by more than two million votes. In the electoral college Truman's 304 votes topped Dewey's 189 and Thurmond's 34. Wallace, who gathered only 1.1 million votes, half of them in New York, gained no electoral votes. Truman's upset victory reflected the accuracy of Clifford's pre-election strategy. Truman did best in areas of New Deal strength as voters adhered to their party identities and voted on party lines. This pattern of party voting meant that Truman was most successful in northern cities, where he attracted the votes of labor, Jews, Catholics, and blacks. He also won over midwestern farmers who had abandoned the Democratic party in the late thirties. Declining prices in 1948 renewed farmer anxieties about an agricultural depression.

THE FAIR DEAL

Truman's victory also returned a Democratic majority to Congress. In January 1949 the president eagerly greeted the Eighty-first Congress with an ambitious legislative program. "Every segment of our population and every individual," he declared, "has a right to expect from our Government a fair deal." Truman's Fair Deal was an extension of Roosevelt's New Deal. It called for increased social security and minimum wages, civil rights legislation, federal aid to education, a program of national health insurance, and a repeal of Taft-Hartley. But Truman overestimated his political strength.

The Fair Deal soon encountered stiff resistance from the true majority in Congress — a conservative coalition of southern Democrats and midwestern Republicans. By controlling the congressional committee system, these groups prevented serious consideration of Truman's proposals. In May 1949 Truman agreed to scrap most of the Fair Deal. Though he remained committed to repealing Taft-Hartley, neither he nor heavy pressure from organized labor could persuade Congress to act. The legislature did extend social security benefits and raise minimum wages. But these benefits were usually insufficient even by the government's standards of living. Congress also enacted a Public Housing Act in 1949 that provided for urban slum clearance and government-funded construction of low-income dwellings. The measure was narrowly passed only because of a severe housing shortage. Yet most of the authorized buildings were never constructed, and the Truman administration was unwilling to challenge an uncooperative real estate lobby.

Truman's drive for civil rights legislation also stalled in Congress. After unsuccessfully attempting to liberalize the Senate's rules regarding filibusters, the administration watched its program languish in committee. Truman demonstrated his commitment to civil rights by rejecting a southern compromise that would have left enforcement powers in the states. But the president recognized the power of the congressional committee system and chose to avoid a hopeless skirmish. The Eighty-second Congress, elected in 1950, failed even to consider a civil rights bill out of committee.

Truman's support of civil rights within the executive branch was also inconsistent. Despite his 1948 order desegregating the armed forces, the military evaded enforcement of the president's decision. In Truman's inaugural parade of 1949, black soldiers marched with whites, but the army blocked full integration by segregating platoons. This pattern of quasi-integration persisted during the Korean War. Moreover, white military officers frequently court-martialed black soldiers on dubious charges. In Europe the military did not even begin desegregation until 1952.

Truman's Department of Justice supported civil rights suits by filing friendly briefs with the Supreme Court. But the FHA continued to accept residential segregation, even after the Court disallowed restrictive covenants. Truman also proved slow to re-establish the FEPC after the outbreak of the Korean War. When he finally created such a committee, he offered no enforcement powers to halt discrimination in war industries. Despite this spotty record, Truman received praise from black leaders. "No occupant of the White House since the nation was born," wrote the NAACP's Walter White in 1952, "has taken so frontal or constant a stand against racial discrimination as has Harry S. Truman." And after deciding not to seek renomination in 1952, Truman became more

General Eisenhower reviews black troops in 1945. The armed services remained segregated until the Korean War. (Dwight D. Eisenhower Library)

outspoken in defense of equal rights for blacks. "The full force and power of the federal government must stand behind the protection of rights guaranteed in the federal Constitution," he told the graduating class of Howard University.

The limitations of Truman's Fair Deal reflected a significant shift in liberal thinking. After the defeat of Wallace, liberals repudiated political association with communism, and in 1950 Wallace himself rejected the Progressive party. The move away from the Left was articulated by Arthur M. Schlesinger, Jr., in *The Vital Center,* published in 1949. Like his mentor, Reinhold Niebuhr, Schlesinger perceived communism and fascism as indistinguishable threats to freedom. Seeking a perfect society, Schlesinger argued, was naive and self-deceptive. Now he called upon Americans to become political "realists," to shun the idealism of perfectionist movements. Such attitudes justified the removal of Communists from public positions. By 1949 the CIO had completed the expulsion of eleven unions.

A BIPARTISAN
FOREIGN POLICY

Schlesinger's defense of power as an instrument of policy translated in foreign affairs to a justification of Truman's Cold War. The administration also obtained valuable support in June 1948, when a bipartisan Senate passed the Vandenberg Resolution, which permitted the United States to participate in a military alliance with the nations of Western Europe. Spurred by the Berlin crisis, the State Department proceeded to negotiate the North Atlantic Treaty Organization (NATO) treaty. In January 1949 Truman announced that the United States would provide military aid to Western Europe; three months later the NATO pact was signed in Washington. Meanwhile, the United States worked feverishly to create a new West German state; and in May 1949 the Federal Republic emerged as a member of the Western alliance.

The NATO pact institutionalized the division of Europe into spheres of influence. Though the treaty obligated the United States to send military assistance to its European allies, State Department planners anticipated no imminent war. Nor did the treaty add to American military power, since the United States still had a monopoly of atomic bombs. The purposes of NATO were primarily political. It forced the nations of Europe to abandon diplomatic independence and to align with the United States. It assured American dominance in Western Europe. "The Atlantic Pact is but the logical extension of the Monroe Doctrine," explained the chairman of the Senate Foreign Relations Committee. The Senate quickly ratified the treaty, but the House proved reluctant to appropriate funds for its implementation.

Then, in September 1949, Truman announced that the Soviet Union had exploded an atom bomb. Within a week the House provided funding for NATO.

The realization that the Soviet Union possessed an atomic bomb demonstrated the futility of atomic secrecy. Yet the political climate of 1949 discouraged cooperation with the Soviet Union. Instead, American policy makers now moved to consider the development of an even more deadly weapon, the hydrogen bomb. Though the Atomic Energy Commission and its civilian advisory committee recommended against building a thermonuclear device, Truman decided to proceed with its manufacture in January 1950. The nuclear arms race continued. By 1951 the United States had successfully tested its hydrogen bomb; within two years the Soviet Union did the same.

The decision to create bigger armaments had important political consequences. In seeking congressional approval of NATO, the administration had given assurances that the defense pact would not alter the status of Germany. By November 1949, however, the army had developed plans for rearming Germany. In 1950 the United States recommended the creation of ten German divisions. This proposal acknowledged a major reversal in European power arrangements since the end of World War Two. France, however, was horrified at the thought of a remilitarized Germany and protested vehemently. The United States overcame these objections by promising to station troops in Europe and by providing economic and military aid. Such assistance was sent to France under the guise of NATO defense. But the French also used this materiel to wage war against liberation movements in the colonies of Indochina and Algeria.

American indifference to economically oppressed peoples was further revealed by the Point Four program, an idea introduced in Truman's inaugural address. Asserting American responsibility to spread "the benefits of our scientific advances and industrial progress" to the "underdeveloped areas" of the world, the president called for a new foreign aid program. Despite the rhetoric, Point Four offered no alternatives to the existing pattern of international economic relations; the "underdeveloped areas" were seen as suppliers of raw materials and consumers of industrial goods. Nor did the program offer to alleviate the endemic poverty of these areas. Even so, the administration could not persuade Congress to appropriate more than a token $27 million in 1950. In practice, Point Four focused less on humanitarian assistance than on providing expert studies to facilitate private business investment. The emphasis on potential profit meant that more Point Four money was invested in industrializing areas like Canada than in impoverished nations like India.

While Americans resisted sending aid to "underdeveloped areas," conservative congressmen criticized the administration for failing to supply adequate assistance to Chiang Kai-shek. Though the State Department opposed such aid, the logic of the Truman Doctrine had obliged the United States to send hundreds of millions of dollars to the Nationalist regime. But the armies of Mao Tse-tung steadily hammered away at Chiang's crumbling forces, capturing American-supplied equipment and winning defections from the Nationalist government. By August 1949 the State Department saw the inevitability of a Communist victory and halted further assistance. "The only alternative open to the United States," asserted a State Department "White Paper," "was full-scale intervention in behalf of a government which had lost the confidence of its own troops and its own people." In December Chiang abandoned the mainland and fled to Taiwan.

Given the logic of containment, the Communist victory could be seen only as a devastating defeat of American foreign policy. The congressional China Lobby attacked the administration for failing to support an anti-Communist ally. Such criticism prevented Truman from seeking an accommodation with Mao. Instead, the United States adopted a policy of nonrecognition that lasted for more than two decades. The debate over military assistance to Chiang also shattered the bipartisan alliance in foreign affairs. After Chiang's defeat, the administration foreign policy was no longer immune from serious Republican attack.

Partisan suspicions were aggravated in February 1950, when Americans learned that Mao had signed a mutual assistance pact with the Soviet Union. Such revelations called for explanations. The "loss" of China and the Soviet explosion of an atom bomb indicated some serious errors of policy. But another ingredient was soon added to the story. In January 1950 Alger Hiss, a former State Department official, was convicted of perjury in his libel suit against Whittaker Chambers, who had accused Hiss of being a spy. The previous discovery of Soviet spies in Canada and the United States, together with the Hiss case, now reinforced the image of the Soviet Union as an internal menace. Republican leaders, believing that the Hiss case was only one strand in a complicated espionage network, condemned the "soft attitude of this Administration toward Government employees and officials who hold or support Communist attitudes."

MCCARTHY AND SUBVERSION

In February 1950 an obscure Wisconsin Republican, Senator Joseph R. McCarthy, discovered a strategy for bolstering his political career by attacking communism in government. "I have in my hands," he told the Women's Republican Club in Wheeling, West Virginia, "a list of 205 [government employees] that were made known to the Secretary of State as being members of the Communist party and who nevertheless are still working and shaping policy in the State Department." In later versions of that speech, McCarthy changed the number of alleged Communists in government, but he stuck to the rest of his story. Drawing considerable attention, McCarthy presented his evidence to the Senate. In a long, rambling speech based on irrelevant files, McCarthy maintained his exaggerated claims.

McCarthy's accusation of Communists in government appealed to the conservative Republican leadership that was looking for grounds to attack the Truman administration. Prestigious politicians like Robert Taft rallied to McCarthy's defense. Such partisan attitudes enabled McCarthy to flourish, even after a Senate investigatory committee, chaired by Millard Tydings, found no evidence to support his charges. In accepting the Tydings report, which described McCarthy's allegations as "a fraud and a hoax," the Senate voted along strict party lines. The pre-eminence of party loyalty defused the effect of the Tydings report and enabled McCarthy to remain a powerful force in the 1950 congressional elections. Taking to the campaign trail, McCarthy reiterated his accusations of "treachery and incompetence" in government. In Maryland he joined the Republican candidate in smearing Tydings with alleged Communist affiliation that contributed to the incumbent's defeat. In California McCarthy helped Nixon destroy Helen Gahagan Douglas, whom he dubbed the Pink Lady. Florida's Claude Pepper, an early critic of Truman's foreign policy, became the Red Pepper and went down in defeat. Illinois's Scott Lucas, Senate majority leader, fell to the conservative Everett Dirksen. McCarthy's impact on these contests remained unclear. But the 1950 elections resulted in a Congress controlled by conservative Republicans.

McCarthy's rash outbursts against communism reflected the political climate in 1950. Two years earlier Senator Karl Mundt and Congressman Nixon had unsuccessfully sponsored legislation for controlling the activities of domestic Communists. Their bill provided for the registration of all Communist organizations, creation of a Subversive Activities Control Board, banning of Communists from defense employment, and denial of such traditional privileges as passports and the use of the U.S. mail. In 1950 the measure was revived as the McCarran Internal Security bill. The new measure authorized the president to declare an "internal security emergency," which permitted the detention of suspected dissidents. Truman promptly vetoed the bill, "because any governmental stifling of the free expression of opinion is a long step toward totalitarianism." Congress nevertheless overrode the veto.

After the 1950 elections HUAC and McCarthy's Internal Security subcommittee continued to investigate disloyalty in government. The major target of their accusations was the State Department, which was blamed for deliberately subverting American foreign policy. Though critical of McCarthy, the administration reacted to these charges not by defending the civil liberties of the accused but by affirming its own anti-Communist credentials. Fearful of provoking further attacks, Truman vacillated on the question of disclosing confidential records to congressional investigators, finally offering some documents but not others.

McCarthy's popularity worried the president. Hoping to prevent further legislation, he decided to appoint a special commission, headed by Admiral Chester Nimitz, to review the government's internal security program. But when Congress delayed authorization of the commission, Truman acted independently. The rules established in 1947 required "reasonable grounds" for dismissal of suspected subversives. In April 1951, however, Truman issued an executive order that introduced a new standard for dismissal. According to the new policy, an employee could be fired when there was "reasonable doubt" about the person's loyalty. The shift in language effectively moved the burden of proof from the accuser to the accused.

Truman's innovation ironically lent credence to McCarthy's charge that existing procedures had been insufficient for preventing subversion. Thus, despite the changes, criticism of the administration persisted. Such pressure led Truman to broaden his loyalty program in 1952 to include civilian consultants in government. Truman also tightened the procedures for classifying government information. In taking these steps, Truman seemed as much interested in thwarting congressional attacks as in preventing actual disloyalty. This yielding to public pressure had the effect of legitimating McCarthy's inquisition.

The willingness of Americans to support the anti-Communist crusade reflected a series of interrelated values. After the high optimism of World War Two, the emergence of a Cold War was unexpected and alarming. These fears were aggravated by a dread of nuclear annihilation; the victims of London, Dresden, and Hiroshima had been innocent civilians. Instead of soothing these fears, the Truman administration intensified them in justifying its foreign policy.

Communism was seen not merely as a political system, but as a threat to the American way of life. Novelists like Mickey Spillane, Hollywood films like *Red Planet Mars* (1952), and a host of popular magazine articles portrayed communist values as a threat to American liberty. Atheism, bureaucracy, and totalitarianism were seen as the antithesis of American religion, family, individualism, and sense of community. Yet these social values already were threatened from within by the rootlessness of American society. "The unity we seek is more than material," declared Thomas Dewey in his 1948 acceptance speech. "Our problem is not outside ourselves. Our problem is within ourselves. . . . Spiritually, we have yet to find the means to put together the world's broken pieces, to bind up its wounds, to make a good society." To conservative Americans, the anti-Communist crusade seemed a logical defense against the disintegration of modern society. Such feelings justified blacklists, loyalty oaths, and public harassment.

THE KOREAN WAR

The sense of crisis provided the background for a reformulation of American foreign policy in 1950. At Truman's request the National Security Council prepared a comprehensive analysis of the world situation in a document labeled NSC–68. The paper reiterated the values that had influenced State Department decision making since 1945. "The Soviet Union, unlike previous aspirants to hegemony," it asserted, "is animated by a new fanatic faith, antithetical to our own, and seeks to impose its absolute authority over the rest of the world." The United States, NSC–68 declared, must be prepared to halt Soviet expansion and to reimpose American-oriented governments throughout the world.

Such lofty goals made it imperative for the United States to establish a global defense system that included hydrogen bombs, the expansion of conventional military forces, and a series of American-dominated alliances. To finance this ambitious program, NSC–68 recommended a quadrupling of the $13 billion national defense budget. This costly plan, however, would face considerable opposition from administration critics in Congress. Moreover, the Soviet Union had avoided any action to justify American intervention. Then, on June 25, 1950, North Korean troops invaded South Korea.

MAP 12.1   THE KOREAN WAR, 1950–1953

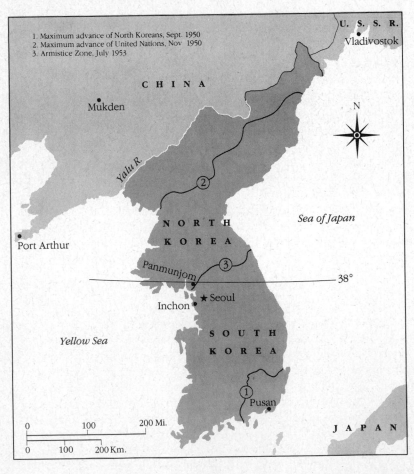

1. Maximum advance of North Koreans, Sept. 1950
2. Maximum advance of United Nations, Nov. 1950
3. Armistice Zone, July 1953

The territorial division of Korea reflected the larger conflicts of the Cold War. According to agreements made at the end of World War Two, the Soviet Union disarmed the Japanese armies north of the 38th parallel, while the United States occupied the area to the south. Both powers spoke about unifying Korea, but neither side wished to risk the dominance of the other. Instead, each global power supported a friendly regime in its sphere of influence. Though the United States extended aid to the South Korean government of Syngman Rhee, the State Department did not view the area as vital to American national security. In January 1950 Secretary of State Dean Acheson specifically excluded Korea and Taiwan from the American defense perimeter in the Pacific.

This statement may have emboldened the North Korean government, headed by the pro-Communist Kim Il Sung. When spring elections indicated the general unpopularity of the Rhee regime, North Koreans began a campaign for national elections that would lead to unification. These national goals may have coalesced with the objectives of the Soviet Union, which feared that the United States was rebuilding Japan as an Asian bulwark against communism. In any case, after a series of mutual border violations, North Koreans, supported by Soviet-built materiel, crossed the 38th parallel.

As the North Korean army advanced quickly through South Korea, Truman moved to halt the offensive. He immediately ordered American assistance to South Korea and directed the navy to sail between China and Taiwan to avoid an invasion of the Nationalist-held islands. The next day the United States called an emergency session of the U.N. Security Council, which, in the absence of the Soviet delegate, branded North Korea as an aggressor and demanded its retreat. As South Korean troops continued to collapse, however, Truman ordered American forces into action. "The attack upon Korea," he declared, "makes it plain beyond all doubt that communism has passed beyond the use of subversion to conquer independent nations." The U.N. subsequently approved Truman's independent action, giving international sanction to American foreign policy.

Truman's decision — as at the times of the Berlin blockade and the Soviet explosion of the atomic bomb — was made without consultation with congressional leaders. Most Americans nevertheless supported the president's action. Truman's claim that he was merely enforcing U.N. policy won the favor of liberals. Sixteen nations eventually participated in the war, but most of the resources came from the United States. Moreover, the American military commander, General Douglas MacArthur, took orders directly and exclusively from United States headquarters.

American forces arrived in Korea just in time to stop a complete North Korean victory. After hard fighting near the southern port of Pusan, the U.N. allies turned the tide of battle, forcing North Korean troops to retreat. At the start of the war, the United States insisted that it was fighting "solely for the purpose of restoring the Republic of Korea to its status prior to the invasion from the north." By September 1950, however, the temptation of wresting territory from Soviet dominance became overwhelming, and the administration authorized an American advance north of the 38th parallel. With the Soviet Union back in the Security Council, the United States resorted to its dominance of the General Assembly to win U.N. endorsement. MacArthur, supremely confident, promised a complete victory by Christmas. But 80 percent of America's 142,000 war casualties followed from this decision.

The invasion of North Korea raised serious questions about the limits of American intervention. In October Truman flew to Wake Island to confer with MacArthur and agreed to allow American troops to proceed to the Yalu River, which bordered China. The decision alarmed the Chinese government, already frustrated by the American defense of Taiwan. China warned the United States not to threaten its borders. When Truman ignored that statement, Chinese troops crossed the Korean border to halt the American invasion. The bloodiest fighting of the war now forced the U.N. armies into a deadly retreat, driving them south of the 38th parallel.

Confrontation with China raised the possibility of another world war, including the use of nuclear weapons. But Truman exercised his power as commander-in-chief to restrain MacArthur's bellicosity and prevented an attack on Manchuria. Truman also responded to international pressure and decided not to use atomic

President Truman and General MacArthur meet at Wake Island to discuss Korean War strategy, 1950. It was the only time the two men met. (Department of State/Courtesy Harry S. Truman Library)

weapons. Yet the administration rebuffed proposals for international mediation of the dispute. Viewing the Chinese as pawns of a Soviet-dominated conspiracy, Truman articulated a domino theory of power that forced him to hold fast in Korea.

By 1951 the battle lines had again stabilized around the 38th parallel. But MacArthur chafed at the limits of American involvement and publicly criticized the president for refusing to wage all-out war. "There is no substitute for victory," he declared. Exasperated by MacArthur's arrogance, Truman fired his general. The decision provoked the wrath of conservatives, who welcomed MacArthur home with extraordinary parades and a unique address to a joint session of Congress. The general took the opportunity to condemn the idea of a limited war. The administration responded, first by reiterating the importance of civilian control of the military, and then by arguing that the Korean War needed to be seen in the context of a broader foreign policy. With Europe uppermost in their minds, American policy makers did not want to provoke Soviet intervention; nor did they wish to alienate their allies in Western Europe. By halting Communist expansion in Korea, the administration could claim a major Cold War victory.

The removal of MacArthur also paved the way for the opening of truce negotiations in June 1951. They lasted for two years, while the fighting continued. The two sides nearly reached agreement on a new boundary line in 1951. But then they disagreed about the repatriation of prisoners of war. The Chinese, following international law, insisted on the return of all prisoners. But the United States, unwilling to return anti-Communists to a Communist state, demanded voluntary repatriation. The impasse was breached only after the inau-

guration of President Dwight Eisenhower in 1953.

The Korean War provided an opportunity for a more aggressive foreign policy throughout the world. Recognizing that the U.N. had approved the Korean action only because the Soviet Union had boycotted the Security Council, the United States moved in 1950 to circumvent the veto power. In a "Uniting for Peace" resolution, the General Assembly announced its right to recommend military intervention in cases of veto in the Security Council. This provision altered the basic assumptions of Big Power diplomacy that had been established at Yalta and in the U.N. Charter. In effect, the United States was announcing the futility of negotiation as a way of establishing world order. Instead, it would use the General Assembly to legislate diplomacy. This situation assumed that the United States would be able to control a majority in the U.N.

The Korean War also committed the United States to supporting reactionary regimes in Asia. Though State Department officials had been prepared to accept a Chinese invasion of Taiwan in early 1950, the outbreak of Korean hostilities provided an excuse to send the Seventh Fleet to protect the besieged island. War with Communist Chinese in Korea exaggerated American fears of a "yellow peril." The prevalence of these attitudes troubled liberals at home. "We will never win the political war in Asia," warned the NAACP's *Crisis,* "as long as Koreans and Asiatics are 'gooks' in the eyes of our fighting men." Yet the specter of a densely populated anti-American Communist China served as a convenient rationale for maintaining an alliance with less perilous Asians in Taiwan and Japan.

These attitudes converged in the formulation of American policy toward Indochina. After the

United States refused to recognize his independence movement, Ho Chi Minh commenced a war of liberation against the French empire. Lacking alternatives, Ho reluctantly accepted assistance from Vietnam's traditional enemy, China. In January 1950 Mao's revolutionary government recognized that of Ho; two weeks later the Soviet Union did the same. Ho's cooperation with Communist nations persuaded the United States to offer additional aid to the French to suppress the liberation movement. After the outbreak of the Korean War, Truman extended this assistance to include military personnel.

In justifying this decision, the Truman administration followed the logic of NSC–68, which saw Indochina as the "key area of Southeast Asia." Besides being a source of "vitally important raw materials" such as rice, rubber, and tin, Indochina had extraordinary strategic value. "If Indo-China went," testified a State Department official in 1951, "the fall of Burma and the fall of Thailand would be absolutely inevitable." These would be followed by Communist victories in Malaya and India.

The State Department was also concerned about the ideological impact of the "fall" of Indochina. The success of a Communist-oriented liberation movement would suggest that world communism was invincible and so create a sense of defeatism in other parts of the globe. Finally, the State Department saw Indochina as the only non-Communist area for Japanese economic expansion. Just as the United States had opposed Japanese restrictions on the Open Door on the eve of World War Two, now American policy makers feared that unless Japan had extended trade opportunities in Southeast Asia, it would be forced into an economic arrangement with Communist China and the Soviet Union. Yet a capitalist-oriented Japan

was an essential aspect of America's containment of Asian communism. These assumptions led to increasing American commitments in Southeast Asia that culminated in the Vietnam War.

The desire to reinforce relations with Japan produced a new treaty in 1951. The pact restored Japanese control of the home islands but allowed American occupation of Okinawa. Japan also agreed to the stationing of American troops on her territory. When Japan's former victims in the Pacific raised the question of reparations, the United States warned against the higher danger of driving Japan into an alliance with Communist nations. The United States nevertheless offered assurances to protect Australia and New Zealand from future attack. These were formalized in the ANZUS treaty of 1951. With such alliances the United States established an anti-Communist barrier against Chinese and Soviet expansion.

American support of Japan as a bulwark against communism paralleled a realignment with the United States's former enemies in Europe. After the outbreak of the Korean War, the United States proceeded with its plans to rearm Germany. To overcome European objections, however, the United States had to agree to station American troops under the NATO command. This policy already had been recommended in NSC–68. But the Adenauer government of West Germany objected to the second-class status implied in the American plan for rearmament. In 1952 a meeting in Lisbon reached a compromise agreement that allowed German forces to enter a multinational European Defense Community (EDC). But the plan was never implemented.

The willingness to establish alliances with former enemies led to American support of Italy and Spain. In 1951 the Western allies agreed to lift military restrictions imposed on Italy in 1945. American policy toward Franco's Spain underwent a dramatic transformation. During World War Two Franco had supported the Axis powers who had helped him come to power in 1939. After the war the United States continued to oppose the Fascist regime. But by 1950 a coalition of conservative congressmen and military officers urged the administration to accept Franco as an anti-Communist ally.

In 1950 the United States extended its first loan to Spain; in 1951 Truman sent an ambassador to Madrid; in 1953 the United States signed a treaty allowing American military bases in Spain in exchange for American economic and military assistance. Like other recipients of American aid, Franco used these funds to suppress domestic revolutionary protest. Meanwhile, within the United States the Veterans of the Abraham Lincoln Brigade, whose members had fought against Franco in the Spanish civil war, was put on the attorney general's list of subversive organizations.

In supporting Spain, Italy, Germany, and Japan against China and the Soviet Union, the United States had radically reversed the Great Power alliance of World War Two. Secretary of State Dean Acheson summed up this transformation in 1952: "We are standing on the threshold of a New Europe and a New World."

SUGGESTED READINGS

The major issues of the Truman years are explored in great detail in Alonzo L. Hamby, *Beyond the New Deal: Harry S. Truman and American Liberalism* (1973). A detailed study of Truman's first administration is Robert J.

Donovan, *Conflict and Crisis: The Presidency of Harry S. Truman,* (1977). Also useful as an introduction to the period is an anthology, Barton J. Bernstein, ed., *Politics and Policies of the Truman Administration* (1970). A convenient collection of primary sources is Barton J. Bernstein and Allen Matusow, eds., *The Truman Administration* (1966).

The domestic policies of the Truman administration are examined in the works by McCoy and Ruetten and by Davies listed at the end of chapter 11. On farm policies, see Allen Matusow, *Farm Policies and Politics in the Truman Years* (1967); for labor, see R. Alton Lee, *Truman and Taft-Hartley* (1966). The Wallace candidacy is described in Richard J. Walton, *Henry Wallace, Harry Truman, and the Cold War* (1976), which contains many primary sources, and Norman D. Markowitz, *The Rise and Fall of the People's Century: Henry A. Wallace and American Liberalism* (1973). James T. Patterson's *Mr. Republican: A Biography of Robert A. Taft* (1972) details the career of the leading conservative.

The domestic anti-Communist crusade is described by Athan Theoharis, *Seeds of Repression: Harry S. Truman and the Origins of McCarthyism* (1971), and Alan D. Harper, *The Politics of Loyalty* (1969). For Joseph McCarthy, see the works listed at the end of chapter 13. A suggestive essay is Les K. Adler and Thomas G. Paterson, "Red Fascism: The Merger of Nazi Germany and Soviet Russia in the American Image of Totalitarianism," *American Historical Review*, 75 (1970). The close relationship between domestic anticommunism and foreign policy is presented in Richard M. Freeland, *The Truman Doctrine and the Origins of McCarthyism* (1972). For the split between liberals and radicals, see Mary Sperling McAuliffe, *Crisis on the Left* (1978).

A sensible and readable introduction to post-war foreign policy is Walter Lafeber, *America, Russia, and the Cold War, 1945–1975* (1976). Also valuable for exploring the origins of American policy is Daniel Yergin, *Shattered Peace: The Origins of the Cold War and the National Security State* (1977). For international economic affairs, see Fred L. Block, *The Origins of International Economic Disorder* (1977). A useful anthology of dissenters from Truman's policies is Thomas G. Paterson, ed., *Cold War Critics* (1971). The Korean War is examined by David Rees, *Korea* (1964) and Ronald Caridi, *The Korean War and American Politics* (1968). Also insightful is Ernest R. May, *"Lessons" of the Past: The Use and Misuse of History in American Foreign Policy* (1973). For a thorough analysis of the Rosenberg case, see Walter and Miriam Schneir, *Invitation to an Inquest* (1973).

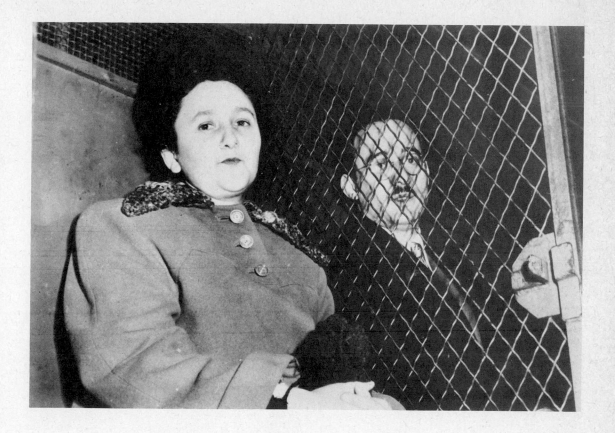

Spotlight: The Case of Ethel and Julius Rosenberg

In June 1953, two New York Jews in their mid-thirties — Ethel and Julius Rosenberg — died in the electric chair for passing secret atomic bomb information to the Soviet Union during World War Two. "I consider your crime worse than murder," Judge Irving Kaufman told the young parents in imposing the death penalty. Their treason, he concluded, "caused...the Communist aggression in Korea, with the resultant casualties exceeding fifty thousand and who knows but that millions more of innocent people may pay the price." President Dwight Eisenhower echoed Kaufman's reasoning in rejecting a last-minute plea for executive clemency. "By immeasurably increasing the chances of atomic war," he declared, "the Rosenbergs may have condemned to death tens of millions of innocent people all over the world."

Throughout the lengthy legal proceedings, however, the Rosenbergs maintained their innocence, even rejecting an offer of clemency from the Eisenhower administration in exchange for a full confession. Instead, the convicted spies insisted that they were victims of a government conspiracy provoked by their leftist political beliefs. There was a political "frame-up," Julius Rosenberg declared, "to establish a fear paralysis among outspoken progressives and to stifle criticism and opposition" to the Cold War. "We are the first victims of American Fascism," alleged Ethel Rosenberg in her last letter. These claims aroused passionate debate at home and abroad, leading thousands of Europeans to protest outside American embassies and to flood the White House with petitions for mercy.

Eisenhower, like his Democratic predecessor Harry Truman, remained unmoved. He argued that a show of compassion would reinforce a Communist belief that the United States was "weak and fearful." Such intransigence reflected the immense symbolic importance of the Rosenberg case. As a symptom of the Cold War, the trial and sentence dramatized the political changes that had occurred in the United States since the Grand Alliance of World War Two. For the Rosenbergs had been found guilty of passing secrets not to the enemy, but to a wartime ally.

Imposing the death sentence also served notice to political dissenters about the consequences of radical opposition. That the Rosenbergs were convicted largely on the testimony of confessed spies who had turned state's evidence to obtain lesser punishments alarmed other radicals who feared similar reprisals from former comrades. Such threats, as Julius Rosenberg predicted, helped to undermine the American Left, especially the Communist party. Fearing further attacks, many leaders of the Communist party went "underground" to prevent a complete destruction of the radical movement. Others simply deserted the party. Both strategies seriously weakened the Communist organization and facilitated the creation of an anticommunist consensus.

The political intensity surrounding the Rosenberg case was closely related to popular fears and misunderstandings about atomic energy. During World War Two, the Office of War Information conducted a successful publicity campaign warning civilians of the importance of secrecy in matters of war production and troop movements. The explosion of atomic bombs over Japan in 1945 seemed to vindicate the lessons of wartime secrecy. At the war's end, military leaders urged that atomic energy remain under military control to preserve an American monopoly over atomic secrets. This position soon met indignant reaction from the nation's leading scientists, who emphasized that the theoretical basis of the atomic bomb was well understood by physicists throughout the world. Congress reacted to a scientists' lobby by establishing civilian control over atomic energy.

Though scientific leaders predicted that other nations could develop atomic bombs in less than a decade, political and military leaders preferred to believe that the Soviet Union lacked the technological expertise to produce atomic weapons for another generation. Such beliefs encouraged the Truman administration to flaunt American atomic power during such crises as the Berlin blockade. These illusions were rudely broken in September 1949 when President Truman announced that the Soviet Union had exploded an atomic bomb. The president emphasized that the Soviet success had been expected by American scientists. But critics of the administration soon charged, in the words of Senator Karl Mundt, that "Communist espionage" had permitted the Soviet Union to acquire "the secrets of our atomic bomb."

These assertions of communist espionage reflected a naive appraisal of Soviet technology, the belief that Soviet science could not compete effectively with capitalist industry. Moreover, as the United States moved quickly to develop a more powerful hydrogen bomb, the idea of American technological superiority was especially comforting. From these assumptions, the only explanation of the Soviet atomic achievement was that spies had passed information to the enemy. Such conclusions ironically were shared by the Rosenbergs' defense attorneys. During the trial, the Rosenberg defense urged that prosecution testimony about the bomb be impounded by the court to prevent the dispersal of "secret" information. (Such trial errors may have resulted from the refusal of other lawyers to enter the case for fear of political reprisal. Significantly, after the trial, disbarment proceedings were begun against the Rosenbergs' lawyer, Emanuel Bloch.)

Suspicions of espionage activity had been nourished in the postwar years by the elaborate confessions of two self-admitted spies, Elizabeth Bentley and Whittaker Chambers, who testified that Soviet agents had infiltrated the United States government. Despite detailed FBI investigations, Bentley's charges led to no indictments. But Chambers's allegations culminated in November 1949, two months after the Soviet explosion, in the second trial of Alger Hiss, a State Department official accused of spying, and resulted in Hiss's conviction for perjury in January 1950. The following month, the British government announced the arrest of Klaus Fuchs, a British scientist who had worked on the atomic bomb, for espionage. Within a week, Senator Joseph McCarthy claimed to have evidence of communist subversion of the State Department.

The Hiss conviction and the arrest of Fuchs seemed to substantiate McCarthy's charge of the existence of an espionage ring in the United States. Government officials began an intensive search for communist spies. The temper of the times may be gauged from a warning of Columbus, Ohio, police officers to local teenagers to be suspicious of "any new member of a group whose background is not an open book" and by a Birmingham, Alabama, ordinance that banished from the city "anyone caught talking to a Communist in a 'nonpublic place,' or anyone who passed out literature that could be traced, even remotely, to a Communist hand." In this atmosphere of distrust, the FBI announced the arrest of Fuchs's American accomplice, a chemist named Harry Gold, in May 1950.

Gold's arrest was followed by several others, including that of a Brooklyn machinist, David Greenglass, who worked at the wartime atomic bomb project in Los Alamos. The outbreak of the Korean War in June 1950 underscored the seriousness of Greenglass's offense and, after intensive FBI questioning, he named as coconspirators his sister and brother-in-law, Ethel and Julius Rosenberg. Other accused accomplices included several of Rosenberg's acquaintances, including a college classmate, Morton Sobell.

Besides an interest in left-wing politics, the members of this alleged spy network shared a common ethnic heritage: they were all Jewish. The idea of an international Jewish conspiracy had been widely circulated among right-wing American groups since the beginning of the twentieth century. The Gold-Greenglass-Rosenberg-Sobell alliance seemed to fit a stereotype of subversive Jews. Government officials therefore took special care to avoid the appearance of anti-Semitism. Chosen as presiding judge was a Jew, Kaufman, as were the chief prosecuting attorney, Irving Saypol, and his assistant Roy Cohn (who later achieved notoriety as chief counsel for Senator Joseph McCarthy). Despite such efforts, however, critics of the case argued that Kaufman, Saypol, and Cohn represented a type of American Judaism different from that of the defendants. Whereas the court officials symbolized the melting-pot tradition of Jewish assimilationism, the Rosenbergs remained closer to their Old World roots, identifying strongly with the victims of Nazi racism, interspersing their language with Yiddish, and living near their childhood homes on the Lower East Side. Moreover, there were no Jews on the jury.

The Rosenbergs were accused of no overt act, merely of "conspiracy" to commit espionage, a crime difficult to substantiate. The government's case hinged primarily on the testimony of their alleged accomplices, Gold and Greenglass. Many states, including New York, limited the applicability of such accomplice testimony, but the federal courts applied no restrictions. Moreover, government officials used the press as a forum in which to assert the guilt of the defendants. During the trial, Judge Kaufman overruled defense objections and permitted questioning of the Rosenbergs' political beliefs, presumably to demonstrate a connection between their left-wing sympathies and their willingness to spy. Such rulings enabled the prosecution to benefit from widespread anti-Communist sentiment and to reinforce the image of an international conspiracy.

The evidence against the Rosenbergs nevertheless remained open to various interpretations. Greenglass claimed, for example, that the Rosenbergs had been rewarded by the Soviet Union with expensive gifts, including a valuable table. The defendants emphasized their relative poverty, however, and insisted that they had purchased an inexpensive table at a New York department store. Not until after the trial was the table located; its markings seemed to corroborate the Rosenbergs' testimony. Similarly, the prosecution attempted to prove that the Rosenbergs had contemplated flight from the country by introducing alleged passport photographs; the government failed, however, to introduce other evidence that implied that the photos were *not* for passports. Subsequent studies also suggest that a hotel registration card, introduced only in photostat, might have been forged in the original.

Despite such problematical evidence, the appellate procedure prevented a rehearing of the trial. Though the Rosenbergs' attorneys carried their pleas to the Supreme Court, they could appeal only judicial *procedures,* not trial evidence. A few days before the execution date in June 1953, however, Supreme Court Justice William O. Douglas stayed the sentence pending further examination of certain legal technicalities. Aware that the Eisenhower administration was negotiating a Korean War truce, Douglas may have hoped that a more peaceful political climate would result in a lesser sentence. But the Eisenhower administration intervened to persuade Chief Justice Fred Vinson to recall the Court to a special unprecedented session, which vacated Douglas's stay. Within two days, the Rosenbergs were dead.

This haste in implementing the death sentence revealed unusual cooperation between the judicial system and the executive branch. Documents released under the Freedom of Information Act indicate that Judge Kaufman consulted with prosecuting attorneys before imposing sentences. The judge also drafted elaborate denials of defense motions prior to even hearing those arguments. He refused to examine new evidence, such as the mysterious table. And to avoid the Rosenbergs' death occurring on the Jewish sabbath, he accelerated rather than delayed the time of execution.

Kaufman's resolution stemmed from his perception of the Cold War. "This country is engaged in a life and death struggle with a completely different system," he declared in rhetoric that had become familiar since the end of World War Two. "All our democratic institutions are... directly involved in this great conflict.... The punishment to be meted out in this case must therefore serve the maximum interest for the preservation of our society against these traitors in our midst."

These ideological imperatives justified loyalty oaths, blacklists, preparation of concentration camps for political prisoners, increased armaments, an aggressive foreign policy, and the execution of the only atomic spies who maintained their innocence. Morton Sobell, accused of indirect complicity and who also maintained his innocence, received a thirty-year sentence (he served eighteen years). David Greenglass faced fifteen years (he served ten); his wife, a confessed coconspirator, was never indicted. (Gold, convicted in another court, received a maximum thirty-year sentence). This pattern of punishment indicates that, Kaufman's language notwithstanding, the severity of the Rosenbergs' sentence reflected not the crime, but their refusal to admit guilt. In a war of moral absolutes — a conflict between American capitalism and Soviet communism — Ethel and Julius Rosenberg remained conscientious objectors.

The ambiguities of the Rosenberg case continue to attract wide interest. There are at least three novels based on the case: Helen Yglesias's *How She Died,* E. L. Doctorow's *The Book of Daniel,* and Robert Coover's *The Public Burning;* a play, Donald Freed's *Inquest;* and a documentary film, "The Unquiet Death of Julius and Ethel Rosenberg." These works emphasize the uncertainties of the evidence and the shadows of doubt that might have led to acquittal in calmer times. They argue strongly that the political climate of the early fifties prevented a fair trial. In 1974, the Rosenbergs' children, Michael and Robert Meeropol, formed a National Committee to Reopen the Rosenberg Case. "To be writing an opinion in a case affecting two lives after the curtain has been rung down upon them has the appearance of pathetic futility," wrote Supreme Court Justice Felix Frankfurter three days after the execution. "But history also has its claims."

Chapter 13

THE EISENHOWER ADMINISTRATION, 1952–1960

By 1952 the Truman administration had lost control of its foreign and domestic policies. Truman's adoption of the principles of containment had wrecked earlier State Department hopes for an international Open Door. Even worse, containment had bogged down in the military quagmire of Korea, a "limited" war that promised neither victory nor an early end. On the home front, Truman's Fair Deal lacked the political base to overcome the opposition of congressional conservatives. In the Senate, Joseph McCarthy continued his campaign to expose alleged Communists in government, capturing headlines by his brash condemnations. Republican leaders, hoping to embarrass the administration, supported McCarthy's actions. Truman's difficulties were compounded by revelations of corruption by high administration officials.

THE ELECTION OF 1952

These problems provided the Republicans with a campaign slogan for 1952 — "K₁C₂": Korea, Communism, Corruption. But despite the Democrats' vulnerability, the Republicans feared a repetition of the disastrous election of 1948. Senator Robert Taft, the leading Republican conservative, worked feverishly to win his party's nomination, believing that the liberal wing offered a poor alternative to the "socialistic" New Deal. "The greatest enemy of liberty," declared Taft in 1952, "is the concentration of power in Washington." Taft also questioned an internationalist foreign policy, believing that heavy expenditures abroad would cause economic collapse at home. These Old Guard attitudes were challenged by Republican liberals such as New York's Thomas Dewey, who accepted a Cold War foreign policy and recognized the impossibility of dismantling the New Deal. They saw Taft's brand of Republicanism as inevitably doomed.

Liberal Republicans turned their attention to a man who claimed to have no interest in presidential politics: General Dwight David Eisenhower. As supreme commander of NATO forces in Europe, Eisenhower refused to take a public political stand. His political beliefs were sufficiently ambiguous for Truman to offer him the Democratic nomination in 1952. Eisenhower was too conservative to run as a Democrat. But unlike Taft, Eisenhower believed in the importance of American military presence in Western Europe. In June 1952 Eisenhower returned from Europe to seek the presidential nomination. The general's immense popularity soon swamped the Taft candidacy. After a brief convention skirmish, Eisenhower captured the Republican nomination in July. As a concession to Taft's supporters, Eisenhower chose the right wing Californian, Richard Milhous Nixon, as his running mate.

The Republican party platform expressed the K_1C_2 formula. "There are no Communists in the Republican Party," the platform boasted, but the Democrats "shielded Traitors to the Nation in high places." Such subversive infiltration had caused the defeat of Chiang Kai-shek and had embroiled the nation in the Korean War. Denouncing the policy of containment as "negative, futile, and immoral," the platform promised to bring "genuine independence" to the "captive peoples" of Eastern Europe. In offering an alternative to containment, this plank appealed to the Eastern European immigrant voters, who traditionally had been Democrats. When linked to the McCarthyite attack on communism, it strengthened Republican support among Catholics. The platform

also adopted a conservative position on civil rights. Though condemning bigotry, Republicans insisted that the state governments had primary responsibility to protect civil rights. This defense of states' rights broadened the party's appeal in the South.

While Eisenhower promised "to lead a great crusade . . . for freedom," the Democrats searched for a party leader. Having announced his own retirement, Truman supported Governor Adlai Stevenson of Illinois. But Stevenson steadfastly refused the candidacy, partly because he wished to remain independent of the incumbent president, and partly because he recoiled from challenging Eisenhower's enormous popularity. While Stevenson hesitated, the contest centered on Georgia Senator Richard B. Russell, an archconservative; Averell Harriman, a liberal Cold Warrior of New York; and Tennessee Senator Estes Kefauver, who had gained national attention through a televised investigation of organized crime. But Russell's conservatism had little support outside the South, Harriman's liberalism threatened to create another Dixiecrat secession, and Kefauver's attack on crime brushed too closely to the big-city political bosses. The Democratic National Convention then turned to the noncandidate Stevenson, who promised to "talk sense to the American people." To balance the party in the South, the Democrats gave the vice presidential nomination to John Sparkman, a segregationist senator from Alabama.

Though Stevenson recognized the handicap of association with the Truman administration, the Democratic campaign revealed a continuity of principles and policies. "In Korea," Stevenson declared, "we took a long step toward building a security system in Asia," and he expressed pride in American "courage to resist that ruthless, cynical aggression." Stevenson also echoed the president's position on domestic communism. Though criticizing McCarthy's attacks on "faithful public servants," the Democratic candidate applauded a "healthy apprehension about the communist menace in our country." Describing communism as the "strangulation of the individual," Stevenson argued that American Communists "have surrendered their right to our trust."

Trying to rid himself of Truman's political liabilities, Stevenson remained cautiously conservative. Despite pressure from Truman, Stevenson took a moderate position on civil rights, emphasizing the importance of state sovereignty. Only after intense criticism from liberals did he endorse a permanent Fair Employment Practices Commission (FEPC). This belated ges-

ture cost Stevenson significant support from blacks, while alienating southern Democrats. Stevenson further aroused southern Democrats by opposing state control of offshore oil wells, a stance that led powerful southern leaders to repudiate his candidacy. Stevenson's hesitancy to attack the Taft-Hartley labor law also offended a traditional Democratic labor constituency, and he nearly lost the support of labor unions. Stevenson's attempt to rise above party strife brought him closer to the Republican camp, blurring the differences between the parties.

While Stevenson struggled to chart an independent course, Eisenhower posed as a candidate above parties. After making a postconvention peace with Taft, Eisenhower scrupulously

MAP 13.1   THE ELECTION OF 1952

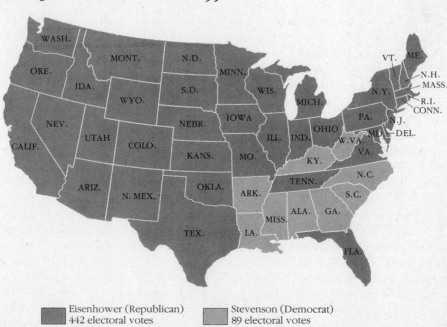

Eisenhower (Republican)
442 electoral votes

Stevenson (Democrat)
89 electoral votes

avoided antagonizing Old Guard Republicans. Though personally insulted by McCarthy's attacks on General George Marshall, Eisenhower's former superior, the nominee quietly deleted a defense of Marshall when speaking in McCarthy's home state of Wisconsin. Eisenhower also avoided direct attacks on Truman, leaving the bitter campaign oratory to Nixon. Eisenhower adopted the beneficent role of great crusader, promising to restore morality to government. He allowed his running mate to hammer away at "Adlai the appeaser... who got a Ph.D. from Dean Acheson's College of Cowardly Communist Containment."

Nixon's role as Eisenhower's shotgun suddenly backfired when newspapers reported that the vice presidential candidate possessed a secret "millionaire's" fund to defray political expenses while serving in the Senate. Democrats immediately used the issue to reply to Eisenhower's accusations about a "mess in Washington." To avoid further embarrassment, Eisenhower's advisers urged him to drop Nixon from the ticket. But while Eisenhower delayed, Nixon seized the initiative. Using Republican party funds, he bought television time to take his case to the public. Sitting behind a desk, a portrait of Lincoln on one side, his wife, Pat, on the other, Nixon explained the sources of his funds and defended his personal honesty. Adopting the folk metaphors of Lincoln, he emphasized that his family had not profited from politics, that his wife still wore a "plain Republican cloth coat," and that despite the criticism he would not return a gift that his daughter had received, a cocker spaniel named Checkers.

The performance was sentimental, but effective. Public opinion rose in Nixon's favor, and Eisenhower decided to keep him in the campaign. The Checkers speech also demonstrated the immense political significance of television. It highlighted the importance of a politician's public image. It suggested that a politician could effectively appeal over the heads of party leaders to the people. For Nixon, the speech not only proved his usefulness to Eisenhower but also gave him a supreme confidence in the medium. In later years he returned to television to win vindication for other aspects of his career, though seldom with the success of his 1952 effort.

Eisenhower tried to avoid direct statements about foreign policy. Though he supported the basic premises of Truman's Cold War, Eisenhower rejected the president's request for a bipartisan approach to foreign policy. Eisenhower endorsed the Republican party platform, drafted by John Foster Dulles, which promised to liberate Communist-dominated peoples. But the candidate avoided militant rhetoric, allowing Dulles and Nixon to speak for him. Eisenhower's position on Korea was equally murky. He approved Truman's intervention, just as he shunned MacArthur's call for all-out war. Yet the war was unpopular, and the Republican candidate blamed the Democrats for bungling the war effort.

Stevenson justified the administration's war policy, arguing that the only "answer" was to "keep it up as long as we have to." But Eisenhower hinted at alternative policies. "If there must be a war," he maintained, "let it be Asians against Asians, with our support on the side of freedom." Eisenhower's military experience enabled him to speak with authority and confidence. Though he possessed no specific proposal for ending the war, he created an image of superior wisdom. Speaking in Detroit on October 24, Eisenhower reiterated his commitment to terminate the war. "That job requires a personal trip to Korea," he declared. "I shall make that trip.... I shall go to Korea." Eisenhower's promise touched the fears and aspirations of a war-weary nation. The strategist of D Day would end the bloodletting of Korea.

Eisenhower's image as a nonpartisan soldier, aloof from the world of crass politics, proved the basis for a landslide victory. Eisenhower captured nearly thirty-four million votes to Stevenson's twenty-seven million and swept the electoral college 442 to 89. Stevenson carried only nine states — all southern or border states. But Eisenhower won in four southern states, breaking the Democrats' "solid South" for the first time since Al Smith's defeat in 1928. Eisenhower also attracted the traditional Democratic vote in the big cities — blacks, Catholics, and immigrants. And on his coattails, he pulled a Republican majority in both houses of Congress.

Republicans exulted in the destruction of the New Deal coalition. The victory of conservatives like McCarthy and the defeat of several of his critics seemed to vindicate the anti-Communist crusade. But the voting statistics also indicated that Eisenhower ran far ahead of other Republicans, including McCarthy. The election of 1952 was an Eisenhower victory, not a Republican one, and the party controlled the House by only eight seats, the Senate by one. During the fifties, voting behavior generally followed party lines. Voters seemed to be less interested in a general political ideology and more sensitive to short-term issues or party affiliation. Even new voters identified strongly with one of the major parties. Eisenhower's ability to avoid a coherent philosophy enabled him to attract a large proportion of independent voters and Democrats. These crossovers supported Eisenhower, but not necessarily other Republicans. The willingness of Democrats to vote for Eisenhower also reflected a consensus of purpose within the two parties. In the South, Republicans attracted newcomers to the region

and uprooted voters who held no loyalty to the entrenched Democratic elite and who appreciated the sense of stability promised by the Republican platform.

WAGING THE COLD WAR

The K_1C_2 slogan, too easily seen as a cynical formula for getting votes, revealed deep-seated fears within American society. By 1953 the dread of nuclear war permeated the country. The federal Civil Defense Administration, created in 1951, disseminated booklets entitled "Survival Under Atomic Attack," which explained the fundamentals of civil defense. Congress appropriated $3 billion for bomb shelters, but an administrator admitted that less than 1 percent of the population would be protected. In New York and San Francisco, school officials routinely issued dog tags to children to facilitate identification of nuclear victims. Radio stations prepared for emergency broadcasting. "I cannot tell you when or where the attack will come or that it will come at all," President Truman admitted. "I can only remind you that we must be ready when it does come." Such oblique warnings fed a remarkable popular interest in flying saucers and mysterious invaders. The Hollywood science fiction film *The Thing* (1951) ended by advising audiences to "Watch the skies!"

Eisenhower's inaugural address spoke to these fears. His words echoed the vision of an earlier president, Abraham Lincoln. (Eisenhower's celebration of Lincoln would later be seen when he chose the sixteenth president's portrait for the basic postage stamp of the period.) Just as Lincoln saw the American nation as the "almost chosen people," Eisenhower also recognized a special relationship with God. As he had done throughout the campaign, the president began his inaugural address with a prayer, beseeching God's guidance during this "time of tempest." Like Lincoln, Eisenhower saw the nation confronting trials and tribulations that would test the divine character of the people. "Are we nearing the light — a day of freedom and of peace for all mankind?" he asked. "Or are the shadows of another night closing in upon us?" For Eisenhower the epochal struggle between light and shadow had brought the United States into inevitable conflict with world communism, a faith that knew "no god but force." "In the final choice," the soldier-president announced, "a soldier's pack is not so heavy a burden as a prisoner's chains."

The metaphors of morality and struggle reflected the new administration's approach to foreign policy. Like the leaders of the Truman administration, Eisenhower and his secretary of state, John Foster Dulles, believed that the Soviet Union was an aggressive nation, seeking to destroy a unique American way of life. Since 1949 the Soviets had enlisted a new, even more dreadful ally: Communist China. In the face of this menace, the Democrats had adopted a defensive strategy that endeavored to contain further Communist expansion.

Eisenhower and Dulles now sought to shift the initiative to the United States. In June 1952 Dulles wrote an article for *Life* magazine, entitled "A Policy of Boldness," that explained the new strategy. Containment, Dulles argued, was designed to protect the status quo, to enable the United States to coexist with the peril of communism. This approach, however, held slim possibilities of eliminating the threat altogether; it was a "treadmill" policy. Moreover, containment was a costly program, requiring heavy expenditures of economic and military

assistance to allies throughout the world. Even the peripheries of the struggle, such as Korea, drained resources from the nation. As an alternative, therefore, Dulles proposed a policy based on principles that became known as "massive retaliation." Instead of waiting for the next Communist advance, the nations of the "free world" should prepare "to retaliate instantly" against the Soviet Union itself, "by means of our choosing." Nuclear weapons aimed at the Kremlin — not at some border area — would deter further Communist expansion.

The doctrine of massive retaliation presupposed American military superiority over the Communist enemy. "Our nation must stand as a solid rock in a storm-tossed world," declared Dulles. In nearly all their public addresses, the leaders of the Eisenhower administration reiterated the importance of strength and power. Such values reflected the traditional warrior code of toughness. But Eisenhower and Dulles added a moral ingredient to the formula. It was not simply that the United States must match the military strength of the Soviet Union, but rather, Dulles and Eisenhower believed, that Communist strength was essentially a façade: as a "godless" people, the Communists were morally rotten at the core. A tough foreign policy based on moral righteousness, therefore, must inevitably defeat the morally weak foe. Eisenhower, moreover, described massive retaliation as a "punishment to be visited upon Russia." The United States, as a Christian country, would implement the wrath of God.

The belief in moral superiority also had a nonmilitary dimension. The United States could wage the Cold War merely by demonstrating its virtue to the "captive peoples" of the world. To carry this message behind the Iron Curtain, the United States established Voice of America broadcasts, which presented American versions of international news. To supplement these programs, Eisenhower advocated the creation of Radio Free Europe in 1949. Ignoring legal restrictions on broadcasting, RFE used propaganda and polemics to agitate for insurrection in Communist countries. Funds for RFE came primarily from the secret budgets of the Central Intelligence Agency. A Free Europe Press, established in 1953, floated propaganda-filled balloons into Communist territories. These activities assumed that moral support would ignite an inherent desire for freedom among "enslaved" peoples. More often, however, the messages exaggerated the United States's commitment to alter the structure of power.

Besides its implications for world affairs, the idea of massive retaliation had distinct domestic advantages. Conservative Republicans, led by Senator Taft, had long dissented from the soaring military budgets of the Truman administration. Eisenhower shared their sentiments. Such budget cutting, however, could not be allowed to compromise the nation's military strength. The emphasis on air power and nuclear weapons provided a prudent solution to the military-budget equation. The "New Look" in military policy enabled the administration to reduce the size of military forces while retaining "massive retaliatory power." This decision enabled Eisenhower to cut $7 billion from Truman's projected military expenses. But Eisenhower's unwillingness to reduce the budget even further aroused the anger of staunch conservatives.

The Republican Old Guard also criticized the president's handling of the Cold War. The Republican party platform had promised to "repudiate all commitments contained in secret understandings such as those of Yalta which aid Communist enslavements." This position reflected a fear of executive independence in foreign policy. But though Eisenhower accepted

The introduction of family bomb shelters revealed the pervasive dread of holocaust in the 1950s. (Wide World Photos)

the statement as a useful campaign strategy, he was reluctant to compromise his own presidential powers. Eisenhower, moreover, did not wish to threaten American claims to Berlin by repudiating the wartime agreements that legitimated the division of Germany. To avoid jeopardizing the European situation, the administration introduced a resolution in February 1953 that renounced diplomacy sacrificing the independence of "captive peoples," but that also ignored the question of Yalta and the decisions of previous presidents. This compromise failed to satisfy Republican conservatives and caused congressional dissent. While Eisenhower was forced to look to Democrats for support, the sudden death of Josef Stalin in March 1953 promised to alter the international situation. The administration took the opportunity to retreat from direct confrontation with congressional conservatives, and the motion never came to a vote.

Eisenhower's success at diverting a controversy failed to alter the conservatives' conviction that executive powers threatened constitutional government. In 1954 Senator John Bricker of Ohio proposed a constitutional amendment requiring that international agreements be approved by Congress before becoming law. This measure challenged not only executive powers but also the internationalist nature of American foreign policy. Supporters of the Bricker amendment pointed out that the U.N. Charter, by affirming human rights, potentially influenced domestic legislation. Eisenhower strongly opposed the Bricker amendment. But because the president believed in a rigid separation of powers, he exercised minimal leadership to defeat the proposal in Congress. Senate Democrats, led by Lyndon Baines Johnson, again saved the president from his own party's conservatives. Though the Bricker amendment obtained a 60–31 majority, it fell one vote short of the necessary two-thirds required for constitutional amendments.

Congressional conservatives also opposed a compromise settlement of the Korean War. They had criticized Truman's initial decision to limit the war, charging the president with appeasing the Communists. But Eisenhower's enormous prestige as a military leader as well as his electoral popularity enabled him to accomplish what the previous Democratic administration was reluctant to suggest. In December 1952 Eisenhower fulfilled his campaign promise to go to Korea. After analyzing the stalemate situation, the new president recognized that a continuation of the ground war would only add to the imbalanced budget. Secretary Dulles joined conservatives in supporting a war for

complete victory. But Eisenhower shunned the use of atomic weapons for several reasons. First, he feared they would provoke Soviet intervention in the war. Second, the United States's atomic arsenal was too small to dissipate in a remote corner of the Cold War. Third, the possible ineffectiveness of such weapons threatened to undermine the immense advantages of atomic diplomacy. As in World War Two, the Korean War had demonstrated the severe limitations of aerial bombardment.

Eisenhower determined to use American military power not for victory but to persuade the Communist People's Republic of China to negotiate a settlement. In his inaugural address, the president announced he was removing the Seventh Fleet from the area separating Taiwan from the mainland, hinting that he was removing an obstacle from an invasion by Chiang Kai-shek. Eisenhower also used diplomatic channels to notify China that the United States might resort to nuclear weapons to drive the enemy to the truce table. After nearly three years of fighting, the Chinese shared American war-weariness. Stalin's death, which introduced the possibility of a shift in Soviet foreign policy, added to China's uncertainty. In March 1953 the Chinese indicated a willingness to resume negotiations.

Peace talks began in Panmunjom, Korea, in April. Both China and the United States accepted the limits of the military struggle. But they still disagreed about the return of prisoners of war. To force the issue, Dulles again introduced the threat of atomic weapons, while the State Department offered a slightly altered proposal. Within three weeks the Chinese accepted, confirming Dulles's faith in tough diplomacy. But Syngman Rhee, the dictatorial leader of South Korea, violently opposed a peace treaty that left his country divided near the 38th parallel. To undermine the settlement, Rhee released twenty-seven thousand prisoners, who vanished into the countryside. American officials quickly intervened, first to assure the People's Republic that the United States had negotiated in good faith, and then to convince Rhee to reconsider his objections. Desirous of an early peace, the Chinese overlooked Rhee's obstructionism and agreed to a final armistice in July 1953.

The end of the Korean War brought most Americans not a sense of celebration, but plain relief. Thirty-three thousand Americans had died to defend an area that State Department officials had admitted was beyond a strategic defense perimeter. Yet congressional conservatives protested that the compromise treaty was actually a vindication of Communist aggression. Republican Senate Majority Leader William Knowland called the settlement a truce without honor, while Taft, then dying of cancer, considered it "extremely unsatisfactory." Eisenhower nevertheless viewed the treaty as a necessary expedient to halt the drain on American resources.

The administration was careful, however, to distinguish the Korean settlement from any semblance of weakness. As a warning to its Communist enemies, the United States joined its allies in stating that further aggression in Korea would have consequences "so grave that in all probability it would not be possible to confine hostilities to Korea." Such threats of massive retaliation were reinforced by the retention in Korea of American military bases, including nuclear-armed missiles. The United States also adopted a multibillion-dollar program of economic and military assistance to shore up the South Korean government. Despite the reactionary internal policies of the Rhee regime, Eisenhower was determined to

stop Communist advances at the 38th parallel. The effect of the Korean treaty, therefore, was to institutionalize the Truman policy of containment in Asia.

Eisenhower's policies toward Europe also revealed basic continuities with those of his predecessor. Though the administration spoke grandiosely about liberating the peoples of Eastern Europe, the principles of massive retaliation were too inflexible to respond effectively to minor crises. When East German workers staged anti-Communist protests in June 1953, Dulles could offer only moral encouragement and $15 million worth of free food. The United States, in effect, accepted the reality of Soviet power in Eastern Europe. Despite its claims to have seized the initiative in foreign policy, the Eisenhower administration could only react to changes elsewhere. Yet this realization of Soviet strength did not produce a desire to negotiate differences. When Stalin's successor, Georgi Malenkov, proposed a treaty to first neutralize Germany and then hold free elections, Dulles rebuffed the idea, arguing that elections must come first. Committed to their world view, Eisenhower and Dulles believed that Soviet power would dissipate because of its own internal weaknesses. While that deterioration proceeded, the United States would watch cautiously and wait.

Eisenhower's reluctance to enter negotiations over Germany reflected the persistence of the containment policy. In seeking to reduce American military expenditures, Eisenhower hoped that the European allies could be persuaded to assume some of the costs. Following the policies of the Truman administration, Dulles pleaded with the allies to ratify the European Defense Community (EDC), an agency that would supplant NATO and permit the arming of Germany without a German general staff. It was this desire to bring Germany into the Western alliance that led Dulles to rebuff a neutralization of the former enemy.

The proposed EDC troubled American allies in Europe. Besides the question of national jealousies, the European nations feared a defense alliance based on massive retaliation and atomic warfare. Such a strategy left ultimate authority on the use of nuclear weapons with the United States. European leaders were also dismayed by Eisenhower's cool response to the apparent moderation of Soviet policy after the death of Stalin. Above all, the French detested the idea of a rearmed Germany. When France delayed acting on the proposed EDC, Dulles attempted to exert additional pressure, suggesting that unless EDC was approved, the United States might undertake an "agonizing reappraisal" of its entire policy toward Europe. Such heavy-handed language, instead of coercing European compliance, underscored Western Europe's dependence on American military strength. Such factors convinced the French to reject EDC in August 1954.

The failure of EDC, however, did not deter American policy makers. Since the United States and Great Britain believed that Germany was essential to the defense of Western Europe, they chose an alternative policy that enabled Germany to rearm under NATO. By 1955 France faced a rearmed Germany that was not limited by the regulatory controls of EDC. "These agreements are founded upon the profound yearning for peace which is shared by all the Atlantic peoples," Eisenhower declared. "The agreements endanger no nation." But the entry of Germany into NATO assured a permanent division of central Europe. In 1955 the Soviet Union initiated the Warsaw Pact, a military alliance that attempted to balance the power of NATO.

SECRET FOREIGN POLICY

The willingness of the United States to dismiss the objections of France, an avowed ally, revealed the self-righteous basis of Eisenhower's foreign policy. Believing that communism was an absolute evil, the United States unilaterally acted on behalf of friendly nations. In the case of other nations, the United States did not hesitate to violate international law when American interests appeared to be threatened. Yet such threats often reflected not a Communist menace but a disagreement over national interest. The Eisenhower administration usually blurred that distinction, claiming that all challenges to the national interest had a Communist base. Such a view could be attributed to a fundamental inability to see the world outside the polarities of what Eisenhower called "light" and "shadow." But in certain situations, there is evidence that the Eisenhower administration deliberately deceived the American people about the nature of international conflict. In concealing their motives, the nation's leaders believed — as in the case of France — that their vision was in the best interests of all.

A major instrument in implementing American policy in unfriendly areas was the Central Intelligence Agency (CIA). Founded in 1947 exclusively as an intelligence-gathering body, the CIA possessed a multibillion-dollar top-secret budget that absolved it of accountability to Congress or the public. In 1953 Eisenhower appointed Allen Dulles, formerly of the Office of Strategic Services and brother of the secretary of state, to head the CIA. Between 1950 and 1955 the CIA tripled in size to fifteen thousand personnel. Besides establishing spy networks throughout the world, the CIA performed secret operations outside the law that facilitated the formal policy of the State Department. The CIA, for example, regularly supported raids from Taiwan to the Chinese mainland. When CIA activities were discovered by other countries, the United States denied the allegations and used the episodes to denounce its enemies as international liars. Several CIA agents languished in Chinese prisons while their employers disavowed their actions. Such dishonesty was justified by the belief that the United States was engaged in mortal struggle against a ruthless, unscrupulous foe. Unsurprisingly, other governments could see the United States in the same light.

The CIA was intimately involved in a coup d'état in Iran in 1953. Two years earlier, the premier of Iran, Dr. Mohammed Mossadegh, had attempted to end British exploitation of the impoverished country by nationalizing the nation's oil wells. The Western-owned oil companies retaliated by instituting a boycott on Iranian oil. Mossadegh appealed to the United States for assistance, but Eisenhower rebuffed him, claiming that "it would not be fair to American taxpayers." The United States did not support a return of the oil wells to Britain; it wanted them for itself.

After Eisenhower's rejection, Mossadegh sought assistance from the Soviet Union. The CIA then stepped in to prevent an Iranian-Soviet alliance. In August 1953 American agents provided crucial military support that enabled the shah to topple the Mossadegh regime. The shah then appointed a premier who was friendly to American interests. In the ensuing negotiations, the nationalized oil wells were replaced by an international consortium, in which American-owned companies held 40 percent interest. By overthrowing the Mossadegh regime, the United States not only broke the British oil monopoly but also placed Iran safely in the non-Communist camp. This realignment was strengthened by American economic assistance to the new Iranian regime.

American intervention in Iran was duplicated in Guatemala in 1954. As in Iran, a popular leader, Colonel Arbenz, attempted to improve economic conditions in his country by enacting land reform and by nationalizing the vast holdings of the United Fruit Company. Arbenz offered a small compensation for the expropriated property, but United Fruit, with the backing of the State Department, rejected the sum. The United States government then began planning to overthrow the Arbenz regime. Through formal diplomatic channels, the State Department urged Arbenz to settle the dispute at the World Court at The Hague. Simultaneously, a secret CIA group began to train an invasion army in nearby Nicaragua and Honduras.

To justify this new version of Dollar Diplomacy, the State Department tried to demonstrate that Arbenz's policies were an opening wedge for "international communism," which would imperil the entire hemisphere. In March 1954 the United States sponsored a resolution at the Tenth Inter-American Conference that declared that Communist control of "any American State" endangered "the peace of America." The motion passed 17–1, with Guatemala alone voting against this new interpretation of the Monroe Doctrine. In May 1954 Arbenz received a shipment of arms from Czechoslovakia, confirming the State Department's worst fears. One month later the CIA-backed army, led by the exiled Colonel Carlos Castillo Armas, invaded Guatemala and defeated Arbenz's forces.

The deposed leader appealed to the U.N. for assistance. But the United States effectively quashed any help by arguing that the Organization of American States, not the Security Council, had proper jurisdiction. "The situation is being cured by Guatemalans themselves," maintained Dulles. After the coup succeeded, however, Dulles took credit for having thwarted "the traitorous tools of foreign despots." In labeling Arbenz a tool of Soviet policy, the Eisenhower administration obtained bipartisan approval. "There is no question here of United States interference in the domestic affairs of any American state," insisted Senator Lyndon Johnson. "We are concerned only with external aggression."

Having argued that the United States had saved Guatemalans from an international conspiracy, the Eisenhower administration arranged to support the new Armas regime with $90 million of economic and military aid. "The United States pledges . . . to help alleviate conditions in Guatemala," assured Dulles, "which might afford communism an opportunity to spread its tentacles throughout the hemisphere." Yet Armas soon returned the nationalized land to United Fruit, provided tax benefits for the large corporation, crushed the labor union movement, and took the vote away from illiterate people, who comprised 70 percent of the population. By defining Arbenz's nationalism as a form of international communism, the Eisenhower administration mustered the political support to restore conditions favorable to American capitalism. But it also aligned itself with the forces of reaction in Latin America.

DOMESTIC CONSERVATISM

American opposition to radical social reform in other countries paralleled the administration's attitudes toward economic development at home. Like most Republicans, Eisenhower initially believed that the swollen budgets of pre-vious Democratic administrations reflected a general "mismanagement" of government. Eisenhower's secretary of the treasury, George Humphrey, was dedicated to a balanced budget by curtailing government expenses. But Eisenhower soon recognized that the administration could not dismantle the social welfare programs of the New Deal. To balance the budget, therefore, the administration reluctantly delayed a tax cut and extended the wartime excess-profits tax to 1954. Despite Humphrey's most frugal efforts and the sharp criticism of Old Guard Republicans, government expenditures remained a basic prop of the American economy.

Eisenhower's economic conservatism emerged more clearly in the debate over control of offshore oil deposits. For more than a decade, the federal government had contested the claims of several coastal states, particularly Texas, Louisiana, and California, to jurisdiction over tideland oil. Since the major oil companies expected beneficial legislation from the state governments, they supported these state claims. In 1946 Congress moved to transfer control to the states. But Truman vetoed the measure, arguing that offshore oil belonged to the nation. In 1947 and 1950 the Supreme Court upheld Truman's position. The Court ruled nevertheless that Congress did have the power to give control of offshore oil to the states.

Conservative Republicans opposed federal control of private business and supported the states' claims. So too did southern Democrats, who saw state control of oil not only in their economic interests, but also as a defense of states' rights. In 1952 these forces pushed through another bill granting jurisdiction to the states. Again Truman vetoed the measure. And before leaving office, Truman reserved offshore oil for the use of the navy.

The new Republican administration determined to reverse Truman's position. Working with southern Democrats, Republicans passed a measure giving control of offshore oil to the states in 1953. Liberals opposed the bill, and Senator Wayne Morse of Oregon staged a twenty-two-hour filibuster in a futile attempt to prevent its enactment. The passage of the Tidelands Oil Act revealed the laissez faire assumptions of the Eisenhower administration. The president personally favored an even more extensive giveaway, but agreed to support his attorney general's defense of federal claims to the continental shelf.

The administration also joined congressional leaders in resisting legislation to alter oil depletion allowances and other tax benefits for the oil industry. This alliance reflected the political strength of southern Democrats from the oil states, especially Speaker of the House Sam Rayburn and Senate Majority Leader Lyndon Johnson, both of Texas. The coalition worked to remove federal controls of natural gas. In 1950 Congress enacted the Kerr bill, exempting natural gas producers from regulation of prices. Encouraged by liberals, Truman vetoed the measure. Eisenhower, however, supported such legislation. But a 1956 bill, which would have removed federal controls, became enmeshed in scandal when an oil lobbyist tried to bribe a senator. To avoid embarrassment, Eisenhower vetoed the bill. The administration, however, relied on a probusiness Federal Power Commission to protect the natural gas industry from strict regulation.

THE ANTI-COMMUNIST
CRUSADE

Eisenhower's belief in the separation of powers influenced his reaction to congressional attempts to purge Communists from government. During the 1952 campaign Eisenhower avoided controversy with such arch-conservatives as Senators McCarthy and Arthur Jenner and endorsed all Republican candidates. After the election Eisenhower continued to appease the conservative wing by naming Scott McLeod, a staunch anti-Communist and McCarthy supporter, to head the State Department's personnel program. Such an appointment, the president felt, would remove conservative accusations that American foreign policy was subverted from within.

Eisenhower also moved to revise Truman's loyalty program. In April 1953 the president issued Executive Order 10450, which decentralized the government's review of employees and placed final responsibility with the separate departments of government. Eisenhower also established a new standard for dismissal. Where Truman required evidence of disloyalty or subversion, the Republican president authorized dismissal on the vague grounds that an individual's employment "may not be clearly consistent with the interests of national security." Under these new guidelines Eisenhower claimed to have removed twenty-two hundred "security risks" in his first year of office. But few were actually charged with disloyalty.

The administration's definition of security risks revealed other underlying assumptions within the Cold War consensus. Besides obvious cases of negligence or criminal acts, Eisenhower's standards for dismissal included "notoriously disgraceful conduct, habitual use of intoxicants to excess, drug addiction, or sexual perversion," as well as insanity. Persons practicing such acts were "risks" because they were vulnerable, weak, and dependent. The Cold War required tough soldiers who would not be dependent on others.

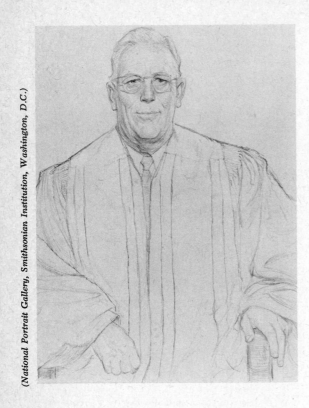

(National Portrait Gallery, Smithsonian Institution, Washington, D.C.)

Earl Warren

1891-1974

"The biggest damfool decision I ever made," Eisenhower remarked of his eight years in the White House, was the appointment of Earl Warren as chief justice of the Supreme Court in 1953. In making the choice, Eisenhower had fulfilled a political debt. As governor of California, Warren represented the liberal wing of the Republican party. He had been Dewey's running mate in 1948 and an important "dark horse" candidate in 1952.

Prior to his Supreme Court appointment, Warren had earned a reputation as an assiduous law enforcement officer in his role as California district attorney and state attorney general. During World War Two, he had advocated confinement of Japanese-Americans. Elected governor in 1943, Warren supported liberal legislation in such areas as health insurance, but had consistently advocated state control and states' rights.

Warren's position on the Supreme Court led to dramatic reversals of precedent. In his first major decision, Brown v. Board of Education (1954), the chief justice dismantled the doctrine of separate, but equal and paved the way for fundamental changes in race relations. The attack on undemocratic practices by the states also led to a Court order for the reapportionment of legislative districts according to the one-person, one-vote principle in 1962 (Baker v. Carr). These rulings altered a traditional political structure that enabled rural elites to ignore numerical majorities.

Warren also became a strong defender of individual rights. In the Yates decision (1957), he concurred in reversing the conviction of leading Communists by differentiating between the theory of subversion and its actual practice. This position led to the eventual overthrow of certain loyalty oaths and state laws against Communists. Under the principle of due process of law, he defended the rights of criminals to legal counsel and fair treatment by police. The Warren-led Court tightened the interpretation of obscenity to limit censorship of speech and the press. In 1962 the Court supported a rigid separation of church and state in denying prayers in public schools. Such opinions earned Warren the hatred of right wing groups such as the John Birch Society, which demanded his impeachment.

Despite the unpopularity of some of his rulings, Warren was widely respected for his personal integrity. President Johnson therefore named him to head a commission to investigate the assassination of President Kennedy. Warren's personal reputation helped persuade political leaders to accept the commission's controversial report. Warren's retirement in 1969 heralded the end of a liberal era of an "activist" judiciary.

Frequent victims of the warrior code were alleged homosexuals. In a single case in 1960, the National Security Administration fired twenty-six employees for sexual deviation. Given the frequency of homosexual contacts reported by Dr. Alfred Kinsey, persecution of homosexuals seemed particularly severe. During the 1952 presidential campaign, Stevenson, who had recently been divorced from his wife, took special care to remain in female company to counter rumors that he was a homosexual. Stevenson's vacillation about running for office reinforced a sense of his weakness. *Life* magazine criticized the candidate's "Softness Toward Communism." Similarly, the anti-Communist *New Leader* praised the political "hards" who were "willing to risk reaction and war ... to fight Communism." In a culture that defined courage in terms of hardness and strength, homosexuals symbolized the "soft" side of all males. Unwilling to accept these characteristics within themselves, political leaders saw nothing wrong in suppressing "weak" men.

The desire to suppress deviant lifestyles closely paralleled an attack on deviant opinion in all levels of government. Shortly after moving into the State Department, Dulles removed several career diplomats, including a group of prestigious China experts who had predicted Mao's victory in 1949. These officers had been accused not of disloyalty but of indiscretion. Dulles also encouraged the departure of George Kennan, viewed as the architect of Truman's containment policy. To replace Kennan as ambassador to the Soviet Union, the administration supported Charles E. Bohlen, an expert on Soviet affairs. But rigid anti-Communists questioned the nomination, pointing out that Bohlen had served Democratic presidents at Yalta and Potsdam. The administration nevertheless decided to stand behind Bohlen. A compromise was reached when Senators Taft and Sparkman examined Bohlen's confidential FBI file. Their favorable report led to senatorial confirmation of the appointment. But Taft indicated the implications of the controversy when he told the president, "No more Bohlens."

The suppression of alternative opinions was revealed dramatically in the case of J. Robert Oppenheimer, the celebrated physicist who had directed the development of the atomic bomb. By 1950 Oppenheimer had expressed serious reservations about further nuclear armament and had opposed the decision to manufacture a hydrogen bomb. Oppenheimer's known association with leftists had aroused suspicions about his loyalty, but the scientist had passed numerous investigations and had maintained his security clearance. In July 1953, however, Eisenhower's director of the Atomic Energy Commission, Admiral Lewis Strauss, began to remove classified documents from Oppenheimer's custody, and in December Strauss asked for the scientist's resignation. Oppenheimer demanded an investigation, which was completed in April 1954. By a 2–1 vote, a special review panel lifted Oppenheimer's security clearance. The scientist was forced to leave the government service.

The attempt to stifle dissenting viewpoints had profound consequences on individual lives, but the administration remained insensitive to these problems. Upon assuming the presidency, Eisenhower inherited a delicate legal case involving the convicted atomic spies Julius and Ethel Rosenberg. Though the only defendants to insist on their innocence, the Rosenbergs had been sentenced to death. Such a punishment revealed a popular but erroneous belief that the Soviet Union lacked the intellectual sophistication to develop atomic weapons without American help. In upholding the sentence, the federal courts cooperated with government prosecutors to assure that unrepentant Soviet sympathizers would receive ultimate punishment. Facing execution in June 1953, the Rosenbergs appealed to Eisenhower for clemency. But the president refused to intervene, charging that the atomic spies "may have condemned to death tens of millions of innocent people all over the world."

"In America," protested the playwright Arthur Miller in *The Crucible,* a 1953 version of the Salem witch trials, "any man who is not reactionary in his views is open to the charge of alliance with the Red hell." Foremost in making such accusations was Senator Joseph McCarthy. "There is only one real issue for the farmer, the laborer, and the businessman," he declared during the 1952 campaign, "—the issue of Communism in government." Such statements proved useful in the election campaign, but members of the Eisenhower administration were concerned when the senator continued his charges after the inauguration.

McCarthy's position as chairman of the Senate Subcommittee on Government Operations provided a forum for his persistent attacks on Communist influence in government. In the spring of 1953 McCarthy and his legal aide, Roy Cohn, staged a series of hearings about the Voice of America, claiming that the organization was a front for leftist groups. McCarthy also meddled in State Department affairs, seeking to "negotiate" a reduction of Greek shipping to China. In April 1953 Cohn and his friend, G. David Schine, embarked on a chaotic investigation of the United States Information Agency in Europe. Their scrutiny of USIA libraries revealed over thirty thousand "subversive" authors, a category that included writers like Theodore Dreiser, Archibald MacLeish, and Arthur M. Schlesinger, Jr. Despite complaints about these absurd charges, the USIA quickly removed several thousand volumes from library shelves.

These attacks finally provoked a presidential response. "Don't join the book-burners!" Eisenhower advised a Dartmouth College commencement audience in June 1953. "Don't be afraid to go into your library and read every book as long as that document does not offend your own ideas of decency." But when asked by the press to elaborate on his comments, the president maintained that he was not referring to McCarthy. Eisenhower was reluctant to clash with McCarthy, fearing a split within Republican ranks and worrying about lending dignity to the senator's crusade. "I will not get into the gutter with that guy," the president declared. The McCarthy problem, he hoped, would wear itself out.

McCarthy's power ended, however, only when he finally outraged the political leadership that had tacitly supported him. In early 1954 McCarthy began an investigation of alleged communism at Fort Monmouth, New Jersey. He soon clashed with General Ralph Zwicker, chastising the officer for his defense of "Communist conspirators." The White House tried to stop McCarthy's criticism, but the senator sidestepped administration pressure. The army responded by releasing documents that revealed McCarthy's attempt to obtain special privileges for Cohn's friend, Private David Schine. Shouting "blackmail," McCarthy insisted on a full investigation of the army. Democratic Majority Leader Lyndon Johnson now saw an opportunity to ruin McCarthy. Like other Democrats, Johnson had avoided a confrontation with the Wisconsin senator, fearing a vicious counterattack. "Joe will go that extra mile to destroy you," he remarked. But Johnson believed that public exposure would also lead

McCarthy to destroy himself. He therefore urged that the Army-McCarthy hearings be televised. For thirty-six days the nation was treated to a spectacle of McCarthy's erratic, irrational behavior. While the senator stormed at witnesses and ignored legal procedures, his public-opinion ratings steadily dropped. In May McCarthy added one year to his denunciation of "twenty years of treason," thus implicating the Eisenhower administration in a coverup of communism. He had gone too far.

In June Republican Senator Ralph Flanders of Vermont introduced a resolution calling for McCarthy's censure by the Senate. In a carefully orchestrated proceeding, a panel of conservative senators recommended censure of McCarthy for conduct that "tended to bring the Senate into dishonor and disrepute." McCarthy continued to rage against the Senate, accusing that body of serving the Communists. But half the Republicans joined the unanimous Democrats in voting McCarthy's censure. Vice President Nixon, presiding in the Senate, deleted the word *censure* from the final document. It was a formality that made no difference. McCarthy's power was broken. He remained in the Senate, politically ineffective, until his death in 1957.

The elimination of McCarthy created an illusion that the Communist witch hunts had ended. But the attack on communism extended far beyond the chambers of Congress, revealing the power of systematic political repression. Libraries removed "controversial" books; school boards and universities dismissed leftist teachers; industries established blacklists to prevent employment of suspected Communists. Such activities won wide support, even from liberals. Minnesota's Hubert H. Humphrey, an early defender of civil rights, supported legislation to prohibit the Communist party. "We liberals," added Illinois's Paul Douglas, "must destroy the Communists if this dirty game is to stop."

THE POLITICS OF CONSENSUS

Despite McCarthy's problems in 1954, therefore, Republican leaders expected the anti-Communist crusade to be an effective campaign weapon in the congressional elections. Eisenhower avoided the emotionally charged issue and contented himself with a nationwide speaking tour on behalf of Republican candidates pledged to his administration. But Nixon, repeating his performance of 1952, attacked the Democrats for their toleration of "the Communist conspiracy in the United States." Neither Eisenhower's prestige nor Nixon's rhetoric could overcome the political effects of an economic recession. More significant was the president's inability to attach his popularity to other Republican candidates. Though Eisenhower could attract a large independent vote, other politicians were linked in the public mind with traditional party labels. In the end, the Democrats won small majorities in both houses of Congress.

The Democratic victories of 1954, instead of creating partisan conflict between the branches of government, actually encouraged cooperation. Rayburn and Johnson, the congressional leaders, shared a conservative outlook that differed only slightly from the president's. Their power in Congress reflected the strength of southern Democrats. Since committee assignments depended on seniority, southerners from the one-party region enjoyed obvious advantages. The patterns of congressional representation also strengthened the conservative group. Urban areas, which traditionally supported liberal candidates, were underrepresented in Congress because state legislatures gerrymandered voting districts to suit local political needs. The imbalances in legislative apportionment were not corrected by the principle of one-person, one-vote until a Supreme Court ruling in 1962.

Reflecting this conservative consensus was Eisenhower's articulation of a philosophy of "modern republicanism." Rejecting the Old Guard Republicans who had criticized Eisenhower's foreign policy and his minimal social legislation, the president suggested that the federal government "must do its part to advance human welfare and encourage economic growth with constructive actions." Such ideas departed from the laissez faire principles of the Republican right wing. But they did not commit the administration to a major program of social welfare legislation. Eisenhower's vision of politics was well summarized by Arthur Larson in his 1956 book, *A Republican Looks at His Party*, a work that the president endorsed. "This is no time to harry the American public from crisis to crisis," Larson advised, "nor to drive breaches between groups for transient political advantage."

This belief in a political consensus encouraged the emergence of an intellectual consensus that dominated the social sciences. The major historians of the fifties, Louis Hartz, Richard Hofstadter, and Daniel Boorstin, described the American past as a homogenized culture without significant class, ethnic, or racial conflict. Racism, for example, became an aberration from the American mainstream that was peculiar to the antebellum South. In sociology and political science, academic scholars stressed the "pluralism" of American society, an interaction of groups that lacked ideological tensions. These trends encouraged the proliferation of American Studies programs that taught the uniqueness and, by implication, the superiority of American culture. The sociologist William Whyte observed in 1956 that most social scientists held a "bias against conflict." Such terms as "disharmony, disequilibrium, maladjustment, disorganization," he remarked, were considered "bad things."

A major unifying force was the Cold War. Democrats and Republicans alike shared a belief in the Communist menace and agreed that the United States had to maintain its military strength. A 1956 survey indicated that there was no correlation between political opinions on domestic issues and support of a tough stand against international communism. Thus Eisenhower's popularity remained high, even though voters might reject other Republican candidates. The relationship between Cold War expenditures and economic prosperity also assured minimal resistance to the administration's budgetary requests for military purposes.

FOREIGN POLICY IN ASIA

Support of the Cold War, however, did not imply a bipartisan foreign policy. Democratic opposition to the principles of massive retaliation led to a major defeat of the State Department's policy for Vietnam in 1954. Since the outbreak of the Korean War, the United States had supported the French attempt to suppress the Viet Minh rebels led by Ho Chi Minh. By 1954 the United States had spent $1.2 billion on military assistance and was financing nearly 80 percent of the total war costs. These expenses included several hundred "technical" advisers. Such intervention was justified by the belief that Vietnam was a valuable source of

raw materials as well as a vital strategic link in the attempt to halt Communist expansion.

Despite American aid, France was unable to defeat the Viet Minh. French opinion, moreover, began to doubt the validity of the war. In April 1954 the French garrison at Dien Bien Phu was surrounded by Vietnamese forces. France faced a major military defeat and appealed to the United States for assistance. Eisenhower had no interest in committing the United States to a ground war in Southeast Asia. Given the doctrine of massive retaliation, however, American assistance would be limited to an air attack, perhaps with atomic weapons. While the French garrison lay under siege, policy makers in Washington debated American foreign policy.

For Eisenhower, Vietnam held the future of Asia. At a press conference in April 1954, the president explained the "falling domino" theory: "You have a row of dominos set up, you knock over the first one, and what will happen to the last one is the certainty that it will go over very quickly." The fall of Vietnam would mean that "many human beings pass under a dictatorship that is inimical to the free world." It would interfere with the acquisition of precious resources. And it would imperil Japanese trade, forcing that ally "toward the Communist areas in order to live." Eisenhower never wavered from this belief that the Viet Minh represented not an anticolonial force, but an instrument of world communism.

The president received differing advice from his closest aides. Dulles and Admiral Arthur W. Radford, chairman of the Joint Chiefs, advocated air attacks to relieve the French, and Air Force General Nathan Twining went so far as to promote an atomic bombing of the Vietnamese countryside. But Army Chief Matthew Ridgway, who as MacArthur's replacement in Korea well remembered the futility of limited warfare, spoke strongly against intervention. Eisenhower then consulted congressional leaders. "Where do the British stand?" asked Richard Russell. The administration admitted that it lacked the support of its allies. The congressmen urged Eisenhower not to act unilaterally.

An international conference to discuss Indochina was scheduled to convene at Geneva in April. British Prime Minister Winston Churchill was unwilling to jeopardize that meeting by supporting American military operations, though Dulles suggested that an air attack would strengthen the allied negotiating position. The administration then used Nixon to send up a trial balloon, proposing American intervention on behalf of the French. Public reaction was highly critical. Meanwhile, the French military position continued to deteriorate. On May 7 the forces at Dien Bien Phu surrendered. "American foreign policy has never in all its history suffered such a stunning reversal," complained Lyndon Johnson in the Senate. "We have been caught bluffing by our enemies." Eisenhower still considered entering the conflict, but the French had lost the will to fight. In June the administration formally rejected the French request for assistance.

The fall of Dien Bien Phu made a diplomatic settlement imperative. In July France signed the Geneva Accords that ended eight years of colonial warfare. According to the agreement, France acknowledged the independence of Vietnam, Laos, and Cambodia. Vietnam was divided temporarily at the 17th parallel, but this division did not imply a political separation of that country. National elections, supervised by an international commission, would be held within two years to unify the country. In the interim, neither zone was to

enter military alliances or allow foreign military bases to be established. These terms required the Viet Minh to surrender portions of the country under their control. But since Ho Chi Minh anticipated an easy electoral victory, he viewed the retreat as a temporary concession.

By acknowledging the validity of a Viet Minh government, if only for the northern portions of Vietnam, the Geneva settlement represented a serious defeat for American foreign policy. Though the United States formally announced that it would respect the Geneva Accords, it refused to sign the agreement. Meanwhile, the Eisenhower administration initiated immediate actions to continue the war against the Viet Minh. Dulles worked to establish a Vietnamese alternative to Ho Chi Minh and succeeded in having Ngo Dinh Diem, an American-educated Catholic seminarian, appointed premier of the French-controlled portion of the country. The administration also rushed a military mission to Vietnam. Headed by Colonel Edward G. Lansdale, who had gained experience fighting Communist Huk guerrillas in the Philippines, the mission performed acts of sabotage and launched a propaganda campaign to discredit the Viet Minh government.

The United States pursued a similar policy through traditional diplomatic channels. Determined to supplant France's role in Vietnam, the State Department by-passed French colonial administrators and transmitted aid directly to the Diem regime. This procedure freed the United States from accusations of supporting European colonialism. But it also had the effect of forcing France to withdraw from Vietnam prior to the 1956 deadline. The United States quickly stepped into the power vacuum. American advisers began to train a large Vietnamese army "to deter Viet Minh aggression by a limited defense of the Geneva Armistice demarkation line." The United States, in effect, was forestalling the possibility of national unification under a Viet Minh government.

These policies were made explicit in July 1955 when Diem announced that he would not honor the Geneva agreement calling for national elections. France and Great Britain protested this decision, but the United States backed Diem. "While we should certainly take no positive step to speed up the present process of decay of [the] Geneva Accords," Dulles declared, "neither should we make the slightest effort to infuse life into them." The United States continued to pour over $1 billion of economic and military aid into Vietnam, financing most of Diem's government expenses. Eisenhower also welcomed Diem in Washington, where the two leaders reaffirmed the struggle against "continuing Communist subversive capabilities."

American support enabled Diem to suppress his political rivals in Vietnam. Diem's soldiers made mass arrests of Communists and non-Communists alike. In 1955 he rigged elections that made him president with 98 percent of the vote. Diem also subverted a land reform program begun by the Viet Minh. Such policies triggered a guerrilla revolt. Though the Viet Minh supported such attacks, the anti-Diem movement originated in the south. In 1959, however, Viet Minh insurgents, many of them native to the south, returned to challenge the Diem regime. To preempt this movement, the United States urged Diem to institute political and social reforms. But Diem refused, leading the American ambassador to notify Washington that "it may become necessary . . . to begin consideration of alternative courses of actions and leaders." This predicament was inherited by President Kennedy in 1961.

While taking unilateral action to support Diem, the United States attempted to use collective security to prevent the further spread of communism in Asia. Learning from the loss of Dien Bien Phu, the administration sought to obtain precommitments from its allies. In September 1954 Dulles signed a Southeast Asia Treaty Organization (SEATO) pact with Great Britain, France, Australia, New Zealand, Thailand, Pakistan, and the Philippines. This treaty provided for mutual defense against either armed attack or subversion and indirect aggression. "An attack on the treaty area would occasion a reaction so united, so strong, and so well placed," boasted Dulles in the language of massive retaliation, "that the aggressor would lose more than it could hope to gain."

The SEATO agreement, however, had inherent limitations that made Dulles's words seem like bombast. Such pivotal nations as India, pursuing a policy of neutrality, refused to cooperate. Moreover, the treaty obliged the eight nations only to consult and then follow normal constitutional procedures. Finally, it was unlikely that massive retaliation would be effective against indirect subversion. The Senate nevertheless ratified the treaty with little dissent. It was never invoked, however, and the agreement was ended in 1977.

The façade of SEATO was soon revealed when the United States made a unilateral decision to defend Chiang Kai-shek's control of the islands between China and Taiwan. Until World War Two, Japan had claimed Taiwan (Formosa) but recognized China's historic claims to Quemoy, Matsu, and the Tatchens. In fleeing the mainland, Chiang maintained control of all these islands. At the outbreak of the Korean War, Truman had ordered the Seventh Fleet to protect these territories from an expected Chinese invasion. But Eisenhower had removed the fleet in 1953, hinting that he was "unleashing" Chiang to attack the mainland. With American support, Chiang also reinforced the island outposts.

In September 1954, while Dulles was flying to Manila to negotiate the SEATO pact, Chinese shore batteries began to bombard Quemoy, and the Peking government called for the "liberation" of Taiwan. The Joint Chiefs of Staff immediately began planning a counteroffensive, including an atomic attack on China. Great Britain opposed such action, viewing Chiang's control of the offshore islands as provocative. Eisenhower recognized that the islands were not crucial to the defense of Taiwan, but he insisted that the Chiang government was part

MAP 13.2 TAIWAN

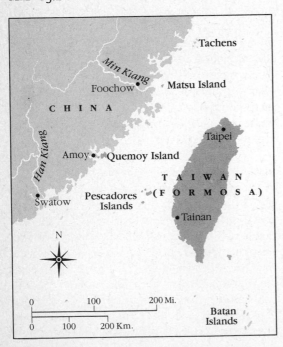

of the "backbone" of American security in the Pacific. In December Dulles negotiated a mutual defense pact with Chiang, but it made no mention of the disputed islands.

After the Chinese captured one of the Tatchen Islands, however, Eisenhower determined to clarify his defense of Taiwan. In January 1955 he asked Congress for authority to use armed forces "to assure the security of Formosa and the Pescadores" as well as "closely related localities." This request for discretionary power to declare war coincided ironically with the Senate's consideration of the Bricker amendment, which would have required legislative cooperation with executive decisions. Yet Congress treated the president's request uncritically, approving Eisenhower's blank check by nearly unanimous votes in both houses. Nor was Eisenhower opposed to using this unprecedented power. As China continued to bomb the offshore islands, the administration prepared for war. But pressure from Asian neutrals persuaded China to relax the tensions. By late spring the crisis had passed.

In supporting the Taiwan government in 1955, however, Eisenhower allowed Chiang to maneuver the United States into supporting a dubious claim to the offshore islands. In subsequent years Chiang took the opportunity to strengthen his fortifications on the disputed territory. But in August 1958 the People's Republic reopened the problem by launching a steady bombardment of Quemoy. Dulles responded to the crisis by reiterating a domino theory that justified defense of the islands, if necessary with atomic power. This position alarmed ally and enemy alike; both Britain and the Soviet Union advised the United States against military intervention. The administration's saber-rattling also brought stern criticism at home. Such pressure forced Dulles to admit that the

United States had no legal obligations to defend Quemoy and Matsu. This position soon eased the crisis. But in defending his bellicose posture, Eisenhower scrupulously insisted that the Formosa Resolution of 1955 granted the president sole responsibility for judging an "appropriate . . . defense of Formosa."

EUROPEAN DIPLOMACY

Eisenhower's assertion of executive prerogatives in 1958 contrasted with his attitudes about presidential diplomacy during his first years in office. Doubting the value of personal negotiations, Eisenhower allowed Dulles to negotiate on his behalf. Eisenhower's hesitancy stemmed from a belief that individual leaders would not significantly alter national policies. Moreover, he feared that a failure of summit diplomacy would only aggravate world tensions. For these reasons Eisenhower preferred to issue broad policy statements and await normal diplomatic responses. In December 1953, for example, Eisenhower addressed the U.N. General Assembly, presenting a dramatic "atoms for peace" proposal that urged international control of atomic weapons. When the Soviet Union reacted unfavorably, however, the president settled for the propaganda advantages and made no counteroffer.

Eisenhower also tried to avoid a meeting of world leaders proposed by Winston Churchill in 1955. He insisted that as a precondition for meeting with Soviet leaders, the former allies adopt a peace treaty with Austria. By 1955 Stalin's successors were anxious to nullify the rearming of Germany by stabilizing central Europe and, to Eisenhower's surprise, agreed to an Austrian treaty. The president's excuse for

opposing a summit conference thus disappeared. In July 1955 Eisenhower attended a meeting with leaders of the Soviet Union, Great Britain, and France in Geneva. The main topics on the agenda — the status of Germany and disarmament — could not be settled. But Eisenhower captured international attention by proposing an "open skies" plan that would allow each nation to observe the other's armaments to prevent surprise attack. The Soviet Union rejected the scheme, viewing it as a threat to its sovereignty.

The Geneva sessions produced no tangible results. The Soviet Union now accepted the division of Germany and took the final steps to establish a separate East German government. But the summit meeting did abate world tension, and the press hailed the peaceful "spirit of Geneva." In his state of the union message of January 1956, Eisenhower acknowledged a new facet to the Cold War. "Communist tactics against the free nations have shifted in emphasis," he declared, "from reliance on violence to reliance on division." To counter this strategy, the president counseled unity and strength. Secretary Dulles was more blunt. In an interview with *Life* magazine, he boasted about the salutary effects of a tough foreign policy. "We walked to the brink and we looked it in the face. We took strong action."

The limits of "brinksmanship" were revealed in two related crises in 1956. In February, the new Soviet leader, Nikita Khrushchev, greeted the Twentieth Congress of the Communist party with an astounding speech that denounced the policies of Stalin. In attacking the "cult of the individual," Khrushchev suggested that Stalin had erred in trying to build a monolithic Communist bloc in Eastern Europe. It was possible, Khrushchev implied, for communism to adapt to local conditions, separate from Soviet control. Two months later, the Soviet

Union dissolved Cominform, the instrument of international Communist conformity.

These liberalizing tendencies encouraged the Communist parties of Eastern Europe to seek independent positions. In the summer, riots in Poland against the Stalinist regime enabled independent Communists, led by Wladyslaw Gomulka, to come to power. With popular support Gomulka negotiated with Soviet leaders and won important concessions for national autonomy. Spurred by Poland's success, mass demonstrations erupted in Hungary, demanding removal of the Stalinist leadership. Despite opposition from conservatives within the Kremlin, Khrushchev accepted the rise of an independent Communist, Imre Nagy. But when Nagy announced that he was taking Hungary out of the Warsaw alliance, Khrushchev felt compelled to restore the solidarity of the Communist bloc. Ordering Soviet tanks into Budapest, Soviet leaders crushed the Hungarian uprising, despite the gallant resistance of poorly armed rebels.

The American response to these dramatic events was negligible. Though Radio Free Europe broadcast moral support, perhaps even exaggerating the United States's commitment to intervene, the Eisenhower administration settled for pious condemnations of Soviet cruelty. The United States introduced a resolution in the Security Council calling for withdrawal of Soviet forces, but the Soviet Union vetoed it. The United States then turned to the General Assembly. By then the rebellion had been broken. Having done nothing to help the rebels, Eisenhower decided to provide sanctuary for thousands of "freedom fighters" who sought asylum in the United States. Eisenhower's failure to act revealed the illusion of an easy "liberation" of Eastern Europe as well as the futility of relying on massive force as an exclusive instrument of policy. American impotence also betrayed serious divisions within the Western alliance.

CRISES IN THE MIDDLE EAST

The importance of oil in the postwar world underscored the economic and strategic value of the oil-rich Middle East. Though the United States supported the independence of Israel, it also took pains to maintain friendship with the Arab states. As part of its professed anticolonialism, the United States encouraged the departure of British forces from Egypt, which was accomplished by treaty between 1954 and 1956. In 1955, however, a successful Israeli attack had demonstrated Egypt's military weakness. The new Egyptian leader, Gamal Abdel Nasser, now sought outside assistance to strengthen his country economically and militarily. While Nasser negotiated with Czechoslovakia to purchase arms, Dulles moved to win Egyptian friendship by offering to finance the Aswan Dam, a giant hydroelectric project that promised to modernize Egypt. Nasser accepted the offer and made a formal application for American assistance.

Dulles's scheme soon ran into congressional opposition. Questioned about the implications of a Middle East arms race, the secretary admitted the possibility of a war between Israel and the Arab states. These fears were aggravated by the formation of an Arab military alliance in April 1956. One month later, Nasser announced his recognition of the People's Republic of China. This decision, together with the Czech arms purchase, lessened the possibility of obtaining congressional approval for Nasser's dam. In July Dulles decided to withdraw his offer to construct the project. "Do nations which play both sides get better treatment than nations which are stalwart and work with us?" asked Dulles piously.

The American reversal humiliated Nasser. One week later the Egyptian leader took revenge by nationalizing the Suez Canal. The seizure alarmed Great Britain and France, who were dependent on the canal for oil. Both nations hinted about the possibility of military reprisal. Dulles opposed such a reassertion of colonialism, fearing that it would drive the Arabs irrevocably into the Communist camp. He proposed as an alternative the creation of an independent canal commission to protect each side's interests. But the idea was unacceptable to all parties. Dulles's refusal to support the Western allies angered them, and they decided to take independent action. While the United States issued a bland statement condemning the use of force in the Middle East, Great Britain and France met with Israel to develop secret plans of attack.

In October Israel launched a surprise attack on Egypt. This conflict provided Great Britain and France with an excuse to intervene to protect the independence of the Suez Canal. The invasion coincided with the Soviet attack on the Hungarian rebels. Faced with a double crisis, the furious Eisenhower demanded that Great Britain and France withdraw from Egypt. So too did Khrushchev, who warned the Western nations about the possibility of a retaliatory attack. The Soviet leader also proposed that his nation join the United States in settling the controversy. This suggestion alarmed Eisenhower, who believed that the Soviet Union would use the conflict as an excuse to acquire power in the Middle East. The United States then rushed to avoid Soviet intervention by unilaterally demanding British and French withdrawal. To strengthen this demand, the

United States halted oil shipments from Latin America to its allies. Such pressure forced a capitulation. By December the allies had removed their forces from the Middle East. The entire episode demonstrated the growing influence of small nations on Big Power diplomacy.

Nasser's successful defiance of the European nations created a power vacuum in the Middle East. Eisenhower moved quickly to prevent the Soviet Union from taking advantage of the situation. In January 1957 the president asked Congress to approve a resolution, known as the Eisenhower Doctrine, "to deter Communist aggression in the Middle East area." Besides requesting a special appropriation for economic and military assistance, the resolution announced that "overt armed aggression from any nation controlled by international Communism" would be challenged by American military forces. As with the Formosa resolution, the president was seeking blanket authority for future executive action.

The proposal instigated a major debate in the Senate. J. William Fulbright of Arkansas denounced the administration's attempt to manipulate congressional opinion by surreptitious news leaks and secret meetings "in an atmosphere of suspense and urgency." He challenged the administration's unusual claim of executive powers and pointed out that Eisenhower offered no specific policy goals. Majority Leader Johnson, however, managed the bill through the Senate, but not before he weakened some of the president's discretionary powers.

The Eisenhower Doctrine became a convenient rationale for United States intervention in the Middle East. In April 1957 the regime of Jordan's King Hussein was threatened by pro-Nasser rebels. The king claimed, however, that the rebellion was really a Communist attack. Understanding the duplicity of language, Eisenhower nevertheless invoked his doctrine and sent the Sixth Fleet into the area to protect the political status quo. In July 1958 a similar distortion of events led the president to order the marines into Lebanon. This dramatic gesture served notice to Arab nationalists that the United States was determined to protect its access to Middle East oil.

THE POLITICS OF MODERATION

The willingness of Democrats to support the administration's foreign policy paralleled a prevailing consensus about domestic politics. Though liberals like Hubert Humphrey and Paul Douglas spoke eloquently about social reform, the Democratic leadership worked closely with Eisenhower's "modern" Republicans to enact minimal welfare legislation. Surveying the political spectrum in 1956, Adlai Stevenson aptly concluded that "moderation is the spirit of the times."

The limitations of this conservative consensus could be seen in the cautious approach to minimum wages, public housing, and health benefits. In 1955 Eisenhower proposed a 90¢-an-hour minimum wage, 35¢ less than organized labor desired, and extension of coverage to include unorganized retail and service workers. Democratic leaders wished to preserve the support of labor unions. But conservatives opposed broadening the coverage to unskilled workers, most of whom were members of racial minorities. Political leaders then agreed to a compromise that raised the minimum wage to $1 an hour but ignored unorganized laborers.

Though the Public Housing Act of 1949 had authorized the construction of nearly one mil-lion dwellings, subsequent appropriations had drastically reduced that figure. The shortage of adequate housing remained critical, especially in the cities. But in 1954 Eisenhower requested only 140,000 units. Congress responded by cutting that number to 75,000 over a two-year period. In the area of health care, political leaders in both branches of government dismissed proposals for national medical insurance as "socialized" medicine. In 1955 the administration endorsed the principle of providing free distribution of the new Salk vaccine to prevent poliomyelitis. But the Department of Health, Education, and Welfare drew a storm of criticism for failing to prepare an adequate program of supply and distribution.

Eisenhower's desire to minimize government involvement in the economy led him to reverse the Democrats' approach to public control of electric power projects. In 1954 the president recommended a revision of the Atomic Energy Act to allow private manufacture and operation of atomic reactors. This legislation led to the first privately run atomic power plants. More controversial was the administration's decision to by-pass the Tennessee Valley Authority in providing electricity for AEC facilities. Eisenhower endorsed an AEC contract with the Dixon-Yates Combine, believing that the federal government should not compete directly with private industry. The idea clashed with the very existence of TVA, long a symbol of New Deal liberalism. Amid charges of corruption, Eisenhower stood by the project. But in 1955 the city of Memphis independently decided to build a power plant that made Dixon-Yates a dead issue.

Despite such squabbles on domestic issues, Eisenhower remained extremely popular. But confidence in the administration was shaken in September 1955 when the president suffered a heart attack. With Eisenhower temporarily disabled, the public worried about the succession of the conservative vice president. Once Eisenhower's recovery seemed assured, the cabinet adopted administrative procedures to minimize Nixon's access to power. The administration also worked to coordinate government operations to avoid a semblance of internal dissension. Eisenhower recovered rapidly, but his health remained an important issue in the election of 1956.

Eisenhower was nevertheless confident about his abilities and resolved to seek a second term. There was no question about his receiving the nomination. In his acceptance speech the president forecast a time of peace and prosperity,

but warned that "it will not be attained by revolution [nor] by the sordid politics of pitting group against group." As president of all the people, Eisenhower would campaign on the principles of consensus. Eisenhower introduced an element of uncertainty for the Republicans when he hesitated to support Nixon as his running mate. The vice president fought back stubbornly and thwarted a weak "dump Nixon" movement.

With Eisenhower's nomination, the Democrats' chances seemed slim. But the race for the nomination saw stiff competition between Stevenson, Kefauver, and Harriman. Stevenson won a first-ballot decision and chose Kefauver as his running mate. The party then adopted a

MAP 13.3   THE ELECTION OF 1956

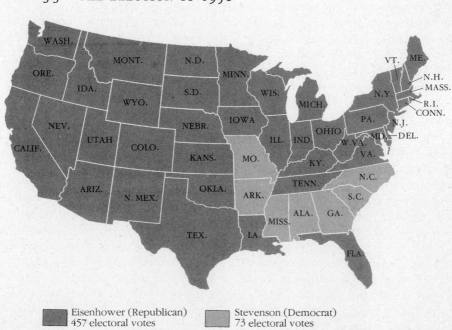

Eisenhower (Republican)
457 electoral votes

Stevenson (Democrat)
73 electoral votes

moderate, noncontroversial platform. Hoping to regain the South, the Democrats wavered on support of the Supreme Court's school desegregation decision. The party's position on foreign policy echoed the Cold War values of the Republican administration.

Stevenson introduced two controversial proposals in the campaign. He called for the end of the military draft and a moratorium on hydrogen bomb testing. These issues played directly to Eisenhower's strength, for the president appeared as an unquestioned authority on military affairs. The outbreak of the Suez crisis and the Hungarian revolt in October provided the Democrats with late-campaign ammunition. But the crisis in foreign policy merely reinforced Eisenhower's appeal as a leader in world affairs. "The butchers of the Kremlin," scoffed Nixon, "would make mincemeat of Stevenson over a conference table.".

Eisenhower's margin of victory exceeded that of 1952. He captured 58 percent of the popular vote and carried all but seven states. But in an unusual situation, other Republican candidates fell far behind the president's pace, and the Democrats regained control of both houses of Congress. This anomalous situation reflected the persistence of party voting habits (there were 50 percent more registered Democrats than Republicans in 1956). Eisenhower could win Democratic support, but lesser Republicans lacked that advantage. The importance of foreign policy issues in the campaign reinforced that trend. Unlike domestic issues, which touched voters personally, international affairs remained distant for most people. Thus voters could follow their personal inclinations to support Eisenhower without upsetting any commitment to specific issues. In 1956 Eisenhower attracted voters in all political spectrums because issues were relatively unimportant.

DOMESTIC DEBATE

Despite his attempt to present a middle-of-the-road program, Eisenhower's second administration was marked by sharp discord with Congress. The first controversy erupted when the president presented a $71.8 billion budget request for 1958. Eisenhower claimed that this figure, the largest peacetime budget ever presented, represented a minimal estimate. But the president's calculations were undermined by Treasury Secretary George Humphrey. "If we fail to economize over a longer period of time," he told a press conference, "I predict ... a depression that will curl your hair." Eisenhower weakened his position further by urging Congress to cut government expenditures as much as possible. These remarks fueled a bitter legislative "battle of the budget." Spurred by conservatives, Congress began to pick apart the president's budget, threatening the administration's entire program. Though Eisenhower attempted to rally public support, Congress held the power of the purse. In the end, the budget was shaved by $4 billion, including $1 billion in foreign aid.

The reduction of government expenditures, instead of strengthening the economy, had the opposite effect. By mid-1957, industrial production had dropped, unemployment increased, and members of the administration were worrying about the economic recession. Eisenhower remained skeptical about the value of government spending to stimulate the economy. But Congress had fewer reservations. Increased appropriations, including public works projects, added over $8 billion to the budget. By September 1958 these funds had halted the recession. But continued government spending also fed an inflation and resulted in large budgetary deficits.

This segregated laundromat epitomized the belief that black people were naturally unclean. (Leonard Freed/Magnum)

While Congress and the president wrangled over the economy, the nation approached a profound crisis over civil rights. During the fifties, major political candidates avoided taking a strong stand on civil rights legislation, lest they offend conservative voters. In his first year in office, Eisenhower promised to end segregation in the armed forces, the federal government, and the nation's capital — all policies that had been initiated by Truman — but otherwise stressed the role of the states and cities in resolving these questions. The Supreme Court desegregation decision of 1954, however, created a new climate of opinion.

The strongest movement for civil rights began in the streets of Montgomery, Alabama, in December 1955. Rosa Parks, a black seamstress, refused to obey a Jim Crow law requiring segregated seating in public buses. Her protest soon mushroomed into a citywide bus boycott led by a Baptist minister, Reverend Martin Luther King, Jr. This direct action not only won the immediate issue, but also demonstrated the advantages of organized black protest.

While whites resisted efforts at desegregation, Eisenhower tried to ignore the problem. "The final battle against intolerance," he remarked in 1956, "is to be fought — not in the chambers of any legislature — but in the hearts of men." The president firmly rebuffed suggestions that he take a strong stand in support of the desegregation of public schools. He did propose legislation that year to protect the voting rights of blacks. A weak measure passed the House, but was quickly killed in the Senate.

In 1957 Eisenhower again requested legislation to protect the right to vote. This proposal now won the support of Lyndon Johnson, who wished to demonstrate his liberal credentials and so enhance his chances for the presidential nomination in 1960. Working behind the scenes, Johnson persuaded southern leaders to drop the filibuster in exchange for a diluted bill. The majority leader then introduced amendments that weakened the administration's proposal. The new bill called for a powerless Civil Rights Commission and authorized the attorney general to seek injunctions for violations of voting rights. Johnson's strategy succeeded, and Congress passed the first significant civil rights legislation since Reconstruction.

The significance of the new law was soon dwarfed by a major defeat of segregation through direct action. In September 1957 Governor Orval Faubus of Arkansas mobilized the National Guard to prevent the integration of Central High School in Little Rock, an action that violated a federal court order. While armed soldiers prevented black students from attending the school, Eisenhower hesitated to act. Faubus's defiance of federal authority raised serious questions about the limits of federal power. These considerations, together with a growing concern about his personal prestige, finally moved the president to action. "Law can not be flaunted with impunity by any individual or mob of extremists," he declared. Three weeks after Faubus challenged federal authority, Eisenhower federalized the National Guard and ordered paratroopers to enforce the court decision. Despite continued mob protest, black students began attending the school.

The school integration case represented more than the breakdown of Jim Crow. In confronting white mobs, blacks learned that personal confrontations could be an effective weapon in the quest for equal rights. In 1957 Martin Luther King helped to organize a coalition of black activists in the Southern Christian Leadership Conference (SCLC). King also led a March on Washington in 1957 that attracted fifteen thousand protesters, a forerunner of later mass demonstrations. Such protests revealed a profound dissatisfaction among blacks at the lack of government response to their grievances. These feelings exploded in a series of spontaneous "sit-in" protests that began in February 1960. Instead of waiting for legislative or judicial sanction, young blacks simply violated Jim Crow laws. Such actions won mass support among northern whites who joined blacks in a national crusade for civil rights. This alliance between white liberals and blacks culminated in mass protests in the next decade.

Disillusionment with traditional institutions was intensified by the astounding news of October 4, 1957: the Soviet Union announced that it had launched an artificial satellite. "The Soviets have beaten us at our own game," declared Lyndon Johnson, "—daring scientific advances in the atomic age." Besides the philosophical shock waves caused by the triumph over the earth's gravitation, the launching demonstrated that the Soviet Union possessed superior rocket technology. The military implications of this superiority were impressive. The dreaded Soviet enemy had developed the capability of delivering intercontinental ballistic missiles (ICBMs) armed with nuclear weapons before the United States possessed sufficient retaliatory power. Within the administration, these fears were confirmed by a secret report prepared by Rowan Gaither. Eisenhower remained calm, however, and rejected Gaither's proposal to begin a national fallout shelter campaign.

The perceived sense of a missile gap fed popular fears of nuclear annihilation. Best-selling books like Nevil Shute's *On the Beach* (1957) and Walt Miller's *A Canticle for Leibowitz* (1959) dramatized the imminence of holocaust. These tensions help to explain the popularity of so-called sick comedians such as Mort Sahl and Lenny Bruce, who poked fun at the precariousness of contemporary institutions. The Eisenhower administration tried to alleviate these fears by denying any military deficiencies. But Democratic leaders took the occasion to criticize the Republican leadership. In the Senate, Johnson backed legislation to create a civilian-controlled space agency, the National Aeronautics and Space Administration (NASA), with expensive facilities in Johnson's home state of Texas. Senator John F. Kennedy of Massachusetts, looking toward the 1960 elections, began a sharp verbal campaign against the administration's handling of the missile gap.

The combination of Sputnik, Little Rock, and the recession, together with a conservative Republican stand on labor legislation, produced landslide victories for the Democrats in the elections of 1958. Democrats controlled the House by a margin of 283–153 and the Senate by 65–35. This majority confronted the administration with powerful opposition to its program. Democrats increased government spending for defense. The party also enacted the admission of Alaska and Hawaii in 1959, but carefully reversed the administration's priorities by welcoming the Democratic state first. Congress also embarrassed the president by denying the nomination of Lewis Strauss as secretary of commerce. Despite these disagreements, however, the administration worked with Congress to

Physicist Werner Von Braun explains the Saturn missile to President Eisenhower, during whose administration the United States strove to bridge the "missile gap." (Dwight D. Eisenhower Library)

enact aid to education, increased support of state unemployment programs, an anticorruption labor law, and a reorganization of the Pentagon.

PRESIDENTIAL DIPLOMACY

Eisenhower's last years in office saw the president increasingly concerned with foreign affairs. Dulles died in 1959, creating an opening for personal diplomacy. In 1958 Eisenhower had sent Nixon on a "goodwill" tour of Latin America. But the vice president had been met by hostile crowds that protested United States economic and political exploitation of the area. The administration dismissed these demonstrations as examples of Communist infiltration. But Adlai Stevenson returned from a trip to Latin America in 1960 with an alternative assessment. "It is foolish . . . to attribute anti-Americanism just to Communist agitation," he maintained. The problem was that the Eisenhower administration "has been basically concerned with making Latin America safe for American business, not for democracy," especially by supporting "hated dictators."

Stevenson's analysis had a small impact on Eisenhower's relations with Cuba. After backing the right wing Fulgencio Batista since 1952, the United States reacted cautiously to the revolutionary government of Fidel Castro that seized power in 1959. Though the administration offered economic aid to Castro, it soon came to distrust the Cuban's anti-American posture and his open acceptance of left wing politics. In May 1959 Cuba enacted agrarian reform laws that nationalized some private American holdings. Eisenhower quickly cut off aid to Cuba and demanded immediate compensation. American antipathy to Castro increased when the Cuban leader summoned the United States to provide massive assistance for Latin American economic reform.

Eisenhower re-evaluated his policy toward Castro in 1960 with an eye toward reversing the Cuban's popularity in Latin America. But relations between the two nations became even worse. In February 1960 Castro announced the sale of sugar to the Soviet Union in exchange for economic and military assistance. Eisenhower feared a Soviet presence in this Amer-ican sphere of influence. He then launched a two-pronged attack. In March Eisenhower ordered the CIA "to organize the training of Cuban exiles, mainly in Guatemala against a possible future day when they might return to their homeland." In public, the president exerted economic pressure by ordering a cut in American sugar purchases. Castro correctly protested that the reduction of sugar purchases was a preparation for an invasion. Khrushchev promptly announced that the Soviet Union would protect the Cuban government. Frustrated by Castro's audacity, Eisenhower severed diplomatic relations in January 1961, leaving the problem for his successor.

While protecting the United States's traditional dominance in Latin America, Eisenhower moved to reduce tension with the Soviet Union without jeopardizing American strength. Since his "atoms for peace" proposal of 1953, Eisenhower had emphasized inspection and control as a precondition for disarmament. In 1956 he had sneered at Stevenson's call for a halt in nuclear testing. But subsequent negotiations between American and Soviet scientists indicated that controls could be instituted. In 1958 the president announced that the United States was ending further nuclear testing. The Soviet Union inaugurated a final series of tests before it too halted similar explosions. The moratorium, however, did not indicate a significant shift of policy, for both powers remained committed to what Churchill called a "balance of terror."

Though liberals pressed for a reduction of the arms race, Eisenhower continued to pursue a Cold War strategy. In 1958 the United States assured West Germany that it would maintain its military obligations in Europe. The rearmament of Germany alarmed the Soviet Union, and Khrushchev decided to use his apparent lead in ICBMs to demand that the Western powers remove their forces from Berlin. He issued a six-month deadline for compliance. Eisenhower rejected Khrushchev's demand, and both leaders spoke about the possibility of World War Three.

These tensions were eased in 1959 when Khrushchev and Eisenhower agreed to engage in personal diplomacy. The Soviet leader toured the United States and met amicably with the president at Camp David. Though substantive issues remained unresolved, Khrushchev quietly lifted his deadline for resolving the Berlin issue and invited Eisenhower to visit the Soviet Union. Encouraged by these trends, Eisenhower began a series of goodwill tours to Asia, Europe, and Latin America.

But in the spring of 1960, relations with the Soviet Union reached crisis proportions. The status of Germany remained a serious problem. A summit conference was scheduled to open in May 1960. The heads of state expressed optimism, but the diplomatic rift remained great. Then on May 5, Khrushchev announced that the Soviet Union had shot down an American spy plane, the U-2. The United States immediately denied the charge, claiming that a "weather plane" strayed from its course. But then Khrushchev produced the CIA pilot, Francis Gary Powers, revealing the American lie.

In seeking to clear his reputation, Eisenhower proceeded to make a series of diplomatic blunders. The State Department replied to the latest evidence by acknowledging the U-2 mission. It also justified such flights by affirming the importance of the "open skies" formula that the Soviet Union had rejected at Geneva in 1955. Khrushchev then lodged a formal protest of American violation of Soviet air space. Working through established diplomatic channels, Eisenhower still hoped to salvage the sum-

Moscow citizens view some incriminating evidence recovered from a U-2 spy plane piloted by Francis Gary Powers and downed by the Russians in May 1960. This incident and the American government's response were later used by Soviet Premier Khrushchev as an occasion for breaking up the Paris summit conference between him and President Eisenhower. (Dwight D. Eisenhower Library)

mit conference with Khrushchev. By claiming ignorance of the U-2 program, the president could rise above the crisis. But Eisenhower's disavowal of knowledge of the spy missions implied that subordinates had taken control of the administration. Such a situation, especially in an election year, threatened the president's power. Eisenhower therefore was forced to acknowledge his complicity. "It is a distasteful but vital necessity," he declared, reminding the

American public of the lessons of Pearl Harbor. Eisenhower's admission destroyed the summit meeting. At the Paris session, Khrushchev denounced the president and refused to negotiate. The Cold War came alive with tension.

The intensification of the Cold War had a profound effect on public opinion. Democratic politicians attempted to lay the blame exclusively at Eisenhower's door. Though careful to maintain a Cold War stance, Stevenson condemned the president for handing Khrushchev "the crowbar and the sledgehammer" to wreck the summit conference. More fundamental, however, the U-2 affair shocked the American public by revealing the duplicity of its government. Eisenhower, who strove to rise above parties, had lied not only to Khrushchev, but also to American citizens. The notion of a credibility gap between the people and their government would haunt American politics for the next two decades.

SUGGESTED READINGS

A comprehensive treatment of the Eisenhower administration is provided by Herbert S. Parmet, *Eisenhower and the American Crusades* (1972). Also helpful is a biography by Peter Lyon on *Eisenhower: Portrait of a Hero* (1974). A detailed collection of primary sources is Robert L. Branyan and Lawrence H. Larsen, *The Eisenhower Administration*, 2 vols. (1971).

The political issues are described in James Sundquist, *Politics and Policy: The Eisenhower, Kennedy, and Johnson Years* (1968). For insights into congressional power, see Rowland Evans and Robert Novak, *Lyndon B. Johnson: The Exercise of Power* (1966). Stevenson's career is described favorably in Stuart Gerry Brown, *Conscience in Politics* (1961), which includes many original sources, and the more detailed study, John Bartlow Martin, *Adlai Stevenson of Illinois* (1976). For Nixon, see the superb analysis by Garry Wills, *Nixon Agonistes* (1970). Voting behavior in the fifties is explained in Norman H. Nie et al., *The Changing American Voter* (1976).

A detailed study of southern politics is Jack Bass and Walter DeVries, *The Transformation of Southern Politics: Social Change and Political Consequence Since 1945* (1976). For the Warren Court, see the relevant chapters of Paul L. Murphy, *The Constitution in Crisis Times: 1918–1969* (1972). Works relating to the civil rights movement are listed at the end of chapter 11.

The best study of McCarthyism is Richard H. Rovere, *Senator Joe McCarthy* (1959). Also helpful on McCarthy's support are Michael Paul Rogin, *The Intellectuals and McCarthy* (1967), and David M. Oshinsky, *Senator Joseph McCarthy and the American Labor Movement* (1976). For McCarthy's relationship to the Senate, see Robert Griffith, *The Politics of Fear* (1970).

A good introduction to Eisenhower's foreign policy is Walter Lafeber's *America, Russia, and the Cold War* (1976). It should be supplemented by Townsend Hoopes, *The Devil and John Foster Dulles* (1973). For the secret foreign policy, see David Wise and Thomas B. Ross, *The Invisible Government* (1964), and Victor Marchetti and John D. Marks, *The CIA and the Cult of Intelligence* (1974).

Chapter 14

THE KENNEDY YEARS, 1960-1963

The Cold War loomed large in the 1960 presidential election. For eight years Eisenhower had extolled the warrior virtues of strength and power. But at the age of seventy, Eisenhower was the oldest man ever to hold the nation's highest office. He now seemed impotent against Khrushchev's indignation, the eruption of liberation movements in Asia and Africa, and anti-American protests in Latin America and Japan. Popular jokes referred to the "Eisenhower doll — wind it up and it does nothing for eight years." In the Senate, John F. Kennedy attacked the president for failing "to maintain the minimum conditions for our survival." "This is not a call of despair," he added. "It is a call for action."

The Massachusetts senator used the theme of Republican immobility in his bid for the presidency. As the youngest candidate (only forty-two when he announced his intention), Kennedy symbolized strength, vigor, and energy. "We've got to get this country moving again," he insisted. But Democratic leaders felt that Kennedy's youthfulness might be an electoral handicap. More problematic was the candidate's Roman Catholic religion. Only one Catholic, Al Smith, had run for president, and he had suffered a devastating defeat in 1928, losing even the "solid" Democratic South.

To remove these doubts, Kennedy entered a series of primary contests against his major rival, Senator Hubert H. Humphrey of Minnesota.

As a native New Englander, Kennedy easily won in New Hampshire. He also triumphed in Wisconsin. But voting analysis revealed that Kennedy carried Catholic voters, whereas Humphrey attracted Protestants. Kennedy's appeal as a national candidate thus hinged on his performance in West Virginia, an impoverished state with a 95 percent Protestant population. Confronting the religious issue directly, Kennedy's expensive campaign overcame traditional Protestant prejudices. He went to the Democratic convention with a clear advantage over his rivals. At the last moment, supporters of Adlai Stevenson tried to draft the two-time loser. But Kennedy held firmly to his delegate support and won a first-ballot nomination. Then, to balance the slate in the conservative South, he chose Majority Leader Lyndon Johnson of Texas as his running mate.

KENNEDY VERSUS NIXON

While the Democratic candidates captured national headlines in their race for the nomination, Vice President Richard M. Nixon quietly called in a dozen years of political debts to cement his support within the Republican party. New York's Governor Nelson Rockefeller briefly challenged the vice president, but Nixon easily won the nomination. The lack of serious opposition cost Nixon national publicity. But he tried to take advantage of the situation by posing as a candidate above party faction. He chose as his running mate Henry Cabot Lodge, who had served as the United States ambassador to the United Nations, where he had earned a popular reputation as a defender of "captive peoples." Republicans expected Lodge to appeal to the anti-Communist ethnic minorities, perhaps to undermine some of Kennedy's Catholic support.

Kennedy's Catholicism remained a controversial subject. He decided to bring the issue to the forefront at the Houston Ministerial Association, a gathering of Methodists that held national interest. "I am not the Catholic candidate," he announced. "I am the Democratic Party's candidate . . . , who happens also to be a Catholic." Kennedy carefully delineated his commitment to the separation of church and state, expressing disbelief that "40 million Americans lost their chance of being President on the day they were baptized." The effect of Kennedy's speech was difficult to determine. But Kennedy rose in favor among black Protestants in mid-campaign when he telephoned support to Martin Luther King, who had been arrested in Georgia. Black evangelicals overcame their doubts about Kennedy's religion and remained faithful to the Democratic party.

Despite Kennedy's handicaps, Nixon recognized that the number of registered Democrats exceeded Republicans. He hoped to attract independents and Democratic crossovers by emphasizing his relationship to President Eisenhower. Contrasting his own experience with Kennedy's youth, Nixon suggested that he had provided leadership within the Eisenhower administration. Yet the president resented such exaggeration. When asked by reporters about Nixon's participation in key administration decisions, Eisenhower replied, "If you give me a week, I might think of one." The negative effects of this statement were aggravated by Eisenhower's minimal activity in support of Nixon's candidacy. At the same time, however, Nixon was forced to defend Eisenhower's policies, including the president's handling of the U-2 affair. Kennedy thus enjoyed the advantage of attacking the party in power. "Mr. Nixon says 'We never had it so good,'" Kennedy remarked. "I say we can do better."

The differences between the candidates were less substantive, more a question of emphasis. In his acceptance speech to the nominating convention, Kennedy proclaimed that the nation stood "on the edge of a New Frontier — the frontier of the 1960's — a frontier of unknown opportunities and peril — a frontier of unfulfilled hopes and threats." Such rhetoric appealed to a national fascination with mobility, with a pervasive sense of rootlessness. Kennedy's willingness to use these metaphors instead of

the traditional Catholic emphasis on roots and a sense of place reflected his commitment to melting pot assimilation. Thus his language easily merged with Nixon's. The vice president's frenetic mobility was symbolized by his decision to visit all fifty states during the campaign. As the race drew to a close, Nixon also embraced the imagery of frontiers and rootlessness. "This country has always been full of the great spirit of conquering new frontiers," the Republican declared.

The substantive similarities between the candidates emerged in a series of nationally televised debates that attracted over 100 million viewers. On domestic matters, both candidates agreed about such goals as economic growth,

MAP 14.1   THE ELECTION OF 1960

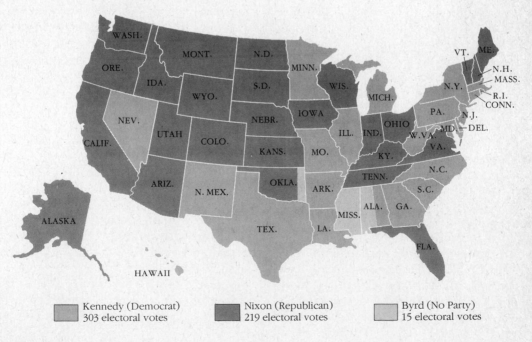

Kennedy (Democrat) 303 electoral votes

Nixon (Republican) 219 electoral votes

Byrd (No Party) 15 electoral votes

aid to the poor, and material progress. They both defended the records of their predecessors, with Kennedy summoning the memory of Roosevelt and Truman, and Nixon boasting about Eisenhower. In foreign policy, the candidates shared the vision of Cold Warriors. The only significant difference was whether to defend Quemoy and Matsu. Kennedy suggested that the islands were not essential to the security of Taiwan; Nixon warned that a retreat from such areas of freedom would "start a chain reaction."

Despite these common assumptions, television highlighted not the candidates' words but their manner of presentation. Radio listeners, who were not distracted by visual appearances, reacted favorably to Nixon's speeches. But the television cameras accentuated the vice president's heavy "five o'clock shadow" and dark eye sockets. His makeup dripped, and his body movements seemed stiff. Suffering from a severe cold, he looked unhealthy, if not unsavory. In contrast, Kennedy brought a dramatic flair to the television screen. He seemed comfortable and confident. The television format, by projecting the candidates as equals, added to Kennedy's national reputation. Subsequent polls indicated that the debates may have influenced as many as four million voters; of these, Kennedy gathered three-quarters.

Such intangible factors had immense significance, for the balloting was extremely close. With nearly sixty-nine million people voting, Kennedy obtained a popular majority of only 118,000 — a margin of one-tenth of 1 percent. Kennedy's electoral victory was a decisive 303–219, but these figures concealed paper-thin majorities in such key states as Illinois and Texas. A switch of only thirty-five thousand votes could have reversed the final decision. Kennedy

also trailed behind Democratic congressional candidates. Though the Democrats maintained control of both houses of Congress, the freshman class of new legislators formed a majority in opposition to the presidential victor. Since southern Democrats frequently aligned with Republicans, the administration lacked a working majority in Congress.

Kennedy's narrow victory revealed significant political trends. In the South, Kennedy's Catholicism reduced his support. But the presence of Lyndon Johnson on the ticket offset this deficiency. Nixon failed to match Eisenhower's success in that region. Yet Republicans carried Virginia, Florida, Kentucky, and Tennessee. Members of the electoral college from Alabama and Mississippi, nominally Democratic, cast their ballots for Harry F. Byrd of Virginia. These patterns suggested a renaissance of the two-party system in the South. In the North, Kennedy captured 78 percent of the Catholic vote. He also won the support of blacks and Jews. The return of these predominantly urban groups to the Democratic party indicated that Eisenhower's popularity was a personal, not a party, phenomenon.

THE KENNEDY PRESIDENCY

With his slender majority, Kennedy was not about to initiate bold departures of policy. He immediately showed his orthodoxy by reappointing J. Edgar Hoover and Allen Dulles to their positions as heads of the FBI and CIA. Kennedy's cabinet appointments also represented the same corporate elites that had served in previous administrations. The president intended to maintain personal control over foreign policy. For secretary of state, he passed over Adlai Stevenson, who was considered too weak a warrior, and chose the hawkish but unassertive Dean Rusk. To head the Department of Defense, Kennedy selected the president of the Ford Motor Company, Robert McNamara, an energetic believer in administrative efficiency and technological expertise. Douglas Dillon, a Wall Street financier and member of the Eisenhower administration, became Kennedy's secretary of the treasury. The most controversial appointment was Kennedy's nomination for attorney general: his brother Robert F. Kennedy. In making this choice, the president not only brought his major political adviser directly into the administration, but also established tight control of the sensitive area of executive law enforcement.

The Kennedy leadership extolled the values of scientific management and cold reason. "Most of the problems...that we now face are technical problems, are administrative problems," Kennedy declared in 1962. "They are very sophisticated judgments which do not lend themselves to the great sort of 'passionate movements' which have stirred this country so often in the past." Matters of foreign policy, the president suggested, "are so sophisticated and so technical that people who are not intimately involved week after week, month after month, reach judgments which are based on emotion rather than knowledge of the real alternatives." Such assumptions not only justified reliance on technical experts, but also allowed the administration to ignore popular opinion.

This optimism about executive leadership reflected a growing acceptance of an activist government. Though conservatives condemned the expansion of government services, a large public consensus had become confident that careful management could solve basic social and economic problems. "There is a recurring temptation to feel that some spectacular and costly action could become the miraculous solution to all current difficulties," admitted President Eisenhower. This confidence in public affairs contrasted with older fears about big government. The inclusion of private questions in the census, for example, had aroused bitter controversy in 1940 and 1950. But in the year of Kennedy's election, such complaints had given way to a silent acquiescence in government intrusion.

Kennedy's promise of dynamic leadership alarmed the outgoing president. In a farewell address to the American people, Eisenhower warned against the temptations of "unrealistic programs." Citing the emergence of a "military-industrial complex," the civilian-soldier urged the nation to be vigilant against "the disastrous rise of misplaced power." He also pointed to the dangers of plundering natural resources and thus jeopardizing the material abundance that had nourished a unique American heritage.

Eisenhower's caution contrasted with the grandiose optimism of Kennedy's inaugural address. "Let the word go forth," Kennedy announced, "that the torch has been passed to a new generation of Americans — born in this century, tempered by war, disciplined by a hard and bitter peace, proud of our ancient heritage." Avoiding the domestic questions that might provoke disagreement, the president spoke to the problems of world affairs. Like his predecessor, Kennedy repeated the warrior virtues of strength, warning of the temptation of "weakness," yet "racing to alter that uncertain balance of terror that stays the hand of mankind's final war." To the rhetoric of the Cold War, the

A youthful President-elect Kennedy listens to outgoing President Eisenhower, the oldest man to hold the nation's highest office. (Wide World Photos)

president added an apocalyptic dimension, describing the nation at "its hour of maximum danger."

During the recent campaign Kennedy had insisted that there was no difference between a Protestant and a Catholic president. Yet the new leader added a distinct, if subtle, Catholic perspective to the Cold War. Like his predecessors, Kennedy defined communism as a total threat to American life. But where earlier Cold Warriors envisioned a dramatic transformation of the forces of evil, Kennedy spoke more about the "burden" of "relentless struggle" with no early or simple resolution. "I do not shrink from this responsibility," he boasted, "I welcome it." Such work "will not be finished in the first one hundred days," he admitted. "Nor will it be finished in the first one thousand days, nor in the life of this Administration, nor even perhaps in our lifetime on this planet." Insisting that the moment of spiritual conversion for the American people would not be easy or instantaneous, Kennedy stated more simply, "Let us begin."

NEW FRONTIERS

Kennedy's world view of steady struggle culminated in his famous appeal: "Ask not what your country can do for you — ask what you can do for your country." To the familiar military summons, Kennedy added the possibility of alternative service. Adopting an idea of Hubert Humphrey, Kennedy established the Peace Corps to bring American technological skills to impoverished areas of the world. Such service, the president hastened to add, "will not be easy." Like American businesspeople and military service men and women, members of the Peace Corps acted as missionaries of the American way of life. By 1963 Kennedy could boast that over one million citizens, including ten thousand Peace Corps volunteers, lived outside the territorial frontiers of the United States, where they served "on a mission of freedom."

The creation of the Peace Corps reflected Kennedy's recognition that the nations of Asia, Africa, and Latin America held the key to the global struggle against communism. The new president pledged his "best efforts" to assist the new nations "to break the bonds of mass misery." Kennedy established a Food for Peace program that shipped surplus food to poor countries. He claimed to be motivated not by international politics, "but because it is right." Unlike Eisenhower and Dulles, Kennedy did not publicly insist that neutral nations take sides in the Cold War. In the former Belgian colony of the Congo, for example, the administration supported a U.N. peace mission that

backed a neutralist government. Yet Kennedy expected U.N. intervention to keep the Soviet Union out of Africa. He therefore allowed the CIA to provide secret cash payments as well as military aid to friendly Congolese politicians. No less than Eisenhower, Kennedy was not prepared to "lose" areas of freedom to communism.

Kennedy's approach to economically underdeveloped nations revealed an inability to understand the dynamics of social change. In his inaugural address, Kennedy called for "a new alliance for progress" in Latin America. Two months later he announced "a vast cooperative effort...to satisfy the basic needs of the American peoples for homes, work and land, health and schools." Promising to bring technical expertise and capital investments, the president envisioned major agrarian reform and public welfare within the context of democratic institutions. These promises were institutionalized at a conference at Punta del Este in August 1961. Pledging $20 billion over ten years, the Kennedy administration predicted rapid economic development that would alleviate the endemic poverty of Latin America while bringing social reform. Such assistance had the indirect advantage of boosting the United States's sagging prestige in the area.

Despite Kennedy's rhetoric about linking social reform to economic growth, the United States had no intention of redistributing wealth and power in Latin America. Fearful of triggering a mass revolution in the image of Castro's Cuba, the administration expected to work through the established elites and business interests. But these groups, though desirous of assistance, had no wish to participate in democratic reform sponsored by North American "Yanquis." Promises of agrarian reform thus

A Peace Corps volunteer teaches students in Nigeria, one of many Americans of all ages who responded to Kennedy's call for active service. (Marc Riboud/Magnum)

brought minimal gains to impoverished peasants.

United States business interests were equally reluctant to risk investment in Latin America. In 1962 Congress approved the Hickenlooper Amendment, which prohibited foreign aid to countries that nationalized or excessively taxed United States corporate property. The next year, the Foreign Assistance Act established an Investment Guaranty program that required recipients of United States aid to insure investors against losses due to nationalization. These requirements protected a conservative economic program. Most aid to Latin America came in the form of loans, rather than grants, that had to be repaid with interest and other service charges (usually amounting to half the face value of the loans). Even these limited funds had to be spent within the United States at prevailing prices. The Alliance for Progress merely protected the United States's traditional markets in the Western Hemisphere.

The Alliance for Progress also promised to blunt the revolutionary appeal of Fidel Castro. During his last days in office, Eisenhower had broken diplomatic relations with Cuba and had encouraged the CIA to plan a military coup.

As a presidential candidate, Kennedy endorsed the overthrow of Castro, describing Cuba as "a hostile and militant Communist satellite." Central to Kennedy's reasoning was the belief that Castro did not represent the Cuban people. These assumptions were reinforced by CIA reports, based on interviews with Cuban refugees, suggesting that anti-Castro sentiment could topple the regime. To increase pressure on Castro, Kennedy persuaded business leaders to boycott Cuban dealings; in March 1961 he prohibited the importation of Cuban sugar.

These efforts culminated in a CIA-planned invasion of Cuba at the Bay of Pigs in April 1961. Using Cuban exiles, the CIA had trained a military force at secret bases in Guatemala. On the eve of the invasion, however, Kennedy received information suggesting that Castro knew about the plan. The president nevertheless approved the scheme. But the CIA planned badly, landing the invaders at an indefensible position and losing critical supplies. At the last moment, Kennedy canceled United States air support, dooming the mission. Most serious, the administration had failed to realize the strong political base of the Castro government.

Though American newspapers had received unofficial leaks about the Bay of Pigs operation, the administration had prevailed upon the major publishers to suppress the story. This policy was encouraged by deliberate lying in official circles. "There will not be, under any conditions, an intervention in Cuba by the United States Armed Forces," the president told a press conference five days before the futile mission. On the morning of the invasion, Dean Rusk issued an equally unreliable statement. "The American people are entitled to know whether we are intervening in Cuba or intend to do so in the future," he maintained. "The answer to that question is no. What happens in Cuba is

for the Cuban people to decide." Nevertheless, the administration steadfastly refused to believe that that was exactly what had happened at the Bay of Pigs.

In justifying the invasion, Kennedy defined Castro in the context of the Cold War. "We are opposed around the world by a monolithic and ruthless conspiracy," he told the nation's leading news editors, "that relies primarily on covert means for expanding its sphere of influence." This "rising din of Communist voices," Kennedy concluded, had to be matched by strong counter-insurgency. The president regretted not the launching of the invasion force but the failure of its mission. The situation also required "self-discipline" at home to "match the iron discipline" of the Communists. Embarrassed by the premature disclosure of the Bay of Pigs operation, Kennedy urged the news media to limit their reporting of world events. "Every democracy," he claimed, "recognizes the necessary restraints of national security."

In the aftermath of the Bay of Pigs, the president moved to strengthen his control over the CIA. Following a McNamara proposal, he established a Defense Intelligence Agency to coordinate military intelligence as a check on civilian operations. Kennedy did not oppose illegal CIA activities against foreign governments. But he limited CIA operations to paramilitary activities that were "plausibly deniable." In 1962 he replaced Allen Dulles with a Kennedy-style technician, John McCone.

In shifting responsibility to the CIA, Kennedy failed to realize the inherent fallacy of his counterrevolutionary assumptions: that Castro, in fact, spoke for the Cuban people. Eighteen months after the Bay of Pigs, the president broadcast an appeal to "the captive people of Cuba" and described their leaders as "puppets and agents of an international conspiracy." Kennedy continued to exert economic pressure on the Castro regime, prohibiting trade with the island. The CIA also endeavored to disrupt Cuban commerce with the Soviet Union, in one case deliberately contaminating a shipload of sugar with bad-tasting chemicals. Secret CIA operations included support of anti-Castro exiles and underworld gangsters who returned to Cuba as guerrillas and assassins.

COUNTER-INSURGENCY IN SOUTHEAST ASIA

Kennedy's inability to understand the Cuban revolution and the nature of the defeat at the Bay of Pigs embroiled him in the political struggles of Southeast Asia. "Thank God the Bay of Pigs happened when it did," Kennedy told Theodore Sorensen six months later. "Otherwise we'd be in Laos now." The Cuban fiasco had taught the president about the risks of ill-prepared military adventures. But he had not grasped the political implications of indigenous revolutionary movements. Laos, instead of spelling a new direction in American foreign policy, proved to be merely a prelude to Vietnam.

As Eisenhower handed the reins of office to Kennedy, the outgoing president apologized for the "mess" in Laos. "You might have to go in there and fight it out." A political coalition established in 1954 had collapsed four years later. The Eisenhower administration had then moved to support an anti-Communist regime. But when the pro-American government used rigged elections in 1960 to exclude both Communists and neutralists, the dissidents organized a coup that triggered a three-sided civil war. As the United States supported one faction, the Soviet Union backed the Pathet Lao.

Upon entering office, Kennedy announced his support for "an independent country not dominated by either side." Unable to see the Laotian crisis as a domestic problem, however, the president warned about the influence of "outside" forces. "We cannot . . . accept any visible humiliation over Laos," he declared. The new administration soon began preparations for military intervention. But the Soviet Union, fearful not only of the United States but also of China, wanted no controversy. Kennedy and Khrushchev agreed to reconvene the Geneva Convention and work for a political settlement based on Laotian neutrality. In reaching this decision, the president overruled the advice of military leaders who favored the use of force. With removal of the great powers, the competing Laotian factions agreed to form a neutralist government in 1962.

Despite the formal settlement in Laos, however, the Kennedy administration decided to create a pro-American regime. Using the foreign aid program, the United States pressured the neutralist government to exclude the Communist faction. Meanwhile, the CIA provided assistance to anti-Communist guerrillas to escalate the military struggle against the Pathet Lao. In 1963 these pressures exploded into open warfare on the Plain of Jarres. United States involvement steadily increased, leading to secret bombing raids against the local Communists. As in Cuba, Kennedy failed to realize the strength of indigenous revolutionary sentiment.

The Laotian controversy soon blurred into the larger United States commitment to South Vietnam. In both countries Kennedy saw Communist aggression "nibbling away" at the forces of freedom. "The complacent, the self-indulgent, the soft societies are about to be swept away with the debris of history," Kennedy warned at the time of the Bay of Pigs. "Only the strong, only the industrious, only the determined, only the courageous, only the visionary who determine the real nature of our struggle can possibly survive." By 1961 the Vietnamese regime of Ngo Dinh Diem was rapidly losing ground to the pro-Communist Viet Cong as well as to non-Communist dissidents. Kennedy believed that the United States had to intervene in Vietnam to halt the erosion of power on the peripheries of the "free world."

MAP 14.2   VIETNAM AND SURROUNDING INDOCHINA

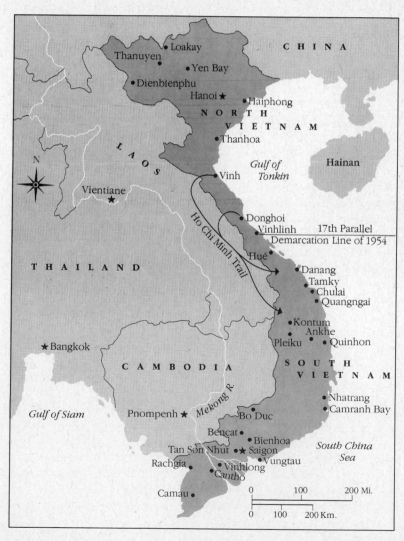

The president supported a policy of counter-insurgency. Where the Eisenhower administration had emphasized the strategy of massive retaliation aimed at the Soviet Union, Kennedy stressed the importance of conventional arms for "brush-fire" wars and guerrilla activity. These beliefs led Kennedy not only to increase American ground forces but also to develop the elite Special Forces (Green Berets), counter-insurgent training centers, and specialized guerrilla equipment. All these forces converged in Vietnam. As General Maxwell Taylor explained in 1963, Vietnam was "a going laboratory" for the study of "subversive insurgency."

Humiliated by his public defeat at the Bay of Pigs and cautious about involvement in Laos, Kennedy decided to act decisively in Vietnam in the spring of 1961. While Vice President Johnson consulted with Diem in Saigon, Kennedy authorized an increase in the number of military advisers and dispatched Green Berets and intelligence agents to engage in covert warfare. The president also invited Diem to request additional ground forces. But the Vietnamese leader opposed American pressure to initiate political reforms and waited until October 1961 to apply for more troops. Kennedy's decisions were reinforced by the vice president's report from Vietnam. Failure to help Diem, Johnson maintained, "would say to the world . . . that we don't live up to our treaties and don't stand by our friends."

As Diem's position continued to deteriorate, Kennedy sent another advisory team, headed by General Taylor and the economist Walt W. Rostow, to Saigon in October 1961. They reported that Diem required massive military assistance, including ground troops. The president, however, was reluctant to commit conventional forces and risk a repetition of the Korean War. Kennedy instead viewed Vietnam from the perspective of the Philippines and Malaya, in which counter-insurgency had proved effective. At the end of 1961, therefore, he authorized an increase of military assistance, including "support troops" and technical advisers. The CIA also began recruiting and training Montagnard mercenaries to fight the anti-Communist crusade. These military activities were augmented by an attempt to pressure Diem to make basic political reforms to win the loyalty of the Vietnamese people. As in Latin America, however, American efforts to promote democratic reform proved futile. Diem remained committed to his own power.

As American aid poured into Vietnam, the level of violence steadily increased. Helicopter warfare initially terrorized the Viet Cong, forcing them to withdraw from exposed positions. In 1962 the National Liberation Front, which represented primarily southern Vietnamese opposed to Diem, indicated a willingness to negotiate a neutralization of South Vietnam. But the Kennedy administration, optimistic about military victory, rebuffed the approach. Meanwhile, the United States persuaded Diem to experiment with political counter-insurgency based on "strategic hamlets." Assuming that guerrilla armies required a popular base, the scheme proposed the physical separation of the peasants behind barbed wire encampments. Lacking contact with the people, the guerrillas would lose their support and disappear. The Diem regime embraced the idea, for it facilitated control of the population. But Vietnamese peasants resented the forced uprooting as well as the pervasive corruption of the government. Nor did the hamlets provide safety from Viet Cong attack.

Despite the failure of the strategic hamlet

program, members of the Kennedy administration remained optimistic about a final victory. "Every quantitative measurement we have," declared McNamara with his typical faith in numbers, "shows we're winning this war." In his 1963 state of the union message, Kennedy boasted that the "spearpoint of aggression has been blunted in Vietnam." The State Department confirmed this optimism by announcing that thirty thousand Viet Cong had been killed in 1962; that figure, however, was twice as large as the estimated size of the entire Viet Cong organization at the beginning of the year. "We can't win," said a GI parody of administrative double talk, "but it's not absolutely essential to pick today to lose."

Exaggerated administration claims stemmed not only from naiveté or poor calculation. They also reflected a determined effort to deceive the American people about the nature of the United States commitment. Government officials systematically avoided publicizing their operations in Vietnam. As in the Bay of Pigs affair, the administration misled the press, offering government news briefings in place of first-hand coverage. Kennedy also tried to suppress unfavorable stories, personally asking the *New York Times* to reassign its Saigon reporter, David Halberstam.

The bad news could not always be silenced. By 1963 the Viet Cong had taken the military initiative, stepping up terrorist attacks against the Diem regime. Equally serious was Diem's refusal to offer political reform. The issue climaxed in 1963 when Buddhist militants protested against Diem's dictatorial policies. South Vietnamese soldiers fired on the crowd, precipitating further demonstrations and bloody reprisals. In June a Buddhist priest dramatically set himself on fire to protest the abuses of

power. Though Americans were horrified by a series of self-immolations, Diem's supporters remained unmoved, scoffing at the "barbecue show" and intensifying a reign of terror.

Such reactions embarrassed the Kennedy administration, but the president took refuge in the domino theory. "For us to withdraw from that effort," he told a press conference, "would mean a collapse not only of South Vietnam, but Southeast Asia. So we are going to stay there." The administration nevertheless began seriously to consider the removal of Diem. When the Vietnamese leader refused to institute political changes, the administration encouraged a military coup. On November 2, 1963, Diem was captured by his own army officers and killed.

Diem's death shocked Kennedy. But the president did not live long enough to revise his commitment to Vietnam. On September 2 Kennedy had acknowledged that the United States could not win the war for the Vietnamese people. "In the final analysis," he said, "it is their war." In the same interview the president rejected the possibility of withdrawal. One month later, however, Kennedy announced that one thousand soldiers would return from Vietnam by the end of the year and that the major United States commitment would end in 1965. Kennedy's decision may have reflected the same misplaced optimism that characterized American policy toward Vietnam throughout the sixties. Yet Kennedy never rescinded his order. Moreover, a high-level meeting in Honolulu on November 20, 1963, agreed to an "accelerated plan" for the withdrawal of American forces. Such shadowy evidence suggests that with Diem out of the way, Kennedy was thinking about a political solution to the war.

KENNEDY AND KHRUSHCHEV

The limitations of Kennedy's policies in Africa, Latin America, and Asia confirmed his world view of "relentless struggle." In the European arena, however, Kennedy spoke a simpler language of military strength. Having campaigned on the issue of Soviet military superiority, the Democratic president did not reverse his position when he learned, shortly after taking office, that there never had been a missile gap. Nor did the new president respond to a cordial letter from the Kremlin or to the friendly gesture of releasing several imprisoned American fliers.

Kennedy instead devoted his first state of the union message to exaggerating the "national peril." Warning that a monolithic Communist conspiracy sought "world domination," the president called for extensive investments in American military defense. Two months later, Kennedy made the first of three military budget requests, asking Congress to appropriate $2.4 billion. Though aware of American missile superiority, he earmarked most of the funding for missile programs. In May, barely a month after the Bay of Pigs disaster, Kennedy requested additional appropriations for conventional weapons and counter-insurgency.

This extensive military buildup reflected the president's belief that the Cold War could be ended — by victory over the Soviet Union. "Let us never negotiate out of fear," he had said in the inaugural address. "But let us never fear to negotiate." Knowing that the Soviet Union trailed far behind the United States in weaponry, Kennedy hoped to create a preponderance of power that would force the Kremlin to accept American terms. In this spirit, he agreed to meet Khrushchev in Vienna in June 1961.

Kennedy underestimated the Soviet position. Though Khrushchev had made conciliatory gestures and was keenly aware of American military superiority, he would not sacrifice Soviet national interest to the bellicose president. The two leaders could easily agree to neutralize Laos, because neither perceived that country to be of vital national concern. But the question of Berlin was less open to negotiation. Reminding Kennedy that World War Two had been over for sixteen years, the Soviet leader demanded that the Western powers sign a final peace treaty that recognized the two Germanys and ended the military occupation of Berlin. Otherwise, he warned, the Soviet Union would sign a separate treaty with East Germany, leaving the Western powers to settle with the de facto regime. Kennedy refused to consider Khrushchev's proposal, insisting that the United States could not abandon its allies in West Berlin. Khrushchev argued that Berlin had no military significance and that he wished only to legitimate the European status quo to reduce further tension. Kennedy remained adamant. "It will be a cold winter," he remarked.

The president returned from Vienna bearing "sober" news for the American people. In a televised speech, Kennedy reaffirmed his intention to maintain American forces in Berlin. This inflexibility, following on the spring military buildup, alarmed Khrushchev. He now capitulated to Kremlin hard-liners and announced a Soviet military buildup to counter American increases. This decision, though a reaction to Kennedy's policies, merely confirmed the administration's view of an aggressive Soviet Union.

Kennedy brought his case to the American people in a grim television broadcast in July

1961. "We do not want to fight — but we have fought before," the president warned in militant rhetoric. "Those who threaten to unleash the forces of war on a dispute over West Berlin should recall the words of the ancient philosopher: 'A man who causes fear cannot be free from fear.'" Kennedy then asked Congress for $3.25 billion, increasing his military requests to $6 billion in his first six months in office. He also increased the size of the armed forces, calling up reservists and extending the draft. Finally, in a gesture that flashed horror through the land, the president asked for increased appropriations for civil defense and bomb shelters. With no consultation, Kennedy was implementing his inaugural promise to "pay any price" to force the Soviet Union to back down on Berlin.

While Americans worried about nuclear holocaust, Khrushchev moved to defend the Soviet position. On August 13, 1961, he authorized the erection of a military barrier to separate East Berlin from the western zones. The Berlin Wall abruptly ended a flood of refugees that was undermining the East German economy. Equally important, the physical barrier symbolized the reality of two Germanys. Despite an extreme crisis atmosphere, Kennedy determined to test the limits of Soviet strategy. He ordered fifteen hundred battle-ready troops to drive from West Germany into West Berlin and commissioned Vice President Johnson to meet them there. Khrushchev decided not to aggravate the situation. American soldiers entered West Berlin peacefully, demonstrating Kennedy's resolve. By September the two powers agreed to negotiate. Having finally managed to bring the United States to the conference table, Khrushchev scrapped his deadline for settling the Berlin question. The crisis passed,

though the talks continued for another ten years. Kennedy's rigidity had brought the world to the brink of nuclear war.

The intensity of the Cold War was dramatized when Khrushchev announced on August 30 that the Soviet Union was ending its three-year moratorium on nuclear bomb testing. Within a week Kennedy declared that the United States had "no other choice" but to resume underground tests. Two days later, *Life* magazine published an article, endorsed by Kennedy, that asserted that a national program of fallout shelters would assure a 97 percent survival rate in case of nuclear war. These grim forecasts precipitated the first major protests against nuclear testing. Peace organizations like the National Committee for a Sane Nuclear Policy (SANE) and the Student Peace Union (SPU) organized mass demonstrations to protest the arms race.

While Soviet tests escalated to the fifty-megaton level (equivalent to fifty thousand tons of TNT), the Kennedy administration aggravated the situation by revealing to Khrushchev that United States intelligence knew the extent of Soviet military weakness. This knowledge enabled Kennedy to propose the resumption of a Geneva Disarmament Conference that would enable the United States to maintain its nuclear advantage. However, France, a nuclear power since 1960, refused to participate, and the Soviet Union introduced its familiar objections to international inspection. With no prospect for a test-ban treaty, Kennedy ordered the resumption of atmospheric tests in April 1962. At the same time, the administration encouraged American scientists to perfect methods of analyzing nuclear explosions as a precondition for a subsequent test ban.

THE CUBAN MISSILE CRISIS

In notifying Khrushchev that the United States had determined the extent of Soviet missile deployment, the Kennedy administration aroused Soviet fears about the imbalance of power. The United States then intensified these concerns by announcing a shift in nuclear strategy in June 1962. Hereafter, American missiles would be aimed not at Soviet cities but at nuclear missile sites. Such targets meant that an American first-strike attack could obliterate Soviet power to retaliate. Khrushchev eventually expected stockpiles of intercontinental ballistic missiles (ICBMs) to reach a level of parity. But in the immediate future, the Soviet leader recognized his vulnerability to American power.

Khrushchev decided to offset this disadvantage by placing less-expensive short-range missiles in Cuba. In the aftermath of *Sputnik,* the United States had pursued a similar policy by establishing missile bases in Turkey and Italy. Khrushchev also anticipated a secondary advantage of bolstering the Castro regime. During the summer of 1962, therefore, the Soviet Union began preparing for the construction of missile sites in Cuba. Word of these preparations reached the United States through Cuban refugees. Senator Kenneth Keating, seeking election in New York in November, publicized these reports and criticized the administration for allowing Communist expansion in the Western Hemisphere. To such charges, the Kennedy administration replied that there was "no evidence of . . . significant offensive capability either in Cuban hands or under Soviet direction." These assurances reflected a private Soviet promise to do nothing that might affect the congressional elections.

Continued surveillance by U-2 aircraft, however, indicated that the Soviet Union was indeed constructing missile sites with a striking range as far as two thousand miles. Kennedy promptly summoned a top-level executive committee to consider an appropriate response. The choices ranged from a military attack, advocated by Dean Acheson, Maxwell Taylor, and the Joint Chiefs of Staff, to a diplomatic retreat, supported by Adlai Stevenson, that involved the trading of outmoded American bases in Turkey for those in Cuba. Within this spectrum a consensus eventually emerged that considered armed intervention only a last resort. Yet the administration rejected the possibility of negotiating the removal of the missiles; Soviet power in the Western Hemisphere, it was believed, was not negotiable.

Kennedy finally accepted a third strategy that did not completely rule out the other two. On October 22, 1962, he presented the situation to the American public. Describing the Soviet intervention as "deliberately provocative," Kennedy demanded "withdrawal or elimination" of all missiles. "We will not prematurely or unnecessarily risk the cost of worldwide nuclear war in which the fruits of victory would be ashes in our mouth," he promised, "— but neither will we shrink from that risk at any time it must be faced." As the world rushed toward nuclear holocaust, Kennedy announced he was establishing a "quarantine" — actually a warlike blockade — to exclude offensive weapons from Cuba. The administration estimated that the missile bases would become operative within ten days. The president appealed to Khrushchev to withdraw "this clandestine, reckless, and provocative threat to world peace."

In confronting Khrushchev publicly, Kennedy avoided traditional diplomatic channels that might have lowered the level of tension. The president also rebuffed a U.N. proposal for a three-week moratorium and determined not to consult with American allies. Such rigidity exaggerated the nature of the crisis. As McNamara pointed out, nuclear warheads in the Soviet Union could inflict much greater damage than the weapons in Cuba. Moreover, Cuba surely would not launch a suicidal attack against the United States. To the contrary, official explanations later claimed that Cuba needed the missiles to prevent an American invasion. But the idea that the missiles did not represent an immediate threat contradicted Kennedy's insistence on a deadline for their removal. A more likely explanation was his desire to settle the crisis before the November elections. In taking his firm position, the president shifted the initiative — and the responsibility — to Khrushchev.

The Soviet leader had not anticipated Kennedy's outraged reaction. Nor had he expected the public humiliation of a diplomatic retreat. In a private letter to Kennedy, Khrushchev protested the demand for an unconditional surrender. Calling American policy "outright banditry," he refused to recognize the naval blockade. But Khrushchev was not about to provoke a war that "would not be in our power to stop." In another emotional letter to the president, the Soviet leader emphasized that the Soviet ships in mid-Atlantic carried nonmilitary goods and that the missiles already were landed in Cuba. He then proposed to remove the weapons, provided the United States ended the blockade and agreed to respect Cuban independence. "Only a madman," Khrushchev wrote, "can believe that armaments are the principal means in the life of a society."

The next day, however, the president received still another message from Khrushchev that stiffened the terms for removal of the missiles. The Soviet leader now demanded the withdrawal of missiles from Turkey in exchange for those in Cuba. This new position, like Kennedy's outrage at the Cuban missiles, was more symbolic than real, for the Turkish missiles were outmoded and the United States already had more deadly weapons aimed at the Soviet Union. Months earlier, the president had even ordered the State Department to negotiate the removal of those missiles from Turkey, but Turkish leaders had been unenthusiastic about losing the profitable bases. Yet in October 1962, Kennedy refused to negotiate the question, partly fearing the effect on American allies in Europe, partly concerned about appearing to compromise with a Communist country on the eve of the elections.

Robert Kennedy proposed a solution to this new dilemma. The United States should ignore Khrushchev's second letter and answer only the first. Kennedy's reply, therefore, made no mention of the Turkish bases. Yet when the Soviet ambassador questioned this omission, the administration explained that Turkey was beyond negotiation; nevertheless, the United States made an informal agreement to remove the missiles from Turkey and Italy. Having preserved its public image, the Kennedy administration was prepared to relinquish the substance of the issue. Khrushchev accepted the arrangement, and the crisis passed. In December Kennedy admitted that the Cuban missiles would not have changed the *military* balance of power. "But it would have politically changed the balance of power. It would have appeared to, and appearances contribute to reality."

TOWARD DÉTENTE

Kennedy's preoccupation with the appearances of power cloaked a more subtle realization about the limits of force. Though Khrushchev's timely withdrawal enhanced the president's reputation, the global position of the United States became worse. Kennedy's victory over the Communist superpower obscured the administration's inability to alter power within a revolutionary society. Castro, Kennedy's Communist nemesis, remained firmly entrenched in Cuba, and the administration had agreed to respect his sovereignty. (Kennedy actually allowed the CIA to continue its anti-Castro activities in violation of his pledge to Khrushchev.) In Europe, France's Charles de Gaulle viewed the missile crisis as the epitome of American arrogance. Appalled by Kennedy's unilateral action, the French leader began to separate from NATO, vetoed British participation in the Common Market, and attempted to create a rapprochement with the Soviet Union.

The brush with nuclear war had a sobering effect within the administration. "One mistake," Kennedy conceded, "can make this whole thing blow up." Yet Kennedy waited for Khrushchev to take the initiative to prevent a recurrence. In December 1962 the Soviet leader suggested the two nations end further nuclear testing. But subsequent negotiations soon bogged down over the question of on-site inspection. In previous discussions this issue served as a convenient excuse to avoid disarmament and a reduction of Cold War tensions. The Eisenhower administration had rejected assurances from American scientists that satellite photographs and distant seismographs could provide adequate detection of nuclear explosions. But Kennedy, more confident about American technology and more fearful of catastrophe, determined to reach agreement.

The president introduced a major re-evaluation of the Cold War in a dramatic speech at American University in June 1963. Assuring the world that the United States did not seek "a Pax Americana enforced ... by American weapons of war," he urged Americans "not to see only a distorted and desperate view of the other side, not to see conflict as inevitable." The United States could not overlook its differences with the Soviet Union. But "we can help make the world safe for diversity," he declared.

The president announced that the United States and Great Britain were sending representatives to Moscow to discuss a test-ban treaty. In addition, he was halting American testing as an act of "good faith." Having set aside the question of inspections (and underground testing), Soviet and American negotiators quickly initialed a treaty banning nuclear tests in the atmosphere. In July 1963 Kennedy presented a summary to the American public, heralding the new treaty as a "first step — a step towards peace — a step towards reason — a step away from war." Kennedy's hopeful rhetoric, however, still had to win approval from the American people, the "military-industrial complex," and a hawkish Congress. Earlier efforts by McNamara to streamline the Department of Defense by curtailing certain military production and closing superfluous military installations had aroused deep public concern. In one Long Island community, for example, the cancellation of a fighter-bomber contract threatened thirteen thousand employees, who protested so loudly that the administration reversed its position. These pressures reflected not just cynical self-interest, but also sincere ideological suspicion of Soviet intentions.

The administration therefore emphasized that the test-ban agreement was a victory for the United States. Since the United States held an undisputed lead in nuclear weaponry, the ban on atmospheric tests would protect that superiority. Nor would the American lead in underground testing be threatened. To win support from his military advisers, Kennedy made assurances that the United States would conduct "comprehensive, aggressive, and continuous" underground nuclear tests. These promises were fulfilled after the Senate ratified the treaty in September 1963. Underground nuclear testing reached a higher level after 1963 than before.

Despite these concessions to the military, Kennedy continued to express interest in reaching a détente with the Soviet Union. "If this pause in the Cold War merely leads to its renewal and not to its end," he warned in an address to the U.N., "— then the indictment of posterity will rightly point its finger at us all." With joint support from the United States and the Soviet Union, the General Assembly passed a resolution condemning the placement of nuclear weapons in outer space. On a bilateral level, the two powers agreed to install an emergency "hot-line" telephone to prevent an accidental conflict. In October the administration announced that the United States would sell surplus wheat to the Soviet Union, a decision that helped the American economy without jeopardizing national security. It represented a symbolic reduction of international tension.

The signs of détente did not indicate a rejection of the Cold War. Though Kennedy welcomed the test-ban treaty, he rebuffed Khrushchev's proposal in July 1963 to formulate a nonaggression pact between NATO and the Warsaw Pact nations. Such an agreement would have undermined the Western alliance and perhaps threatened American dominance in Western Europe. To bolster American influence, the president journeyed to Europe in the summer of 1963, where he reiterated the Cold War polarities first stated by President Truman.

Kennedy emphasized the global dimension of the American commitment in a speech in West Berlin. "Two thousand years ago the proudest boast was 'civis Romanus sum' [I am a Roman citizen]," the president declared, quoting the words of another apostle, Paul. "Today, in the world of freedom, the proudest boast is 'Ich bin ein Berliner.'" Like the early Christians, Kennedy reaffirmed the impossibility of compromising with atheistic evil. In 1959 Khrushchev had expressed his faith in the historical inevitability of a communist victory when he told Eisenhower, "We will bury you." Kennedy remained wedded to a similar, though opposite, belief. In a speech intended for delivery in Dallas on November 22, 1963, the president defined his sense of historical destiny: "We in this country, in this generation, are, by destiny rather than choice, the watchmen on the walls of world freedom."

POLITICS AND THE DOMESTIC ECONOMY

President Kennedy's willingness to seek global confrontation contrasted with his position in domestic matters. Certain of American strength in world affairs, Kennedy did not negotiate "out of fear." But at home, the administration lacked a firm base of power. Kennedy's slim electoral victory reflected the divided opinion of the electorate. A Gallup poll in January 1961 indicated that 42 percent hoped the president would pursue moderate policies; 24 percent hoped he would be more conservative; 23 percent desired a liberal position. Within Congress, an old conservative leadership, backed by the seniority system, jealously guarded its power and its prerogatives. This cautious mood was

Betty Friedan

1924-

"Is that all?" By popularizing and legitimating that simple question, Betty Friedan stimulated a fundamental re-examination of the fifties truism that the American woman would achieve maximum fulfillment as wife and mother, as housewife and homemaker. Her book of 1963, The Feminine Mystique, which challenged the prevailing mythology of domestic bliss, sold three million copies and reached an estimated readership five times as large.

Born to immigrant Jewish parents in Peoria, Illinois, Friedan studied psychology and social science at Smith College and the University of California, Berkeley. "I didn't want to be like my mother," she later recalled. Friedan worked as a journalist during World War Two, but lost her job to a returning war veteran. She was fired from another job because of pregnancy, in violation of a union contract. In 1949, she explained, there was no term to describe "sex discrimination."

During the fifties, Friedan lived in various suburbs of New York, raising three children. She continued a free-lance journalist career and wrote articles for such magazines as Harper's, Good Housekeeping, Redbook, and Mademoiselle. For a piece about her Smith College classmates fifteen years after graduation, Friedan conducted a survey of their attitudes and feelings. It revealed a profound unhappiness among college-educated, middle-class women. But the article was rejected by the editors of women's magazines.

Friedan turned instead to her book. "Something is very wrong with the way American women are trying to live their lives today," she began. "It is no longer possible to ... dismiss the desperation of so many American women." Friedan proceeded to demolish the "happy housewife" syndrome of postwar society and argued that middle-class women required a *sense of* personal *fulfillment to be truly satisfied.*

Having identified a major social problem, Friedan joined other feminists in seeking its resolution. In 1966 she helped found the National Organization for Women (NOW) "to bring women into full participation in the mainstream of American society now" and served as its first president until 1970. She also helped establish the National Women's Political Caucus in 1971, but split publicly with other feminist leaders over political strategy. Friedan described her career after 1963 in It Changed My Life *(1976).*

revealed prior to inaugural day when Vice President–elect Johnson, recently the efficient Senate majority leader, offered to lead the Democratic caucus. Johnson's former colleagues rebuffed the idea and reaffirmed the separation of powers. Congress had served notice that it would be reluctant to follow the new administration's leadership.

Kennedy's precarious position reflected the legislative strength of southern Democrats who, though nominally members of the president's party, frequently joined with Republicans to thwart consideration of liberal measures. To overcome the conservatism of the House leadership, Speaker Sam Rayburn proposed an expansion of the Rules Committee to increase its liberal membership. By threatening House traditions, the scheme aroused deep southern resentment, but Rayburn managed to pass the measure on an extremely narrow vote. The victory removed only one obstacle, however, and southern legislators continued to crush or dilute such liberal administration proposals as an increase in minimum wages and federal aid to education.

Kennedy's major concern was to rejuvenate the economy. Believing that a healthy capitalist structure was essential to effective rivalry with world communism, Kennedy had criticized the Eisenhower administration for failure to stimulate economic growth. Never doubting the possibility of unlimited expansion, the Democratic president promised to bring the economy to a 5 percent growth rate per year. These political concerns were made especially acute by a severe recession that was causing 7.7 percent unemployment by January 1961. To combat the recession, Kennedy proposed increased unemployment benefits, depressed-area development programs, and additional public housing. Congress moved slowly to enact these measures.

Meanwhile, the economy showed signs of improvement.

Kennedy's economic advisers, particularly the liberal Walter Heller, urged more vigorous federal spending. But the administration was unwilling to challenge a conservative Congress on that issue. Fearing that deficit spending would antagonize the business community, Kennedy instead proposed a tax credit for new investment in plant equipment. By stimulating business expansion, this measure would simultaneously attack unemployment and provide the basis for long-term growth. To compensate for the loss of tax revenue, however, Kennedy also requested tax reforms that would close such corporate loopholes as expense accounts, earnings on dividends, and foreign income. But these changes attacked the interests of the wealthiest and most powerful groups, and Congress delayed action until 1962. Meanwhile, heavy government spending for military defense boosted the sagging economy.

As the recession passed in 1961, Kennedy turned his attention to controlling inflation. In January 1962 the president's Council of Economic Advisers issued a series of "wage-price guideposts" that recommended noninflationary increases. Though business leaders resented the administration's desire to manage the economy, the wage-price formula made no effort to alter the existing patterns of corporate wealth. The guidelines for price increases remained imprecise and subject to corporate manipulation. But wage increases were directly linked to corporate production. The administration did not envision employees obtaining a larger share of corporate profits. "Forcing wages up ahead of productivity," Kennedy asserted, "can only weaken our efforts to expand the economy."

Despite this conservative outlook, the wage-price controls produced a major clash between the president and the nation's largest industry — steel — in the spring of 1962. As part of its anti-inflation program, the administration had persuaded the United Steelworkers Union to accept a modest pay increase. Central to the arrangement was the steel industry's promise to hold the price line. But in April 1962 Roger Blough, president of U.S. Steel, notified the president that he was raising steel prices an inflationary $6 per ton. Other steel companies announced they would follow Blough's lead.

"My father once told me that all steelmen were sons of bitches, and I did not realize until now how right he was," Kennedy remarked. He then launched a strenuous campaign to force the steel industry to rescind the increases. Administration officials pleaded with friendly steel executives to hold the old price line. McNamara instructed the Defense Department to purchase only from low-price manufacturers, and Robert Kennedy ordered the Justice Department to investigate the possibility of illegal price fixing. These pressures led Inland Steel Corporation to reject a price increase, creating a domino effect within the industry. Kennedy had ably defended his economic strategy.

The president's assertion of the government's economic power aroused the hostility of business leaders. These negative feelings were reinforced by a slumping stock market. In May 1962 Wall Street prices touched the lowest point since the Crash of 1929. This trend reflected the belated impact of the recession of 1960–1961, which had reduced corporate earnings. But the president's stand on steel prices disheartened the business community, which blamed the administration for the downturn.

Kennedy responded to this crisis in confidence by emphasizing his support of business. At the Yale University commencement in June 1962, the president pleaded for an end to "sterile acrimony." The interests of government and business, he insisted, were the same. Kennedy proceeded to challenge certain fallacies in popular thinking. He argued that the government was not too large and that its growth since World War Two had been slower than other sectors of the economy. The president also denied the evils of deficit spending, pointing out that federal government indebtedness had increased less than private and local government debts. Finally, Kennedy minimized the economic importance of business confidence in government, observing that previous recessions had come during popular administrations. "What is at stake is not some grand warfare of rival ideologies," the president maintained in the language of consensus, "but the practical management of a modern economy."

The Kennedy administration moved quickly to demonstrate its commitment to business prosperity. A lowering of margin requirements on the purchase of securities stimulated the stock market. In July 1962 the Treasury Department liberalized the scale of depreciation allowances for business equipment, thus encouraging the replacement of older machinery. Congress also enacted the proposed tax credit on new investments as well as a diluted tax reform package that maintained specific benefits for business. Kennedy endorsed new legislation for the marketing of drugs that proved favorable to the pharmaceutical industry. In the field of space technology, the administration favored private control of a communications satellite corporation, thus permitting private business to benefit from the government's space program.

The commitment to business interests culminated in Kennedy's support of foreign trade. Since the latter part of the Eisenhower administration, the United States economy had suffered a serious imbalance of foreign payments,

largely because of heavy spending for foreign military bases. In 1961 Kennedy created a special position in the Defense Department to encourage the sale of American arms to foreign nations. Besides bringing profits to arms manufacturers, this policy linked business prosperity to American foreign policy. Kennedy also continued Eisenhower's policy of trying to persuade the NATO nations to pay a larger proportion of the common defense. As an inducement, Kennedy proposed the creation of a Multilateral Nuclear Force (MLF) in 1962. But United States insistence on an absolute veto over the use of nuclear weapons offended the allies, and the idea was never implemented.

Indicative of the erosion of the Western alliance, the European nations also thwarted Kennedy's hope for expanded international trade. In 1962 the president presented a trade expansion bill as his major legislative concern. Such a law, Kennedy declared, "could well affect the unity of the West, the course of the Cold War, and the economic growth of our Nation for a generation to come." In response to intense administration pressure, Congress enacted a measure in 1962 that permitted the president to negotiate across-the-board tariff reductions. In the tradition of the Open Door, Kennedy expected this legislation to increase American trade with the European allies. His hopes were rudely assaulted, however, when France vetoed British participation in the Common Market, and the prospects of Atlantic economic unity diminished.

In seeking ways to strengthen the economy, Kennedy discarded his initial belief in a balanced budget and embraced the "new economics" of John Maynard Keynes. In 1961 the president had rejected the advice of his Council of Economic Advisers to cut taxes to stimulate economic expansion. By 1962, however, Kennedy accepted the theory that a tax cut would increase consumer spending, lift the "fiscal drag," and thus increase the rate of economic growth. Kennedy's willingness to experiment with deficit spending aroused conservative opposition, and he waited until January 1963 to submit his proposal to Congress. Kennedy's plan called for a $13.6 billion reduction of taxes, most of it on individual incomes, as well as significant tax reforms to shift the tax burden toward the upper brackets. But the president clearly was more committed to the tax cut than to reform, and he offered little protest when Congress whittled away the reform provisions. The measure, not enacted until the Johnson administration, provided the basis for an extraordinary surge of economic growth.

THE CIVIL RIGHTS CRISIS

Kennedy's reluctance to challenge congressional conservatives influenced his stand on the question of civil rights. Recognizing the political strength of southern Democrats, the administration tried to appease the conservative leadership. Kennedy responded quickly to southern patronage demands, awarded federal construction projects to southern states, and raised the level of price supports on cotton. More important, the president declined to introduce civil rights legislation or issue strong executive orders.

Shortly after taking office, Kennedy created a Commission on Equal Employment Opportunity (CEEO), headed by Vice President Johnson, and charged it with ending discrimination on work done under government contract. But the CEEO preferred voluntary compliance and seldom punished violators. During the 1960 campaign Kennedy claimed that Eisenhower could eliminate federal support of segregated housing "with the stroke of the presidential pen." But the Democratic president became remarkably silent when that power passed into his own hands. Hoping to win congressional approval for a Department of Urban Affairs, Kennedy refused to challenge segregated housing. Not until 1962, after Congress defeated his efforts, did Kennedy act to end segregation in federally funded housing. More than previous administrations, however, Kennedy appointed blacks to government positions and allowed them to work in areas other than race relations.

Kennedy's limited support of equal rights for blacks reflected more than a fear of southern power. Like other liberals, the president believed that changes in race relations could not be forced on the nation. He placed his hopes for racial justice not on new legislation but on enforcement of the voting rights provisions of the Civil Rights Acts of 1957 and 1960. According to his premises, Attorney General Robert Kennedy would file suits on behalf of black plaintiffs, thereby guaranteeing black suffrage and providing the basis for black political power. He believed that other changes would follow from these beginnings. But Kennedy's inertia, after acquiring 70 percent of the black vote in 1960, belied his premises. Moreover, he weakened even the minimal possibilities of obtaining favorable rulings by appointing segregationist judges to federal courts in the South. One Kennedy appointee openly referred to blacks as "niggers" and "chimpanzees."

The administration's failure to support civil rights reform angered the black community. Instead of waiting for government action, black activists determined to force legal change by

A black minister protects his house from night riders after becoming the first black to register to vote in his Louisiana parish in sixty years. (Bob Adelman/Magnum)

violating segregationist laws. Following the nonviolent, direct action of Martin Luther King and the sit-in demonstrators of 1960, the Congress of Racial Equality (CORE) launched a series of "freedom rides" in 1961 to force integration of interstate commerce and transportation. Busloads of freedom riders were met by angry white crowds who attacked them while FBI agents looked on. The administration justified its refusal to intervene by stressing its lack of jurisdiction in matters of state and local control.

The public violence nevertheless forced Kennedy to act. The administration sent federal marshals into the South and obtained court injunctions against interference in interstate bus travel. At the same time, Robert Kennedy called on the freedom riders for a "cooling-off period." An indignant Martin Luther King agreed only to "a lull." "We had been cooling off for 100 years," protested James Farmer, organizer of the freedom rides. "If we got any cooler we'd be in a deep freeze." Meanwhile, Attorney General Kennedy petitioned the Interstate Commerce Commission to issue an order prohibiting segregation in interstate travel.

After an initial rebuff, Kennedy exerted behind-the-scenes pressure that led to the desired ICC ruling in September 1961.

In reacting to the freedom rides, the administration revealed its preference for avoiding direct confrontation outside the legal framework. This tendency emerged clearly in a lengthy power struggle over the integration of the University of Mississippi in September 1962. James Meredith, a black air force veteran, had obtained a federal court order allowing him to register at the all-white school. But Governor Ross Barnett spoke for the southern leadership when he announced his refusal to comply with the ruling. The Kennedy administration determined to enforce the law. Following the precedent of Eisenhower in 1957, Kennedy federalized the National Guard and sent regular army troops and federal marshals to the area. But the administration was especially careful not to threaten local authority. Even when bloody riots erupted, Attorney General Kennedy allowed state officials to maintain their power. Nor did the government attempt to punish Barnett for violating the law.

While the administration sought to heal the breaches caused by the civil rights movement, liberal activists began a voter registration campaign in the South. Such activities brought them into contact with a police and legal system that violated basic constitutional rights with impunity. As in the case of the freedom rides, civil rights workers discovered that the federal government was reluctant to provide adequate protection. Denying its jurisdiction, the administration refused to confront traditional southern power. This failure to act aroused widespread indignation among blacks and stimulated further mass protest. To quiet this dissent, Kennedy proposed a civil rights bill in February 1963. "We are committed to

achieving true equality of opportunity," he declared, "because it is right." Yet the president's message called only for accelerating prosecution of voting rights violations, the authorization of federal funds to encourage school desegregation, and the extension of the Civil Rights Commission. Unmentioned were the broader questions of equal rights or the extralegal protests sweeping the land.

Black leaders rejected Kennedy's caution. In the spring of 1963, King's Southern Christian Leadership Conference (SCLC) carried the civil rights crusade to Birmingham, Alabama, purportedly "the most thoroughly segregated big city" in the nation. King's nonviolent strategy aimed at producing so much "creative tension" that segregationist leaders would feel compelled to negotiate a peaceful settlement. The American Gandhi was not mistaken. After several weeks of noisy but relatively peaceful demonstrations, the local police chief, "Bull" Connor, attempted to end the movement by attacking the protesters with clubs, fire hoses, and dogs. This violence steeled the nerves of black demonstrators and, because of wide television coverage, sent waves of outrage throughout the country. The Kennedy administration at last intervened, pressing Alabama business leaders to settle the issues. In May a shaky truce was reached.

The Birmingham confrontation — and the many other demonstrations it spawned — convinced Kennedy to stand behind strong civil rights legislation. "We face . . . a moral crisis as a country and as a people," he told a television audience in June 1963. "It cannot be met by repressive police action. It cannot be left to increased demonstrations in the streets." Kennedy then introduced a new civil rights bill that prohibited racial discrimination in public accommodations, authorized the attorney general to initiate suits to desegregate public schools, sought to improve black employment opportunities, and incorporated the administration's earlier proposal to protect voting rights. Black activists questioned some of the legal loopholes that remained in the bill. But few doubted the clarity of Kennedy's moral position.

While Congress began to consider Kennedy's civil rights package, black leaders decided to stage a show of strength by organizing a March on Washington. The president initially discouraged such a demonstration, fearing that it would inflame passions and embarrass the administration. But the civil rights leadership refused to retreat. On August 28, 1963, 250,000 marchers converged in the nation's capital to affirm their commitment to civil rights. "I have a dream," Martin Luther King told the assemblage. "I have a dream that...the sons of former slaves and the sons of former slave-owners will be able to sit together at the table of brotherhood." King's passionate language electrified the crowd.

Other voices in Washington, however, presented an alternative vision of the black future. John Lewis, head of the Student Non-Violent Coordinating Committee (SNCC), attacked the Kennedy administration for its "immoral compromises" with conservative politicians. "If any radical social, political, and economic changes are to take place in our society," he maintained, "the people, the masses must bring them about. In the struggle, we must seek more than mere civil rights; we must work for the community of love, peace, and true brotherhood." Three months later, Lewis's language was echoed in a speech by the black nationalist leader, Malcolm X. Calling for a revolutionary consciousness, he scoffed at the limited horizons of racial integration. "A revolutionary," he asserted, "is a black nationalist."

RADICAL POLITICS

These broad statements, transcending the traditional dialogue of political parties, perplexed the political leadership. "Extremism," as it was called, aroused the specter of Communist subversion. Conservatives like Ross Barnett accused civil rights organizations of acting as "Communist fronts," while liberals like Arthur M. Schlesinger, Jr., identified black radicals with Mao Tse-tung. Such labeling reflected an inability to perceive or understand indigenous radical activity; it was the same logic that saw Fidel Castro and Ho Chi Minh as mere puppets of Moscow.

The confusion of radicalism with communism permeated the political establishment. As the Kennedy administration became committed to supporting Martin Luther King, it strove to purge radicals from the civil rights movement. Secret wiretaps of King's telephone by the FBI indicated that one of his associates may have been sympathetic to communism. President Kennedy personally warned King of such associations and persuaded the black leader to break relations with this supporter.

Kennedy's fears about Communist influence reflected not so much his concern about national security as his dread of Communist taint. Long after Joseph McCarthy was dead, communism still conjured up visions of ultimate evil. Prominent Communists continued to face economic and political discrimination. Leftist entertainers like the singer Pete Seeger were denied access to television programs and college campuses. At Queens College in New York, school officials simultaneously banned speeches by the Communist leader Ben Davis and Malcolm X, precipitating the first major student strike for free speech in 1961. The next year, the same college administration placed the en-

Malcolm X, addressing a Black Muslim audience in 1961, emphasized the importance of preserving a black identity in white America. (Eve Arnold/Magnum)

tire student editorial board on probation for attacking HUAC. Kennedy's support of international diversity had made few inroads at home.

The attack on student radicalism reflected the perpetuation of an academic philosophy called *in loco parentis* (in the place of the parent). Under its principles, university officials claimed the right not only to guide students' intellectual development, but also to supervise their personal lives. Student involvement in the civil rights movement stimulated strenuous protests against these paternalistic

values. Attacks on the university system merged with a broader vision for a humane society in the radical organization Students for a Democratic Society (SDS). In a position paper known as the Port Huron Statement (1962), SDS founder Tom Hayden condemned the "poverty, waste, elitism, manipulation" that characterized mainstream politics. Ironically, until 1966 SDS bylaws banned affiliation with Communists.

The awakening of student protest on the Left mirrored the emergence of a radical politics of the Right. As liberal Democrats and "modern" Republicans joined in a political consensus that accepted government participation in the economy and minimal social welfare legislation, orthodox conservatives condemned the betrayal of such traditional American values as individualism and laissez faire. Equating social reform with alien "un-American" forces, extreme conservatives concluded that "Communist influences are now in almost complete control of our Federal Government." In 1958 Robert Welch, a wealthy business leader and former director of the National Association of Manufacturers, founded the secret John Birch Society to agitate against the alleged "Communist conspiracy." Funded largely by small-business executives, such right wing organizations not only opposed domestic liberalism but also objected to an internationalist foreign policy, including participation in the U.N., foreign aid, or negotiation with the Soviet Union. Though numerically weak, the radical Right was particularly vocal.

Conservative opinion was also enjoying a renaissance within the major political parties. As the administration endorsed a more aggressive civil rights movement, the conservative ideology spread through the South. "This is like a dictatorship," Mississippi's Ross Barnett protested against federal authority. "It looks like we're being kicked around." Southern Democrats spoke loudly about deserting the national party. Taking advantage of these resentments, Republican Senator Barry Goldwater of Arizona offered an orthodox alternative. In his best-selling book, *The Conscience of a Conservative* (1960), Goldwater criticized "the encroachment of individual freedom by Big Government," defended states' rights, attacked forced school desegregation, called for the return to a "free" marketplace, and urged a more

vigorous waging of the Cold War. The program promised to create a new conservative coalition.

Kennedy's advisers feared that Goldwater would drain the president's support in the South and Southwest. A popular bumper sticker — "Kennedy for King — Goldwater for President" — indicated the liability of civil rights. In Texas the Democratic party had split into warring camps, threatening the party's electoral chances. For this reason Kennedy decided to keep the Texan Johnson as his running mate in 1964. Yet Texas remained a hotbed of anti-Kennedy sentiment. In October 1963 U.N. Ambassador Stevenson had been pushed and spat upon by an angry crowd in Dallas. With an eye on the next presidential election, Kennedy decided to go to Texas in November to mend his political fences and reunite the state's Democratic party.

SUGGESTED READINGS

A brief survey of the Kennedy years is Jim F. Heath, *Decade of Disillusionment: The Kennedy-Johnson Years* (1975). Two Kennedy workers have written extensive but uncritical studies: see Arthur M. Schlesinger, Jr., *A Thousand Days* (1965), and Theodore Sorensen, *Kennedy* (1965). More insightful of Kennedy's policies is Bruce Miroff, *Pragmatic Illusions: The Presidential Politics of John F. Kennedy* (1976).

The election of 1960 is described in Theodore H. White, *The Making of the President: 1960* (1961). For a more detailed statistical analysis of voting patterns in the fifties and sixties, see Norman H. Nie et al., *The Changing American Voter* (1976). Kennedy's problems with Congress are explored in Tom Wicker, *JFK and LBJ: The Influence of Personality upon Politics* (1968). The Kennedy administration's relationship to the civil rights movement is analyzed critically in Victor S. Navasky, *Kennedy Justice* (1971), and more favorably in Carl M. Brauer, *John F. Kennedy and the Second Reconstruction* (1977). The problems of economic policy are described in Jim F. Heath, *John F. Kennedy and the Business Community* (1969).

A critical analysis of Kennedy's foreign policy is Richard J. Walton, *Cold War and Counterrevolution* (1972). The main issues of the Cuban missile crisis are discussed in an anthology, Robert A. Divine, ed., *The Cuban Missile Crisis* (1971), and David Detzer, *The Brink* (1979). Kennedy's attitude toward Viet-nam is explored in portions of Ernest R. May, *"Lessons" of the Past* (1973). For the CIA, see the works listed at the end of the chapter 13. A detailed study of the German question is Curtis Cate, *The Ides of August: The Berlin Wall Crisis, 1961* (1978).

There is a vast literature on the Kennedy assassination. The best starting point is an anthology, Peter Dale Scott, Paul L. Hoch, and Russell Stetler, eds., *The Assassinations: Dallas and Beyond* (1976). Extremely provocative in relating Kennedy's assassination to American foreign policy is Carl Oglesby, *The Yankee and Cowboy War: Conspiracies from Dallas to Watergate and Beyond* (1976). For the social context, see Bradley S. Greenburg and Edwin B. Parker, *The Kennedy Assassination and the American Public* (1965).

Spotlight: The Kennedy Assassination

Kennedy's mission ended abruptly under a hail of bullets in Dallas on November 22, 1963. As the presidential motorcade passed near the downtown area, Kennedy was shot and killed by sniper fire. In the ensuing confusion, eyewitnesses disagreed about the sequence of events. Dallas police quickly arrested a mysterious character named Lee Harvey Oswald, who claimed to be a "patsy" for unknown conspirators. Before he could be tried, however, Oswald was killed by a Dallas nightclub owner, Jack Ruby, who allegedly had connections with the criminal underworld. Lyndon Johnson, who had accompanied Kennedy to his politically divided home state, took the presidential oath of office in Texas before returning to Washington with the slain president's body.

The assassination of John Kennedy had a profound impact on American society and culture. Because of its suddenness, news of the killing wrenched the American people from the routines of their daily lives. People would later remember exactly what they were doing when they first heard the news. As word of the shooting spread from Dallas, people everywhere crowded around televisions and radios seeking further information. The sophistication of the public media made the assassination a national event, an experience that was shared simultaneously throughout the country and the world. Surveys later revealed that 92 percent of all Americans learned of the assassination within two hours and that more than half of all Americans watched the same television coverage of the event. Millions of citizens were glued to their television sets on November 24 and watched Jack Ruby murder the suspected assassin. As Pearl Harbor had shocked an earlier generation of Americans, the assassination of Kennedy and its aftermath touched the lives of the entire nation.

This shared experience created a unique moment in American history, a time when normal activities stopped because of the weight of the tragedy. On the day of the president's funeral, schools and businesses were closed to enable all people to share in the national ritual. As a Catholic, Kennedy received the last rites of the church. But even the hoary traditions of the Catholic church paled before a dramatic display of national symbols — a riderless black horse, a military cortege, the playing of taps. This secular pageantry brought people together on an emotional level, reinforcing a sense of national identity.

A fundamental ingredient of these unifying themes was Kennedy's public image. Where previous presidents emphasized their wisdom and experience, Kennedy celebrated youth and energy. His family's touch-football games were noted for their vigor and intensity. The president boasted about physical fitness, encouraging people to embark on fifty-mile hikes. The Kennedy family, with its young children, suggested growth and strength. The president projected these attributes in his frequent television appearances. He was a master of the visual media, combining physical grace with sharp wit. "Washington had...become the Hollywood of the upper middle class," chided critic Roger Hagan. "Through the slick media, every mannerism of the first family...reverberates through the suburbs of the land."

Kennedy's vigor starkly contrasted with the impotence of death. His assassination symbolized the imminence of everyone's death and intensified a pervasive death fear within American culture. Despite the obvious knowledge that all people die, American society traditionally tried to ignore the inevitability of death. Jessica Mitford's exposé of the funeral industry, *The American Way of Death* (1963), illuminated some of the strategies Americans used to avoid confronting death and dying. In Dallas, for example, the funeral parlor that provided Kennedy's coffin possessed a "Slumber Room" where survivors could view the dead. Makeup devices were designed to conceal ugly wounds and bodily disintegration. The Kennedy assassination undermined these charades. Kennedy was not in "slumber" and his head was too badly mutilated to be exposed; he was dead.

The death anxiety within American society had intensified during the Kennedy administration. Since the atomic bombing of Hiroshima in 1945, Americans had lived in close proximity to annihilation. Kennedy had admitted that "a simple clash could escalate overnight into a holocaust of mushroom clouds." He had taken the nation to the brink of nuclear calamity during the Cuban missile crisis, acknowledging that "American citizens have become adjusted to living daily on the bull's-eye of Soviet missiles." Despite Kennedy's claim of adjustment, Americans dreaded the possibility of mass death. "We may be the last generation in the experiment with living," protested the Port Huron Statement. And conservatives complained, in the words of Senator Goldwater, of "a craven fear of death."

This fear of human annihilation was accentuated by a new image of the global condition. As part of his Cold War strategy, Kennedy had committed the United States to an elaborate program for the exploration of outer space. In 1961, after America's first astronaut, Alan Shepard, rode a missile three hundred miles, the president announced a bold and costly program to place human beings on the moon by the end of the decade. "No single project," he explained, "will be more impressive to mankind." One year later John Glenn became a national hero by circling the earth three times. "This is the new ocean," Kennedy proclaimed, "and I believe the United States must sail on it."

Though he defined space exploration as a competition with the Soviet Union, Kennedy appreciated the implications for the rest of mankind trapped by the earth's gravity. Distant photographs of earth demonstrated the smallness and frailty of the blue planet. Despite the rhetoric of new frontiers and new oceans, Kennedy realized that the earth was mankind's only home. "We all inhabit this planet. We all breathe the same air," he declared in his American University speech of 1963. "We all cherish our children's future. And we all are mortal."

The imminence of global death was closely related to concern for the living environment. The discovery of radioactive fallout in the form of strontium 90 had initially perplexed scientists. In 1955, however, the Atomic Energy Commission assured the public that only animals who ate contaminated grasses would be endangered. Human beings, the AEC insisted, were exempt from the radioactive chain. Such statements clashed with the emerging science of ecology, which stressed the interrelatedness of all life. In a carefully documented book, *Silent Spring* (1962), the biologist Rachel Carson described the pervasive danger of the uncontrolled use of pesticides. "The question is whether any civilization can wage relentless war on life without destroying it," she warned.

The ecology movement, the space program, the rumblings of the Cold War — all spoke to a culture preoccupied by cataclysm. The killing of Kennedy reduced this imminence of mass death to human proportions. The slain president personified what could happen to anyone and to everyone. This sense of heightened vulnerability helps to explain the popular fascination with the Kennedy assassination and the Kennedy family survivors. The thirst for information, as evidenced by the proliferation of newspaper and magazine articles, reflected a psychological attempt to master the events by learning about them. It also betrayed an unwillingness to accept the finality of death.

Anguished by the Kennedy assassination, Americans sought appropriate ways to commemorate the dead president. Kennedy memorabilia — pictures, charms, jewelry, and books — found ready customers, even in the gloomy Christmas season that followed the assassination. Local governments named and renamed public buildings after Kennedy. The space center at Cape Canaveral became Cape Kennedy (later changed back under the Nixon administration); New York's Idlewild Airport switched to JFK; and a new arts complex in the nation's capital was called the Kennedy Center. The president's grave at Arlington National Cemetery became an overnight shrine. These monuments attempted to provide an earthly immortality to ease the nation's psychic loss.

To explain the national trauma, President Johnson created a nonpartisan commission, headed by Chief Justice Earl Warren, to investigate the circumstances of the assassination. Though he selected the most prestigious political leaders, Johnson imposed one serious handicap. He insisted on a final report before the elections of 1964. This rigid timetable resulted in a sloppy report that failed to answer basic questions about Kennedy's death. Released in October 1964, the Warren Report concluded that Kennedy had been killed by the dead assassin, Oswald, who had acted alone and who in turn had been killed by Ruby, acting alone. A 1966 Gallup poll found that a majority of American citizens doubted the validity of the report, and yet a majority also opposed reopening the case.

In assessing Oswald's motives, the Warren Commission stated simply that the assassin was a "loner" who suffered from an "inability to enter meaningful relations with people." As for Ruby, the report attributed his actions to extraordinary grief at the Kennedy assassination. Such flimsy explanations encouraged the proliferation of alternatives. Oswald's interest in Cuba led to two mutually exclusive possibilities. The first explanation saw Oswald as a Communist agent, taking revenge on Kennedy for the Bay of Pigs and for CIA attempts to assassinate Castro. A second scenario saw Oswald as an enemy of Castro, working with Cuban refugees and international criminals and seeking to eliminate Kennedy because of his refusal to support further anti-Castro operations. Few students of the Warren Report, however, accepted the finding that Oswald acted alone.

Though Oswald's motives remain unexplained, the willingness to ascribe his actions to insanity or mental disturbance reflected a dominant attitude toward political violence. Even Oswald's legal defender, Mark Lane, described the unknown assassins of Kennedy as "motivated by diseased minds." Throughout American history, presidential assassins like John Wilkes Booth and Charles Guiteau have been dismissed as insane. Later assassins such as Sirhan Sirhan (who shot Robert Kennedy), Charles Bremer (who attacked George Wallace), and Lynette Fromme (who tried to kill Gerald Ford) have equally been silenced by claims of insanity. Another assassin, James Earl Ray (who killed Martin Luther King) pleaded guilty and avoided political testimony. This pattern of enforced silence minimized the significance of assassination as a political act.

Kennedy's assassination triggered a wave of similar crimes that included (in addition to the ones mentioned above), the murder of Malcolm X and the American Nazi George Lincoln Rockwell. These murders reflected political polarities that could not be resolved within the existing political institutions. But to avoid an examination of the need for such extralegal politics, American leaders ruled these acts, by definition, to be insane. Political assassination nevertheless had an internal logic as well as a rational (if unpleasant) objective. The failure of the government to confront these issues assured the perpetuation of popular conspiracy theories about the rash of political violence in the sixties.

The political ramifications of the Kennedy assassination were intimately related to the emotional power of the tragedy. "For me this one act has made all other acts irrelevant and trivial," declared one student. Such sentiments may have had a significant effect on the traditional patterns of voting. In the three presidential elections before Kennedy's assassination, voting behavior indicated that most people ignored the content of political issues and expressed a simple preference for one of the two major parties. Between 1960 and 1964, however, there was a sharp increase in the proportion of voting according to issues and a simultaneous decrease in the importance of party affiliation. This shift in voting habits became a clearer trend in subsequent elections.

The growing emphasis on political issues rather than party labels reflected the political style of a new generation of voters who reached their majority during the Kennedy and Johnson years. Unlike older voters, these newer constituents perceived politics as immediate and personal. Such moral questions as the arms race and civil rights touched deeply in the lives of ordinary citizens. Viewing politics as a system rather than as a random series of events, the new voters formulated politically consistent responses. Such changes remain difficult to explain. But the impact of Kennedy — both in life and in death — on young people illuminates one level of motivation. As a source of idealism, Kennedy's stature was magnified by his tragic death.

For the Kennedy assassination, above all, was an emotional event. In reacting to the murder, Americans spontaneously created an idealized sense of community, an idealized feeling of national harmony. Sharing their shock and their fear, Americans believed they could transcend the differences that separated them. For this reason, they responded favorably to Johnson's call for a consensus. Such idealized hopes, however, were impossible to obtain in the political world of American society. Yet Americans continued to measure their political problems against idealized standards of community. The disillusionment of subsequent years, particularly among young people, could be traced to the high level of early aspiration. In death, Kennedy created what had eluded him in life — a broad affirmation of community that transcended the differences of established politics.

Chapter 15

THE LOST CONSENSUS, 1964-1968

Five days after the assassination of John F. Kennedy, Lyndon Baines Johnson appeared before both houses of Congress. "All I have, I would have given gladly not to be standing here today," he said quietly. The former vice president and Senate majority leader pledged to lead the nation to a consensus in domestic affairs and singled out civil rights legislation as a fitting tribute to the late president. "Let us here highly resolve that John Fitzgerald Kennedy did not live or die in vain," Johnson stated. "Let us continue."

KENNEDY LEGACY

The new president moved quickly to assure an orderly and smooth transition of power in a na-

tion traumatized by the events of the Kennedy assassination. To win national confidence in his leadership, Johnson telephoned the fifty governors, consulted with former Presidents Truman and Eisenhower, and conferred with business, labor, and civil rights leaders. He also insisted that Kennedy's aides remain in the new administration. New Frontier appointees such as Secretary of State Rusk, Defense Secretary McNamara, and National Security Adviser McGeorge Bundy continued to play central roles in the foreign policy of the Johnson years.

By early 1964 Johnson chose three legislative priorities — a tax cut, civil rights, and antipoverty legislation. Tutored by Economic Adviser Walter Heller, Kennedy had asked for a $10 billion tax cut in 1963. The request marked a deliberate attempt to use deficit spending to stimulate private spending, and Heller predicted that higher tax revenues would accompany increased consumption. Although the House passed Kennedy's proposal two months before his assassination, fiscal conservatives in the Senate and business leaders remained uneasy over large deficits. Johnson won the tax cut through personal persuasion and by slicing Kennedy's proposed budget to under $100 billion. Passed in February 1964, the $11.5 billion personal and corporate income tax cut was the new president's first legislative triumph. It marked the institutionalization of the deficit and stimulated a 7 percent boost in the gross national product in 1964. National production continued to rise through 1966, while both unemployment and inflation sank to 3.8 percent, a dramatic indication of fiscal success.

Kennedy's second legacy was the call for a civil rights bill to prohibit racial discrimination in voting, public accommodations, and employment. Before his death Kennedy had lined up sufficient congressional support to pass a civil rights law, but expected southern members of Congress to weaken some of its provisions and reject others. Johnson succeeded in prevailing upon the House to pass an uncompromised bill in February 1964, but faced a seventy-five-day filibuster in the Senate. In mid-June, Illinois Republican Senator Everett Dirksen decided to support Johnson's civil rights bill as "an idea whose time had come." With the added strength of northern Republicans, two-thirds of the Senate voted to invoke cloture, ending debate and killing the southern filibuster. It was the first time the Senate had ever voted cloture on a civil rights issue. The Civil Rights Act of 1964 gave the federal government the power to sue to desegregate accommodations and public schools. It attempted to outlaw the denial of equal job opportunity in all but the smallest businesses and unions and allowed the federal government to monitor state voting records. For black Americans and their supporters, the Civil Rights Act was a step toward the dream of equal opportunity, but conservatives such as Senator Barry Goldwater objected to extending the power of federal government to local and community affairs.

Johnson's third priority in 1964 was poverty legislation. In a commencement address at the University of Michigan, the president asked students to join "in the battle to build the Great Society." America could be more than rich and powerful, Johnson preached, and he committed the nation to "an end to poverty and racial injustice." The president believed that medical care, education, job training, and racial equality could complete the New Deal by finally assuring equal opportunity for all Americans. The Economic Opportunity Act, signed in August 1964, focused on training programs for the young and loans and grants for self-help projects initiated by local communities. The bill's Community Action program was important to the president because it called for "participatory democracy" of the poor to break the cycle of poverty. The law also established a Job Corps for youth, and VISTA (Volunteers in Service to America) — a domestic Peace Corps. Sargent Shriver, Kennedy's Peace Corps director, headed the Office of Economic Opportunity (OEO), which administered the multibillion-dollar program. Beginning in 1966, OEO also created Headstart, a "prepackaged" program for local agencies that provided intensive preschool training for the children of the poor.

When Congress adjourned for the fall election campaign of 1964, most of the president's legislative goals had been fulfilled. They included a $1 billion housing program, federal grants for mass transportation, extensive loans to college students, and massive aid for college construction. Johnson also expanded a Kennedy pilot project into a full-scale food stamp program for the working poor. Much of Congress's work was based on Kennedy concepts, but it was Johnson's legislative skill and his rapport with southern conservatives that translated New Frontier intentions into political accomplishments. LBJ also benefited from a "honeymoon" relationship with Congress, stimulated in part by election-year restlessness.

THE LANDSLIDE OF '64

As Johnson's programs were signed into law, Barry Goldwater emerged as the Republican candidate for the presidency. The conservative senator's followers mounted a grassroots campaign to select convention delegates from non-primary states and reverse a thirty-year domination of the Republican party by eastern liberals. Like the Taft movement of the 1950s, Goldwater partisans sought a break with party acceptance of the New Deal and managerial liberalism. The climactic point in the Goldwater drive came in the California primary, where the senator won a tight victory over Governor Nelson A. Rockefeller of New York. Rockefeller symbolized eastern liberalism and corporate power, and had recently divorced his wife and then married a younger woman, herself divorced. At the Republican Convention in San Francisco, Rockefeller was roundly booed by Goldwaterites, while a liberal resolution renouncing "extremist groups" such as the John Birch Society was decisively defeated. Following his first-ballot nomination, Goldwater selected William Miller, a conservative New York congressman, as his running mate. In his acceptance address, Goldwater responded to charges that his views on defense, race, and anticommunism mirrored those of the right wing Birch Society. "Extremism in the defense of liberty is no vice," he inserted in the middle of the routine speech, "...moderation in the pursuit of justice is no virtue." The convention came alive with boisterous chanting, but to many Americans the specter of political fanaticism appeared unsettling.

Goldwater enthusiasts, particularly in Anglo-Protestant areas of the South and Southwest, insisted that lawlessness was the major domestic issue of the era. The Goldwater candidacy was the first to embrace the "social issue," the discomfort experienced by many Americans over personally frightening aspects of social change in the sixties. Violence in the streets, political corruption, aimlessness among youth, anxiety among the elderly, and loss of spiritual meaning in the culture were themes that Goldwater articulated. Refashioning the traditional call for personal accountability, Goldwater held social permissiveness responsible for a "growing menace" to "personal safety, to life, to limb, and property." He also opposed the Civil Rights Act because it required government to interfere with social and personal relations. "In Your Heart, You Know He's Right," Goldwater bumper stickers proclaimed.

Goldwater extended his critique of mainstream liberalism to the administration's handling of the hostilities in Southeast Asia. "Failure in the jungles of Vietnam," he cried, "proclaims lost leadership, obscure purpose, weakening wills, and the risk of inciting our sworn enemies to new aggressions and new excesses." The senator held out the use of nuclear defoliants as a possible option for cutting insurgent supply lines and called for increased air power. He even labeled the president "soft on communism." But Goldwater's "cowboy" style of from-the-hip commentary frequently got him into trouble. Soon he was clarifying remarks about social security, TVA, and nuclear warfare. Goldwater's mercurial style inspired a television commercial, sponsored by the Democratic party, that showed a little girl picking petals from a daisy in a mock countdown and was followed by a quick shot of a nuclear explosion. The narrator assured that Lyndon Johnson was for peace and military restraint. Republican protests subsequently banned the advertisement from TV screens, but it did point to Goldwater's vulnerabilities.

Johnson did not enter the Democratic primaries. National attention focused on Governor George C. Wallace of Alabama, who took 34 percent, 30 percent, and 43 percent of the vote against Johnson stand-ins in Wisconsin, Indiana, and Maryland. Political commentators described the Wallace vote as a "backlash" against civil rights agitation and integration, but the conservative Democrat directed most of his rhetoric toward liberal paternalism and big government. Wallace's surprising success revealed lower-middle-class restlessness with the consensus of managerial liberalism and its disregard of their own struggles for survival.

It was black activism, however, that obsessed Johnson with the dangers of strife and violence at the Democratic Convention. Earlier that summer the Student Non-Violent Coordinating Committee (SNCC) had invited one thousand white activists to participate in a voter registration campaign in Mississippi. But the integrated crusade met with violent repression from vigilantes and local authorities who resented outside interference. "Mississippi Summer" brought one thousand arrests, numerous church burnings, bombings, and beatings, and the murder of three civil rights workers. Although only twelve hundred blacks were registered during

the summer's bloody events, a contingent of SNCC workers and new black voters came to Atlantic City to demand political representation. Calling themselves the Mississippi Freedom Democratic party, they argued that the all-white delegation from Mississippi should be unseated because black citizens were unable to participate in their selection. When both sides refused to compromise, the regular delegates, most of whom supported Goldwater, stalked out of the convention, and the embittered Freedom Democrats sat-in at the vacant seats.

Johnson had hoped for a unified convention. But concern with party harmony and fears of another assassination prompted presidential aides to request the FBI to eavesdrop on Martin Luther King and SNCC. Johnson's worried assistants also received minute-by-minute phone calls concerning "potential trouble" from confidential informants who had infiltrated the civil rights camp. While the president agonized about racial strife in Atlantic City, he also withdrew Attorney General Robert Kennedy from consideration for the vice presidency. Anxious to move beyond his predecessor's shadow and easily intimidated by intellectuals and the chic Kennedy people, Johnson announced his decision to leave Kennedy off the Democratic ticket by shrewdly revealing that no member of his cabinet would be selected. Instead, the president nominated a liberal of good standing in the party, Minnesota Senator Hubert Humphrey.

Johnson and Humphrey proclaimed an electoral politics of consensus by defending civil rights legislation and calling for moderation in Vietnam. "We seek no wider war," the president responded to Goldwater's plea for military escalation, as he denounced those who would "supply American boys to do the job that Asian

Lyndon Johnson used the politics of consensus to construct a 61 percent plurality in the 1964 presidential election. Johnson won over 90 percent of the black vote. (Frank Wolfe/Lyndon Baines Johnson Library)

boys should do." But, significantly, Johnson added that he had not "chosen to retreat" and turn Vietnam over to the Communists. The Johnson-Humphrey ticket scored a record 61 percent plurality in the 1964 election, amassing 43 million votes. Goldwater and Miller carried only Arizona and five states in the Deep South, while the Democrats won over 90 percent of the black vote. Similar to Roosevelt's victory in 1936, the Johnson landslide provided the president with better than two-to-one majorities in both houses of Congress. The election also inflated Johnson's conception of presidential authority and bolstered his consensus view of the nation and the world. With an overwhelming electoral mandate, Lyndon Baines Johnson had achieved political independence and a unified nation.

Facilitated by a procedural change that allowed new legislation to by-pass the conservative House Rules Committee, the liberal Eighty-ninth Congress passed aid to education, Medicare, and a Voting Rights Act in 1965. The education bill overcame a controversy about assistance to private schools by basing aid on the number of low-income families in each school district, while a Higher Education Act, passed later in the year, provided college scholarships and fellowships. But these laws enabled the federal government to influence local political decisions. As early as April 1965, the commissioner of education ruled that school districts had to show a "good faith substantial start" toward desegregation or lose federal funding. A year later the Office of Education issued tighter guidelines, declaring an end to "paper compliance with desegregation orders." As appropriations for education reached $10 billion by the late sixties, therefore, conservatives objected that federal aid was threatening local control over schools.

Johnson also pushed for the health care bill for older Americans that Kennedy had feared pressing. With the president's approval, congressional leaders put together a compromise that incorporated Republican demands for voluntary medical insurance to cover doctors' fees and drug costs. But the heart of the Medicare package provided for hospital and nursing home care for Americans over sixty-five through payroll taxes administered by social security. In addition, the bill provided "Medicaid" grants to states that enacted health programs for poor and indigent people of all ages. By 1970 the cost of state health care nearly equaled that of Medicare. But although the Great Society medical programs were a step toward the comprehensive health scheme that Harry Truman had proposed in 1948, the government had no control over service fees, and medical costs increased drastically for all patients.

The most dramatic Great Society reform was the Voting Rights Act of 1965. The twenty-third Amendment to the Constitution, ratified early in 1964, outlawed the poll tax in federal elections, long a barrier to black voting in the South. But as "Mississippi Summer" and Martin Luther King's marches in Selma, Alabama, demonstrated, white resistance to black balloting remained violent in the Anglo-Saxon South. Accordingly, Johnson summoned a warlike joint session of Congress in March 1965 to request federal protection for blacks who tried to register to vote. The president's words were astounding. First, he compared the Selma demonstrations to Lexington, Concord, and Appomattox as turning points in "man's unending search for freedom." Then, borrowing the language of the civil rights movement itself, the first southern president since Woodrow Wilson told the nation that "All of us ... must overcome the crippling legacy of bigotry and injustice — and we *shall* overcome."

Signed in August, the Voting Rights Act abolished the literacy test and empowered the attorney general to assign federal examiners to register voters in those states still practicing political discrimination. Applied to state and local elections as well as federal, the law marked a revolution in southern political life. Over 400,000 new black voters were registered by examiners in the next year. By 1968 one million southern blacks had been added to the voting lists.

The Great Society reached its apex in 1965. The president approved a $1 billion Appalachia Assistance program, most of which went to road building in the economically depressed region embracing eleven states. A $7.8 billion housing bill included rent supplements to low-income families, but that part of the appropriation was postponed because of strong Republican opposition. Johnson also made the Department of Housing and Urban Development a cabinet-level office, and followed that with approval of the Demonstration Cities and Metropolitan Development Act. The latter appropriated $900 million for intensive attacks on urban blight and established "incentive" grants to encourage metropolitan planning. While Congress more than doubled funding for OEO, it also provided federal grants and loans for public works in "depressed" areas. The consensus approach of the Great Society was symbolized by congressional abolition of the national-origins quota system for immigration. Although immigration was limited to 390,000 a year, close relatives of American citizens and those with special talents and skills were now favored instead of particular nationalities. By 1972 immigrants accounted for 23 percent of the nation's population growth.

RACIAL TURMOIL IN
THE CITIES

The Great Society brought dramatic gains for blacks in national affairs. Robert Weaver was appointed the first black cabinet member in history when he assumed directorship of the Department of Housing and Urban Development. Johnson also named the first black woman to a federal judgeship and appointed Thurgood Marshall, former counsel of the NAACP and the great-grandson of a Maryland slave, as the first black ever to serve on the Supreme Court. In 1966 Massachusetts elected Republican Edward Brooke the first black senator since Reconstruction. Despite these gains, however, moderate leadership found it increasingly difficult to contain the mixture of impatience, rage, and black consciousness that accompanied heightened aspirations and unchanging realities for most black Americans.

Passage of the Voting Rights Act marked the last triumph for the nonviolent and integrated civil rights movement. After 1965 national at-

tention shifted to the 53 percent of the black population that lived outside the South. Many of these Americans lived in decaying ghettos in the older industrial cities of the Northeast and Midwest. The very areas to which southern blacks had migrated since World War One were those in which technology was replacing low-skilled service jobs and from which factories were leaving for the suburbs and the South and West. The exodus of manufacturing plants from the old rail centers and the transition to a sophisticated service economy were disastrous for the black labor force. For example, the Department of Labor reported in 1968 that black Americans were more than three times as likely as whites to be in poverty and twice as likely to be unemployed. Unemployment among black youths in 1966 was 27 percent, compared to 12 percent among young whites; median income for blacks was $4,481 and $7,517 for whites.

As demands for welfare and social services increased in the inner cities, middle-class whites and businesses undermined the needed tax base by moving to the suburbs. By the sixties, America's great cities increasingly were inhabited by the segregated, unemployed, poor, and the elderly. Welfare, housing, and jobs all were inadequate in such a setting. Mothers receiving Aid to Dependent Children, the fastest growing welfare program of the decade, were allotted 21¢ a meal per person in Chicago in the early sixties. Despite the Johnson poverty program and OEO rhetoric, life for most ghetto Americans remained depressingly unchanged throughout the decade.

Shortly after the signing of the Civil Rights Act of 1964, the powder keg exploded. One hundred ghetto rebellions occurred between 1964 and 1967 in the most violent period in American history since the Civil War. Property damage from the disturbances approximated $750 million. The riots began in New York's Harlem, when an off-duty white policeman shot and killed a black youth who allegedly drew a knife. The result was an angry rampage by blacks that destroyed over one hundred businesses, brought hundreds of arrests, and left over one hundred injuries. The Harlem Riot was followed by similar outbreaks in Brooklyn, New Jersey, Philadelphia, Chicago, and Rochester. The following summer, Watts went up in smoke. Watts was a corner of Los Angeles with high dropout rates, 30 percent unemployment, and a long tradition of police harassment. Rioting, arson, shooting, and looting resulted in thirty-six deaths, one thousand injuries, four thousand arrests, and massive property destruction in August 1965. As young blacks chanted "burn, baby, burn," twenty-three thousand National Guardsmen occupied Watts during the six-day riot. But a new sense of power and pride in black identity seemed to emerge from the Watts Rebellion.

By 1966 militant black leaders such as Stokely Carmichael of SNCC were predicting another "long hot summer." Not surprisingly, Carmichael was arrested for inciting a riot when the mayor of Atlanta was toppled from the roof of a car. In Chicago, Martin Luther King had just begun an "open city" campaign when three nights of rioting resulted from a police decision to turn off fire hydrants used for relief from the stifling heat. At King's request, Mayor Richard Daley agreed to set nozzles on hydrants and obtain federal funds for ghetto swimming pools. Later in the summer King led marches for integrated housing into the white ethnic neighborhoods of southwest Chicago, where he and his followers were jeered and pelted with rocks and bottles.

King warned in 1967 that at least ten major cities were ready to explode in racial violence. The summer brought 150 separate riots. In Detroit one week of devastation resulted in forty-three deaths, two thousand injuries, five thousand homeless people and $50 million property damage. Sociologists described the Detroit disturbances as a "commodity riot" in which both whites and blacks helped themselves to goods, but indiscriminate shooting by police and the inexperienced National Guard aggravated racial tension. In Newark, New Jersey, one of the first northern cities with a black majority, severe economic competition with whites and the worst housing in the nation set the stage for the 1967 riot. Twenty-six people died in what the governor's Select Commission later described as "excessive and unjustified force" by police and National Guardsmen. Reports indicated that law enforcement personnel vandalized black businesses and shot ghetto residents indiscriminately. The following year a poll of Newark rioters indicated that 58 percent did not believe the United States worth fighting for. The racial mood of 1967 was conveyed by SNCC leader H. "Rap" Brown, who urged black demonstrators in Cambridge, Maryland, to "burn this town down if this town don't turn around and grant the demands of Negroes."

The riots of the mid-sixties frightened and angered many Americans, particularly white ethnics living in adjoining communities to the blacks. Reacting to the violence, President Johnson appointed a National Advisory Commission on Civil Disorders in 1967, chaired by Governor Otto Kerner of Illinois. The commission's report, issued in February 1968, declared that the United States was "moving toward two societies, one black, one white, separate and unequal." The riots, concluded the distinguished and biracial panel, resulted from white racism and ghetto conditions created, maintained, and condoned by white society. The commission urged a massive commitment to housing, education, welfare, and jobs, as well as better law enforcement techniques. But the president, by then preoccupied by issues of foreign policy, remained silent on the Kerner Commission findings.

CORPORATE WEALTH AND EMPIRE

Despite increased activity in education, housing, and health, federal spending on goods and services barely kept pace with the rising gross national product of the sixties. Income distribution remained lopsided in the prosperous decade. For example, the wealthiest fifth of American families received over 45 percent of the nation's personal income in 1966, whereas the lowest fifth took in a bare 3.7 percent. Tax loopholes underlined the pattern. More than 150 persons with income surpassing $200,000 paid no taxes in 1968. Outstanding tax-exempt bonds, a refuge for wealthy investors, amounted to nearly $86 billion in 1963. Oil-depletion allowances also worked to the advantage of corporations like Atlantic Richfield, which paid no taxes out of a $145 million income in 1967. The percentage of federal revenues coming from corporate income taxes actually dropped from 20 percent in 1955 to 12 percent in 1970.

The sixties produced booming prosperity for American corporations. Profits jumped $12.5 billion, or 57 percent, between 1960 and 1964, as technology continued to play a vital role in American capitalism. Pneumatic conveyors, copying machines, videotape recorders, piggyback freight, jet aircraft, and containerization in ocean shipping were sixties innovations that increased efficiency and profit making. Furthermore, corporations provided a wide variety of low-cost items with new synthetics in textiles and construction, plywood, and freeze-dried foods. Lucrative military and space contracts, particularly in the "sun belt" extending from Southeast to Southwest, also stimulated corporate prosperity and consolidation. By the end of the decade, 71 percent of the profits in manufacturing went to the four hundred largest producing firms in the nation, and half of premium stock was held by large banks, insurance companies, and financial brokers.

The scope of corporate enterprise became an issue of public policy in the sixties. Critics charged that the interaction of private business with public officialdom, an American reality since World War Two, did not always benefit the nation. Personnel shifted easily between corporate management and the federal regulatory boards that set industry standards. When companies with federal contracts got into financial trouble, government assistance frequently assured continued operation, and few government officials attempted to protect consumer interests. But Ralph Nader, a private citizen, worked to publicize the problems facing the ordinary consumer. His book, *Unsafe at Any Speed* (1965), chronicled the vulnerabilities of General Motors' Corvair. Senate hearings in 1966 revealed that the world's largest corporation had investigated Nader's personal life in order to discredit his work. A jury award brought Nader $280,000, which he used to establish research centers to monitor the varying quality of American consumer products. The young lawyers attracted to the campaign called themselves Nader's Raiders, and also investigated mining safety, radiation hazards, pollution, union corruption, and tax inequities.

Sixties prosperity relied substantially on overseas activity. As investment in the Common Market countries of Europe doubled, the total value of American-owned plants and equipment overseas surpassed $100 billion by the end of the decade. Standard Oil of New Jersey, for example, sold more oil in Europe than in the United States. While American firms exported $35 billion worth of goods each year by mid-decade, foreign subsidiaries of American "multinationals" annually sold another $45 billion. By 1967 American corporations funded 80 percent of the vital European computer business and owned half of all modern industry in Britain. As the decade closed, the United States controlled nearly three-fourths of the world's oil and produced most of its machinery, electronics, and chemicals. Through the dissemination of technological products and practices, sophisticated corporations had assumed the mission of "Americanizing" the rest of the planet.

One of the most effective tools of American corporate prosperity was foreign aid, which surpassed $6.6 billion a year during the sixties. Aided by a 1968 "additionality" clause, which required foreign-aid recipients to "buy American," four-fifths of overseas assistance came back to the United States in spending on American products. Loans through government bodies such as the Agency for International Development (AID) and the Export-Import Bank helped underdeveloped nations meet the interest required by congressional foreign aid, but kept these nations in financial subservience to the United States. American assistance also maintained contracts for corporations based at home, as when food shipments to famine-stricken India were held up in 1966 while American oil companies negotiated to establish fertilizer plants in that nation. Military aid, particularly in Latin America, accustomed foreign governments to American products and

technology, and trained police and military forces. Such assistance helped to maintain social structures in which conservative elites exerted power and preserved investment stability for American corporations.

The conservative approach to foreign policy was clearest in Latin America, where Johnson adviser Thomas C. Mann proclaimed that the United States hoped to foster economic development and private investment, not social reform. As a result, Kennedy's Alliance for Progress floundered, and land reform, literacy, and distribution of wealth barely increased in the impoverished region. American preference for stability at any cost surfaced when the United States quickly recognized a repressive military regime after a Brazilian coup in 1964. Significantly, the coup officers who overthrew the constitutionally elected government had been trained under AID military assistance.

Johnson's Latin American policy crystalized with the invasion of the Dominican Republic in 1965, when constitutionalists took to arms to restore a president overthrown by the army. Already the beneficiaries of a $5 million American loan, the Dominican generals asked for American military assistance to "help restore peace." Johnson decided to intervene on the frantic advice of his Dominican ambassador, who alleged that fifty-three Communists were leading the constitutionalist movement. On television, the president explained that he was sending in the marines to save American lives and to prevent a "band of Communist conspirators" from wreaking disorder in an explosive situation. Enunciating a Johnson Doctrine, the chief executive proclaimed that "the American nations cannot, must not, and will not permit the establishment of another Communist government in the Western Hemisphere." Eventually, twenty-four thousand American troops supervised the creation of a new provisional government, but the hasty Dominican intervention seemed an overreaction by a great power to a minor dispute not central to its interests. Unilaterally, Johnson had decided that another Castro-type revolution in the hemisphere would not be tolerated.

The major instrument of American foreign policy in Latin America was not the military, but the Central Intelligence Agency. With little hindrance the CIA practiced "covert interference" in the internal affairs of poor countries that the United States wished to control or influence. Techniques included blackmail, bribery, forgery, bombing, sabotage, daily espionage, propaganda, disinformation (deliberate circulation of false information), psychological warfare, military training, and paramilitary activities. Financial support to individuals, political parties, private organizations, unions, and businesses also was common practice. American foreign policy advisers believed that the Cuban Revolution had stirred the forces of instability in the hemisphere. Their intention was to use the CIA to promote stability through assisting local governments to build up security forces and put down the violent Left. If economic growth and political stability were to continue, friendly governments needed time in which to effect the reforms that would prevent communism.

The CIA financed mass urban demonstrations against the leftist government in Brazil shortly before the 1964 coup. In Ecuador agency operatives worked to strengthen non-Communist trade unions and disrupt the revolutionary Left. Through agency auspices the State Department and AID funneled up to $20 million into the Chilean elections of 1964, where they were successful in contributing to the defeat of Salvador Allende, the Marxist candidate. In Peru the CIA secretly loaned helicopters, arms, and Green Beret training to the government effort to head off a guerrilla insurgency in the eastern jungles. During 1967 agency special operations officers assisted the Bolivian army in tracking down world revolutionary Che Guevara, who was quickly executed by the Bolivian government.

The same philosophy led to CIA intervention in the Congo in 1964, where agency mercenaries used American B-26 bombers to carry out regular missions against insurgents, while CIA money and arms supported the pro-Western government. In Laos, where American troops were prohibited by the 1962 Geneva Accords, the CIA maintained a private army of thirty-five thousand mountain tribesmen and recruited and financed another seventeen thousand Thais. Bombing and supply missions were flown by pilots hired through Air America, the agency's proprietary company in Southeast Asia. The secret program, not revealed until 1971, cost about $70 million a year.

By the end of the decade, American military power was awesome. The United States had 429 major and 2,972 minor military bases across the globe in thirty countries, and one million American service men and women were based overseas. The nation's military arsenal included one thousand nuclear-armed intercontinental missiles and seventy nuclear-powered and armed submarines. In fact, America's nuclear storehouse amounted to the equivalent of fifteen tons of TNT for every person in the world. The total tonnage of its navy was greater than that of all other nations combined. Costs for the military establishment ran to $216 million a day. Between 1945 and 1970, American taxpayers spent $1 trillion (one million millions) on defense. Yet, the late sixties brought the United States to the worst military and political disaster in its history, as military and techno-logical power proved impotent in Southeast Asia.

VIETNAM

One of Lyndon Johnson's first acts as president was to confer with Ambassador to South Vietnam Henry Cabot Lodge. Lodge delivered the grim news that attacks from the guerrilla arm of the National Liberation Front (NLF) had increased sharply. Johnson, who had presented Kennedy with a glowing firsthand report on American prospects in Vietnam in 1961, told Lodge that he was "not going to be the President who saw Southeast Asia go the way China went."

The nature of Johnson's commitment in Vietnam, however, differed significantly from that of Kennedy. In the last days of his life, Kennedy had ordered a reduction of American forces in Vietnam and had indicated a dissatisfaction with a military solution. But he had not publicized the changing direction of his policy. Moreover, prominent members of the New Frontier, such as Secretary Rusk, continued to favor full military operations.

After meeting with Lodge, therefore, Johnson canceled the withdrawal of troops and approved a program to accelerate covert attacks against North Vietnam and operations into Laos. Under secret plan 34A, implemented February 1964, hired Asian sabotage teams parachuted into North Vietnam, conducted commando raids against transportation targets, and kidnapped Vietnamese to gain intelligence information. American destroyers also patrolled the Gulf of Tonkin, while PT boats bombarded North Vietnamese coastal installations.

As Johnson continued to speak publicly against American military involvement in Vietnam, he proceeded with a covert war. He promised economic aid to both Vietnams if Hanoi would keep within the temporary border erected by the 1954 Geneva agreements. If not, he warned, the United States would devastate North Vietnam. In May 1964 the State Department secretly drafted a congressional resolution for a declaration of war. A CIA National Intelligence Estimate predicted that no other nation, with the possible exception of Cambodia, would succumb to communism if Laos and Vietnam fell. But Johnson, like his three predecessors in the White House, believed in the domino theory and in the need to maintain American credibility.

South Vietnamese ships began bombarding several North Vietnamese islands in the Gulf of Tonkin in July 1964. American destroyers, fit for electronic intelligence, accompanied them. When three North Vietnamese PT boats fired on one of the destroyers in what the United States described as international waters, four American fighter planes strafed the attackers. On August 4 the Americans claimed a second attack on the destroyer and a sister ship, although a subsequent report blamed "freak weather effects, and an overeager sonar man" for that impression, and the North Vietnamese vehemently denied the allegation.

Johnson, nevertheless, ordered an air reprisal on PT boat bases in North Vietnam. Addressing the American people on national television, the president assured that a "positive reply" was "being given as I speak to you tonight." Although American commitment would "be redoubled by this outrage," the president said, "we still seek no wider war." On August 7 Johnson went to Congress with a reworded version of the May declaration of war. The

MAP 15.1   SOUTH VIETNAM

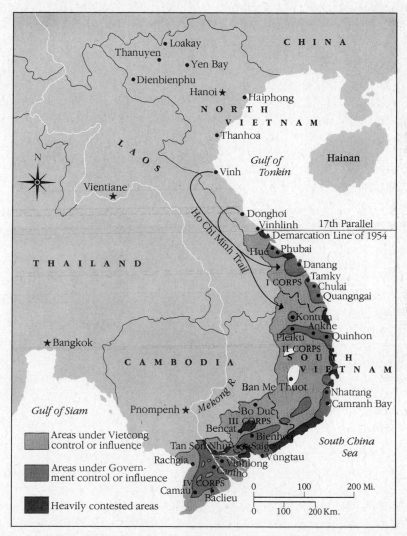

Areas under Vietcong control or influence

Areas under Government control or influence

Heavily contested areas

© 1966 by the New York Times Company. Reprinted by permission.

Tonkin Gulf Resolution stated the "Congress approves and supports the determination of the President as commander-in-chief to take all necessary measures to repel any attack against the forces of the United States and to prevent further aggression." The resolution passed the House 416–0 and the Senate 88–2, with only Wayne Morse of Oregon and Ernest Gruening of Alaska dissenting. A Harris poll also showed 85 percent approval of the air strikes against North Vietnam. The administration had stopped short of a full declaration of war, careful not to antagonize China or the Soviet Union. But Johnson had won a free hand to conduct a war by presidential discretion, and he continued to cite the Tonkin resolution as the legal basis of his Vietnam policy. This interpretation had a precedent in the Formosa Resolution of 1955.

As the United States increased its opposition to North Vietnam, street fighting by students and Buddhists erupted against the increasingly authoritarian regime in South Vietnam. On Christmas Eve 1964, an American billet in the heart of Saigon was blown up, killing two GIs and injuring eight. Johnson refused the strong response called for by the Pentagon. The turning point instead came in February 1965, when a company of NLF insurgents attacked an American base at Pleiku in the central highlands, killing 9 Americans and wounding 140. "They are killing our men while they sleep at night," a disturbed president told a congressional briefing. Johnson then announced Operation Flaming Dart, a program of retaliatory air strikes against North Vietnam. The president believed that the Pleiku attack was directed from Hanoi, perhaps even Peking, and vowed that he would not be scared out of Vietnam.

In response to American bombing raids, the Soviet Union and North Vietnam announced a "mutual aid" treaty in which the Soviets would supply antiaircraft weapons. A few days later the American barracks at Qui Nonh was blown up, killing twenty-three Americans. At this point the State Department retreated to a fixed position and rejected a French offer to arrange negotiations. Placing the conflict within the context of Cold War balance of power, Defense Secretary McNamara told a House committee that the United States would not leave Vietnam because China was making it a test of the Sino-Soviet rivalry. But McNamara's assistant secretary, John McNaughton, privately estimated that only 20 percent of American war aims concerned Chinese expansion and that merely another 10 percent involved a better life for the Vietnamese. The remaining 70 percent, McNaughton conceded, incorporated the necessity of avoiding a humiliating defeat for the United States. No doubt should ever be left, McNaughton stated in a top-secret Pentagon memorandum, "regarding American policy, power, resolve, and competence."

By March 1965 Operation Rolling Thunder began a full-scale bombing of North Vietnamese military installations. Poor accuracy marked the air force strikes, as North Vietnamese antiaircraft quickly discovered the direct routes flown by pilots anxious to add to their number of sorties. The result was a high loss of planes and indiscriminate bombing of schools, hospitals, and other civilian targets. Meanwhile, 3,500 recently arrived marines, still classified as "advisers," took the offensive for the first time in the American involvement on the ground, and Johnson authorized an additional 100,000 troops for Vietnam duty. The president explained his position at an address at Johns Hopkins University. We do not seek territory in Vietnam, he stated: "We fight because we must fight if we are to live in a world where every country can shape its own destiny." Johnson spoke of the commitment of the United States "to strengthen world order," to sustain the confidence of those who depend on America. "To withdraw from one battlefield means only to prepare for the next," the president explained. In conciliation, he proposed a $1 billion "Marshall Plan" for the Mekong Valley of South Vietnam. A Gallup poll showed that 61 percent of the sample approved the increased troop allotments. Johnson's decision to use ground troops in offensive action was designed to maintain enough force to prevent the Communists from winning, but not enough to antagonize China into full participation. The president was demonstrating that a limited war could be fought with conventional weapons.

By the summer of 1965, however, the war was no longer limited. American ground troops began their first full-scale combat offensive, engaging in "search-and-destroy" missions. In the air, B-52s flew three thousand miles from Guam to drop 750-pound bombs on suspected Viet Cong strongholds in South Vietnam. By the end of the year, American and South Vietnamese air attacks on the South surpassed seventy thousand strikes. December brought the first air strikes against industrial targets in the North, including a power plant just outside the chief North Vietnamese port of Haiphong. At Christmas Johnson declared the beginning of a thirty-seven-day bombing halt and sent emissaries around the world to explore possibilities for peace. But the stumbling block to negotiations was the refusal of the United States to recognize the National Liberation Front as a political force independent of North Vietnam. The administration contended that the North Vietnamese had invaded South Vietnam, and thereby denied that the United States had become embroiled in a civil war. When North Vietnamese infiltration continued during the bombing pause, American attacks on the North resumed.

Johnson would go no further than an offer to withdraw troops and end the bombing once a peace settlement was achieved.

Just as Congress approved a $14.7 billion supplemental expenditure for Vietnam, Johnson flew to Honolulu to embrace South Vietnamese leaders Nguyen Cao Ky and Nguyen Van Thieu and to pledge "social revolution" for the South and 385,000 more troops. Meanwhile, the resumption of bombing early in 1966 brought public hearings on Vietnam policy by the Senate Foreign Relations Committee. Led by Committee Chairman J. William Fulbright of Arkansas, several senators questioned the legality of the undeclared war and listened to retired Lieutenant General James A. Gavin become the first military man to oppose the war. Former State Department troubleshooter George F. Kennan, author of the containment policy toward the Soviet Union, testified that he felt "bewildered" by the commitment to defend a nonessential South Vietnam. In contrast, Ambassador to South Vietnam General Maxwell Taylor maintained it was essential to demonstrate the failure of "wars of liberation." It was clear that the administration had staked its reputation at home and abroad on the successful conclusion of the Vietnam War.

"We do not seek to enlarge this war," Johnson insisted in May 1966, "but we shall not run out on it." He testily predicted there would "be some Nervous Nellies and some who will become frustrated and bothered and break ranks under the strain." But bringing consensus to Vietnam was no easy task. In Danang and Hue, South Vietnamese marines were compelled to put down antigovernment demonstrations, as Ky led the forces capturing Buddhist pagodas. A new program of "pacification" began with the training of South Vietnamese cadres in the spring of 1966, but NLF control only increased in the northern provinces. Furthermore, elections promoted by the United States only proceeded when "neutralists," "pro-Communists," and areas under insurgent influence were excluded.

Starting in June 1966, the United States began to bomb central Hanoi. "We must continue to raise the price of aggression at its source," Johnson explained in the language of militant retaliation. The goal of American bombing had changed from breaking the enemy's will to cutting supply lines. But the CIA and Defense Intelligence Agency reported that sixteen months of bombing had brought "no measurable direct effect on Hanoi's ability to mount and support military operations in the South." One pilot in every forty sorties was lost in the bombing program. Johnson promised that the United States would stop bombing if the North Vietnamese pledged to send no more troops south, but Hanoi responded that peace depended on withdrawal of all American troops and bases and peaceful reunification of the two Vietnams. In turn, Johnson informed American allies in Asia that South Vietnam must be preserved. The president also made a surprise visit to a military base in Vietnam, where he gave a rousing speech urging American soldiers to "come home with that coonskin on the wall." The warrior mentality still prevailed. Back in the United States for the congressional elections of 1966, the president reminded Americans that they were "outnumbered fifteen-to-one" in the world and that "we have what they want."

But Johnson's efforts were to no avail. Military advisers repeatedly made the error of assuming that lessened Viet Cong combat operations indicated diminished capability, when the VC only were adapting new strategies after American escalations. Furthermore, American denial of civilian damage from the bombing in North Vietnam was belied when the *New York Times* published firsthand reports by correspondent Harrison Salisbury that described the destruction in central Hanoi. By the fall of 1966, Defense Secretary McNamara, disillusioned by plane and pilot losses, rejected a Pentagon troop request for the first time and privately called for a new initiative toward a political settlement. When McNamara vetoed General Westmoreland's plea for 300,000 more troops early in 1967, the defense secretary commissioned a systematic study of Vietnam policy, later to be called the Pentagon Papers, to re-examine the original strategies behind the war. McNamara eventually settled on fifty-five thousand more troops, assuring a half-million-man ground force for 1968. But by December 1967, Johnson's impatience with the ambivalence of his Pentagon chief led to McNamara's resignation and appointment to the World Bank.

As Americans confronted regular North Vietnamese troops, casualty figures jumped feverishly. In one battle a mistaken air force strike against an American position killed thirty GIs. Meanwhile, the NLF controlled the timing and terms of nearly four-fifths of the military engagements in the southern provinces by mid-1967. In turn, pacification in the South became increasingly bloody.

Beginning as a counter-insurgency program to win "hearts and minds," pacification evolved into a terror campaign that herded refugees into "strategic hamlets" for "protection" from guerrilla insurgents. To destroy Viet Cong hideouts, bases, and sources of food, American planes dropped napalm, defoliants, and herbicides in South Vietnam. Napalm burned everything it touched, including the skin of human beings, while fragmentation bombs hopelessly destroyed internal organs with millions of tiny particles that could not be detected by X rays.

MAP 15.2   THE TET OFFENSIVE, 1968

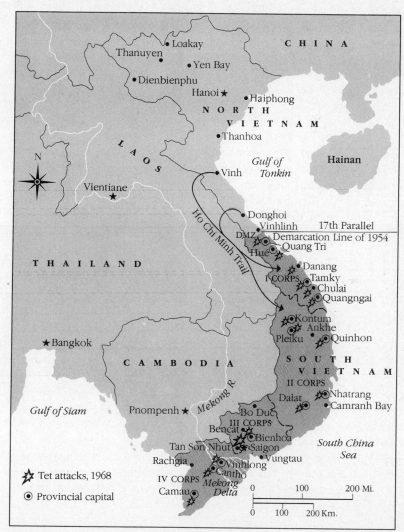

Reprinted by permission from TIME, *The Weekly Newsmagazine; Copyright Time Inc. 1968*

Bombing in the South was indiscriminate and lethal to civilians who often were listed in "body counts" as "suspected Viet Cong." After villages were bombed, peasants were relocated, a strategy promoted by American social scientists as "forced urbanization." These campaigns also involved the arrest and interrogation of suspected members of the "Viet Cong infrastructure." Aided by a central computer in Saigon that assigned "neutralization" quotas for each province, teams of Vietnamese "Revolutionary Development" units conducted systematized kidnapping, torture, and assassination programs in the villages. The CIA, which trained and supervised the Vietnamese cadres, estimated the death toll from this Operation Phoenix to be at least twenty thousand.

The futility of the American effort in Vietnam was brought home by the Communist Tet Offensive in February 1968, a coordinated attack on every major city in South Vietnam planned in conjunction with internal revolutionary uprisings. In Saigon a commando attack on the United States Embassy brought five American deaths and a six-hour battle with marine guards and military police. For twenty-eight days, the Communists held Hue, the capital of old Vietnam, where they executed police officials and pro-Americans, while block-by-block fighting, bombing, and shelling continued incessantly. The South Vietnamese, in turn, executed Buddhists, students, and teachers as "VC collaborators." An estimated thirty-two thousand insurgents were killed during Tet, while over four thousand Americans lost their lives and nearly twenty thousand were wounded. Although the Communists withdrew from the major cities they had captured, the Tet Offensive destroyed any war optimism still surviving in the United States, and more than half the American people turned against the

war for the first time. Despite Pentagon claims of victory, Tet demonstrated that the Viet Cong and North Vietnamese only had to survive in order to prevent the United States from "winning" the war. It also revealed the impotence of a South Vietnamese Army unable to defend positions without American air or artillery assistance.

Several aspects of the Tet confrontation were particularly disturbing. At Khe Sanh three hundred marines were killed in a seventy-seven day siege by surrounding North Vietnamese regiments. Following the battle, the Americans abandoned the position as of no value. In the Mekong Delta one thousand pro-Saigon villagers were killed by American artillery and air strikes. The commanding air force major explained that "it became necessary to destroy the town to save it." In the village of Son My, an untested company in the Americal Division was unable to find an NLF batallion that army intelligence had located in the area. Tense and under pressure to build up the VC body count, Lt. William L. Calley's men lined up over four hundred villagers, mostly old people, women, and children, and shot them all. The My Lai massacre, not disclosed until 1969, was reported in army records as an important victory involving enemy sniper attacks and fierce fighting. By the end of March 1968, however, Pentagon and presidential credibility concerning the war were exhausted.

THE WAR AT HOME

As dissent against the Vietnam War escalated, the Johnson administration adopted measures to impose a consensus by force. Beginning in 1968, the FBI applied its counterintelligence capacities to further what Bureau Director J. Edgar Hoover saw as a crusade "to expose, disrupt, and otherwise neutralize the activities of the New Left." Records of "black-bag jobs" (burglaries) against "domestic subversive targets" were placed in a special "Do Not File" file. COINTELPRO, as the Bureau called its program, also attempted to widen the rift between radical organizations through falsely attributed letters and undercover agents. In California, COINTELPRO agents hired a prostitute infected with venereal disease to seduce New Left leaders and discredit them with campus followers.

But the FBI's major target was Martin Luther King. Hoover feared the civil rights movement might produce a "black messiah" who would unite American blacks in a movement to disrupt society. When Attorney General Robert Kennedy authorized wiretaps on King's telephones in 1963, the FBI went further and placed "bugs" (electronic recording devices) in his bedroom. Kennedy desired to ascertain Communist influence on King and approved the taps on a trial basis. But stung by the minister's attacks on Bureau handling of civil rights cases, the FBI conducted a full-scale public relations vendetta to discredit and intimidate King.

FBI activity was duplicated by other intelligence agencies. Following the Watts riots in 1965, army intelligence began to gather information to be used when troops were called to police civil disturbances. A "domestic war room" in the Pentagon treated campus and urban demonstrators as "insurgents" whose actions aided the Communists. By 1968 the army had compiled 100,000 dossiers on antiwar activists and elected officials and employed one thousand undercover agents to spy on American citizens. During the summer of 1967, Johnson also

established a Special Operations Group in the CIA. "Operation Chaos" kept files on seventy-two hundred Americans and trained agency recruits by assigning them domestic surveillance of dissidents, demonstrators, and even "suspicious" members of Congress. The program also instituted wiretaps and break-ins against radicals and featured a computerized index that included the names of 300,000 individuals and organizations. Since the CIA charter prohibited agency domestic operations, Operation Chaos was blatantly illegal. But when the CIA attempted to convince Johnson that domestic dissent was independent of foreign funding, the president was reluctant to accept the findings.

Johnson had hoped to finance the war without cutting Great Society funding. But as war costs rose to $2 billion a month by 1966, Johnson admitted that "guns and butter" were not always compatible. In a year of record federal spending overseas, Congress abolished the school milk program and sliced money for education. While Democrats defeated Republican attempts to dismantle OEO, Congress required that community action funds be channeled through public officials, and the antipoverty agency struggled along on half its projected funding.

Despite the need to cut spending, Johnson desired to forestall social strife by keeping the Great Society alive. Korean War veterans won educational aid in 1966, while the president signed a bill that raised minimum wages by one-fourth and covered farmworkers for the first time. The 1967 school aid bill was the largest in history and was followed the next year by an urban development package that provided the most generous housing allotment since 1949. Johnson also approved creation of a cabinet-level Department of Transportation and signed a $330 million model cities bill. A

Robert Francis Kennedy

1925-1968

The death of Robert Kennedy signaled the end of hope in a turbulent era desperately in need of conciliation. Kennedy had served as the New Frontier's principal power broker — presidential campaign manager in 1960, attorney general, and personal adviser to his brother's presidency. A tough Irish-American who believed in Cold War vigilance, he helped to fashion counter-insurgency in Vietnam and personally supervised the CIA's covert campaigns in Cuba and elsewhere. But Dallas tore his world apart, and Kennedy began a new career in 1964 as the junior senator from New York.

Affected by his own personal tragedy, Kennedy used his Senate prestige to push for greater commitments toward those without privilege or power. He visited Cesar Chavez's grape strikers in California, took testimony on malnutrition in Mississippi, conducted hearings on the squalor of reservation life in New Mexico. In an eloquent denunciation of American materialism, he warned in 1967 that "We cannot measure national spirit by the Dow-Jones Average, nor national achievement by the gross national product."

Kennedy was not among the first to question the Vietnam War. But early in 1966 he issued a cautious call for a coalition government in Saigon. A year later Kennedy took the Senate floor to condemn the administration's bombing: "We are all participants.... We must also feel as men the anguish of what it is we are doing." In November 1967 he delivered a spontaneous tirade on national television against American slaughter of the Vietnamese. Commentators began to speculate on his availability for the presidency, but Kennedy was too much of a professional Democrat to risk splitting the party in a personal vendetta against an incumbent president. Once again, however, he was moved by events beyond his control.

The eighty-five-day campaign of Robert Kennedy stirred an emotional groundswell never before seen in American politics. Kennedy proposals for a draft lottery, corporate ghetto development, and Vietnam negotiations were modest. But "Bobby" symbolized the lost idealism of the New Frontier, the flickering hope that all classes and races really could share in the American Dream. He campaigned on the streets, jacket off, tie loose, and sleeves rolled up. Excited crowds swarmed along the primary trail just to touch his hand.

When Martin Luther King was assassinated in April 1968, Kennedy went directly to a ghetto street gathering in Indianapolis and shared his own feelings of loss by quoting the Greek poet Aeschylus. A nearby graffiti explained his remarkable following among American blacks: "Kennedy white but alright./The one before, he opened the door." But the secret to the Kennedy campaign was the compassion he expressed toward all the nation's working people and dispossessed. Despite his stance against the war, the tough-minded senator scored heavy primary pluralities in white districts that had previously supported George Wallace.

Robert Kennedy was the only leader of his era who might have united white working people, antiwar students, and the racial minorities in a coalition for change. At the Democratic Convention in Chicago, members wept and sang the "Battle Hymn of the Republic" in his memory.

truth-in-lending bill, signed in 1968, required that consumers be told the costs of loans and installment plans in terms of annual rates.

Although these were substantial accomplishments for a nation at war, ghetto and campus rioting hurt further liberal proposals. When Johnson followed King's "open city" campaign in Chicago with submission of an equal housing bill in 1966, two attempts to end a Senate filibuster failed, and the administration settled for a $40 million appropriation for rat control in city slums. Congress responded to campus antiwar disorders in 1968 by stipulating that students convicted of disruptions could not receive federal funds.

Congressional uneasiness with domestic programs also reflected the soaring inflation precipitated by spending for the war. By 1968 the defense budget reached $70 billion. Johnson had prevailed upon Congress to suspend Kennedy's investment tax credit and had accelerated depreciation allowances in 1966, but these minor tax increases proved insufficient. The president suffered a severe legislative setback the following year when Congress refused to accept his war tax surcharge, preferring either spending cutbacks or tax reform. Johnson finally won a 10 percent surcharge on individual and corporate income taxes in 1968. But to satisfy fiscal conservatives, he was forced to accept a restriction on domestic spending and federal employment of civilians. The delay in taxing inflated profits and incomes. This inflation combined with war spending to bring a phenomenal rise in the federal deficit. From $3.8 billion in 1966, the deficit leaped to $8.7 billion in 1967 and a catastrophic $25.2 billion in 1968. As a result, the consumer price index rose 5 percent in 1968 alone.

Wartime inflation was particularly harmful to the elderly and others on fixed incomes, as well as to the forty million Americans who constituted the working class. But Americans of modest income feared tax increases that would aggravate their financial burdens, while the banking community worried that raised interest rates would discourage installment buying and home purchases. Given the widespread reluctance to cut defense in wartime, public opinion responded to the threat of inflation by calling for cutbacks in liberal welfare programs. Deficit spending under Kennedy and Johnson actually had stimulated business activity more than government programs. But as the financial pressures of the Vietnam War built up after 1965, many Americans began to resent reforms that seemed to benefit professional program administrators, dissatisfied students, and rebellious minorities. Although statistics continued to emphasize the poor standing of blacks in income and employment, many working-class and middle-class whites believed that hard-earned tax dollars were benefiting blacks while they were left to face an intolerable economic squeeze on their own.

The conservative backlash to the Great Society surfaced in the congressional elections of 1966. Stressing "crime in the streets" and the need for "law and order," Republicans gained forty-seven seats in the House and three in the Senate. Democrats warned that education, jobs, better housing, and an end to discrimination were needed to eliminate domestic strife, but were hampered by the realization that Great Society spending had to be reduced in the face of war costs. In Georgia, segregationist Lester Maddox, who had defied the Civil Rights Act of 1964 by chasing blacks from his restaurant with a pistol, was elected governor in a runoff in the state assembly.

"Law and order" meant that voters were sensitive to the increase in offenses against persons, which more than doubled between 1960 and 1968. In New York City a special election defeated by a 2–1 margin the creation of a civilian review board to monitor police. Concern over crime also resulted in the Crime Control and Safe Streets Act of 1968, which provided grants to upgrade local law enforcement, authorized wiretapping with a warrant, and banned interstate shipment of handguns and their sale to minors. As a response to urban rioting, the law disqualified from federal employment anyone convicted of a riot-related felony. Most important, the omnibus bill attempted to reverse *Miranda* v. *Arizona*, the Supreme Court decision of 1966 that ruled that police must inform criminal suspects of their rights. The Crime Control Act responded to conservative ire about "permissiveness" toward criminals by providing that voluntary confessions were admissible in federal trials.

This concern over social and economic disorder enabled Alabama Governor George Wallace to attract a massive following by 1968. Wallace won extensive working-class support in rural and small-town areas of the South, but elsewhere his support was divided equally between working people and the middle class. A large segment of the Wallace movement also consisted of noncollege youth, polarized to the Right by the confrontation politics of campus radicalism. Wallace articulated deeply held resentments toward liberal government programs, ghetto rioting, and student rebellion, but also emphasized the importance of property rights and local government. When he announced his presidential candidacy in the American Independent party in February 1968, Wallace promised to maintain social peace with "30,000 troops with two-foot-long bayonets." He called for repeal of civil rights laws and a forceful pursuit of the war in Vietnam. To emphasize his confidence in the military, Wallace chose former Air Force Chief of Staff Curtis Le May as his running mate. Le May dampened the Wallace upsurge with a thoughtless quip about bombing North Vietnam back to the Stone Age. But the campaign also spoke to grassroots impatience with the two major parties.

Despite Wallace's prowar appeal, blue-collar support of the war was only 1 percent above that of the rest of the nation in 1966. Late in 1967 a national sample disapproved of Johnson's handling of the war by a 68–22 percent margin, but also viewed peace demonstrations as "acts of disloyalty against the boys fighting in Vietnam." Those who defended the war felt the president had the facts. Even if he did not, sentiment to support the troops was very strong. A New York City march "supporting our men in Vietnam" attracted seventy thousand people in 1967.

THE CHAOS OF '68

Although the administration put on a bold front, the Tet Offensive brought an end to the Johnson war policy and ushered in the most calamitous year in American political history since the Civil War. Westmoreland continued to request at least 200,000 more troops and mobilization of the reserves. His proposal would have added $12 billion to war costs already reaching $30 billion a year. But Clark Clifford, who had replaced McNamara as defense secretary, found extensive "dove" sentiment among top Pentagon civilians. Poring over pessimistic military and CIA reports, Clifford discovered that the past year's bombing had only tripled North Vietnamese infiltration rates. Beginning in February 1968, Clifford quietly rallied sup-

port within the administration for a reduction of the costly war effort. On March 12 antiwar Senator Eugene McCarthy astounded the nation by taking 42 percent of the vote in the New Hampshire Democratic primary. Four days later Robert Kennedy announced his candidacy for the presidential nomination. On March 18, 139 members of the House called for a congressional review of the administration's war program. Four days later Johnson relieved Westmoreland of the Vietnam command and summoned a meeting of the Senior Informal Advisory Group.

The March 22 conference included twelve of the most prestigious members of the nation's foreign policy, business, and law establishment, men who constituted the cream of the American corporate elite. Nearly all had approved the escalation of bombing in 1967. But present policy, a majority concurred, could not achieve its objectives without the use of unlimited resources for another five years. This was impossible, the group counseled, without citizen support and budgetary sacrifices. Former Treasury Secretary Douglas Dillon, former Undersecretary of State George Ball, former Deputy Defense Secretary Cyrus Vance, and Wall Street luminary John McCloy, all of whom saw Europe as the proper arena for American economic expansion, emphasized the strain on the dollar abroad and the threat to international monetary stability. Generals Omar Bradley and Matthew Ridgway vacillated in support of the bombing. But the climax to the meeting came when former Secretary of State Dean Acheson, whom Johnson deeply respected, argued that the bombing was more damaging to the administration in Washington than the regime in Hanoi. Acheson described the Joint Chiefs of Staff as "mad" and said the president's speeches were so out of touch with reality that "nobody could believe them." The war had brought a loss of national purpose, Acheson warned, and eclipsed the "most critical priority of all"—the home front.

Johnson and his advisers had believed that wars of national liberation were Communist efforts to wear down the West and eventually surround the United States and Europe with hostile forces. They had faith that American power and idealism could stop Communist revolts, even when they occurred against corrupt and authoritarian regimes. Strong leadership, Johnson believed, could overcome obstacles at home and abroad. He hoped to be remembered as a great president. But the twelve "wise men" whom Johnson had summoned buttressed Senator Fulbright's 1965 observation that the nation was "losing its perspective on what exactly is within the realm of its power and what is beyond it." Following the meeting, Clifford told Johnson that a "peace speech" was in order for the television talk the president had scheduled to precede the Wisconsin primary. Johnson resisted, but the polls had turned against him, the press spoke of a "credibility gap," and hostile demonstrators greeted him at every turn. On March 31 Johnson stunned the nation when he explained that "I shall not seek, and I will not accept, the nomination of my party for another term as your president." He also announced suspension of bombing above North Vietnam's 20th parallel and indicated a willingness to include the NLF in peace negotiations.

Johnson hoped that his withdrawal from the presidential race would encourage peace prospects and lead to the healing of bitter wounds at home. But the difficulty of achieving domestic peace was underscored when Martin Luther King was assassinated by a self-proclaimed white racist on April 4, the day after the North Vietnamese had agreed to peace talks. Riots immediately erupted in black ghettos across the country. Whole blocks between the White House and the Capitol were burned out after three days of looting and arson in predominantly black Washington. In Chicago, Mayor Daley ordered police to "shoot to kill arsonists and shoot to maim looters." All told, rioting occurred in 168 cities and towns, producing forty-three deaths and two thousand arrests. But within a week of King's death in Memphis, Congress passed Johnson's long-delayed open housing bill. The Civil Rights Act of 1968 banned racial discrimination in the sale and rental of about four-fifths of the nation's housing. It also outlawed crossing interstate lines with intent to incite riot or disorder.

Johnson's withdrawal opened up the possibility of an antiwar Democratic candidacy. Minnesota Senator McCarthy had announced his intention to test rising sentiment for a negotiated settlement late in 1967. When college and peace volunteers presented him with an awesome organization, McCarthy broadened his criticism with attacks on an arrogant military and an overextended presidency. Government's role was to liberate people, not to organize them, he preached, as young activists flocked to the "get clean for Gene" crusade. Conservatives also responded to McCarthy's emphasis on limited government, lessened expectations, and personal honesty.

Robert Kennedy, who was elected senator from New York in 1964, moved more slowly to an antiwar stance. Up to 1968, Kennedy was reluctant to split the Democratic party by challenging an incumbent president. But following the New Hampshire primary, Kennedy told Clark Clifford that he would seek the nomination if the president did not create a special commission to explore a wider peace approach. Johnson vehemently rejected the proposal. Kennedy then announced his candidacy, believing that the McCarthy crusade had demonstrated the political futility of the president's position. He called for a Vietnam peace settlement based on political compromise, arguing that the nation should not subordinate the national interest to an "incompetent military regime," and linked Vietnam to neglect of domestic issues. Kennedy's compassion and enthusiasm attracted a wide spectrum of minorities, working-class Catholics, labor supporters, and students. On June 4 he won the California primary. But minutes later, Kennedy was assassinated by Sirhan Sirhan, a Palestinian who opposed Kennedy's pro-Israel position.

The assassinations of Kennedy and King had a devastating effect on the majority of the American people. It seemed that only death awaited young men of vision and energy, that attempts to stop the killing in Vietnam were futile. As it became clear that Vice President Humphrey, who entered the presidential race late in April, would take the nomination, peace activists and young radicals went to Chicago to demonstrate at the Democratic Convention. Inside the convention hall, Mayor Daley had erected the most elaborate security measures in American political history. A private security force issued electronically scanned passes to delegates and used force to control reporters, delegates, and visitors. A minority platform report, sponsored by Senators McCarthy, George McGovern, and Edward Kennedy, called for an unconditional end to the Vietnam bombing,

MAP 15.3   THE ELECTION OF 1968

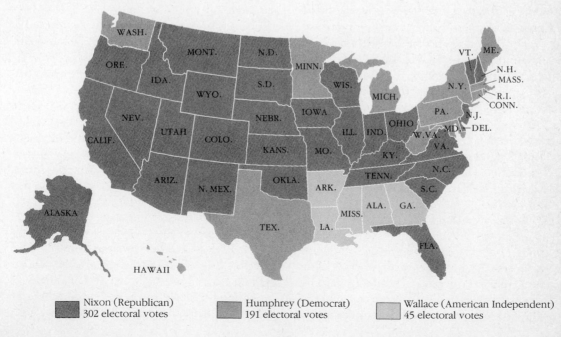

Nixon (Republican)
302 electoral votes

Humphrey (Democrat)
191 electoral votes

Wallace (American Independent)
45 electoral votes

negotiated withdrawal, and a Saigon coalition with the NLF. But the doves were unable to overcome administration pressure, and the measure failed by a 3–2 margin. While clubbed and Maced demonstrators on Chicago streets chanted "The whole world is watching!" the presidential balloting proceeded on the convention floor. Rising to nominate George McGovern of South Dakota, who had won the endorsement of Kennedy's California delegates, Senator Abraham Ribicoff denounced "Gestapo tactics on the streets of Chicago." Daley shot to his feet, shouting obscenities at the speaker, and the hall erupted in pandemonium.

Backed by organized labor and the party professionals, Humphrey easily won the nomination. But the Democrats were so badly split that the vice president's chances seemed slim. Humphrey's major problem was achieving an independence from the Johnson war policy that would not offend the party mainstream. For Americans sickened by the war, Humphrey's enthusiastic support of the hawk position was unforgivable. In October he finally broke with Johnson, announcing in Salt Lake City that he would risk an unconditional cessation of all bombing. From then on, Humphrey and running mate Edmund Muskie rose dramatically in the polls, but it was too late. Even Johnson's last-minute announcement on October 31 that he had completely stopped the bombing was not enough to erase the image of chaos and violence that voters associated with the Chicago convention.

While the Democrats wrestled with the war, Richard Nixon sailed to an easy Republican nomination. Overcoming the image of "loser," the former vice president took primary after primary, cultivating a new aura of maturity and mellow reflection. Although he did not provide details, Nixon pledged new leadership to "end the war and win the peace in the Pacific." He hinted at a Great Power settlement of the conflict and the creation of a new global balance of power. Nixon pictured the strongest nation in the world tied down in an endless war, unable to manage its economy, and overwhelmed by lawlessness. He promised to "bring the American people together," and chose Maryland Governor Spiro T. Agnew for the vice presidency.

On election day Nixon and Agnew won by less than a percentage point. Wallace's Independent party, which hoped to deprive anyone of an electoral college plurality and send the contest into the House of Representatives, amassed nearly 14 percent of the vote. Surprisingly, much of the Democratic coalition of labor, blacks, Catholics, Jews, and urban voters held together in 1968. But in the South, Humphrey scored less than 30 percent, and Nixon and Wallace carried 57 percent of the national electorate.

The turbulent events of the sixties shook faith in the political system. A government credibility gap and violent dissent brought widespread alienation from conventional politics. Accordingly, independents rose from 22 percent of the electorate in 1965 to 30 percent by 1969. But alienation was not necessarily helpful to the youthful insurgents of the Democratic party and the Movement Left. By decade's end, six-sevenths of all voters were over the age of thirty and the great majority of voters, as conservative political analysts indicated, were "unyoung, unpoor, and unblack." As 1968 ended, the American death toll in Vietnam passed thirty thousand, and a half million troops remained in that distant outpost of national aspirations. A weary nation looked to Richard Nixon to restore tranquillity at home and a dignified peace abroad.

SUGGESTED READINGS

A thorough synthesis of the politics of the Great Society appears in the relevant chapters of Jim F. Heath, *Decade of Disillusionment: The Kennedy-Johnson Years* (1975). Segments of Alexander Kendrick, *The Wound Within: America in the Vietnam Years, 1945–1974* (1974), trace the connections between Johnson foreign policy and domestic developments. A useful history of the sixties is William L. O'Neill, *Coming Apart: An Informal History of America in the 1960s* (1971). Two anthologies that address the political controversies of the era are Jerome M. Mileur, ed., *The Liberal Tradition in Crisis: American Politics in the Sixties* (1974), and Marvin E. Gettleman and David Mermelstein, eds., *The Great Society Reader: The Failure of American Liberalism* (1967). Peter Joseph, *Good Times: An Oral History of America in the Nineteen Sixties* (1974), offers excellent material from interviews with prominent Americans of the decade.

The economics of the corporate state are analyzed in John K. Galbraith, *The New Industrial State* (1967). A useful synthesis that includes material on sixties business consolidation is Robert L. Heilbroner and Aaron Singer, *The Economic Transformation of America* (1977). G. William Domhoff, *Who Rules America?* (1967), presents considerable data on the economic elite, while urban renewal and ghetto problems are addressed in several essays in Alexander B. Callow, Jr., ed., *American Urban History: An Interpretive Reader with Commentaries* (1969).

Johnson's domestic political problems are analyzed by Eric Goldman, *The Tragedy of Lyndon Johnson: A Historian's Personal Interpretation* (1969), and Thomas Powers, *The War at Home: Vietnam and the American People, 1964–1967* (1973). The brief essay on Johnson in William A. Williams, *Some Presidents, from Wilson to Nixon* (1972), combines New Left analysis with sympathies toward the president as a southerner. See also George E. Reedy, *The Twilight of the Presidency* (1970). Johnson's political opponents are described in Richard Rovere, *The Goldwater Caper* (1965), David Halberstam, *The Unfinished Odyssey of Robert Kennedy* (1968), and Lewis Chester, Godfrey Hodgson, and Bruce Page, *An American Melodrama: The Presidential Campaign of 1968* (1969).

The Vietnam War is placed into the perspective of the battle against communism in the relevant chapters of Walter LaFeber, *America, Russia, and the Cold War, 1945–1971* (1972). Walt W. Rostow, *The Diffusion of Power* (1972), presents an overview of foreign policy from the standpoint of the Kennedy-Johnson administrations, while *The Pentagon Papers* (1971) presents the documents instrumental in American decision making in Vietnam since 1945. Richard J. Barnet, *Roots of War: The Men and Institutions Behind U.S. Foreign Policy* (1972), places Vietnam within the context of national security management. For a critique of liberal intervention in Vietnam, see Halberstam, *The Best and the Brightest* (1972). Johnson's abandonment of escalation in 1968 is treated by former Pentagon official Townsend Hoopes, *The Limits of Intervention* (1972). Relevant chapters in Gabriel Kolko, *Roots of American Foreign Policy* (1969), offer a radical critique of the war and can be supplemented by segments of the more informal Felix Greene, *The Enemy: What Every American Should Know About Imperialism* (1970). The most informative work on the CIA is Victor Marchetti and John D. Marks, *The CIA and the Cult of Intelligence* (1974).

Chapter 16

FRAGMENTATION OF AMERICAN SOCIETY, 1960-1980

"We stand on the edge of a New Frontier," President John Kennedy proclaimed in 1961. "It would be easy to shrink from that frontier —to look to the safe mediocrity of the past." Like Theodore Roosevelt in 1901, Kennedy asked young Americans to reject a life of comfort and personal pleasure for one of hardship and military discipline. "I am asking each of you," the president continued, "to be new pioneers on that New Frontier." And Kennedy pleaded for young people to "pay any price, bear any burden, meet any hardship" to make that New Frontier a success.

The nation's first Catholic president thus attempted to revitalize the urban-industrial frontier first conceived by Roosevelt and the Progressive leadership. By involving standards of sacrifice and collective heroism, Kennedy also recalled the pattern of social values established by middle-class Anglo-Protestants during the Progressive years. So too did another Catholic, Vincent Lombardi, coach of the professional football team, the Green Bay Packers. In the 1960s Lombardi became the most important spokesman for football as the game that taught the virtues of military discipline. Like Kennedy, Lombardi stressed the necessity of victory. "Winning," he declared, "isn't everything. It is the only thing."

THE CRISIS OF ADOLESCENCE

The emergence of Catholic leaders such as Kennedy and Lombardi in the 1960s demonstrated that the prosperity brought by World War Two had lifted many Catholics out of working-class and into middle-class status. By the sixties, Irish Catholics had achieved levels of income and education approaching that of such Anglo-Protestant groups as Episcopalians and Presbyterians. But the rise of Catholic leaders not only signified Catholic assimilation to Anglo-Protestant middle-class values; it also revealed underlying weaknesses in that middle-class structure. Such figures as Kennedy and Lombardi were popular precisely because established middle-class people as well as recent entrants into that class were apprehensive that their children were losing a sense of discipline and ambition.

The first signs of a youth rebellion were directed against a social pattern constructed at the end of the nineteenth century. The white Protestant upper middle class in the 1890s had pressured American children into embracing a new pattern of adolescence. This pattern reflected basic economic changes in post–Civil War society. By the beginning of the twentieth century, most young members of the upper middle class could no longer expect to become independent businesspeople. Instead, job opportunities for them increasingly were found in large corporations or in government bureaucracies. Economic success increasingly depended on advanced education. But lengthy schooling extended the time of a child's dependence on parents and schools. Consequently, social, sexual, and economic independence for upper-middle-class youth was to be delayed at least until the age of twenty-two. To fill the years between fourteen and twenty-two, a special youth culture, centered on competitive sports, gradually evolved under the guidance of adults.

At the beginning of the twentieth century, the most important of these sports was football.

The game had developed in the late nineteenth century as an elite activity for the 5 percent of young men who went to college. In football, a successful play required every member of the team to move at the same time. The young men who played football frequently became corporate executives who had the responsibility to get thousands of employees to start work at the same time. Football reflected the rhythms of corporate competition, not mere rivalry as between independent farmers or small businessmen. Team cooperation and precision approximated the discipline of competing armies. Unlike baseball, a sport in which the length of innings was unpredictable and the pace frequently was relaxed, football involved the pressure of playing against the clock.

The upsurge of professional football after 1945 coincided with the rapid increase in the number of American college students. In 1940 only one-sixth of the eighteen-year-old population went on to college. But the dramatic increase of automation in industry and the mechanization of agriculture meant that most new jobs were to be found in the white-collar sector. As a result, young people were encouraged to go beyond high school in preparation for the changing job market. By expanding state teachers colleges into more diversified institutions and establishing new state colleges and junior colleges, it was possible by 1965 to enroll 50 percent of all teenagers into higher education.

As many children of Catholic blue-collar workers moved up to white-collar status between 1945 and 1965, however, the offspring of the Anglo-Protestant establishment were reacting to a profound contradiction of values. The growth of a corporate economy since 1920 had fed upon the stimulation of consumer demand. Consumerism accelerated as the baby boom of 1940 to 1958 increased average family size to almost four children. As larger numbers of young people began to move through high schools and colleges in the early 1960s, advertisers quickly turned to this vastly expanded youth market. To take advantage of the affluence of so many middle-class children, corporate advertisers stressed how separate the young were from parents and encouraged youngsters to buy products designed especially for them.

The marketing of these special records, clothes, food, and movies intensified the problem of identity for young men. Under the pattern of adolescence developed in the 1890s, youngsters were expected to learn discipline to contain their energies before they left home to compete successfully for careers. Young men were supposed to avoid all kinds of pleasures that might weaken that discipline. They were encouraged to dress in scout uniforms and march in the woods under the direction of adults and were urged to train for uniformed competitive sports under the same kind of leadership. But advertising told them to enjoy pleasure and relax at home as their mothers and fathers did. By the 1960s, mass media suggested that almost everyone was going on to college and that careers were easily available. Why then should American youngsters discipline themselves in preparation for a world of ruthless competition when there was a world of plenty?

Much of the development of a generation gap in the 1960s, therefore, came from a rebellion by upper-middle-class children against the late-nineteenth century idea of adolescence held by their parents. But it is clear that this counterculture built on attitudes that had been causing contradictions within the lifestyle of the middle class since at least the 1920s.

Most of the young men and women of the upper middle class during the 1960s rejected the delay of social and sexual independence demanded by the old style of adolescence. They had begun to identify in the late 1950s with Elvis Presley because they saw him as a representative of lower-income whites and blacks who still became socially and sexually independent at an early age. By 1964 the Beatles, a musical group whose members were raised in the slums of Liverpool, England, had become a much more powerful and explicit symbol of teenage sexuality. By the mid-sixties, sexual expression by rock musicians on stage was much more explicit than that of Elvis Presley or Chubby Checker at the end of the fifties. The total liberation of the body became a major objective of the counterculture in the 1960s.

WOODSTOCK NATION AND THE NEW ADOLESCENCE

As many middle-class youths rebelled against the restraints or inhibitions that characterized the old model of adolescence, they began to claim the right to sexual and social independence during their college years. This rebellion radically changed college lifestyles. Until the 1960s college administrations acted on the philosophy of *in loco parentis*. The administrators, especially the deans of men and women, had the responsibility of seeing that the students did not act like adults in making social and sexual decisions. Strict dormitory regulations were established. Both male and female students were required to be in their rooms at a certain hour in the evening. Sexual mixing was strictly forbidden. All of these regulations broke down in the 1960s to the point where at some

With the great increase in national wealth after World War Two, middle-class Americans from every part of the country began to visit Reno and Las Vegas, Nevada, where gambling was legal. The emergence of Las Vegas as a center of middle-class recreation indicated how dramatically patterns of middle-class morality and economic values had changed since 1900. (UPI Photos)

colleges male and female students shared the same dormitories.

The majority of middle-class young people compromised their rebellion and accepted continued economic dependence on their parents until graduation from college and entrance into the work force. A minority, however, "dropped out" of college; some even dropped out of high school and refused to enter the "straight" economic lifestyle of the "establishment." Many of those who remained in school occasionally used drugs, especially marijuana, as a sign of their rebellion. The old principle of adolescence had insisted that no consciousness-altering drugs, including alcohol, should be available to the young. Yet the lifestyle of the suburban middle class from 1920 to 1960 increasingly included "cocktails" as an important part of social life, especially parties. Drinking was well established among college youth by the 1950s, so another form of consciousness-altering drug was necessary to show independence from the ways of the older generation. For the dropouts, something stronger than marijuana was needed to prove independence, and they often found it in LSD or heroin. Yet some of the drug takers were motivated by more than the desire for independence from their parents. The Beat poets of the 1950s, for example, had used drugs to free themselves from the consciousness of "square" society and to find a higher and more spiritual reality. A significant number of young people used drugs for this purpose as they searched for new religious inspiration throughout the 1960s and 1970s.

From 1965 to 1969 high school and college students, most of them still economically dependent on their parents, provided the audience for "hard" and "acid" rock music bands like the Rolling Stones. Long-haired rock performers symbolized a dropout way of life that completely rejected the morality and discipline of the older generation. "You can't trust anybody over thirty," they shouted. Jim Morrison of the Doors explained that "We make concerts sexual politics" and boasted that he could sustain an erection through a two-hour concert. It was support from college students that made a public figure of the Harvard psychologist, Timothy Leary, who advocated freedom through drug taking. "Remember, man," he insisted, "a natural state is ecstatic wonder. Don't settle for less." And it was attention from college students seeking new values that made the novelist Ken Kesey and his Merry Pranksters a focus

of national controversy as his group traveled across the country in its psychedelic bus, liberating people with music, drugs, and sex. Janis Joplin, a successful rock singer who died of a drug overdose, proclaimed, "I never hold back, man. I'm always on the outer limits of probability." Dropping out as a fantasy for college students reached a climax in August 1969 when 400,000 gathered at a rock festival in rural New York before returning to classes in the fall. This Woodstock festival seemed to be filled with a spirit of love and gentleness, drugs, sex, and music. For many it marked the end of a materialistic, war-loving America and the birth of a spiritual, peace-loving "Age of Aquarius."

But another festival in 1969 at Altamont, California, featuring the Rolling Stones, ended in violence when one member of the audience was kicked to death. At the same time, a dropout group headed by Charles Manson murdered several affluent people, including a pregnant movie star, Sharon Tate. By the end of the 1960s it was becoming clear that the most important community of dropouts, the Haight-Ashbury district in San Francisco, was overwhelmed by violent crime that fed on extensive drug taking. It was also becoming clear that corporate advertisers were profiting handsomely by exploiting fantasies of dropping out. Rock music itself was big business, and producers, record companies, agents, and some rock stars rapidly became wealthy. So did the importers and manufacturers of drugs. Corporations also profited by selling love beads, head bands, blue jeans, and even "hip" cosmetics and hair accessories. Likewise, the producers of movies that celebrated the rebellion of the young against the establishment — *The Graduate, Easy Rider, Alice's Restaurant, Bonnie and Clyde* — expected to make money and did.

By 1970, then, some of the excitement of dropping out had lost its appeal. But conservatives, many of whom believed that the turmoil over competing lifestyles in the 1960s was caused by a few misguided young people who would straighten out when they had to earn a living, were still uneasy during the 1970s. While no coherent movement of cultural and political dissent survived the seventies, significant signs of social breakdown characterized the decade. Consumption of drugs, including marijuana, angel dust, cocaine, and heroin, increased, while use of alcohol spread even into grade school.

The seventies also witnessed a rapid rise in the number of illegitimate children, most of whose mothers were in the ten-to-fourteen-year age group. As girls became sexually active at earlier ages, delinquency and crime rates rose dramatically among them. Most disturbing, the suicide rate for young people tripled during this period.

The fact that the youth rebellion of the 1960s reflected the changing values of adult culture is suggested by the confusion of the courts in defining obscenity and pornography. Departing drastically from the purity crusade of the late nineteenth century, the Supreme Court had ruled at the end of the 1950s that underground literary classics such as D. H. Lawrence's *Lady Chatterly's Lover,* Frank Harris's *My Life and Loves,* and *Fanny Hill* could no longer be barred from the mails or confiscated by American customs officers. Grove Press immediately became a major publisher of books that formerly would have been classified as pornographic. Pornographic movies came out from underground and were shown openly. Nudity and sexual language also became a standard part of movies made by major Hollywood studios. Yet government officials continued to cen-

sor "hard-core" pornography and attempted to maintain a distinction between good and bad sexuality.

Younger men in the "square" middle class of the 1950s participated in this sexual revolution by making *Playboy* magazine a success. The magazine featured photographs of nude young women. Playboy clubs provided sexual titillation for successful young businessmen. Businessmen also were customers in restaurants featuring "topless" waitresses and lingerie shows at lunch time. By the 1960s Las Vegas, Nevada, became established as a center to which businessmen from every part of the nation came to relax. They watched shows featuring Hollywood stars, gambled, and were entertained by the many attractive young women in the city.

The rejection of traditional middle-class morality by young people who remained within the economic system was dramatized by the new lifestyle practiced by professional athletes in the 1960s. Professional football proved so popular on television that the American Football League was organized to challenge the National Football League for lucrative contracts from the major TV networks. This expansion led to a bidding war for college stars. A quarterback from the University of Alabama, Joe Namath, was signed in 1964 to a $400,000 bonus to play for the New York Jets of the new league. Namath's bonus and salary began a trend to higher salaries as professional athletes in all sports realized that they worked in show business. Hiring lawyers and business managers, they rejected the tradition that players never questioned team owners or the discipline set by managers. A new emphasis on personal expression and personal fulfillment replaced spartan loyalty to the team. Namath led this change by emphasizing his personal hair and clothing style and by leading a lifestyle more like that of a movie star than of the traditional professional athlete. Soon Namath was making more money from TV commercials, linking his personal image as a "swinger" to a variety of products, than he did from his football salary. Another athlete, Jim Bouton, a former major league baseball player, changed the public image of athletes considerably when he wrote *Ball Four* (1970), a humorous account of the game that revealed the off-the-field pleasure seeking of his teammates.

The trend from self-discipline to self-indulgence among professional athletes was another indication of the confusion of values among middle-class Americans. Professional athletes were grown men who were supposed to remain socially dependent on their leaders as long as they played the game. Until the 1960s they were seen as permanent adolescents. Under the patterns of adolescence that prevailed between the 1890s and the 1960s, young people were to show their dependent status by leaving all important decisions to their elders. But these attitudes were altered in the 1960s, and professional athletes demanded recognition of their adult dignity and formed players' associations to bargain with team owners.

ANTIWAR PROTEST AND A NEW LEFT

The rebellion of college students against the traditional pattern of adolescence went beyond the rejection of *in loco parentis*, which had given college administrators the right to regulate students' sexual lives. It extended to politics as well. The leaders of Students for a Democratic Society (SDS), for example, saw the major difference between the "New Left" and

the "Old Left" of the 1930s as the attitude toward discipline. Adults of the various Marxist parties of the 1930s expected college students to follow their leadership blindly and accept a military discipline of unquestioning loyalty within the party. SDS, however, which criticized universities for not allowing students to participate in making decisions, was equally critical of the absence of participatory democracy in the parties of the Old Left. SDS leaders also were inspired by writers such as Paul Goodman, Norman O. Brown, and Herbert Marcuse who berated the way modern capitalism forced people to repress their imaginations, the capacity of their bodies to experience pleasure, and their instinct for play. But Goodman, Brown, and Marcuse argued that Soviet Russian communism was as repressive as capitalism and that Old Left organizations in the United States encouraged this kind of repressiveness.

SDS leaders expected the economic slowdown and rising unemployment of the Eisenhower administration to continue under President Kennedy. They expected increasing numbers of poor people to join them in a reform movement that would bring a decentralized economy run cooperatively by local groups. These local groups would make decisions through participatory democracy. But the depression did not come and the white and black poor in the urban slums and impoverished countryside did not become involved in radical actions. Nevertheless, the growth of anti–Vietnam War attitudes among middle-class students and their parents between 1964 and 1968 led SDS to believe that a major new radical movement was developing in America.

The first massive student protest of the sixties came in Berkeley, California, in the fall of 1964 when the Free Speech Movement

(FSM) arose over a university prohibition of on-campus recruiting and fund raising for the civil rights movement. Eight hundred students were arrested at a sit-in at Berkeley's Sproul Hall. After FSM, middle-class students began to see themselves as an oppressed class whose training was designed to place them in the bureaucracies of the corporate order. "There's a time when the operation of the machine becomes so odious," FSM leader Mario Savio told the Berkeley students, "that you can't take part. . . . And you've got to put your bodies upon the gears . . . and you've got to make it stop."

By early 1965, students concerned with domestic issues such as racism, poverty, corporate power, and the military-industrial complex began to connect overseas military activities with social injustice at home. SDS shifted its focus from participatory democracy for working people to the Vietnam War. Student radicals saw the war in Asia as a pilot project of counter-insurgency designed to demonstrate that the United States would not tolerate change in economically underdeveloped areas. But SDS changed antiwar protest by placing responsibility for Vietnam on liberals tied to the corporate structure. Weeks before the bombing of North Vietnam began in March 1965, SDS had planned a small April march for Washington, D.C. To everyone's surprise, twenty thousand people attended the demonstration. By then, teach-ins on the war had begun at major universities. At Berkeley twelve thousand students and faculty participated in a Vietnam Day teach-in.

As draft calls rose to forty thousand a month in mid-1966, rallies, marches, teach-ins, and draft-card burnings increased. Young men refused induction orders, thousands deserted the armed forces, and more fled to Canada or Europe to avoid the draft. At Fort Hood, Texas, three men refused orders for duty in Vietnam. Protesters sat-in at military induction centers and harassed on-campus job recruiters for the military, CIA, and defense contractors such as Dow Chemical, which produced napalm.

While the Johnson administration remained aloof from criticism, Vietnam protest became massive. In 1967, "Stop the Draft Week" at the Oakland Induction Center, led by the pacifist group Resistance, resulted in a battle of several hours between police and twenty thousand demonstrators. That November over 100,000 protesters surrounded the Pentagon, while in New York City 300,000 people marched to protest the Vietnam War. Weeks later a new phase of the antiwar movement commenced when Father Philip Berrigan and three other members of the Catholic Ultra-Resistance poured ox blood on draft files in Baltimore. The following year Berrigan, his brother Daniel, and six other Catholic radicals burned the draft files of a Maryland town with homemade napalm. The Catonsville Nine submitted to voluntary arrest and revealed that they had followed napalm instructions from a Special Forces handbook. All nine were convicted in the fall of 1968. At Fort Jackson, South Carolina, army doctor Captain Howard Levy was court-martialed for refusing to train Green Berets in dermatological warfare.

BLACK AND WHITE RADICALS

White radicals and antiwar activists hoped that their cause would benefit from the simultaneous rebellion of black college students against racism. Up to 1964, the nonviolent civil rights movement in the South had won the support of both established black organizations such as the NAACP and CORE and the white liberal community. But by the mid-sixties, signs of stress were apparent in this coalition. Little had been done to desegregate schools in the South after the Supreme Court decision of 1954 and segregation was increasing in northern schools. The rise of black voting had not affected politics in the southern states. Major liberal newspapers in the North, like the *New York Times*, criticized the sit-ins and freedom rides. Young blacks began to see — just as SDS leaders had insisted — that there was a very strong and unresponsive establishment. President Nathan Pusey of Harvard University, for example, when challenged about the university's lack of a concern for social justice, replied, "Our purpose is just to invest in places that are selfishly good for Harvard. We do not use our money for social purposes."

Many young blacks who wanted to reject this establishment, however, perceived white liberals and white radicals as part of it. Antagonism toward whites on the part of young black activists reached a deep intensity by 1966. As murders of blacks who defied southern racial taboos continued, James Meredith, who had been the first black student at the University of Mississippi, began a "March Against Fear" into Mississippi to enroll the state's 450,000 potential black voters. As soon as Meredith crossed the state line from Tennessee, he was wounded by a sniper. The disrupted march was resumed by a broad spectrum of national black leadership.

Earlier that year the Student Non-Violent Coordinating Committee had abandoned nonviolence, excluded whites from membership, and chosen the militant Stokely Carmichael as director. While Martin Luther King and his followers continued to preach nonviolence on the March Against Fear, Carmichael took up

the rhythmic cry of "Black Power, Black Power" and predicted another "long hot summer." The new phrase electrified the media and frightened whites throughout the nation, although to most blacks its purpose was to instill a sense of pride and identity. "If we are to proceed toward true liberation," Carmichael stated, "we must set ourselves off from white people."

Throughout the rural South in the 1960s, most blacks, like this cottonpicker, remained economically dependent on white landowners and were kept isolated from political participation. (Bruce Davidson/Magnum)

In the growing black ghettos in the cities, in contrast to many areas in the rural South, blacks worked to liberate their children from psychological dependence on whites by teaching black pride, as in this school in Harlem. (Charles Gatewood)

Even a black novelist like James Baldwin, who had many white friends, explained the riots and violence of the 1960s as a response to the terrible history of the exploitation of blacks by whites. "To be a Negro in this country," Baldwin said, "is to be in a rage all the time." Eldridge Cleaver, then emerging as a Black Panther leader, voiced agreement with whites in the New Left that Americans needed to be liberated from the repressive discipline that robbed the human body of its freedom. In his best-selling book, *Soul on Ice* (1968), Cleaver found that blacks still had that freedom, expressed by the spontaneity of sexual life in the black community. But Cleaver had little hope whites could share that liberation.

Malcolm X was a major black leader who did call for the cooperation of radicals of every race against the establishment. Malcolm Little became a convert to the Black Muslim faith while in prison. To symbolize his liberation from white domination, he changed his name to Malcolm

X. A persuasive speaker and organizer, Malcolm began to question the Black Muslim doctrine of voluntary black segregation from "evil whites." He broke from the Black Muslims after he came to believe that the great oppressive force in the world was capitalism and that the economically oppressed of all colors, including whites, must work for a socialist alternative to capitalism. But Malcolm X was assassinated in Harlem in 1965. His killers probably were blacks who opposed his ideology, although white law enforcement never satisfactorily explained the circumstances.

The spirit of Malcolm's teachings, however, resurfaced in the Black Panthers, organized in Oakland the following year. Founded by Bobby Seale and Huey P. Newton, the Panthers monitored ghetto police and addressed the needs of poor blacks by providing free breakfasts for schoolchildren and establishing health clinics. To dramatize their right to bear arms against police "occupying" black communities, the Panthers marched into the California legislature with loaded rifles and shotguns. When Newton was arrested for murder in an Oakland confrontation with police, the Panthers began a long and insistent "Free Huey" campaign. By 1968 the Black Panther party had devised a ten-point program embracing Marxist concepts of self-determinism and the end of "welfare colonialism."

The FBI and local police forces harassed all black radicals, but they were most eager to destroy the Black Panthers. By 1969 two of the major Black Panther leaders, Eldridge Cleaver and Bobby Seale, had fled the country to escape legal harassment. Another leader, Bobby Hutton, had been killed, and the last, Huey Newton, was in prison. In December 1969 Chicago police officers staged a late-night raid on the headquarters and living space of the city's Panther party. The attack, directed with FBI assistance by Illinois State Attorney Edward V. Hanrahan, resulted in the killing of Panther leaders Fred Hampton and Mark Clark. Although none of the occupants of the house fired a shot and Hampton was hit by bullets while sleeping, a county court subsequently acquitted Hanrahan and thirteen others of conspiracy to obstruct justice. But the Chicago murders and other police raids against Panthers enraged black activists and white radicals.

Black leaders often were torn between the philosophy of separate black power and their desire to stop the Vietnam War by cooperating with white antiwar activists. They were aware that young blacks suffered casualties in Vietnam in greater proportion than whites. SNCC was the first black organization to oppose the war, initiating the "Hell, no, we won't go!" chant in daily demonstrations at the Atlanta induction center. Julian Bond, SNCC's communications director, twice was denied his seat in the Georgia legislature for antiwar statements before the Supreme Court ordered his reinstatement. By the spring of 1967, Martin Luther King proposed that the civil rights and antiwar movements merge, calling the American government the "greatest purveyor of violence in the world." Meanwhile, heavyweight boxing champion Muhammad Ali was arrested for refusing induction in the army after he claimed conscientious objector status as a Black Muslim minister. "No Viet Cong ever called me 'nigger,'" he explained in defense of his refusal to fight. Boxing authorities quickly stripped Ali of his crown.

The Chicago "New Politics" Convention of 1967 provided an opportunity for a coalition between black power advocates and antiwar activists. But although the convention platform

Eldridge Cleaver

1936-

Eldridge Cleaver was the most powerful symbol of revolutionary change in America in 1968. Cleaver had been paroled from prison only two years earlier. But it was his history as a juvenile thief, as an alienated man of senseless violence, and then as a political prisoner that gave Cleaver much of his power as a critic of the establishment. Raised in the Los Angeles ghetto, he fell into trouble with the law for petty theft and the sale of marijuana before he was out of grade school. Cleaver received a long prison term for assault with intent to rape and murder in 1958. In prison, he began to read the writings of Malcolm X. Imitating this new-found hero, Cleaver converted to the Black Muslim faith and rejected the anarchy of his early life. While still in prison, he began to study Afro-American history. He also began to write about his personal life, placing it within the context of the white racism that he saw as the dominant force in American society. When Malcolm X left the Black Muslims and began to preach that capitalist exploitation of whites and blacks must lead to a coalition of the oppressed of every color, Cleaver made the same change in emphasis.

Some of his writing, which showed great artistic skill, was smuggled out of prison and published in Ramparts, a journal of radical lay Catholics. Cleaver's literary talents were quickly recognized, and he signed a contract to write a book for a major publisher. With backing from members of the white literary community, he was paroled in 1966, and his book, Soul on Ice, published in 1963, became a best seller. But Cleaver came out of prison searching for the kind of political radicalism suggested by Malcolm X. He found this radicalism in the Black Panthers. The Panthers had started in Oakland, California, hoping to lead young ghetto blacks out of a life of apathy and petty crime into a life of political and economic radicalism. Like Malcolm X, the Panthers were ready to work with radical whites dedicated to social revolution.

Cleaver was an excellent speaker and soon was reaching large white audiences in opposition to the war in Vietnam. A group of white radicals in California persuaded Cleaver to be the presidential candidate of their Peace and Freedom party in 1968. The nomination gave him further opportunity to speak against American colonialism. Governor Ronald Reagan put pressure on the parole board to warn Cleaver to stop his political speeches. He refused. But J. Edgar Hoover had ordered the FBI to harass the Panthers, and local police were encouraged to suppress Panther activity. In April 1968, police in Oakland moved against a group of Panthers including Cleaver. Two policemen were wounded when the Panthers resisted, and a Panther leader, Bobby Hutton, was killed while Cleaver and another leader were wounded. Appeals by his lawyers kept Cleaver out of jail until November 1968, but he fled the country rather than return to prison. After seven years in exile in Cuba, Algeria, and France, Cleaver returned to the United States to face court proceedings. His return in 1975, he said, was prompted by his loss of faith in Marxist materialism and his conversion to Christianity.

called for "revolutionary change" and "open draft resistance," the gathering split over Panther demands that blacks be given half the leadership positions. The following year, the Panthers managed to win the support of white radicals through the Peace and Freedom party. The party ran Eldridge Cleaver, the Panther author, for president and stressed peace in Vietnam as well as self-determinism for blacks.

Cooperation between black and white radicals also came at Columbia University in the spring of 1968, when separate groups of black and white students took over two university buildings for several days. The students were protesting both university ties to the war through the Institute for Defense Analysis and the proposed construction of a gymnasium in a park separating Columbia from Harlem. SDS leaders who mobilized the white protesters saw the Columbia confrontation as an opportunity to promote the radicalization of students. The occupation, which ended with seven hundred arrests and rough handling by New York police, set the tone of confrontation for more than three thousand campus protests during 1968. Although most concerned Vietnam, student issues and demands for black studies also figured heavily, and for the first time arson and bombings marked student protests. SDS, which hoped to use the university as a stepping-stone to revolution, claimed 100,000 members in 1968. When President Johnson's Committee on Student Disorders, headed by Harvard law professor Archibald Cox, made its report that year, it described the college generation of the period as "the best informed, the most intelligent and the most idealistic this country has ever known." But the committee noted that the university had become the "surrogate for all the tensions and frustrations of American policy in Vietnam."

Despite instances of cooperative activity, however, there was no major national coalition of white and black radicals by the end of 1968. Nor had SDS been able to persuade most college students to become politically active. The majority of young people expressed their rejection of the establishment through the development of alternative lifestyles rather than through politics. Most antiwar activists, young or middle-aged, believed that the economic and social system was sound and could be brought back to health by ending the war. And the overwhelming majority of antiwar activists as well as most of the youth in the counterculture were strongly critical of the violence on the campuses in 1968. It was not surprising, then, that SDS membership declined after 1968.

The turn toward radical violence in 1968 came partly from the assassinations of Martin Luther King and Robert Kennedy and from the Chicago convention of the Democratic party. Because the New Left was unable to bring a strong economic radicalism to challenge established Democratic leaders, dramatic protests in Chicago came from the Yippies, a New York–based group devoted to irreverent anarchism and cultural revolution. These activists called for a "Festival of Life" to counter the August "Convention of Death." Most peace groups declined to join the Chicago demonstrations, but Mayor Richard Daley's refusal to accommodate any form of protest attracted media attention. Stressing law and order, Daley directed Chicago police to prevent protesters from camping out in city parks. Tension between police and demonstrators mounted until the evening of August 27, when crowds of protesters surged toward the convention headquarters. Blocked from marching on a convention busily ratifying the war, some of the protesters began to pelt police with sticks, bottles, and sexual taunts. The police charged furiously into the crowd with clubs, tear gas, and Mace. The president's National Commission on the Causes and Prevention of Violence later described the Chicago battle as a "police riot" involving "unrestrained and undiscriminate" attacks against many people "who had broken no law, disobeyed no order, made no threat." But most Americans blamed the demonstrators for the chaos in Chicago.

Increasingly isolated from mainstream opinion, political radicals became more violent after 1968. The Weathermen, a remnant of SDS that included newly radicalized women, came to Chicago in October 1969 to take part in "Days of Rage." Protesting government prosecution of the leaders of the 1968 convention protests, they "trashed" cars, banks, and businesses. The police used their guns to restore order and arrested three hundred persons. After Chicago, Weather leaders such as Mark Rudd and Bernadine Dohrn became underground fugitives.

Organized in secret "affinity groups," the Weather Underground initiated a series of dramatic bombings to demonstrate the vulnerability of the social system. The most controversial of the bombings killed a graduate student in August 1970 at a research facility at the University of Wisconsin. No longer could radicals claim that bombings were directed only against property. Such radical activity aroused the opposition of leaders of organized labor, who rejected both economic radicalism and the antiwar movement. "We are members of the capitalist society," George Meany, the head of the AFL-CIO declared. "We are dedicated to the preservation of the system, which rewards the workers." During the 1960s many young blue-collar workers, wearing hard hats, disrupted peace marches as they chanted, "God bless the establishment."

White blue-collar workers, who often had Catholic or evangelical Protestant backgrounds, had difficulty relating to New Left leaders, who usually were raised in families connected to established Protestant churches or to the Jewish community. Many blue-collar workers came from families that had been struggling to reject their ethnic backgrounds and to be accepted as Americans. They could not understand the New Left leaders whose families were part of the American establishment and who now wanted to reject that Americanism. In May 1970 construction workers attacked a peaceful demonstration of college students on New York's Wall Street, injuring about forty. A few days later twenty thousand supporters of the "hard-hats" paraded down Broadway in a show of support for the war. President Nixon subsequently met with a delegation from construction and longshoremen's unions, confiding that he found their actions "very meaningful." But the president's courting of labor leaders was not fruitful. By 1972, Gallup polls indicated that blue-collar workers were more critical of Nixon's war policies (44 percent opposed) than the general public (39 percent opposed).

As campus protest abated, disaffection and antiwar activity began to penetrate the armed forces, where most soldiers came from low-income families. In such an atmosphere, career soldiers in Vietnam were openly ridiculed, and rumors spread of widespread murder of officers. The army eventually created separate companies for those who refused to go into action. Readily available Asian heroin contributed to sixteen thousand drug-abuse-related military dismissals in 1969 and 1970. At home, twenty-seven military prisoners were tried for mutiny at the San Francisco Presidio. Antiwar activists

provided support and meeting places for GI dissenters by establishing coffee houses close to military bases. A Concerned Officers Movement spoke out against the war, and twelve thousand men joined Vietnam Veterans Against the War (VVAW). In April 1971, two thousand Vietnam veterans rallied in Washington, as scores of decorated soldiers, some in wheelchairs, threw their medals on the steps of the Capitol. By then, a Gallup poll indicated that 61 percent of the American public believed Vietnam to be a "mistake." "How do you ask a man...to die for a mistake?" VVAW spokesman John Kerry asked the Senate Foreign Relations Committee in testimony that accompanied the powerful demonstration.

Discontent also reached the nation's prisons by the early seventies, particularly among blacks tutored by the street-wise Black Panthers. In 1970 three black California "Soledad Brothers," including the political writer George Jackson, were charged with the slaying of a white prison guard. Jackson's young brother attempted to kidnap the trial judge as a hostage. The resulting shoot-out, in which the judge and the younger Jackson were killed, only led to the arrest of communist philosopher Angela Davis, who was accused of supplying the weapons. After spending sixteen months in jail, Davis was acquitted by an all-white jury in June 1972. But George Jackson had been killed the previous August in an alleged escape attempt from San Quentin. Increased politicization and racial consciousness also contributed to a rebellion at New York's Attica prison during September 1971. Over one thousand inmates at the overwhelmingly black and Puerto Rican institution took ten guards as hostage in response to crowded conditions and bitter charges of racial abuse. Inmates insisted on personal negotiations with Governor Nelson Rockefeller, but when the governor refused, nine guards and thirty-one prisoners were killed in the ensuing attack by fifteen hundred armed state troopers. Attica remained a bloody symbol of brutality and racial hostility in seventies America. Ten weeks later a similar outbreak at New Jersey's Rahway prison ended peacefully when Governor William Cahill assured prisoners that their demands would be considered.

Despite the failure of radical movements to bring substantive social change, activists had successfully underscored the moral bankruptcy of the Vietnam War and contributed to pressures for withdrawal of ground troops. But violent and disruptive tactics, no matter how effective in unsettling the nation's leaders, appeared to most Americans as the irresponsible acts of a handful of unrepresentative "crackpots." These attitudes were dramatized in 1974 when members of the secret Symbionese Liberation Army (SLA) kidnapped San Francisco communications heiress Patricia Hearst. The SLA won considerable publicity when it demanded free food for the poor as part of Hearst's ransom. The group then released tapes in which Hearst claimed that she had converted to the revolutionary crusade. Indeed, the heiress participated in a dramatic robbery of a San Francisco bank. When leaders of the terrorist organization subsequently were killed by Los Angeles police, Hearst escaped, only to be captured by the FBI in September 1975. Back in the protection of her family, she pleaded that the traumatic kidnapping had destroyed her sense of individual will. After serving twenty-two months in prison for the bank robbery, Hearst was pardoned in 1979 and resumed her place in San Francisco society. The SLA affair only re-emphasized the isolation of remnants of the revolutionary Left from the American people.

BLACK POWER AND AFRO-AMERICAN CULTURE

By 1969 there seemed little hope for an easy and quick revolution that would instantly convert all Americans to the counterculture of the dropouts or to the decentralized communal economics and participatory democracy of the New Left. But the groups who wanted to return to what they believed was the unity and optimism of the liberal establishment under President Kennedy were equally disappointed. Liberal historians and sociologists in 1960 used a melting pot theory to explain the development of American history. They argued that all groups that were different from the Anglo-Protestant middle class — blacks, Native Americans, Chicanos, Catholic and Jewish immigrants from Europe — were in the process of being assimilated to the Anglo-Protestant middle-class lifestyle. The advocates of black power challenged this view. Although blacks had been stripped of their African languages and forced to speak and write English for hundreds of years, black intellectuals insisted in the 1960s that there was a vital Afro-American culture. While this was most obvious in music, they argued that there also were survivals of African culture in the way in which American blacks understood religion, defined family values, and saw the nature of the world.

As he lost the ability to identify himself with the white culture for which he had written his early plays, the black dramatist LeRoi Jones changed his name to Imamu Baraka. In his books of essays, *Home* (1966) and *Raise Race Raze Rays* (1970), he spoke of giving up the white ideal of being an independent artist to accept the African ideal of the artist as a spokesperson for the community. Other major black writers such as John Oliver Killens joined this movement to Afro-American unity. In Killens's novel *And Then We Heard the Thunder* (1962), the hero rejects the goal of making it as a leader in white society. He too rejoins the black community as he affirms his roots. "This is me. Proud black American me, whose ancestors came from great Africa." Other black novelists in the 1960s and 1970s who celebrated the Afro-American community, stressing its values of communal sharing in contrast to Anglo-Protestant competitive individualism, included John William (*Captain Blackman,* 1973) and Ernest J. Gaines (*The Autobiography of Miss Jane Pittman,* 1971).

Black college students used confrontation tactics to force college authorities to establish black studies departments or programs where black literature, history, and family patterns could be seen as alternatives to white culture rather than as inferior forms of white culture. The students were supported by the scholarship of both black and white professors who concluded that there was a history of a strong, separate Afro-American culture. These scholars had to become sensitive to oral tradition before they were able to understand how African cultures were passed from one generation to another. One of the scholarly discoveries was the existence of an African tradition of an extended family among American blacks that was different from the tradition of the nuclear family among whites. The extended-family tradition stressed cooperation rather than competition. Unlike the white nuclear family, in which parents had total responsibility, cousins, uncles, aunts, and grandparents were encouraged to help raise children. There was also evidence of a separate black English with different rules of grammar. Afro-American tradition stressed the interrelatedness of all things in contrast to the white middle class, which divided things into separate parts.

Black English encouraged children to think in terms of this interconnectedness.

CHICANO CULTURE AND ACTIVISM

The example of black power inspired other Americans to seek identity in their social and ethnic groups. The founding rally of the Italian-American Civil Rights League attracted fifty thousand people to New York's Columbus Circle in June 1970. In Brooklyn, New York, working-class Jewish youth organized a Jewish Defense League (JDL) to protect synagogues and schoolchildren in a racially tense neighborhood. And elderly Americans sought to advance their social and political needs by forming the Gray Panthers. The closest replica of the black power movement, however, surfaced among Mexican-Americans, the most rapidly growing group of Americans. While the birthrate of blacks remained slightly higher than that of whites, it tended to follow the major population pattern of American society and had dropped since 1958. But the Chicano birthrate remained high, as did the birthrate in Mexico. Population growth and poverty in Mexico continued to encourage immigration to the United States after World War Two. Between 1945 and 1965, five million Mexican workers, or braceros, were brought into the United States to cultivate and harvest vegetable crops. Under the labor contracts, they were expected to return to Mexico when the harvest ended. Many did not and many more crossed the border as illegal aliens. In the ten years following World War Two, four million were apprehended by American authorities as they crossed the border and were sent back to Mexico. These figures indicate the

Cesar Chavez was a leader of the 1960s effort to unionize migrant farm workers. Chavez believed that the many Chicano workers could gain economic strength only as they liberated themselves from psychological dependence on Anglos (white Americans) by developing pride in their Mexican-American heritage. (Paul Fusco/Magnum)

massive scale of the illegal immigration and point to the probability that millions were not apprehended. By 1970 Chicano population counted in the census approached ten million, but estimates were much higher, and migration from Mexico continued with equal intensity throughout the 1970s.

This Spanish-speaking population was joined by a million Puerto Ricans. Concentrated in New York and Chicago, Puerto Ricans were pushed toward the United States by a high birthrate and the poverty of that American colony. Miami, Florida, also developed a huge district of Spanish-speaking people who had fled the Communist revolution in Cuba. Spanish-speaking radio stations were popular in Miami, New York, and Chicago as well as in every major city in the Southwest. Public schools in Spanish-speaking communities also established bilingual education.

Organized in a similar fashion to the NAACP, a League of United Latin American Citizens (LULAC) had begun to work for the civil rights of Spanish-speaking Americans before World War Two. Both the NAACP and LULAC represented middle-class groups who hoped for assimilation in white society, and both turned to the courts to end patterns of segregation in the schools and denial of citizenship rights. Chicanos in the Southwest, for example, like blacks in the South, were not allowed to serve on juries. As blacks became more active in politics and moved to challenge Jim Crow patterns, Chicano leaders such as Edward Roybal in Los Angeles worked to get their people involved in politics and social action through the Community Service Organization. This activity led by 1960 to the Political Association of Spanish-Speaking Organizations (PASO).

About the same time that young black-power advocates were questioning efforts by moderates to end discrimination and integrate into white society, young Chicanos began to choose brown power over integration. The Brown Berets, like the Black Panthers, carried weapons to show that they would not retreat before the threat of Anglo violence. Using confrontation tactics, young Chicanos forced college administrations to establish Chicano studies programs or departments. Magazines like *El Grito, Bronze, El Machete,* and *La Raza* were published to raise social and ethnic consciousness. The scholarly journals *Aztlan: Chicano Journal of the Social Sciences and the Arts* and the *Journal of Mexican-American History* began publication to serve as a foundation for college programs throughout the country. The renaissance of black novelists, poets, and dramatists was paralleled by a renaissance of Chicano novelists such as Raymond Barrio, Richard Vasquez, and José Antonio Villarreal; poets such as Miguel Ponce, Tomás Rivera, and Roberto Vargas; and painters such as Malaguias Montoya and Esteban Villa.

Another major parallel between the development of black and brown power was the similar style of leadership expressed by the Chicano leader Cesar Chavez and the black leader Martin Luther King, Jr. At the time of his assassination in 1968, King had turned his attention from civil rights to the problems of poverty facing so many blacks. He had gone to Memphis, where he was killed, to encourage a strike of the city's sanitation workers. That spring, as thousands of blacks camped out near the Lincoln Memorial, SCLC carried out King's plan for a poor people's demonstration in Washington. Fifty thousand people, half of them white, then participated in a "Solidarity March" to reaffirm the slain minister's dream.

Like King, Chavez was able to appeal to the conscience of middle-class whites by reminding them of the exploitation of his people and by using Christian imagery to challenge the complacency of the establishment. Chavez, a deeply religious man who used the Virgin of Guadalupe as the symbol of his struggle for social justice, emerged as a national figure in 1965 for his leadership of Mexican-American grape pickers in California. Like King, Chavez preached nonviolence as he moved his National Farm Workers Association to improve the working conditions and pay of farmworkers throughout California. And, like King, he did reach the conscience of many white Protestants. But unlike the black minister, Chavez was able to appeal to many newly middle-class Catholics who had left the problems of the poor behind when they moved from the slums of the central cities to the suburbs.

Still another parallel between the two movements was the increasing rejection of the nonviolent positions of King and Chavez by young radicals. Reies Lopez Tijerina, a Chicano from New Mexico, shared the attitudes of black leaders who had become impatient with the possibility of reform through the legal system or with the appeal to the conscience of middle-class whites. Tijerina asked Chicanos in New Mexico to remember the outrage of the 1890s when they had been cheated out of their land. Emphasizing especially the return of the land that villages held in common before the coming of the Anglos, Tijerina armed his followers and urged them to take back what belonged to them. Like many black militants, Tijerina was jailed for his challenge to the establishment.

Deep bitterness developed in Texas where José Angel Gutierrez developed a political party, La Raza Unida, to win Chicano control of the twenty counties in south Texas in which they were the majority. This bitterness was similar to that which developed throughout the South in the 1960s as blacks started to win political control in those counties where they were the majority. The fierce efforts of Anglos (white Americans) in the Southwest and South to retain control of rural counties where either Chicanos or blacks were the majority was similar to efforts by whites in northern and southwestern cities to keep growing black or Chicano populations from getting political power.

Rudolfo "Corky" Gonzales was a Chicano urban leader in Denver, Colorado, in the 1960s. Chicanos were not the majority in Denver, but through his organization, the Crusade for Justice, Gonzales encouraged the Chicanos to use their political power as a large minority to bring about changes in the school and welfare system.

All the major Chicano political and cultural leaders of the 1960s, like the blacks, contrasted their social system of extended families, with less stress on individual achievement and more emphasis on social justice, to that of Anglo-Protestant competitive capitalism. Militant Chicano leaders conveyed a sense of a separate

culture with deep roots in an ancient past. They noted with pride that Spanish culture had been absorbed and reshaped by the Aztec culture of northern Mexico and what was now the southwestern part of the United States. These notions led Chicanos to distinguish themselves sharply from the Catholic culture that had come to America from modern Europe. They pointed to the separate styles of church architecture and art and to separate traditions such as that of the Virgin of Guadalupe with different festivals and feast days. By the 1960s the hierarchy of the American Catholic church, largely Irish-American, was forced to admit that it had underestimated the cultural strength of the Chicanos and it began to appoint, for the first time, Chicanos as bishops in such states as Texas and New Mexico.

NATIVE AMERICAN CULTURE AND MILITANCY

Young American Indians in the late 1960s joined young blacks and Chicanos in rejecting the melting pot ideal. Their affirmation of red power mirrored declarations of black and brown power. Communication among Native American groups had been increasing since 1944, when the National Congress of American Indians (NCAI) was formed. Using this network, Native American leaders intensified their pressure on the national government to end the presence of the Bureau of Indian Affairs (BIA) on reservations. True local government, they argued, had not been achieved because of continued interference by BIA agents in tribal life. By the 1960s younger Indians were growing impatient with the inability of the NCAI to win more tribal autonomy and formed the more militant National Indian Youth Council. After 1966 some adopted confrontation tactics, marching on the BIA in the nation's capital and sitting-in on college campuses to force the establishment of American Indian departments or programs.

Native American militancy in the 1970s partly resulted from the doubling of Indian population to one million between 1945 and 1975. Once the United States Public Health Service replaced the BIA in providing Indian medical services at the end of World War Two, improved health care permitted Native Americans to experience a higher birthrate than that of the rest of the nation. Despite the persistence of higher mortality rates among Indian infants than among other American infants, the nation's Indian population grew. Half the population was concentrated in settlements in cities such as Los Angeles, San Francisco, Chicago, and Minneapolis by 1970. Here urban Indians

In 1973, American Indian Movement (AIM) leaders seized Wounded Knee, South Dakota, by force and held it for several months against armed pressure from the FBI. As in the case of dramatic acts by black and Chicano leaders, the purpose of this seizure was to help liberate American Indians from their psychological dependence on whites. (UPI Photos)

formed Native American centers that emphasized pride in cultural traditions.

Although urban settings provided opportunities for cultural cohesion, unemployment and
poverty characterized Native American life in
the city. Average yearly income for urban Indians was $1,500 in 1960. And because of poor
food and bad living conditions, the average life
span of an Indian was forty-four years compared to sixty-six for a white. These circumstances encouraged the growth of urban radicalism among Native Americans in the early
1970s. Groups such as the American Indian
Movement (AIM) demanded greater economic
and political activity for Indians in the cities
and on the reservations. Led by urban Indians
such as Clyde and Vernon Bellecourt and Russell Means, AIM members seized Wounded
Knee, South Dakota, in 1971 to dramatize demands for autonomy. For two months before
they surrendered, the warriors exchanged gun-
fire with the FBI who surrounded their outpost.
The FBI had worked closely with local police
forces to suppress radicalism among Native
Americans as well as among Chicanos and
blacks.

While Native American radicalism captured
the imagination of young Indians in the cities,
some of the traditional tribes found it difficult
to follow their lead. The Navaho, for example,
at 150,000 members the largest tribe in the nation, rejected radical politics because they had
resisted white influence on their reservations
and sought no demands from the white power
structure. The Pueblo followed a similar pattern. But even off the reservations, most Indians held to tribal traditions. The Cherokee
of Oklahoma, whose reservation had been destroyed in the 1890s, continued to demand that
their children speak the native language at
home, despite the pressure of public schools.

ECOLOGY AND THE
LIMITED FRONTIER

Although a much smaller group than blacks
or Chicanos, Native Americans probably had
a greater impact on the imagination of young
white people in the 1960s and 1970s. Seeking
ties to a tradition of mysticism and the use of
hallucinogens, the counterculture began to explore Native American sources. In *The Teachings of Don Juan: A Yaqui Way of Knowledge*
(1968) and several sequels, Carlos Castaneda
portrayed a "separate reality" of magic and
spiritual enchantment conveyed to him by an
ancient desert medicine man. But countercul-
tural youth also wanted to redefine America
as a peaceful home. They hoped to end the tradition that Americans were warlike conquerors
of new frontiers. The pattern of adolescence
developed around 1900 asked young people
to find their heroes among winning football
players, winning soldiers, or winning cowboys.
Many of the songs, stories, and movies of the
counterculture, however, celebrated antiheroes,
losers who refused to find fulfillment in the
wars of conquest by the establishment. For the
counterculture, Native Americans had represented admirable values in defending their
homes but had been defeated by evil men for
three hundred years. The counterculture hoped
to learn from Indian experience how to survive
defeat by the establishment.

In questioning militant heroes, young people
found support in Joseph Heller's 1960 novel,
Catch-22. Heller presented World War Two
as an absurd experience. In the senseless context of insane bureaucracies, there was no possibility of heroism as young men had been
taught to believe in it. The only sane act for
the hero, Yossarian, was to drop out and row
away on a life raft. The successful movie

M*A*S*H and the TV program with the same name also presented a war without heroic action against the enemy. The only heroism came from small acts of kindness to and support of the people who shared personal suffering, trapped in a way of life they didn't believe in.

The cowboy as a hero who conquers frontiers collapsed as a believable figure both in the movies and on the TV screen during the 1960s. Movies of the 1960s and 1970s such as *The Ballad of Cable Hogue, McCabe and Mrs. Miller, Ride the Whirlwind,* and *Little Big Man* removed the glamour of the conquest and replaced heroes with confused and sometimes evil men. The TV western also became absurd in the 1960s. The first TV westerns for children at the beginning of the 1950s such as the "Lone Ranger" presented heroes who lived outside of society in the open spaces of the frontier. Holding to a personal code of honesty and justice, the hero drew strength from nature to ride into towns and overcome the corrupt elements there. Then he rode back into boundless prairies and mountains. By the end of the 1960s, however, the most important TV westerns like "Bonanza," the "Big Valley," and "High Chaparral" had heroes who were protecting the boundaries of their property. As long as the western hero was presented as someone who rode away from society, the lack of women on the frontier did not seem odd. But when a group of men, as in "Bonanza," were living as a permanent society without women, the situation became absurd.

The Indian political leader and writer Vine DeLoria, Jr., argued in *God Is Red* (1973) that the frontier experience of whites was ending and that they must learn from the Native American to live with America as a home. DeLoria agreed with Chief Luther Standing Bear that "the white man does not understand America. The roots of the tree of his life have not yet grasped the rock and the soil. But in the Indian, the spirit of the land is still vested."

DeLoria appealed to the sciences of biology and physics developed in the white man's universities to show the falseness of the social, economic, and political life of the whites. White science, he argued, taught that the earth is our home and must be conserved, but white economics and politics considered the earth as a frontier to be conquered. DeLoria was correct about white science. By the 1960s biologists such as Paul Ehrlich in *The Population Bomb* (1969) argued that endless population growth was based on the hope of a limitless frontier. But with the closing of that frontier, Ehrlich and others called for an end to population growth. An organization, Zero Population Growth, attempted to persuade American political leaders to work for population control. By the late 1960s, environmentalists began to emphasize that humans live within the circle of the earth's atmosphere and must limit the pollution discharged into the air from industry and cars. Congress and state legislatures soon passed laws to control air, water, and land pollution. The national government and the states also created environmental protection agencies.

Although such legislation was enforced haphazardly, government concern with the environment won endorsement from ecologists. In *The Closing Circle* (1971), Barry Commoner argued that since nature works in vast cycles to regenerate the earth's air, water, and land, human economy must adapt to the cycles. Straight-line economic growth or progress conflicted with natural cycles. Some major economists such as Nicholas Georgescu-Roegen, who wrote *The Entropy Law and the Economic Process* (1971), were converted to the views of the biologists and physicists and rejected the possibility of continued economic growth. A group of scientists from many nations published a study in 1972, *The Limits of Growth,* that warned that the growth economy was rapidly exhausting the earth's resources. According to their computer analysis, catastrophic breakdown would come by the end of the century if limits to growth were not set by human beings.

This "subversive" science of ecology gave intellectual authority to Afro-Americans and Chicanos as well as to Native Americans because their traditions, like ecology, emphasized that everything was interconnected. It also gave authority to those in the Anglo-Protestant counterculture who, in the 1960s, followed the leadership of the Beat poets of the 1950s. Allen Ginsberg and Gary Snyder expressed the sense of being within nature in their poems. They were attracted to Asian philosophy because it taught humanity to find truth within the universe rather than to seek to analyze the universe by standing outside it, as modern Europeans and Americans believed possible.

Ironically, the landing of an American astronaut, Neil Armstrong, on the moon on July 20, 1969, served to dramatize the ecological perspective that humans live within the circle of the earth. President Kennedy had included the sending of men to the moon as an important part of his New Frontier philosophy. Although President Eisenhower declared that "anybody who would spend $40 billion in a race to the moon for national prestige is nuts," Kennedy persuaded Congress to fund the Apollo project. Dr. James E. Webb, the director of the National Aeronautics and Space Administration (NASA), expressed Kennedy's motivation when he remarked, "With a billion people already allied against us, and the emerging nations weighing events . . . the United States must present the image of a can-do nation, with which they can confidently align their futures."

NASA was encouraged to ignore problems of safety in an attempt to reach the moon by 1967, the fiftieth anniversary of the Russian Revolution. On January 27, 1967, the astronauts Virgil I. Grissom, Roger B. Chaffee, and Edward H. White died in a rocket malfunction. But when Armstrong walked on the moon in 1969, President Nixon declared it was "the greatest week since the Creation."

The moon landing, however, did not inspire most Americans to see traditional frontier heroes conquering the vast expanses of space. Instead, looking back at the blue and living earth from the dead moon in the black coldness of outer space, many people felt for the first time that their planet was an island home. Viewed from the moon, the earth was an exceptional and precious gift to be preserved.

WOMEN'S LIBERATION

Unlike Afro-Americans, Chicanos, and Native Americans, women of the white Protestant middle class did not bring a sense of oppression into the 1960s. The ethnic and racial minorities kept alive traditions that told of ancestors who had not been dominated by whites and of cultures that hoped to be liberated from that domination. But middle-class women, who shared the wealth, security, and status of fathers, husbands, and sons, had no such memories or awareness of a shared culture. Nevertheless, a strong sense of women's liberation emerged by the end of the sixties and continued to grow in the 1970s.

Middle-class women had proved their strength during World War Two when they worked in vital industries. Then, after the war, popular novels and films encouraged women to relinquish their jobs to men and return to their homes. But as establishment institutions were called into question by the counterculture and the minority cultures in the 1960s, middle-class women became aware of the way in which they had been taught to see themselves as weak and helpless.

The first major statement of this middle-class women's liberation was Betty Friedan's *The Feminine Mystique* (1963). The large sales of the book showed that many women could see, with Friedan, the contradiction between the ideal middle-class woman as "young and frivolous, almost childlike; fluffy and feminine; passive, gaily content in a world of bedroom and kitchen, sex, babies, and home" and the way in which most women, as members of the lower-income majority, held the least rewarding jobs in the economy.

Many middle-class women became angry as they discovered how they had been persuaded since 1920 not to seek professional careers. Unlike the feminists of the Progressive era, however, they also demanded a place in business as well as in the professions. And they were not satisfied to be an example of purity for male politicians. They wanted to share leadership with men in important political institutions. Agitation by a small group of professional women led President Kennedy to establish a National Commission on the Status of Women. Soon every state had established such commissions. Under the Civil Rights Act of 1964, women, like blacks, were to be protected against discrimination in hiring and in wages. It was now against the law to deny a woman a job because of her sex or to pay her less than a man for the same work. The Equal Employment Opportunity Commission (EEOC), however, moved very slowly to protect women under these provisions.

But some middle-class women grew impatient and organized the National Organization for Women (NOW) in 1966. NOW focused its energy on the passage of the Equal Rights Amendment (ERA) to the Constitution, which would prohibit sex discrimination. NOW also worked to end sex discrimination in private industry. Middle-class women showed their concern for lower-income women by asking for maternity leave rights for working women and government-financed day-care centers for preschool children. Like middle-class men, women of the middle class believed that each individual could find justice in the marketplace if equal educational facilities were provided and racial and sexual discrimination was ended. These women reformers did not share the hostility to the marketplace held by the counterculture and the New Left and did not accept the concern for social, rather than individual, justice in the traditions of the Chicanos, Native Americans, and Afro-Americans. Middle-class women who were college faculty members organized a Women's Equity Action League (WEAL) to protect their interests, as did the women in national government with their organization of Federally Employed Women (FEW).

The National Women's Political Caucus worked to have women accepted as leaders of the major political parties, and both the Republicans and the Democrats moved to include more women as delegates to their conventions. Congresswomen Shirley Chisholm and Bella Abzug initiated reforms in the Democratic party to increase the percentage of female convention delegates from 10 percent in 1968 to 40 percent in 1972. During the 1970s an increasing number of women were elected to state legislatures, governorships, and Congress, although their numbers remained far below the proportion of women in the national population.

The goals and successes of middle-class women reformers were very different, therefore, from those of women reformers during the Progressive era. So were the goals and successes of women radicals. Some college women from the middle-class establishment participated in the development of the New Left and joined the civil rights movement to destroy the Jim Crow system in the South. As they became sensitive to the injustice of established institutions in the early 1960s, many women radicals also became sensitive to "sexism." They angrily objected to the "male chauvinism" that denied them a leadership role in radical movements, just as they were denied a leadership role in the establishment. Women activists frequently were told by male radicals that their major contribution to the cause was to provide sex for the male leaders. These men, wrote Elizabeth Janeway, still believed that it was a "man's world" and there was a "woman's place" apart from that world. Kate Millett wrote *Sexual Politics* in 1969 to show how all men held women in contempt.

Radical women were able to come together quickly and powerfully because their work for the New Left or civil rights in the early 1960s had brought women from every section of the country in contact with each other. As the counterculture developed its own magazines such as the *Berkeley Barb, Village Voice,* and *Rolling Stone,* the radical women began to publish their own journals: *Off Our Bodies, Ain't I a Woman,* and *Majority Report.* A magazine that tried to provide a common ground for middle-class and radical women was *Ms.,* which became a financial success after it began publication in 1972.

One radical group, Redstockings, insisted that "We identify the agents of our oppression as men. Male supremacy is the oldest, most basic form of domination. All other forms of exploitation and oppression (racism, capitalism, imperialism) are extensions of male supremacy." By the early 1970s these radicals seemed to have experienced the same kind of frustration that the male-dominated New Left had developed by 1969. They were not able to recruit a large group of followers committed to the belief that women must segregate themselves from men. Neither had the radicals from middle-class backgrounds found a way to communicate with women from lower-income groups or from the black, Chicano, and Native American cultures.

A third group of women, represented by Elizabeth Janeway, Carolyn Heilbrun, Alice Rossi, and Gloria Steinem, seemed to suggest another alternative for women. These women looked to an "androgynous" society in which men would be free to develop their feminine characteristics and women, their masculine attributes. In such a world, there would not be a sharp distinction between home and marketplace. Both men and women would feel comfortable and competent at home, in rearing children, and in making a living.

GAY LIBERATION

The youth rebellion of the 1960s directed much of its energies against the patterns of traditional adolescence that placed rigid definitions on the behavior of men and women. Traditional roles dictated that men were strong and competitive and that women were weak and passive. But a decade of role questioning made it possible for homosexuals to consider making their identities public and to develop movements for gay pride and gay power. Homosexuals, an estimated 10 percent of the population, had been under special pressure in the 1950s to hide their identities. The anticommunist crusade led by Senator Joseph McCarthy had associated homosexuals with communism. In the federal civil service in Washington, D.C., and in the artistic community in Hollywood, the two areas under greatest pressure from McCarthy, one could be fired from a job for no other reason than suspected homosexual tendencies. As recently as 1964, Walter Jenkins, an official in the Johnson administration, was forced to resign because it was revealed that he had a homosexual experience.

But the Kinsey reports had indicated that 37 percent of all males and 28 percent of females had had at least one homosexual experience some time during their lives. Homosexuals were reassured by these reports that they were a significant part of the population. During the 1950s, middle-class homosexuals began to develop organizations such as One Inc., the Mattachine Society, the Society of Individual Rights, and the Daughters of Bilitis to protect their civil rights and to provide psychological support for their members. Like early black civil rights organizations, they tended to work quietly through the courts. An aggressive public demand for gay rights, however, emerged among young homosexuals at the end of the 1960s. The development of this gay rights movement had many parallels with the development of women's liberation.

Many women's liberation leaders had become rebels against the establishment by participating in the civil rights movement for blacks, in the antiwar movement, or in the New Left. They had become angry, however, when these movements for social change declared that they were interested only in changing relationships between men and not in changing the traditional roles of women and men. Many homosexuals had the same frustrating experience in the 1960s. They had participated in the civil rights and antiwar movements and had called for economic change; young lesbians had participated in women's liberation. But none of these movements, including women's liberation, had questioned the traditional relations between "straight" and "gay" people. All had assumed that being gay was abnormal and unnatural. All had declared that liberation was for "straight" people, not for "queers." By the end of the 1960s, young gays had developed anger against both the establishment and the various reform movements. They also had developed skills of organization and political activism through participation in protest movements.

By the end of the decade, therefore, the situation was ripe for an explosive demand by gays for their own rights. When police raided a gay bar, the Stonewall Inn, in New York City in June 1969, homosexual patrons no longer accepted police brutality as customary and fought back for the first time. Gays in New York and many other cities used this event to declare the beginning of gay power as they shouted, "Out of the closets, into the streets." With some success, gays began to pressure states to end laws against sex acts by consenting adults of the same sex. They also asked city and state governments to include homosexuals in civil rights legislation that barred discrimination in jobs and housing. On the second anniversary of the Stonewall Inn raid, the New York Gay Activists Alliance held a commemorative march in which ten thousand paraded from Greenwich Village to Central Park. Marches were also held in Boston, New Orleans, and San Jose. By 1971, when Jack Baker, a law student and affirmed homosexual, was elected president of the student association at the University of Minnesota, student homophile groups had been established on seventy campuses.

Gay lifestyles also influenced seventies youth culture. By the end of the decade, both working-class and middle-class young people were dancing to "disco" music, a fusion of persistent Afro-American or Latin rhythms accompanied by electronic synthesizers. The "discotheque" had originated with exclusive nightclubs for the "jet set" wealthy in New York City during the late sixties. By the early seventies, gay clubs in New York had adopted the format in which glamorously attired clients responded to recorded music with precise and expressive dance movements. As heterosexual couples were attracted to the disco beat, the music, dance, and clothing became a hallmark of American culture and were celebrated in the popular film *Saturday Night Fever*. By the late seventies the disco beat provided the background for television commercials, police serials, and even network sports coverage. Despite disco's origins in gay culture, however, the end of the decade also witnessed the birth of an antihomosexual movement. Led by Florida singer Anita Bryant and a number of major evangelical leaders, local citizens' groups succeeded in 1978 in eliminating homosexuals from inclusion in the civil rights ordinances of Miami, St. Paul, and Wichita, Kansas.

MIDDLE AMERICA AND MORAL CRISIS

The upsurge of social conservatism at the end of the 1970s continued the themes stressed by George Wallace and Richard Nixon in 1968. Another limitation on seventies conservatism

Lower-middle-class and blue-collar workers in the South, who were largely evangelical Protestant, and in the North, where many were Catholic, were confused by the social ferment of the 1960s. Under pressure to send their children to college, these "middle Americans" especially felt the need for young people to discipline themselves if they were to win a white-collar job. They were bitter, therefore, when they saw upper-middle-class college students setting bad examples, as campus agitators called for an increase in student administrative leadership and a furthering of sensual pleasure. Americans from the lower middle class and from blue-collar industries became even more bitter when they saw the major institution of establishment authority, the Supreme Court, accept this "permissiveness." The Court, for example, had voted against compulsory prayers and Bible reading in the public schools. Other Court decisions seemed to accept pornography and obscenity. These Americans believed that the Court was protecting criminals when it moved to protect the rights of people accused of crimes. The Court also appeared permissive to conservatives in ruling that laws restricting the sale and distribution of birth control methods were unconstitutional. As reported crime rates rose rapidly in the late sixties, criminal activity was associated with the permissiveness of the Supreme Court and the Anglo-Protestant establishment. Early seventies television featured a host of serials that celebrated the courage and wit of law enforcement officials upholding moral order.

By the mid-1970s, however, President Nixon's appointments to the Supreme Court had reversed the trend toward protecting the rights of the accused and the rights of privacy against police searches. The Nixon majority also seemed to reverse the Court's liberal tradition concerning civil rights. In the Bakke decision of 1978, the Court ruled against the use of racial quotas in the affirmative action admission policies of medical schools. Since 1965, it had been the policy of the national government to encourage such programs to overcome historical patterns of racial, ethnic, and sexual discrimination. Now some black leaders, such as Jesse Jackson, wondered if the Bakke decision marked the final collapse of efforts to establish greater social justice in the United States.

As mass media became open to gay and feminist critiques, a number of women with leaders such as Phyllis Schlafly banded together to preserve the traditional role of women as homemakers. They focused their efforts on blocking passage of the Equal Rights Amendment (ERA). Playing upon widespread resentment toward the middle-class cosmopolitans of the women's liberation movement, these activists succeeded in delaying, and perhaps defeating, passage of ERA by state legislatures in the late 1970s. When the Supreme Court ruled that laws against abortion were unconstitutional, these women attempted to enact a constitutional amendment that would permit legislation to bar abortions. And by 1980 they had succeeded in getting many state legislatures to cut back funding of abortions for poor women and had won severe restrictions on the use of federal funds for low-income women who wanted abortions.

Evangelical ministers such as the Reverend Carl McIntire and the Reverend Billy James Hargis had been attempting since the 1950s to build a political movement to stop social permissiveness. But although many Americans were drawn to social conservatism in the 1970s, the spread of the Charismatic and Pentecostal movements among Protestants and Catholics focused the energies of such conservatives on personal conversion, not social action.

Another limitation on seventies conservatism in middle America was the acceptance of new forms of birth control such as the pill by young women of southern Protestant background and northern Catholics. This change caused a special crisis of authority among Catholics, since the church hierarchy in Rome and the United States remained firmly against both "artificial" means of birth control and abortion. Surveys revealed, however, that while 40 percent of Catholic women used unapproved forms of birth control in 1960, the proportion had increased to 70 percent in 1970. The Catholic church, therefore, failed to function as a foundation of social conservatism in the 1960s and 1970s. Furthermore, the Catholic community faced considerable disarray in the 1960s as five thousand priests and forty-five thousand nuns left their callings and the number of young men preparing for the priesthood dropped from fifty thousand to eighteen thousand. Weekly attendance at Mass fell from 70 percent to 50 percent of Catholic parishioners, and participation in monthly Confession dropped from 37 percent to 17 percent. More dramatically, acceptance of the Pope's authority dropped from 70 percent to 40 percent.

The strongest academic criticism of permissiveness in the 1960s and 1970s came from Jewish intellectuals who had been accepted by the Anglo-Protestant academic community in the 1940s and 1950s. Writing in such magazines as *Commentary,* these critics attacked the way in which establishment leaders made concessions to the counterculture and the black, Chicano, and Native American minorities. Meanwhile, Jewish religious and social organizations focused increased energies on moral and financial support for Israel. The Jewish retreat from political liberalism took a different form in the 1970s when a number of young

Jewish intellectuals joined with young white Protestants and blacks to develop a neo-Marxist interpretation of American society. The academic professions of history, political science, sociology, anthropology, economics, and philosophy no longer were able to stop young professionals in those fields from becoming Marxists. Other young Jews were attracted to Asian religions. Still others turned back to ancient Judaism to find communal traditions and ethnic identity.

Given these deep confusions in the Protestant, Catholic, and Jewish communities, it was not surprising that no organized movement of social conservatism developed in the United States in the 1970s. Some sociologists in the late sixties had predicted a "blueing of America." They believed that the breakdown of the 1900 pattern of adolescence among the children of the white Protestant elite would open the door of upward economic mobility for the children of lower-middle-class and blue-collar workers. Symbolized by their love of President Kennedy and Coach Lombardi, these children were still willing to accept the discipline of delayed social and sexual maturity. They were still willing to compete hard. They still thought it was worthwhile to win a place in the establishment. But the "blueing of America" never completely arrived. Studies of young noncollege workers in the early 1970s found them moving rapidly toward some of the values that emerged on college campuses in the mid-sixties.

While only one out of ten college students identified with the New Left in 1967, many young people on campus had lost a great deal of respect for authority, police, and institutional religion. Two-thirds of the students believed that the country was run by big business and not by Congress or the president. And between 1967 and 1971, a very strong antiwar attitude

developed. While half of those polled were ready to support a war to protect national interest in 1967, only 30 percent supported that kind of war in 1971. One of three believed in war for national honor in 1967, but that ratio dropped to one out of five in 1971.

Between 1965 and 1971, polls indicated a steady movement toward permissiveness among college students. The trend was toward the acceptance of premarital sex, the use of marijuana, and the toleration of homosexuals. Further studies revealed that young noncollege workers, who constituted three-fifths of those between the ages of eighteen and twenty-two, resisted these changes until 1969. But young workers began to shift rapidly away from the old adolescence between 1969 and 1973. In 1960, one out of five young blue-collar workers wanted more sexual freedom; this ratio increased to one out of two by 1973. Two out of three had found premarital sex to be morally wrong in 1960, but only one of three did in 1971. In 1973, half of the noncollege youth accepted homosexual relationships between adults, although in 1969, three out of four had condemned that activity. Two of three had opposed abortions in 1960, but this had dropped to one of two in 1973.

Blue-collar youth had disagreed with college students on the value of organized religion, patriotism, and hard work in 1969. But by 1973 they shared the skepticism of college students on these issues. Support for organized religion among noncollege youth dropped from 65 percent in 1969 to 40 percent in 1973. Support for patriotism also fell from 60 percent to 40 percent during those four years. Belief that hard work always pays off dropped even more sharply, from 80 percent to 50 percent.

For young men and women in blue-collar jobs, the loss of blind loyalty to authority made them question the lack of worker participation in making decisions in the plants where they were employed. Job satisfaction became as important as wages. Polls indicated that many wished workers owned the businesses and factories where they spent so much of their lives. This discontent forced some business executives to become more sensitive to the feelings of their employees and to develop more flexible working schedules. No major changes occurred in the 1970s, however, toward significant participation of workers in decision making about the jobs they performed.

Despite the popularization of certain values and practices introduced by sixties counterculture, however, most of the nation's forty million working-class people continued to cling to many of their own traditions and outlooks. For example, several hundred thousand Americans in campers and pickup trucks continued to flock to the annual auto races at the Indianapolis Speedway. Camping out with ample supplies of hamburgers, beer, and country music, these vacationers conducted communal celebrations that rivaled the intensity and shared feelings of Woodstock. While disco music pervaded radio, television, and the movies by the late seventies, transplanted southerners, westerners, and other urban workers continued to listen to recorded country music. Based in music centers such as Nashville, Tennessee, and Austin, Texas, country music lamented the loss of family and community roots while simultaneously exploring the urban experiences of adultery, divorce, drinking, and alienating work.

The 1970s witnessed renewed sensitivity toward working-class culture and ethnic identity. By the end of the decade, Hollywood had produced successful films such as *Blue Collar, Norma Rae,* and *The Deer Hunter* that portrayed both the frailties and courage of those who worked the assembly lines, mills, and blast furnaces. As white ethnics began to organize for political power and cultural influence in the major industrial cities, films such as *The Deer Hunter, Rocky, The Godfather* and *The Godfather, Part II* depicted vital religious and social traditions among the nation's eastern and southern Europeans. Prodded by books such as Michael Novak's *The Rise of the Unmeltable Ethnics* (1971), major universities in urban centers began to establish programs in ethnic studies.

THE NEW AGE

The loss of social cohesion in American life in the 1960s and 1970s prompted many young people to search for spiritual alternatives. Because of the loss of faith in established religious institutions, the spiritual searching of young people often took them toward Oriental mysticism. Zen, Tibetan Buddhism, Yoga, I Ching, and other Asian philosophies and disciplines grew in popularity, particularly among middle-class youth. Much of the Charismatic movement within Catholicism shared the rejection of modern materialism in favor of increased spirituality. Such concern also appeared among "Jesus Freaks." These young Christians criticized the lack of spirituality among established Protestant denominations. They also were less willing to give their loyalty to the national government, capitalism, and the nuclear family than were the older group of evangelical Protestants. Like some of the counterculture and radical political experimenters of the early seventies, many of these groups established live-in communes in both rural areas and large cities.

While such religious developments were not threatening to the majority of the nation's people, the growth of spiritual cults disturbed American notions of individual free will. Groups such as Esalen, the Church of Scientology, the Hari Krishnas, and the disciples of the Korean Sun Myung Moon demanded total commitment and involvement by their members. By the late 1970s the parents of some cult members had turned to professional "deprogrammers" to reverse the brainwashing allegedly perpetrated by these organizations. The worst fears of anticultists were confirmed, however, when over nine hundred members of the California-based People's Temple committed mass suicide in 1978 in Guyana under orders from their spiritual father, Reverend Jim Jones.

Although the Jonestown suicides pointed to the dangers of cultism, the rampant concern for spirituality in the seventies went beyond fads and charismatic leaders. Writers such as William Irwin Thompson (*At the Edge of History,* 1971) spoke of a "planetary consciousness" that tied intuitive speculation to the experiments of the modern physical sciences. Novelist Tom Robbins, whose *Even Cowgirls Get the Blues* (1976) infused descriptions of counterculture antics with Oriental mysticism and biophysics, proclaimed that such "holistic" synthesis marked the dawn of a "new age." Holistic thinkers were particularly critical of the way in which modern medicine separated the mind from the body, treating the body as a machine. The mechanical tendencies of the medical establishment also treated one part of the body in isolation from the other parts. Holistic medicine accused the medical establishment of neglecting both the role of nutrition and exercise and the importance of the mind and spirit in individual health. George Leonard's *The Ultimate Athlete* (1975) provided an example of the attempt to combine body, mind, and spirit. Leonard argued that

true athletics was spiritual and involved "entering the realm of music and poetry, of the turning of the planet, of the understanding of death." The 1970s produced widespread acceptance by middle-class Americans of natural pathology, Chinese acupuncture, meditative techniques for treating illness and disease, and body exercises such as jogging.

Asian philosophies of wholeness gained new prestige when scientific experiments confirmed that the mind could influence such bodily states as the pulse and breathing rate. Scientific equipment also suggested that half the brain had artistic and imaginative qualities that were neglected or repressed by the educational system. Psychologists such as Robert Ornstein in *The Psychology of Consciousness* (1972) and Paul Watzlawick in *The Language of Change* (1978) called on modern psychology to give up its materialistic approach to human behavior because of this evidence.

Young physicists such as Fritjof Capra in *The Tao of Physics* (1975) also argued that the major developments of twentieth-century physics had broken down the distinction between spirit and matter. For Capra, the logic of physics was similar to that of Oriental mysticism. These changes in psychology and physics toward a more spiritual definition of reality were paralleled in popular culture by two very successful movies in 1977 and 1978, *Star Wars* and *Close Encounters of the Third Kind.* These films were very different from most of the science fiction movies of the 1950s that portrayed the invasion of Earth by hostile aliens from outer space. The heroes of the fifties movies had been scientists who produced atomic weapons for the military to use against aliens. In *Star Wars* and *Close Encounters,* however, evil was represented by military power that used atomic weapons. The heroes, who did not represent centralized power, gained strength from a sense of unity with a spiritual universe. "The Force be with you" was the religious statement of *Star Wars*. And for Americans torn apart by nearly two decades of social and cultural ferment, *Close Encounters* concluded with the promise that "We are not alone."

SUGGESTED READINGS

Two useful overviews of the 1960s are Ronald Berman, *America in the Sixties* (1968), and William O'Neill, *Coming Apart* (1972). Joseph Kett, *Rites of Passage,* and Kenneth Keniston, *The Uncommitted* (1965) and *Youth and Dissent* (1971), analyze the crisis of adolescence. The first major study of the youth rebellion is Theodore Roszak, *The Making of a Counter Culture* (1969). Richard King, *The Party of Eros: Radical Social Thought and the Realm of Freedom* (1972), describes some of the philosophic heroes of the youth culture, as does Robert Hunter, *The Storming of the Mind* (1972). Another excellent description of the new values is Philip Slater, *The Pursuit of Loneliness* (1970). The new religious perspectives of the decade are discussed in William Braden, *The Age of Aquarius* (1970), Robert Wuthnow, *The Consciousness Reformation* (1976), and Charles Glock and Robert Bellah, eds., *The New Religious Consciousness* (1976). The most recent study of the major cultural expressions of the 1960s is Morris Dickstein, *Gates of Eden* (1977).

Cultural confusions in the white Protestant establishment are explored in E. Digby Baltzell, *The Protestant Establishment* (1964), Peter Schrag, *The Decline of the WASP* (1976), and Ralph Brauer, *The Horse, the Gun, and the Piece of Property: Changing Images of the T.V. Western* (1975).

The factors leading to the emergence of a New Left after the sterility of the Old Left in the 1940s and 1950s is the subject of John P. Diggins, *The American Left in the Twentieth Century* (1973), Peter Clecak, *Radical Paradoxes: Dilemmas of the American Left, 1945–1970* (1973), and Irwin Unger, *The Movement* (1974).

The major principles of the ecology movement and its challenge to technology and economic growth can be found in Paul Sheperd and Daniel McKinley, eds., *The Subversive Science* (1969), Barry Commoner, *The Closing Circle* (1971), Nicholas Georgescu-Roegen, *The Entropy Law and Economic Process* (1971), and Victor Ferkiss, *The Future of Technological Civilization* (1974).

Vine DeLoria, Jr., *God Is Red* (1973), uses these ecological principles to criticize white Protestant values. Other studies of the recovery of cultural confidence by Native Americans are Helen Hertzberg, *The Search for an American Indian Identity* (1971), Stuart Levine and Nancy Lurie, *The American Indian Today* (1965), and Stan Steiner, *The New Indians* (1968). Matt Meier and Feliciano Rivera, *The Chicanos* (1972), and Rudolfo Acuna, *Occupied America: The Chicano's Struggle Toward Liberation* (1972), describe the resurgence of Chicano culture.

An overview of changes in the black community is Benjamin Muse, *The American Negro Revolution: From Violence to Black Power* (1968). Excellent descriptions of the dramatic changes in black literature are Addison Gayle, Jr., *The Way of the New World: The Black Novel in America* (1976), and

Eugene B. Redmond, *Drum Voice: The Mission of Afro-American Poetry* (1976).

Barbara Deckard, *The Women's Movement* (1975), Betty Gorburg, *The Changing Family* (1973), and Gayle Graham Yates, *What Women Want: The Ideas of the Movement* (1975), discuss the patterns of change among women. An excellent oral history of the origins of the women's movement can be found in Sara Evans, *Personal Politics* (1979).

Michael Novak, *The Rise of the Unmeltable Ethnics* (1971), Richard Krickus, *Pursuing the American Dream: White Ethnics and the New Populism* (1976), and Daniel Yankelovich, *The New Morality* (1974), analyze the stresses and confusions among blue-collar Americans.

Chapter 17

THE SEARCH FOR AUTHORITY, 1968-1980

Despite the major cultural changes of the 1960s, President Richard Nixon attempted to create a political administration based on traditional values of order, discipline, and strength. Elected amid the social chaos of 1968, Nixon represented the attempt to restore the discipline that Anglo-Protestant culture expected of its youth. The president's critique of permissiveness and his personal enthusiasm for the collectivized competition of football set the tone for an administration that sought to counter the pleasure seeking of the middle class with renewed respect for authority and national power.

NIXONIAN SOCIAL MANAGEMENT

Conforming to a pattern originally set in the New Deal, the Nixon White House moved to centralize policy making at the expense of Congress, the cabinet, and the permanent regulatory agencies. With Roy Ash of Litton Industries at the helm of a key reorganization task force, the Nixon administration began to adapt techniques of corporate management to national planning. Ash assumed responsibility for the Office of Management and Budget (OMB), which monitored the managerial practices and performance of the federal agencies. Under "Management by Objectives" procedures, borrowed from private corporations, all agencies listed their annual goals so the president might choose the highest priorities. Nixon also appointed presidential counselor John Ehrlichman to head a new Domestic Council. Modeled on the National Security Council, the DC formalized the transfer of policy making to the White House by acting as the president's planning board.

Ehrlichman's Domestic Council used cabinet officials to chart national policy, but Nixon went outside the cabinet system to appoint Harvard's Daniel Moynihan to lead an Urban Affairs Council. Moynihan's systems approach to urban policy prompted the president to maintain Great Society programs such as Model Cities and OEO, and encouraged Nixon to endorse the idea of a nationwide growth policy. Through Moynihan's influence, the president also created a controversial commission on population growth and family planning. Nixon's desire to fuse national planning with management efficiency was evident in his 1971 message on government reorganization, which recommended that bureaucratic overlapping be ended by consolidating domestic policy making in four broad categories — natural resources, community development, human resources, and economic affairs. But reorganization threatened vested interests accustomed to working with congressional oversight committees, and Congress never followed through on the idea.

Although Nixon had been elected as a budgetary conservative, he understood that government management could encourage social stability. Accordingly, federal spending, as a percentage of the gross national product, continued to rise during the Nixon years. By 1975 government outlays for income maintenance surpassed defense costs for the first time in history. Rising government assistance was reflected in the expansion of Aid to Dependent Children (ADC), a welfare program that covered two million youngsters in 1960 and twelve million in 1975. By the mid-1970s, thirteen million American families were receiving government food stamps. Nixon and Moynihan hoped to reduce the cumbersome welfare bureaucracy and channel money directly to the poor. Accordingly, the president introduced a $6 billion Family Assistance Plan in 1969. In order to satisfy Republican conservatives, Nixon denied that FAP was a guaranteed income program and misleadingly labeled it "workfare." But the president's bill did not include strict work requirements, and conservatives objected to its provision of at least $1,600 a year to every poor family. Ironically, the plan was killed in the Senate when liberals feared inadequate support levels for the poor and objected to Nixon's rhetoric. In reprisal, the president made major cuts in Great Society programs such as Head Start, the Job Corps, and OEO. By 1975 twenty-five million Americans still lived below the poverty line.

While centralizing procedures in the federal bureaucracy, Nixon attempted to revitalize state and local governments. The president's 1971 State of the Union message called for a "New American Revolution" through revenue sharing between the federal government and the states, a proposal first made by a Lyndon Johnson task force. Despite much rhetoric over the "New Federalism," however, general revenue sharing provided no more than 5 percent of state and local funds, while the federal government continued to control spending through larger outlays for "special programs." Although conservatives hoped to reverse the erosion of local control that had marked federal policy making since the New Deal, problems of inflation distracted the Nixon administration from that goal.

Several developments contributed to the inflation that characterized the years after 1965. Between 1965 and 1975 the nation spent $600 billion on weapons. But massive foreign aid and overseas investment brought a resulting troublesome export of dollars, in annual balance-of-payment deficits of $20 billion. So great was the flow of capital abroad that by 1974 the foreign earnings of American multinational corporations constituted 30 percent of all corporate profits after taxes. This "dollar drain" reduced the supply of gold reserves in the United States and contributed to rising corporate debt, which reached $1.3 trillion in 1974. Corporate debt, in turn, increased the competition for credit and accelerated interest rates and further inflation.

Inflation disrupted the social stability that Nixon sought, as it reduced spending power and eliminated savings. The national median housing price, for example, had been within reach of two-fifths of the nation's families in 1965. By 1971, however, only one-fifth could afford such a price. Inflation also aggravated relations between labor and management, since both worker productivity and real wages began to decline after 1966. A wildcat strike by 100,000 Teamsters tied up trucking in the Midwest and West Coast during the winter of 1969–1970 and was followed by a long strike of auto workers. But civil servants, teachers, and hospital workers also joined unions to strike for better pay against the government itself. A spontaneous walkout of postal workers, for example, briefly disrupted mail deliveries in 1970; but the president threatened to use troops and the strike was abandoned.

Nixon began to fight inflation by extending Johnson's 10 percent tax surcharge, vetoing a bill to expand public works in the cities, and declaring a ninety-day freeze on wages, prices, and rents in 1971. The president also created a Cost of Living Council to monitor rising costs. Nixon's freeze marked the first peacetime price control in history, but by the end of the year he was forced to devalue the dollar to stop further inflation. Fearful that stringent economic control might slow the economy and boost unemployment, the president relaxed wage and price regulations in 1973. But a government-subsidized sale of 8.5 million tons of grain to the Soviet Union contributed to a 20

percent leap in retail food prices that year, and Nixon resorted to another freeze. When that proved ineffective as well, the president conceded that inflation was beyond the immediate control of the government, and a discouraged administration allowed economic controls to expire in 1974.

Just as the administration gave up its war on inflation, it found itself confronted with an energy squeeze. In 1973 one-third of the nation's oil was imported, a proportion that approached one-half by the late seventies. Estimates suggested that half the 12 percent leap in the 1974 consumer price index stemmed from dwindling energy resources and soaring fuel costs. Nixon appointed Colorado Governor John Love to a newly created Energy Policy Office in June 1973 and allotted $100 million for energy research. But in October, Middle East oil-producing nations declared an export embargo against the United States to weaken American support for Israel. The embargo dramatized American dependence on foreign oil sources, and the price of imported petroleum quadrupled in three months. By February 1974, motorists lined up for hours to buy gasoline, as the major oil distributors held back on supplies. Americans who paid 35¢ a gallon in mid-1973 paid 50¢ a gallon by early 1975.

Nixon responded to the escalated energy crisis by replacing Love's office with a new Federal Energy Administration, headed by Deputy Treasury Secretary William E. Simon. He also signed legislation that permitted construction of a pipeline from northern Alaskan oil fields owned by the major oil producers. Opposed to rationing, Nixon sought a symbolic commitment to energy conservation by lowering the maximum speed limit to 55 mph. Although energy consumption did not decrease dramatically, slower speeds reduced traffic fatalities by one-fifth, and Congress made the speed reduction permanent late in 1974. The president also announced Project Independence, an effort to make the nation self-reliant in energy. But estimates placed the costs of energy independence at $1 trillion. When Nixon vetoed a bill to tax oil profits in March 1974, most Americans suspected that the "energy crisis" was a ruse to pad corporate dividends. Not until the later seventies did automobile manufacturers respond with production of smaller and more efficient vehicles. Whatever the size of their cars, Americans remained skeptical about the energy crisis and continued to insist on individualized forms of transportation.

Despite a strong beginning, the Nixon administration pulled back from concepts of national planning. The president created an Environmental Protection Agency (EPA) in 1970 to consolidate the government's antipollution programs and later asked Congress to establish various controls over private resources. But the Nixon presidency failed to meet the twin challenges of inflation and energy conservation and never followed up on initial interest in growth and population policy, land-use planning, and explicit national goals. All that remained of Nixonian innovations in social management were the reforms that strengthened the president's control of the federal bureaucracy and that consolidated power in the White House.

THE REVIVAL OF SOCIAL CONSERVATISM

Throughout the sixties, liberal cosmopolitans had defined the issues and solutions to national problems with little sensitivity to lower-middle-class and working-class people. Exaggerating the political influence of minority voters, the professional middle class, and the young, New Frontier and Great Society administrators had attempted to erect a homogeneous society built upon corporate precepts of cooperation and goodwill. But liberal social programs seemed to suggest that the government was concerned only with the rich and the very poor. And by this time millions of ethnic Americans had internalized traditional values of hard work, obedience to law and order, respect for authority, self-reliance, and patriotism. As welfare spending, ghetto rioting, illegal antiwar protests, and youth rebellion crescendoed in the late sixties, ethnic and lower-middle-class Americans found their conventional lifestyles and values ridiculed by the media and the liberal intelligentsia.

Many white Americans resented the attention given to black demands in the late sixties and expected blacks to adhere to white standards and values. Like George Wallace, Nixon played upon these sentiments in appeals for law and order and in suggestions that "black capitalism," not political activism or cultural independence, would bring equal opportunity. In a policy that Domestic Adviser Moynihan described as "benign neglect," the Nixon administration discouraged the use of federal power to ensure racial integration in the work force and the schools. When the Labor Department prepared to order minority representation on federal construction jobs in 1972, Nixon characterized quotas as "a dangerous detour away from the traditional value of measuring a person on the basis of ability." Twelve days later the department announced that "proportional representation" was a goal, not a requirement, of federal contract compliance.

School integration provided a more complex issue for the administration. While Nixon gave verbal support to equal opportunity, he opposed cutting off funds for school districts that did not comply with judicial orders for integration. Nevertheless, the Department of Health, Education, and Welfare began to withhold funds from certain northern communities and ordered hearings on racial discrimination in Boston schools. Meanwhile, the Supreme Court unanimously approved school integration through busing, although Chief Justice Warren Burger also indicated that racially balanced schools were not required in all cases and that "unwarranted" decisions for busing had been made in the past.

Opposition to busing combined elements of racial prejudice with sincere concern for neighborhood schools and community stability in working-class districts of the inner cities. Nixon felt compelled to respond to these sentiments by publicly reaffirming his personal distaste for busing. The president also proposed a judicial moratorium on busing directives, during which Congress could consider whether to deny the courts further power to order them. While the NAACP accused Nixon of bringing Jim Crowism back to the nation's schools, a federal court

City police escort school buses at the peak of the busing controversy in the Boston school district. Bunker Hill Monument appears in the background. (Nick Passmore/Stock, Boston)

postponed the busing of 300,000 students in Detroit. Yet school desegregation proceeded at an increasing pace in the Nixon years, and the president's resistance proved largely symbolic.

While Nixon failed to slow the pace of school integration, he attempted to show that the Democratic Congress was "soft" on crime. The administration introduced a controversial court reorganization bill for Washington, D.C., labeling it a model for national crime legislation and a warning to "criminal forces." Although the bill provided police and judges with no more power than they already possessed, it legitimized "preventive detention" and certain warrantless searches. To constitutionalists such as Senator Sam Ervin of North Carolina, the bill clearly violated four of the ten amendments in the Bill of Rights. But Congress shared the president's sensitivity to law and order and passed the package in a surprise move in 1971.

Nixon attracted social conservatives by placing blame for society's permissiveness on the liberal Supreme Court. Court decisions involving abolition of prayer in public schools, reapportionment of state legislatures, and protections for criminal suspects had encouraged sixties conservatives to support Nixon's promise to appoint nonactivist justices. When Chief Justice Earl Warren retired in 1969, Nixon chose Warren Burger, a moderate Minnesota Republican, as Warren's replacement. But when a second vacancy occurred that year, the president followed Attorney General John Mitchell's "southern strategy" and nominated Georgia Judge Clement Haynsworth. When the Senate questioned a conflict of interest in Haynsworth's judicial record, however, he became the first Supreme Court nominee in forty years to be rejected. Nixon responded by appointing another southerner, Harold Carswell. But Senate inquiry revealed that Carswell

had made white supremacist statements in a 1948 election campaign, and his nomination was rejected as well. Infuriated, Nixon lambasted the Senate for "regional discrimination" and claimed that his power of appointment had been abrogated by liberals hostile to a strict interpretation of the Constitution. Yet the president eased the tension by selecting another Minnesota moderate, Harry Blackmun.

The Court fight demonstrated Nixon's determination to attack liberal institutions with conservative principles. By the end of his first term, the president succeeded in appointing two more conservatives to the increasingly cautious Supreme Court. Although the Burger Court outlawed domestic "national security" wiretaps without judicial permission and prohibited states from interfering with most abortions, it generally followed Nixonian lines of social conservatism. Court decisions limited the immunity of witnesses from prosecution, allowed non-unanimous jury verdicts in state criminal cases, and compelled news reporters to testify before grand juries. The Burger Court also facilitated enforcement of the death penalty by ruling that state capital punishment was constitutional if the appropriate statutes were worded carefully and applied without discrimination. The Court further pleased Nixon conservatives by opening the door to "local option" on obscenity and pornography censorship in 1975.

DÉTENTE AND ESCALATION

Despite his rhetoric over domestic discipline and order, Nixon believed that the presidency was concerned primarily with foreign affairs. The most innovative aspect of his administration was the movement toward relaxation of tensions with both China and the Soviet Union. Ever since the Communist Revolution of 1949, the People's Republic of China had remained unrecognized by the United States. Cold Warriors, including Nixon himself, continually warned that recognition would entail abandoning the Nationalist government on Taiwan (Formosa) and would legitimize Communist subversion against established regimes. Beginning with Harry Truman, each Cold War president backed away from conciliatory steps toward China, fearful of appearing "soft" on communism. But when the Chinese made diplomatic overtures in 1969, Nixon reasoned that he could win concessions from both China and the Soviet Union if he took advantage of the deepening rift between the two rivals. Accordingly, the president began to establish communication with the Chinese and eased restrictions on American travel to the mainland. By 1971 Nixon no longer referred to "Red China" and he encouraged an American table tennis team to go to Peking. When the athletes were received warmly, the United States announced the end of a twenty-one-year embargo on Chinese trade and accepted Peking's seating in the United Nations several months later.

The China détente was formalized when the president toured the Communist nation early in 1972. Although the visit was largely nonsubstantive, millions of Americans witnessed the highly publicized event through satellite television. Nixon and Chinese Premier Chou En-lai released a joint communiqué that pledged the two nations to "peaceful mutuality," but the most important part of the negotiations involved an American promise to withdraw military forces from Taiwan and accept Peking's contention that the island historically belonged to China. Three months after Nixon had achieved détente with the People's Republic,

he traveled to Moscow. President Johnson had met amicably in 1967 with Premier Alexei Kosygin, but that meeting was not substantive. This time, Nixon and Communist party leader Leonid Brezhnev signed a Strategic Arms Limitation Treaty (SALT), limiting construction of antiballistic missile sites and nuclear delivery systems. Although the treaty did not rule out the development of new weapons, the Nixon-Brezhnev talks produced agreements on Berlin and trade. In July 1972 the United States agreed to sell the Soviets $750 million worth of grain, about one-fourth of the entire American crop. When Brezhnev visited Washington the following year, the two leaders signed additional pacts covering nuclear arms, cultural exchanges, and peaceful uses of atomic energy.

Like Johnson, Nixon held out the promise of peace in Southeast Asia. But détente with China and the Soviet Union only heightened the president's desire to maintain credibility — the image of national strength and determination in global affairs. "Precipitate withdrawal" from Vietnam would be a "popular and easy course," Nixon told the American people in 1969, but he warned that defeat and humiliation would bring the "collapse of confidence in American leadership." Although the president believed in both the rightness of the war and the need to end it, his fear of surrender brought the United States four more years of destruction in Southeast Asia.

Once Nixon indicated willingness to resume the bombing of North Vietnam in early 1969, the North Vietnamese responded with a fresh offensive, and the president ordered a new "pacification" program in the Mekong Delta. As the nation's chief executive sought "peace with honor," bombing of villages, destruction of crops, and removal of peasants once again characterized the bloody conflict. By mid-1973, the Nixon administration had unleashed four million tons of bombs on Indochina; twice the tonnage ordered by Johnson and one and one-half times the total dropped on Europe and Asia in both World War Two and the Korean War.

Despite Nixon's refusal to accept a Communist victory in Vietnam, he understood how massive commitments of fighting men had destroyed the Johnson presidency. Accordingly, as disaffection mounted among soldiers and the domestic public, the president announced a Nixon Doctrine by which ground troops would be withdrawn while the United States escalated the air war and provided economic and military aid to the South Vietnamese. Amid massive antiwar demonstrations in the fall of 1969, Nixon told a television audience that "we are Vietnamizing the search for peace," and began to move toward an all-volunteer army. By the spring of 1970 the president had withdrawn 110,000 troops and announced a "Vietnamization" program to train the South Vietnamese Army to assume the burden of the fighting.

As Nixon stepped up troop withdrawals, however, he continued to expand the war. Fearful of public opinion at home, the president ordered the secret bombing of insurgent forces in Cambodia during March 1969. To prevent disclosure of the covert air war, conducted even without the knowledge of the secretary of the air force, military officers established a bombing command system outside ordinary channels and falsified or destroyed all records of sorties. But in 1970 Nixon went public when he told a stunned nation that twenty-five thousand American and South Vietnamese ground forces had entered Cambodia in an "incursion" designed to "shorten the war." The object of the invasion, the commander-in-chief explained, was "cleaning out major North Vietnamese and Vietcong occupied territories," and destroying

the "main headquarters for the entire Communist military operation in South Vietnam." The president also hoped to bolster the anti-Communist military regime that recently had taken control of the Cambodian capital.

For Nixon, Cambodia was a test crisis whose importance lay in the manner in which Americans revealed themselves to the world. The president proclaimed that the United States could not act "like a pitiful, helpless giant" and confided that he would rather be a one-term president than see the nation become a "second-rate power" and be defeated for the first time "in its proud 190-year history." Referring to an "age of anarchy both abroad and at home," Nixon emphasized American will and determination by resuming the bombing of North Vietnam.

Failing to find Communist insurgents, American ground troops withdrew from Cambodia two months later, pulling out on the very day that Congress passed a prohibition against their continued presence. But in February 1971 the president revealed that the South Vietnamese Army had invaded Laos with American air support. American bombing in Laos had not abated since the early sixties, but the invasion represented a new tactic, and the administration placed a news blackout on the inept attack. American planes also continued daily bombings in North Vietnam in what the Pentagon described as "protective-reaction air strikes" to cover withdrawing American forces. By the spring of 1972, however, South Vietnamese troops were in chaotic retreat from the northern provinces, and the Communists were moving into the central highlands. Angered and faced with the failure of Vietnamization, Nixon announced the mining of North Vietnamese ports. Three months after his triumphant visit to the People's Republic, the president labeled the

North Vietnamese "international outlaws" and ordered the bombing of railroad lines leading to China. He also instructed the air force to hit industrial targets in populated areas of North Vietnam and sent American B-52s to attack the Vietnamese dike system. Nevertheless, polls showed that 60 percent of the American public believed that the president was doing everything he could to end the war.

One month before the 1972 presidential election, National Security Adviser Henry Kissinger and North Vietnamese negotiators secretly agreed to a military cease-fire. Under Soviet influence, North Vietnam had decided to postpone a political settlement but won the right to keep its military units in the South. As the Nixon administration stopped the bombing of the North, Kissinger confidently proclaimed that peace was at hand. But when South Vietnamese leaders rejected the truce, Kissinger abruptly announced the suspension of negotiations and resumption of the air war. In the "Christmas Bombing" of 1972, B-52s attacked populated areas and wiped out a children's hospital at Bach Mai resulting in hundreds of casualties. Despite private and official criticism from world leaders of all ideologies, the Nixon administration offered little explanation for the most intensive bombing in military history. But it was clear that the United States supported Saigon's reluctance to relinquish South Vietnamese territory held by the Communists and that Nixon and Kissinger hoped to build up fears of American retaliation should North Vietnam overwhelm the South.

Nixon finally announced a Vietnam peace agreement that would "end the war and bring peace with honor" in January 1973. But there was little in the accord that could not have been negotiated when Nixon assumed office four years before. During that time, twenty thousand Americans lost their lives and fifty thousand more were wounded in Vietnam, while South Vietnam suffered even more casualties than it had in the Johnson years. The formal peace settlement provided for the withdrawal of the twenty-five thousand remaining American troops in exchange for American prisoners of war. But the peace treaty also provided official recognition of the National Liberation Front by the United States and resolved the nineteen-year controversy over the two Vietnams by declaring the 17th parallel a provisional boundary instead of a political or territorial dividing line.

Although the truce did not affect American bombing in Cambodia, military involvement in Vietnam ended with withdrawal of the last troops and return of the remaining POWs in March 1973. The administration arranged a televised homecoming for the released pilots, but nothing could erase the fact of American capitulation in the most unpopular war in the history of the United States. Altogether, the Vietnam War left over 56,000 Americans dead, more than 300,000 wounded, over one million Vietnamese slaughtered, and ten million homeless. But the injury to national cohesion went far beyond the awesome destruction and the $140 billion in war costs.

THE FAILURE OF NATIONAL UNITY

Continuation of the Vietnam War proved fatal to the Nixon administration and to social peace at home. When the "twelve wise men" of the corporate elite had informed President Johnson that the war was unwinnable in 1968, they anticipated a reversal in American policy. Like-

Protesters gather at the Moratorium against the War,
Washington, D.C., 1970. (Charles Gatewood)

wise, most Americans assumed that Johnson's
abdication signified an imminent end to hostilities. But the slow pace of Nixon's withdrawal broadened the base of antiwar sentiment. By the fall of 1969, 57 percent of the
country favored a specified deadline for complete disengagement. On October 15, Vietnam
Moratorium Day, 40,000 demonstrators marched
in Washington, 65,000 rallied in New York
City, and 100,000 gathered on the Boston Common to hear Senator Edward Kennedy propose
total withdrawal within the year. A second
moratorium in November brought out the largest political gathering in American history.

While peace rallies and marches occurred
across the nation, more than 250,000 demonstrators gathered at the Washington Monument. When ten thousand protesters were tear-
gassed in front of the Justice Department,
Attorney General Mitchell remarked that "it
looked like the Russian Revolution." But one
million Americans had demonstrated peaceably
against the war in the fall campaign.

College campuses were relatively quiet until
Nixon announced the invasion of Cambodia
in April 1970. But escalation of the war literally set the nation's universities on fire. At Kent
State in Ohio, Governor James Rhodes called
in the National Guard to prevent further demonstrations after students burned the campus
Reserve Officers' Training Corps building. Just a
few days before, Vice President Agnew had denounced student unrest and urged Americans
to "act accordingly." Rhodes blamed the Kent
violence on agitators "worse than the Brown
Shirts, the Communist element and also the
night riders and the vigilantes." On May 4,
Kent State students failed to respond to a dispersal order at a noon rally and threw rocks
and bottles at guardsmen firing tear gas. Finding themselves surrounded, several of the tense
guardsmen wheeled around and fired rifle shots
into the crowd, wounding nine and killing four.

The Kent State deaths electrified a nation
already shocked by news of the Cambodian
invasion. University presidents had warned
Nixon that there was no hope of restoring
peace on American campuses without ending
the Vietnam War. Following Kent State, Interior Secretary Walter Hickel wrote Nixon
that "youth in its protest must be heard." But
Agnew responded to the killings by blaming
"elitist" permissiveness toward "psychotic and
criminal elements" for the "traitors and thieves
and perverts...in our midst." The president

appeared more uncertain. He assured the nation that the Cambodian invasion would not exceed a twenty-one-mile limit and would be over in three to seven weeks; he also told reporters that he knew "how deeply" antiwar protesters felt and that "everything that I stand for is what they want." On edge and unable to sleep one evening, the president made fifty-one late-night telephone calls and spoke to Kissinger eight times. Finally he left the White House to engage several antiwar demonstrators in small talk beneath the Lincoln Memorial at 5 A.M.

Never before in American history had white students been fired upon by forces of the state. Within days, student strikes closed 350 universities and colleges, while hundreds more suspended classes. As ROTC bombings, window smashing, and building occupations broke out across the nation's schools, the American system of higher education ceased to function. At Jackson State in Mississippi, two black students were killed when police inexplicably fired on a college dormitory. But at most institutions, moderates channeled activism into letter campaigns, antiwar petitions, and doorbell ringing. Under a plan devised at Princeton, some colleges gave released time for students who wished to campaign for antiwar candidates in the fall elections.

The student strikes of 1970 made it clear that social peace and continuation of the war were incompatible, but the massive disruptions marked the last cry of campus protest. The Kent State shootings intimidated further demonstrations in a period in which draft calls were falling off and students increasingly were concerned with a declining job market. Yet thirty thousand demonstrators arrived in Washington during May 1971 to protest the invasion of Laos by blocking traffic and employing civil

disobedience to disrupt the functioning of the capital. Monitored by a joint command of the CIA and local police, twelve thousand people were swept off the streets in the largest mass arrest in American history. But the arbitrary arrests involved widespread suspension of legal procedures in the first assignment for the administration's Intelligence Evaluation Committee. Four years later a federal court awarded $12 million in damages to those who had been improperly detained.

Like Johnson and his Cold War predecessors, Nixon believed that the fight against world communism was a test of the president's personal character. But the Vietnam War politicized all aspects of American life, and the federal government lay in the front lines of the attack on institutional leaders and traditional sanctions of authority. Starting with the Johnson administration, the government acted to stem the tide toward anarchy and political disrespect, fearing the very existence of the nation to be at stake. Johnson's Department of Justice prosecuted baby doctor Benjamin Spock, Yale chaplain William Sloane Coffin, and two others for aiding draft evasion in 1968. Through the Internal Security Division of the Justice Department, the Nixon administration continued to use the courts and unauthorized wiretaps to suppress dissenters. In 1969 a federal grand jury indicted eight leaders of the 1968 Chicago demonstrations, accusing them of conspiracy and violation of the antiriot provisions of the Civil Rights Act of 1968. The explosive trial of the Chicago Eight became a showplace for radical protest and revolutionary culture. Insisting that the government was using the case to discourage dissent, Yippies Jerry Rubin and Abbie Hoffman wore long hair, talked back to the judge, introduced songs as evidence, and displayed NLF flags. When Black Panther

Bobby Seale would not proceed without his bedridden attorney, Judge Julius Hoffman ordered Seale gagged and chained. Judge Hoffman cited defendants and their lawyers for 175 acts of contempt during the five-month trial. The jury verdict in 1970 erased the conspiracy charges but found five of the defendants guilty of individual intent to incite riot. Four of the

contempt citations were upheld in another trial in 1973, but charges against Seale, who won a separate trial, were dropped.

Although federal grand juries collected information on radicals and antiwar groups, prosecution frequently faltered in court. A grand jury indicted the imprisoned Berrigan brothers and five others in 1970 for conspiracy to kidnap

MAP 17.1   THE THRUST INTO CAMBODIA

Reprinted by permission from TIME, *The Weekly Newsmagazine; Copyright Time Inc.* 1970

National Security Adviser Kissinger. But another jury failed to convict them two years later when the prime evidence turned out to be a whimsical letter delivered to Philip Berrigan through an FBI informer. Thirteen Black Panthers also were acquitted of conspiracy to bomb New York City department stores in 1971, while a New Haven jury failed to agree on a verdict in a case that charged Seale and other Panthers with conspiracy to murder an alleged police informant.

Not satisfied with court proceedings, the Nixon administration mounted an intense public relations campaign against antiwar activism and radical violence. Assistant Attorney General Richard Kleindienst called for the repression of "ideological criminals" in 1969 and described the antiwar movement as "national subversive activity." Meanwhile, the president told a South Dakota college audience that "fundamental values" were "under bitter and even violent attack in America" and that "We have the power to strike back if need be, and to prevail." Stung by massive antiwar activity in November 1969, the president called demonstrators a "vocal minority" and appealed for support from the nation's "silent majority."

But it was Vice President Agnew who assumed the burden of the administration's attack on the moratoriums of 1969, referring to antiwar activists as an "effete corps of impudent snobs who characterized themselves as intellectuals." Within its first year of office, the Nixon White House had become convinced that liberal-dominated institutions such as the Supreme Court, mass media, and universities were preventing the president from reaching the silent majority. Agnew complained to a Des Moines audience that a "tiny enclosed fraternity of privileged men" in TV journalism distorted presidential addresses through the "instant analysis" that followed televised speeches. He contended that "a small band of network commentators and self-appointed analysts" had tried to obstruct the president's effort to bring peace to Vietnam. The implications of the vice president's criticism were crystalized when the newly confirmed chairman of the Federal Communications Commission requested transcripts of the network commentaries on Nixon's Vietnamization speech. And White House communications director Herbert Klein threatened that if the networks and press did not correct their bias against the president, "you do invite the government to come in."

Agnew also had criticized the print media for concentrating on bad news instead of good. But the day following the November moratorium, newspapers published the first reports on the recently uncovered My Lai massacre. The highly publicized case resulted in a military trial and the 1971 murder conviction of Lieutenant William Calley. While the army brought minor coverup charges against a brigade commander, Calley was the only career officer to be convicted. The case brought an emotional burst of support for the defendant from Americans who insisted that Calley had only performed his military duty. Another segment of opinion held that he had been made a scapegoat for American brutality in Vietnam. Intervening in the volatile case, Nixon promised to review the final sentence and permitted Calley to live in his own quarters at a military base. A military review court later reduced the lieutenant's sentence to twenty years.

Nixon's intervention in the Calley case indicated his desire to win support from patriotic blue-collar ethnics and the lower middle class. His encouragement of working-class patriotism was part of an administration effort to construct an image of national war enthusiasm. To counteract protests over Cambodia and Kent State, White House aides also created bogus citizen groups such as the Tell It To Hanoi Committee, while the Republican National Committee signed hundreds of names to form letters endorsing administration policy.

The climax to the Nixon campaign came during the congressional elections of 1970. In order to defeat candidates it described as "radical-liberals," the White House created its own Committee for a Responsible Congress. Nixon visited ten states in four days during the campaign, making his own prestige and student demonstrations the central issues. In San Jose the president jumped on top of a car and made the peace sign, deliberately provoking a crowd of protesters into angry response. "As long as I am president," Nixon declared, "no band of violent thugs is going to keep me from going out and speaking with the American people." Meanwhile, Agnew referred to domestic rebels as "misfits" and "garbage." By the 1970 elections, however, much of the American public had tired of the administration's abrasiveness and desired social peace. Speaking for the Democratic candidates on election eve, Maine's Senator Edmund Muskie castigated the administration for a "politics of fear." The next day, Republicans gained two seats in the Senate but lost nine congressional seats and eleven governorships.

WATERGATE AND
POLITICAL REPRESSION

The public relations campaign and court action against radicals proved insufficient for an administration that continually found itself beset by threats to social order. When the liberal

New York Times publicized the secret bombing of Cambodia in 1969, the White House ordered the FBI to install "national security" wiretaps on the telephones of four newsmen and thirteen administration aides. To stop further leaks, White House assistants hired two former police agents as private investigators, but their tasks included surveillance of Senator Edward Kennedy, a potential candidate for the 1972 presidential campaign. Kennedy had driven his car off a bridge during a late-night accident at Chappaquiddick, Massachusetts, drowning a woman who was a former campaign aide. Questions concerning the senator's relationship with his companion, in addition to his delay in reporting the accident, made Kennedy a logical choice for White House undercover investigations.

By 1970 Nixon pressed for a coordinated program of domestic intelligence to counter the threat of internal dissent. Following the Cambodian invasion, presidential aide Tom Huston drafted a proposal for an interagency intelligence unit composed of the FBI, CIA, National Security Agency, and the Pentagon intelligence agencies. The illegal Huston Plan called for burglary, wiretapping, mail openings, campus informants, and monitoring of international communications, but the presidentially approved program was implemented for only five days before FBI Director Hoover squelched it. Hoover feared disclosure of the unlawful procedures and hoped to maintain FBI control of domestic security. Despite the demise of the Huston Plan, however, the FBI continued its counterintelligence program against radicals, the CIA carried on illegal domestic spying, and the NSA maintained electronic surveillance of international messages. In late 1970 the White House settled for an Intelligence Evaluation Committee to coordinate surveillance of radicals.

The crisis atmosphere of 1970 produced another administrative offensive when Marxist candidate Salvador Allende was about to be confirmed as president by Chile's national assembly. Kissinger privately warned that Allende would pose "massive problems" for the United States in Latin America and told the president's national security advisers that they could not "stand by and watch a country go communist due to the irresponsibility of its own people." Nixon quickly ordered the CIA to organize a Chilean military coup. When that did not materialize, government and private lending agencies refused credit to Chile, creating unbearable pressures on that nation's economy, while the CIA continued to provide funds to opposing politicians, friendly media, and anti-Communist unions. Between 1970 and 1973 the United States spent $8 million in the covert effort to turn Chile against its elected president. Finally, Allende was assassinated in a bloody coup in 1973, and a military regime abolished Chilean democracy.

When the *New York Times* began to publish the secret Pentagon Papers in 1971, the Nixon White House faced still another self-created crisis. McNamara's study of the Vietnam War focused on the continuity of government duplicity during the Kennedy and Johnson administrations. But National Security Adviser Kissinger feared that future leaks might threaten Soviet and Chinese confidence in the American ability to conduct secret negotiations. Shortly after federal courts refused to permit the government to stop publication of the Pentagon study, Nixon authorized creation of a Special Investigations Unit (the "Plumbers") to prevent administration leaks. When Daniel Ellsberg, a former Defense Department planner, confessed that he had released the papers to expose government lying and help end the war,

the Plumbers burglarized the office of Ellsberg's psychiatrist to gain information that could be used to discredit the former Pentagon aide. Ellsberg and Anthony Russo were indicted for espionage and conspiracy in 1971, but the government dropped the charges when it refused to produce wiretap logs that contained conversations involving the defendants. Presidential assistants John Ehrlichman, Charles Colson, and others subsequently were convicted of various charges related to the smear campaign against Ellsberg, and in 1974 a federal court ruled that a president had no constitutional right to authorize a break-in, even when national security and foreign intelligence were involved.

As the 1972 presidential election approached, the Nixon administration turned its intelligence capacity to more partisan matters. Since 1970, the Internal Revenue Service had been using tax audits to harass individuals and organizations with "extremist views and philosophies" and had provided confidential information about these targets to intelligence and law-enforcement agencies. But in 1971 the White House prepared an "enemies list" of 280 individuals whom it perceived to be allies of the Democratic party. The list of those to be audited included liberal congressmen, labor leaders, prominent media and show business personalities, and Democratic fund raisers and contributors from the corporate world. But the IRS declined to pursue these partisan demands. Nevertheless, Nixon operatives began undercover investigations of Republican antiwar presidential candidate Paul McCloskey, Democratic candidate Edmund Muskie, Democratic Party Chairman Lawrence O'Brien, and syndicated columnist Jack Anderson. In February 1972 Anderson reported on a memo from a lobbyist for International Telephone and Telegraph. The memo referred to an arrangement by which the Department of Justice had approved an ITT merger in return for a $400,000 contribution to the Republican National Convention. When John Mitchell resigned as attorney general in March to become the president's campaign manager, his successor, Richard Kleindienst, faced hostile confirmation hearings in the Senate. Although Kleindienst finally was confirmed, he pleaded guilty in 1974 to false Senate testimony about the ITT affair.

During the 1970 elections, the White House had channeled $400,000 in secret funds into the Alabama gubernatorial primary in a futile effort to defeat George Wallace, a possible presidential candidate for 1972. Desiring to place Nixon above the battle of the re-election drive, Chief of Staff H. R. Haldeman organized a Committee to Re-Elect the President (CRP) in 1971. With the assistance of Commerce Secretary Maurice Stans and the president's personal attorney, four hundred "dummy" corporations directed secret corporation campaign funds to CRP. Although oil companies, airlines, and defense contractors contributed substantially in an effort to win preferential government treatment, the leading donor was the Associated Milk Producers, which hoped to assure administration continuance of price supports with a $422,000 stipend. While Republicans stalled passage of a campaign disclosure law early in 1972, financier Robert Vesco contributed another $200,000 to Nixon's campaign. Vesco was under investigation by the Securities and Exchange Commission for an alleged $250 million looting of mutual funds. A subsequent trial acquitted Maurice Stans and John Mitchell of influence peddling in the case, although Vesco had fled to Costa Rica with the president's nephew.

CRP made extensive use of the unprece-dented $55 million collected by its fund raisers. The committee directed intelligence operations against the strongest Democratic contenders for the presidential nomination and worked covertly to support the weakest. A "dirty tricks" operation issued false and misleading literature "signed" by Democratic candidates and engaged in other pranks designed to embarrass the Democrats. A particularly effective ploy involved a letter planted in a conservative New Hampshire newspaper that accused front runner Muskie of making a derogatory reference to New Englanders of French-Canadian descent. Furious and exhausted from campaigning, Muskie appeared in the snow outside the newspaper office and wept as he vehemently denied the contrived charge. The emotional outburst signaled the decline of the candidate's fortunes.

As George McGovern became the most likely candidate for the Democratic nomination, CRP began to focus on the Democratic National Committee and Chairman O'Brien. Accordingly, CRP Director Mitchell approved a covert entry into Democratic headquarters at Washington's Watergate building complex. When a wiretap on O'Brien's telephone malfunctioned, however, the CRP team returned for a second entry. On June 17, 1972, five CRP operatives were arrested for burglary inside the Watergate office of the Democratic party.

Although presidential press secretary Ron Ziegler dismissed the entry as a "third-rate burglary," CRP and White House aides began an immediate coverup. Americans would not discover the fact for two years, but Nixon personally conducted preliminary steps in the Watergate coverup. Acting on an idea suggested by Mitchell, the president ordered aides to request the CIA to stop an FBI inquiry into the source of Watergate funds. To protect Nixon, frantic aides improvised a day-to-day conspiracy. Wiretap records were destroyed at CRP headquarters, campaign officials lied to the FBI and grand jury, incriminating evidence was removed from a White House safe, and law-enforcement agencies were subjected to pressures for "cooperation." When those measures proved insufficient, Haldeman and Ehrlichman devised an elaborate scheme to provide "hush money" to the Watergate defendants. Yet at an August press conference, Nixon pretended that his counsel, John Dean, had completed a Watergate investigation for the White House. "I can state categorically," the president declared, "that no one in the White House staff, no one in this administration, presently employed, was involved in this very bizarre incident."

NIXON'S RE-ELECTION

Campaigning as an outright opponent of the Vietnam War, Democrat George McGovern brought an evangelical message of peace and social concern to newly enfranchised young voters, middle-class reformers, and racial and cultural minorities. The Twenty-sixth Amendment to the Constitution, ratified in 1971, awarded the vote to eighteen-year-olds, bolstering the South Dakotan's hopes for a new Democratic coalition. Winning the largest number of delegates in the 1972 primaries, McGovern broadened his emotional antiwar stance by denouncing inflation, unemployment, and administration connections to big business, while promising tax reform and a shift of spending from defense to social needs. George Wallace had used the busing issue to take the largest popular vote in the primaries. But Wallace was

shot in May 1972 by an assailant with no apparent political motive, and the resulting paralysis left him unable to continue the campaign. With the failure of mainstream candidates such as Muskie and Hubert Humphrey, McGovern had little competition at the Democratic Convention in Miami. Following the McGovern Committee reforms of 1968, party delegates had been chosen in primaries, caucuses, and other elections during the convention year. As a result, four-fifths of the 1972 delegates were attending their first national convention. The new rules also required equitable representation for certain social groups. Consequently, women constituted 38 percent of the Democratic delegates, blacks 14 percent, and those under twenty-five 13 percent. In addition, over one hundred delegates publicly acknowledged themselves as homosexuals.

The climate for the McGovern candidacy had been prepared by New Left critiques of the war, black and radical demands for social justice, and the counterculture of middle-class youth. McGovern enthusiasts believed that the Democrats finally had rejected both party bosses and the Vietnam War. Even Mayor Daley of Chicago was unseated when the Illinois delegation was cited for violating party reform rules. But as the McGovern revolution attempted to replace the New Deal coalition with a "politics of conscience," working-class ethnics felt deserted. Even though 1972 polls showed that a greater percentage of blue-collar workers were critical of Nixon war policies than the general sample, working-class Americans associated the McGovern candidacy with draft card burning, campus destruction, street riots, and disrespect for national values. These fears were crystalized when the convention defied McGovern staffers and openly debated culturally abrasive issues such as abortion, gay rights, and the le-

Frank Rizzo

1920-

Frank Rizzo, an Italian-American, a high school dropout, and a career police officer, won national headlines when he was elected "law-and-order" mayor of Philadelphia in 1971. As police commissioner, Rizzo was known as a "tough cop." Called from a formal dinner in 1969, he confronted an angry disturbance at a black housing project with a nightstick jammed into his tuxedo. When four policemen were shot in West Philadelphia the following summer, Rizzo proclaimed that the black neighborhood was no longer "civilized" and warned that the "only other thing we can do now is buy tanks and start mounting machine guns." Blaming the attacks on Black Panthers, whom he described as "imbeciles," the commissioner personally supervised a raid on a Panther house during which suspects were stripped naked on the street.

Rizzo won the 1971 election because he understood the fears and resentments of Philadelphia's working-class ethnics. As street crime skyrocketed in the early seventies, inner-city Americans became increasingly impatient with "liberal" judges and permissive schools. Large numbers of Italians, Irish, Poles, and Jews also believed that public agencies were spending hard-earned tax dollars on "handouts" to blacks and racial minorities. Rizzo promised law and order without tax increases and talked about preserving neighborhoods, decent families, and public morality. "I'm a man of action who gets things done," he told Philadelphians in 1971. "Nobody owns Frank Rizzo."

But once in office, Rizzo did nothing to stop the increase of inner-city crime. In a city in which two-fifths of the population was black and in which 90 percent of black crimes of violence were directed against other blacks, Rizzo's rhetoric only heightened racial antagonism.

Unlike ethnic leaders such as Barbara Mikulski of Baltimore and Steve Adubato of Newark, Rizzo never addressed the substantive problems of urban working people, black or white. Rizzo closed the public hospital, permitted schools and public housing to deteriorate, raised wage and real estate taxes by 30 percent, and tried to hide an $80 million budget deficit. While claiming that social welfare costs were exorbitant, Rizzo padded city payrolls with personal favorites and accepted $130,000 in private funds to refurbish his own office. As hundreds of city jobs were exempted from the civil service merit system, Rizzo assumed control of a $65-million-a-year patronage system. Charged with awarding city contracts in exchange for loyalty to his machine, the mayor became the first public official in history to take a lie detector test and fail. When a newspaper ridiculed the fiasco with an offensive satire, union allies surrounded the daily's headquarters and physically prevented its distribution.

Frank Rizzo was a product of seventies disillusion with governments that could no longer produce what they promised. But unlike Governor Jerry Brown of California, who initiated state policies based on ecological and fiscal limitations, Rizzo had no program whatsoever. Like Richard Nixon, he concentrated on destroying his enemies by building his own power base. Proclaiming that "Rizzo Means Business," the mayor of Philadelphia won re-election in 1975 with the support of the loyal ethnics and downtown business interests. The following year Jimmy Carter campaigned against Rizzo bossism in the Pennsylvania presidential primary. But in the November election, the Rizzo machine provided Carter with the Democratic victory margin in the state. Moments after the network announcement of Carter's triumph, the president-elect telephoned Frank Rizzo. "You really knew what you were talking about," Carter said in thanks. The ethnic political machine, refurbished by the social tensions of seventies urbanism, still was alive and well in American politics.

galization of marijuana. Although McGovern tried to communicate his vision of a just society in ordinary language, a carelessly presented plan for a guaranteed income conveyed confusion about economics. The fatal blow to the campaign came, however, when newspaper reports indicated that vice presidential candidate Thomas Eagleton had been hospitalized several times for emotional depression. McGovern first gave Senator Eagleton a "1,000 percent" public endorsement, then asked for his resignation, thereby creating an image of indecisiveness and hypocrisy. R. Sargent Shriver carried the Kennedy mantle onto the 1972 ticket, but McGovern's strength as a trustworthy candidate had been irreparably damaged.

The Republican Convention provided a stark contrast to the openness of the Democratic conclave. Security was so tight at convention headquarters that delegates could not leave their hotels without a badge. Three thousand "Young Voters for Nixon," organized and paid by White House advance men, paraded through convention festivities reciting "Four more years, four more years!" Surpassing Johnson's 1968 efforts at Chicago, the Nixon White House scripted the entire convention proceedings and platform, deriding capture of the Democratic party by a radical clique and repeatedly depicting the chaos of the McGovern convention. "Let us reject," Nixon stated in his acceptance speech, "the policies of those who whine and whimper about our frustrations and call on us to turn inward. Let us not turn away from our greatness."

Nixon's campaign followed the strategy outlined in Kevin Phillips's *The Emergent Republican Majority* (1969), which sought a new coalition of Wallace voters, white southerners, urban supporters in the Southwest, working-class Catholics, suburbanites, and rural Americans. These voters had not benefited from costly welfare programs erected after World War Two, and many depended on military defense spending for their livelihood. While McGovern charged that the administration was "the most corrupt in history," the president placed himself above politics and pointed to Kissinger's negotiations with the North Vietnamese. The results of the Nixon strategy were spectacularly successful. The president received 61 percent of the popular vote, nearly equaling Johnson's landslide of 1964, and carried every state in the electoral college except for Massachusetts and the District of Columbia. While McGovern took only 29 percent of the southern vote, Nixon reversed Democratic domination of the white ethnics by winning a majority of Catholics, Irish-Americans, and Italian-Americans. But in a show of widespread political apathy, less than 55 percent of eligible voters cast ballots in the 1972 election, and 39 million qualified Americans did not even register to vote.

Following the balloting, Nixon consolidated his hold on the federal bureaucracy and cabinet by appointing White House loyalists. To reduce "big government," the president also vowed to cut back domestic spending. In October 1972 the Senate had killed a Nixon request for a $250 billion limit on congressional spending. Three months later the president impounded $12 billion already appropriated by Congress, including a water pollution bill that Congress had overridden a Nixon veto to pass. Continuing his austerity program, the president appointed an acting director of OEO and instructed him to liquidate the antipoverty agency. Program reductions followed in the Job Corps, Model Cities, slum rehabilitation, and aid for education, science, and health. Critics argued that Nixon had converted a financial management technique into an instrument for thwarting congressional will and asserting the president's own priorities.

Ever since the Cambodian invasion of 1970, Congress had been debating the enactment of a time limit for the entire American presence in Southeast Asia. Shortly after Kent State, two congressmen broke away from an official Vietnam tour to visit Con Son penal island, where they discovered tiny concrete cells set in the ground and covered with bars. The shackled inmates of the "tiger cages" turned out to be political prisoners of the South Vietnamese government. The following year, two thousand Vietnam Veterans Against the War shocked the nation by throwing their battle medals on the steps of the Capitol and pleading with senators to end the "mistake" in Vietnam. Stung by the deteriorating military situation, demoralization at home, and prohibitive war costs, the Senate voted to end the entire foreign aid program in 1972 if the administration did not bring the disruptive war to a close. Five months after the Vietnam truce of early 1973, Nixon finally accepted a congressional deadline on funding for the continued bombing of Cambodia. To assure no repetition of presidential wars, Congress also overrode a Nixon veto to pass the War Powers Act in November 1973. The law provided a sixty-day limit on the commitment of troops abroad without congressional consent and stipulated that CIA activities were to be reported to Congress "in a timely fashion." Despite Nixon's strong objections, Congress was beginning to repair the erosion of its foreign policy powers, reversing a trend that had characterized national politics since World War Two.

THE WATERGATE COVERUP AND NIXON'S FALL

While McGovern attempted to connect the Watergate break-in to the White House in the 1972 campaign, the early stages of the coverup succeeded in confining prosecution to the original seven defendants. But by the time the Watergate trial opened in January 1973, two of the men, E. Howard Hunt and James McCord, had received promises of executive clemency from presidential assistants in return for continued silence. At the close of the trial, federal judge John Sirica read a letter from McCord that charged that the other defendants had committed perjury and that "higher-ups" were involved in the Watergate break-in and coverup. A former CIA employee, McCord resented what he believed to be a White House attempt to place blame for Watergate on the agency. But Hunt, another CIA veteran, continued to press for executive clemency and $130,000 for the four Cuban-American burglars and himself. Hunt had participated in the break-in at the office of Ellsberg's psychiatrist and warned that he might have to review his decision to remain silent. On March 21 counselor Dean brought the Hunt demands to the president's attention at an Oval Office meeting, outlining a "cancer on the presidency" and estimating that eventual hush-money payments could reach $1 million. Instead of backing away from the coverup, Nixon ordered an immediate $75,000 payment to Hunt. The next day the president told Mitchell: "I don't give a shit what happens. I want you all to stonewall it, let them plead the fifth amendment, cover-up or anything else, if it'll save it — save the plan."

By April 1973, however, McCord's revelations had triggered an outpouring of evidence that implicated top White House and campaign aides in the Watergate break-in and coverup. In an apology to journalists, press secretary Ziegler declared all previous White House statements on Watergate "inoperable." Nixon then announced the dismissal of Dean and the resignation of Attorney General Kleindienst and the president's two key assistants, H. R. Haldeman and John Ehrlichman. But Nixon denied personal involvement in the Watergate coverup. To satisfy critics, the president nominated liberal Republican Elliot Richardson to be the new attorney general and stated that Richardson could appoint a Watergate special prosecutor. When the Senate insisted on the appointment before confirming the new attorney general, Richardson named Harvard's Archibald Cox, a former solicitor general in the Kennedy administration.

The Watergate crisis escalated in May 1973 when a special Senate committee, chaired by Democrat Sam Ervin, began a televised investigation of the scandal. Nixon responded to charges of his personal involvement in Watergate by admitting that he had ordered aides to restrict early stages of the Watergate probe on grounds of "national security." But former presidential counsel Dean testified about Nixon's continuing knowledge of the coverup and provided evidence of the administration's illegal manipulation of the IRS and the intelligence agencies. Dean's staggering allegations, however, were surpassed by the committee's discovery that the president had installed secret tape-recording devices in his own offices in the White House.

Once the existence of the White House tapes was disclosed, Nixon was forced to battle both the Ervin Committee and Special Prosecutor Cox in an attempt to withhold the evidence that could implicate him in Watergate crimes. The president's attorneys claimed that executive privilege gave Nixon the right to preserve the confidentiality of conversations with advisers. But in October 1973 the Circuit Court of Appeals upheld Judge Sirica's decision to review personally nine subpoenaed tapes. In response, the White House proposed that Senator John Stennis, an elderly Mississippi conservative, review the tapes and provide summaries to Sirica and the Ervin Committee. Nixon's counsel also requested that the special prosecutor relinquish the right to further subpoenas. When Cox rejected the offer, the president stunned the nation by firing him and abolishing the special prosecutor's office. Attorney General Richardson and his deputy, William Ruckleshaus, both resigned rather than carry out the Cox firing.

The "Saturday Night Massacre" brought what the White House described as a firestorm of protest, including 250,000 genuine telegrams to the president's office. Nixon's popularity, registered by Gallup at 68 percent following the Vietnam cease-fire in early 1973, plummeted to 27 percent, and pro-Nixon newspapers deserted the president in droves. The White House had not anticipated the massive response to the Saturday Night Massacre, and relinquished the disputed tapes to Sirica a few days later. Nixon also appointed Leon Jaworski, a Houston lawyer, as special prosecutor. But to Jaworski's chagrin, the White House now claimed that three of the nine tapes did not exist, while the others contained gaping blank spots, including one that lasted eighteen and one-half minutes. A technical panel appointed by both the White House and the special prosecutor later reported that the eighteen-and-

one-half-minute gap was caused by five separate manual erasures.

By the end of 1973 the president was on the
defensive. Fifteen officials and key aides, including Vice President Agnew, already had resigned from the administration. Agnew had
pleaded "no contest" to charges of income tax
evasion in early October. The vice president
also had been under investigation for conspiracy, extortion, and bribery, all part of a
"kickback" scheme in which he had received
bribes from Maryland contractors for nearly ten
years. Adhering to the succession provisions of
the Twenty-fifth Amendment, ratified in 1967,
Nixon nominated House Republican leader
Gerald Ford for the vice presidency, and Congress quickly confirmed him. But Nixon had
his own financial problems as well. Shortly
after the Cox firing, the IRS announced that
it was re-examining the president's back taxes.
In response to questions concerning his personal finances, Nixon told a televised meeting
of newspaper editors that "People have got to
know whether or not their president is a crook.
Well, I'm not a crook." The president released
a sweeping personal financial report, but questions remained concerning the back-dating of
a gift of vice presidential papers, large tax de-
ductions, financing of personal properties, and
home improvements at public expense. Several
months later the IRS reported that the president of the United States owed over $450,000
in back taxes and interest penalties. Concerned
over possible criminal activities in the White
House, the House of Representatives voted
406–4 in February 1974 to authorize the Judiciary Committee to initiate impeachment proceedings against Nixon.

The rest of the president's term involved a
futile effort to release as little evidence as possible to the Judiciary Committee and the special prosecutor. With great fanfare, Nixon
publicized a carefully edited version of some
subpoenaed tapes in April 1974, but the cynical and manipulative quality of White House
conversations prompted even Republican Senate leader Hugh Scott to describe them as "de-
plorable, shabby, disgusting, and immoral. . . ."
The turning point of the Watergate drama
came in July when the Supreme Court decided
unanimously that the president had to surrender the subpoenaed tapes. A claim of presidential privilege based on confidentiality, the Court
ruled, "cannot prevail over the fundamental demands of due process of law."

As Nixon prepared to turn over the tapes,
the Judiciary Committee voted three bills of
impeachment against the president. They
charged Nixon with obstruction of justice,
abuse of power, and unconstitutional defiance
of committee subpoenas. Judiciary supporters
of the president had insisted that available evidence was not solid enough to produce a "smoking gun." But in August the "smoking gun"
emerged when the president's attorneys forced
the White House to release transcripts of
Nixon's conversations with Haldeman six days
after the Watergate break-in. The president
had clearly directed his aide to order the CIA
to call the FBI off aspects of the Watergate
inquiry. Now Nixon admitted that he "was
aware of the advantages this course of action
would have with respect to limiting possible
public exposure of involvement by persons connected with the re-election committee." Nixon
also confessed that he had kept the crucial
evidence from his own lawyers and Nixon supporters on the Judiciary Committee, and that
portions of the newly released tapes were "at
variance with certain of my previous state-

ments." The president admitted that impeachment by the full House was a foregone conclusion, but hoped that the charges were not sufficiently serious to merit conviction in a Senate trial.

Despite Nixon's hopes, however, public opinion had turned against him and no more than fifteen Senators out of one hundred still supported the president. On August 8, 1974, the thirty-seventh president of the United States announced an unprecedented resignation. The following day at noon, as Nixon flew to San Clemente, Gerald Ford took the oath of office. "Our long national nightmare is over," the new president told the nation. "Our constitution works. Our great republic is a government of laws and not of men."

FORD AND CARTER

President Ford faced a nation shaken by the traumas of Vietnam and Watergate. But government credibility suffered another blow when the president announced one month later that he was pardoning Richard Nixon "for all offenses against the United States which he ... has committed or may have committed" during his presidency. The Judiciary Committee quickly initiated hearings to discover whether Ford had made assurances to Nixon before the resignation. But the new president insisted "There was no deal, period," and explained that the pardon was designed to remove the disruptive Watergate issue from the national spotlight and move on to the future. Yet the majority of Americans believed that Nixon should go to jail for his crimes, and Ford never recovered his initial popularity. In the reaction against the former president, Congress angrily

reduced Nixon's transition funds and nullified an arrangement by which the General Services Administration had provided Nixon with custody of White House documents and tapes. White House tapes in possession of the special prosecutor and John Dean's testimony proved crucial in the coverup convictions of Nixon aides H. R. Haldeman, John Ehrlichman, and John Mitchell in January 1975.

Ford nominated former New York Governor Nelson Rockefeller to fill the vice presidential vacancy. But Rockefeller, whose family fortune exceeded $1 billion, faced hostile questions about extensive loans and gifts to state officials and family financing of a vicious biography of a former political opponent. In the post-Watergate atmosphere, such ethical issues received careful congressional scrutiny. When the vice president finally took the oath of office in December 1974, the United States had the first nonelected presidential and vice presidential team in history.

Despite Nixon's vetoes, Congress had acted vigorously during the 1974 economic recession. It passed the first housing bill since 1968, added $25 billion to public school assistance, revived OEO, and provided nearly $12 billion for a six-year program of mass transit. To counteract joblessness, which climbed over 7 percent by late 1974, Congress also created an emergency work program and extended unemployment benefits and coverage. Other reforms included new federal standards for private pension plans and a presidential campaign finance bill. The campaign reform law, another legacy of Watergate, provided the first use of public money to finance presidential campaigns and primaries and limited private contributions and campaign spending. Proponents argued that the law separated presidential politics from the power of money, but significantly, Congress refused to extend coverage to its own election campaigns.

When Congress ignored Ford's key anti-inflation proposal — a 5 percent tax surcharge on corporations and the middle and upper class — and easily overrode a veto to extend veterans' education benefits to Vietnam servicemen, the president took his antispending crusade to the voters. But Watergate and the Nixon pardon worked against Ford in the congressional elections of 1974. Democrats gained forty-three seats in the House to give them more than a two-thirds majority and captured another four seats in the heavily Democratic Senate. Despite their overwhelming numbers, however, the Democrats were not able to erect an independent program. Congress scaled down a Ford tax cut, ended depletion allowances for large oil corporations, and curbed investment tax shelters. But congressional leaders had to compromise with the president on a temporary energy package. To reduce energy use and stimulate fuel production, Ford had pushed for increased oil prices and the deregulation of natural gas. But under great pressure from constituents, congressional Democrats found price increases unacceptable. The Energy Policy and Conservation Act of 1975 provided oil price controls for forty months by scheduling a temporary rollback to be followed by gradual increases. Congress and Ford came to another compromise when the president reluctantly agreed to sign over a $2.3 billion loan to New York City. Burdened by the urban dilemma of rising welfare costs and a decreasing tax base, New York had come close to defaulting city bonds in 1975.

With Henry Kissinger implanted as secretary of state, Ford attempted to continue Nixon's emphasis on balance of power in foreign affairs. The United States and the Soviet Union signed an arms agreement in late 1974 that limited the number of offensive strategic nuclear weapons and delivery vehicles. Kissinger also continued his peace mission in the Middle East, where American energy needs dictated the stabilization of hostilities in the oil-rich area. Through his efforts, Egypt and Israel concluded an interim peace agreement in October 1975 that brought the withdrawal of Israeli troops from Sinai passes and oil fields and furthered negotiations toward a final political settlement. Nevertheless, the American Jewish community began to be concerned with the administration's tilt toward the Arabs.

Awakened by Watergate and Vietnam excesses of presidential prerogative, Congress resisted administration efforts to conduct an independent foreign policy. When the agreement between Egypt and Israel called for stationing of American technical observers, for example, Kissinger was closely questioned about secret commitments to Israel. Congress also forced a partial embargo on arms deliveries to Turkey, which had invaded the Greek island of Cyprus, and undercut Kissinger by denying the Soviet Union most-favored-nation status in trade until it relaxed restrictions on emigration, particularly for Soviet Jews and other dissenters. Furthermore, Congress defeated administration requests for increased military aid to South Vietnam. Without American air support, the strategic retreat of South Vietnamese forces from the central highlands turned into a rout, and Communist divisions easily swept south. On April 30, 1974, an emergency helicopter evacuation completed the removal of one thousand Americans and fifty-five thousand Vietnamese dependents from Saigon. A few hours later General "Big" Minh surrendered South Vietnam to the parading soldiers of the Provisional Revolutionary Government, Saigon was renamed Ho Chi Minh City, and the war was over. "This closes a chapter in the American experience," Ford announced laconically.

Like no other event in American history, the Vietnam War showed the limits of American power, and Ford indicated that the lessons of the debacle had been learned. Yet one month later the president sent troops to recapture an American merchant ship taken by an over-zealous outpost of Cambodian Communists. The *Mayaguez* incident was quickly resolved at the cost of several American casualties, but it indicated a presidential reluctance to accept both the American loss of pride in Southeast Asia and the tarnished image of the United States as a guarantor of world order.

Congress also rebelled against further administration moves in mineral-rich Africa. Press accounts had revealed that the CIA was covertly aiding an anti-Soviet faction in a civil war in the former Portuguese colony of Angola. Backing away from the possibility of another Vietnam entanglement, Congress ignored Kissinger's pleas and prohibited further military aid in a rider to the defense appropriation bill. Ford bitterly condemned Congress members who had "lost their guts" and derided an "abdication of responsibility," but he promptly acceded to their demands. Never before had Congress exerted such control over foreign policy conducted by the CIA.

The determination to supervise the CIA stemmed from revelations publicized in 1975 by the Senate Select Committee on Intelligence Activities. Public hearings sustained newspaper accounts of illegal surveillance, LSD experiments on unsuspecting subjects, political spying and mail openings at home, and covert attempts to overthrow other governments and murder their leaders. A system of "plausible denial" shielded presidents from specific knowl-edge of unsavory details. Testimony also indicated that the CIA and other intelligence agencies spent $7 billion to $17 billion each year.

Public bitterness over Watergate made personal trust a key issue in the presidential campaign of 1976. Former Georgia Governor Jimmy Carter emerged as the Democratic front runner after defeating a host of party contenders in a series of early primaries. Espousing a combination of southern populism and economic conservatism, Carter spoke quietly, talked of replacing the professionals in Washington, and promised to restore ethical moralism to foreign policy. At the most harmonious Democratic Convention in memory, a unified party rallied behind Carter and liberal vice presidential nominee Walter Mondale. It was the Republicans who were divisive in 1976, however, as California's Ronald Reagan attacked Ford from a conservative perspective and criticized the Nixon pardon. But Reagan's effort faltered in the closing weeks of the campaign, and Ford won the nomination in a close convention vote. The president chose another midwesterner, Kansas Senator Robert Dole, as his running mate.

Carter emerged from the Democratic Convention with a thirty-three-point lead in national polls. Intent on winning the presidency in his own right, Ford campaigned strenuously on the need to curb spending, but fell short by two percentage points and two million votes. In the electoral college, the tally was a close 291 to 241. Although the president carried the entire West except for Hawaii, Carter rode the strength of Mexican-American votes in Texas and strong black support to sweep the entire South. Moved by regional pride and an affinity with Carter's roots in evangelical Protestantism, black and white southerners provided the can-

THE DEMOCRATIC WHISTLESTOP

DEMOCRATIC WHISTLES

a train for a change

Jimmy Carter campaigned in 1976 to restore trust to presidential government. (Peter Southwick/Stock, Boston)

didate with 90 percent of his national plurality. As a result, Ford joined Republicans William Howard Taft and Herbert Hoover as the only twentieth-century presidents to be denied second terms by voters.

As the United States celebrated its 1976 bicentennial, Americans seemed to have lost confidence about the course of social events. Inflation, Vietnam, and Watergate acted to diminish faith in strong presidents and their global aspirations. But dependence on overseas raw materials and sources of energy, as well as a changing world balance of power, introduced elements of complexity in the nation's foreign policy that Americans found frustrating.

Carter continued to request increases in the defense budget and criticized Soviet treatment of dissidents as a violation of international standards of human rights. But to the dismay of conservatives, the administration also laid the groundwork for a less militant foreign policy. After a lengthy Senate debate, the president signed a new Panama Canal Treaty in 1978. The agreement provided for full Panamanian control of the canal by the year 2000, although the United States reserved the right to intervene to preserve the neutrality of the Canal Zone. The treaty also required payment of nearly $1 billion in compensation to Panama. Andrew Young, Carter's black ambassador to the United Nations, worked to refashion the American image in the Third World by denouncing apartheid in South Africa. Young also defended the administration's refusal to recognize the government of Zimbabwe Rhodesia until the dominant whites permitted political participation by black revolutionary organizations. While Carter continued to denounce both Cuban and Soviet involvement in central and eastern Africa, the United States confined itself to supplying airlifts and verbal denunciations when secessionist guerrillas violently overran several towns in pro-American Zaire during 1978.

Following the foundations laid by Nixon and Kissinger, Carter moved to stabilize relations with China and the Soviet Union. The United States formally exchanged ambassadors with the People's Republic on New Year's Day, 1979. But the president received criticism even from liberal Democrats such as Senator Edward Kennedy for severing diplomatic ties with Taiwan at the insistence of the Chinese. The administration appeared willing to suffer this political discomfort because it hoped for stabilization in Southeast Asia and increased trade with China. But promises of peaceful order in Asia seemed uncertain when the Chinese briefly invaded Vietnam in response to armed Vietnamese interference in Cambodia. Despite a Chinese warning that an aggressive Soviet Union stood behind Vietnam's expansionism, Carter moved toward another arms agreement with Moscow. SALT II, signed by the president in May 1979, proposed to establish further areas of equity between the two superpowers in certain nuclear missile systems. But congressional

conservatives, whose number moderately increased in the 1978 elections, hesitated to push détente because of growing Soviet influence in Africa, Cuba, and the Middle East.

American energy needs directed much of Carter's attention to the oil-rich Middle East. As revolution and armed conflict rocked Afghanistan, North and South Yemen, and Iran, the president hoped to promote Mideast stability by arranging a peace agreement between Egypt and Israel. Following a dramatic visit to Jerusalem by Egypt's Anwar Sadat in late 1977, Carter brought Sadat and Israeli Premier Menachem Begin to Camp David for a personal summit. When further negotiations stalled early in 1979, the president flew to the Middle East to continue his low-key diplomacy. Egypt and Israel finally signed the historic peace treaty in Washington in April 1979. The treaty provided for Israeli withdrawal of military forces and civilian settlers from the Sinai Peninsula. In return, Egypt agreed to open the Suez Canal to Israeli ships and end its economic boycott against Israel. Full diplomatic relations between the two nations were scheduled for 1980. Separate provisions of the treaty also committed the United States to military and economic assistance to both countries. The most controversial stumbling block to Mideast stability, however, continued to be the fate of Palestinians living in Israeli-occupied territories. To the dismay of Arab critics, the 1979 treaty provided for a five-year transition period in which the final status of the Palestinians would be negotiated.

Just as Carter was succeeding in attaining peace between Egypt and Israel, a massive social revolution was overturning American interests in Iran. But for the first time since the advent of the Cold War, American leaders were faced with a hostile revolution that had no ties to Soviet or Chinese communism. Led by the Moslem cleric Ayatollah Ruhollah Khomeini, hundreds of thousands of Iranian nationalists overthrew the pro-American Shah Mohammed Reza Pahlavi in early 1979. Khomeini's followers demanded a Moslem state that would withdraw from military cooperation with the United States and limit sales of oil to the West. Underestimating the fervor of the revolutionary movement, Carter first indicated support for the shah and then watched helplessly as most of the dictator's military and political supporters deserted to the Khomeini forces.

Following the Iranian revolution, corporate and government leaders in the United States feared the spread of Moslem nationalism to Saudi Arabia and other sources of Mideast oil. Accordingly, American corporations began to store crude oil in case of future import problems. By the spring of 1979, the nation faced another gasoline shortage and increased prices at the pump. Carter continued to press Congress for a comprehensive energy program that would include deregulation of oil and natural gas prices and a contingency plan for rationing automobile fuel. But Congress had difficulty in determining how heavily the oil corporations should be taxed and placed strict limits on the president's power to implement rationing. The prospects for energy production appeared even more grim when a nuclear power plant near Harrisburg, Pennsylvania, leaked radioactive steam and gas into the atmosphere for several days in April 1979. The worst accident in the history of the nuclear industry brought cries of protest from antinuclear power activists, who argued that utility corporations had not yet devised safe means of controlling radioactive waste and that nuclear plants were inefficient producers of energy.

The energy impasse typified the administration's difficulties in solving domestic problems in the late 1970s. Rampant inflation, unhindered by a presidential request for a 7 percent limit on wage increases, seemed to aggravate the normal competition of pressure groups and organized lobbies in Congress. As a result, the administration retreated from earlier endorsements of comprehensive tax reform and national health insurance. Inflation and loss of faith in government also stimulated a national taxpayers' revolt. Led by Governor Edmund G. Brown, Jr. of California, whose constituents had placed a ceiling on property taxes through a voters' initiative, some Americans began to call for a constitutional convention to compel a balanced federal budget. Brown also talked of the need to preserve the ecological balance of the planet while seeking possibilities for the development of outer space. Despite Brown's planetary concerns, and despite Senator Edward Kennedy's entry into presidential politics late in 1979, most Americans closed the decade in sour confrontation with the realities of rising prices and economic stagnation. For the people of the United States, a century that began with the opening of overseas frontiers reached its closing stage with a retreat from military adventurism and troubled concern over the question of national and economic limits.

SUGGESTED READINGS

The Nixon years are outlined with brilliant insight by Jonathan Schell, *The Time of Illusion: An Historical and Reflective Account of the Nixon Era* (1975). The relevant chapters in Alexander Kendrick, *The Wound Within: America in the Vietnam Years, 1945–1974* (1974), describe the interplay between the Vietnam War and political ferment at home.

See also Weldon Brown, *The Last Chopper: The Denouement of the American Role in Vietnam, 1963–1975* (1976).

For portraits of the Nixon administration, see Rowland Evans and Robert Novak, *Nixon in the White House* (1971), and William Safire, *Before the Fall* (1975). Battles over law enforcement and the Supreme Court are described by Richard Harris, *Justice* (1970) and *Decision* (1971). The appropriate section of Otis L. Graham, Jr., *Toward a Planned Society: From Roosevelt to Nixon* (1976), presents a detailed account of Nixonian social management and administrative innovation. Gary Wills, *Nixon Agonistes: The Crisis of the Self-Made Man* (1971), offers a critical psychological study of the thirty-seventh president.

Overseas investment and the weakening of the seventies economy are summarized in the concluding sections of Gabriel Kolko, *Main Currents in Modern American History* (1976), which may be supplemented by appropriate segments of Arthur S. Miller, *The Modern Corporate State: Private Governments and the American Constitution* (1976). A provocative assessment of seventies economic and political trends is Kirkpatrick Sale, *Power Shift: The Rise of the Southern Rim and Its Challenge to the Eastern Establishment* (1975). The relevant chapters of Stanley Aronowitz, *False Promises: The Shaping of American Working Class Consciousness* (1974), dramatize seventies labor discontent.

Explorations of the dissatisfaction of ethnic Americans include Richard Krickus, *Pursuing the American Dream: White Ethnics and the New Populism* (1976), and Michael Novak, *The Rise of the Unmeltable Ethnics: Politics and Culture in the Seventies* (1972). For a specific illustration, see Joseph R. Daughen and Peter Binzen, *The Cop Who Would Be King:* *The Honorable Frank Rizzo* (1977). The conservative response to the counterculture and radical protest is described in Richard Scammon and Ben J. Wattenberg, *The Real Majority* (1970).

For Watergate, see *The Senate Watergate Report: The Final Report of the Senate Select Committee on Presidential Campaign Activities* (1974) and House Judiciary Committee, *Impeachment of Richard M. Nixon, President of the United States* (1974). Two informative Watergate memoirs are H. R. Haldeman with Joseph DiMona, *The Ends of Power* (1978), and John Dean, *Blind Ambition: The White House Years* (1976), while the road to disclosure is chronicled by Carl Bernstein and Bob Woodward, *All the President's Men* (1974). The vice presidential scandal is presented by Richard M. Cohen and Jules Witcover, *A Heartbeat Away: The Investigation and Resignation of Vice-President Spiro T. Agnew* (1974).

The most comprehensive treatment of foreign affairs in the early seventies is Tad Szulc, *The Illusion of Peace: Foreign Policy in the Nixon Years* (1978). National security management is brilliantly analyzed in Richard J. Barnet, *Roots of War: The Men and Institutions Behind U.S. Foreign Policy* (1972). For CIA activities in Chile and elsewhere, see Victor Marchetti and John D. Marks, *The CIA and the Cult of Intelligence* (1974). Illegal agency activities at home are chronicled by the *Report to the President by the Commission on CIA Activities Within the United States* (1975). For a critical assessment of Carter, see Robert Shogan, *Promises to Keep: Carter's First 100 Days* (1977). A sobering essay on loss of faith and ecological and economic challenge in the seventies is Robert L. Heilbroner, *An Inquiry into the Human Prospect* (1974).

Spotlight: The Meaning of Watergate

The expansion of twentieth-century presidential power began with the New Deal. Franklin D. Roosevelt presided over the permanent presence of executive agencies in the economy and an ongoing mobilization in global politics. Following World War Two, full employment and material benefits derived from large corporations at home, positive direction from executive government, and domination in the world economy. But continued economic expansion depended on open access to the rest of the world. As the Soviet Union began to consolidate its sphere of influence, American global interests could not be sustained without huge government expenditures.

Two developments coincided with the evolution of the Cold War. First, the government encouraged Americans to see national aims as individual goals, articulating foreign policy as a messianic crusade against global communism. Second, the tools of management, bureaucracy, and military technology merged in a massive national security establishment. The expanded office of the presidency presided over both developments. The chief executive assumed personal responsibility for defining and implementing the national security. Presidential elections in the Cold War period hinged on the perceived ability of candidates to manage a gigantic military-industrial complex under the pressure of global conflict.

Roosevelt and Truman had set precedents for unlimited presidential action in the national interest during World War Two. Secrecy, deception of the public, and mobilization of all resources for uncontained violence emerged as accepted methods of total warfare. Nuclear technology furthered the need for government secrecy. The Cold War widened definitions of vital national security, causing security managers to believe that policy making was too complex for people to understand. The Central Intelligence Agency conducted covert foreign policy, accountable only to the National Security Council and the president. Presidential and military advisers remained responsible only to the Oval Office. By the sixties, presidential managers from the corporations, military officers, and national security bureaucracy constituted a powerful elite unaccountable to the American people.

Administrative consolidation depended on the passivity of those Americans not included in the ruling hierarchy. But after 1945, members of various outgroups began to challenge the managerial consensus. Urbanization brought minority groups together so that each could mount organized pressure and protest. Expanded media and education raised expectations and permitted people with common problems to find each other. By the sixties, the nation confronted a civil rights revolution among minorities and a cultural revolution within the middle class that seriously threatened the established administrative authority.

Social and political consensus collapsed entirely as the Vietnam War dominated public attention. To the national security establishment, Vietnam symbolized American will to prevail in world affairs. To the dissidents, however, the war symbolized government malignity and hypocrisy. Believing that control was necessary to limit turmoil and preserve social institutions, military and intelligence agencies turned their attention to "national security" enemies at home. To do so they imported "dirty tricks" and espionage techniques customarily employed overseas. But the major threat of the Vietnam years was to national political consensus, not internal security. Both Presidents Johnson and Nixon rejected CIA reports that insisted that domestic radicals were not supported by foreign governments.

Nixon's first wiretaps were necessary only because the president refused to reveal administration war policy to Congress and the American people. Even some of the president's own national security aides disagreed with him.

As intelligence gathering increased in the sixties and seventies, the line between national security management and partisan politics disappeared. In 1962 President Kennedy moved jurisdiction of internal security from the National Security Council to the attorney general's office headed by his brother. A year later Attorney General Robert Kennedy ordered FBI wiretaps on Martin Luther King to clear associates of King before the administration endorsed his leadership of the civil rights movement. During the campaign of 1964, President Johnson's press secretary requested FBI reports on all persons employed in Goldwater's campaign office. CIA and army surveillance during the Johnson years provided data on antiwar members of Congress, and the FBI passed purely political information about United States senators to the president. During the closing days of the 1968 election campaign, Johnson ordered FBI surveillance of a woman close to the South Vietnamese government to determine whether the Nixon camp intended to sabotage the Vietnam peace negotiations.

The Nixon administration attempted to consolidate the cumbersome national security bureaucracy by hiring its own operatives. But Nixon's undercover agents quickly systematized the gatherings of political intelligence. Other aides attempted to harass political opponents through the IRS. By distorting the statutory purpose of the regulatory agencies, Nixon's people moved toward a permanent perpetuation of their own power. The use of "dirty tricks" in the 1972 campaign was another effort to deprive those without power of equal competition with those who held power. CIA techniques of forgery, false advertising, disinformation, espionage, and finally burglary invaded the two-party system.

But it was the Watergate coverup, not the break-in, that brought down the Nixon administration. Through overconfidence in the ability to manipulate public opinion with the prestige of the presidency, Nixon nearly destroyed the office. Instead of burning the lethal White House tapes, he tried to withhold evidence through incantations of executive privilege, national security, and the integrity of the presidency. But the case continued to surround him, as a vigilant judiciary, a revitalized press and Congress, and an uneasy public cooperated to preserve the nation's institutions. The Saturday Night Massacre of October 1973 informed the country that a president who had agreed to a set of rules wished to change them when he seemed to be losing. The Nixon transcripts conveyed an image of White House amorality and cynicism. Fully a third of the taped conversations were devoted to rehearsals for public lies.

Johnson had seriously eroded the credibility of the presidency with lack of candor about Vietnam. Nixon seemed to leave little hope that any integrity remained. In 1975 Americans also learned that Presidents Eisenhower and Kennedy had indirectly sanctioned CIA assassination plots against foreign leaders. Ford's pardon of his predecessor added to these doubts.

Triggered by the disruptive war in Southeast Asia, Watergate arose from an attempt to repair fault lines in a thirty-year Cold War consensus. The imperial presidency was its immediate victim. But the national intelligence establishment, from which Nixon operatives borrowed their techniques, remained intact. Though more accountable to congressional oversight and less prone to covert activism abroad, policy-making elites remained shrouded in secrecy. By the time President Carter assumed office in 1977, Watergate, the Vietnam War, and domestic dissent were distant memories. But while the excesses of presidential power had been temporarily curbed, Americans had yet to come to terms with the true meaning of national security.

Index

Index

Abraham Lincoln Brigade, 277, 377
Abzug, Bella, 507
Acheson, Dean, 326, 355, 373, 377, 434, 477–478
Acheson-Lilienthal plan, 352
Adubato, Steve, 535
Advertising
  and election of 1952, 328
  between 1945 and 1960, 328
  and television, 341
  and youth, 485
AFL-CIO, *see* American Federation of Labor-Congress of Industrial Organizations
Africa, 425, 465, 542
Afro-American culture, 491–495, 534
Agency for International Development (AID), 464–465
Agnew, Spiro T., 480, 526, 529–530, 539
Agricultural Act(s)
  of 1948, 325
  of 1949, 325
  of 1956, 325

Agriculture, 323–325, 332, 499–501
Aid to Dependent Children (ADC), 461, 518
Alaskan pipeline, 519
Ali, Muhammad, 493
Allende, Salvador, 465, 531
Alliance for Progress, 425–426, 464
American Federation of Labor (AFL), 329–331
American Federation of Labor-Congress of Industrial Organizations (AFL-CIO), 330–331, 496. *See also* Congress of Industrial Organizations (CIO)
American Independent party, 476–477
American Indian Movement (AIM), 504
American Indians, *see* Native Americans
Americans for Democratic Action (ADA), 354, 358, 364
Anderson, Jack, 531–532
Anti-communism, 359, 380
  and Hollywood, 359–360
  and Senator McCarthy, 370–371, 381, 385, 397, 400–402
Anti-Inflation Act, 293

ANZUS treaty, 376
Arbenz, Colonel, 395–396
Armas, Carlos Castillo, 395–396
Armstrong, Neil, 506
Ash, Roy, 517
Asimov, Isaac, 315
Associated Milk Producers, 532
Atlantic Charter, 285
Atom Bomb, 314–316
   and Cold War, 351–353, 368, 381
   and Rosenberg case, 379–384
   and Truman, 314, 389
   and World War Two, 303–304
Atomic Energy Act (1946), 314
Atomic Energy Act (1954), 410
Atomic Energy Commission (AEC), 314–315,
   368, 410, 451
Attica riot, 497–498
Automobiles, 513
   and energy crisis, 519–520
   and environment, 315–316
   between 1945 and 1960, 321

Badoglio, Marshal Pietro, 285
Baker, Jack, 509
Baker v. *Carr*, 398
Bakke case, 511
Baldwin, James, 492
Ball, George, 477
Baraka, Imamu, 498
Barnett, Ross, 444–445, 447
Barrio, Raymond, 501
Baruch, Bernard M., 277, 352–353
Batista, Fulgencio, 416
Battle of the Bulge, World War Two, 308
Bay of Pigs, 427–428, 452
Beatles, the, 485
Begin, Menachem, 544
Bellecourt, Clyde, 504
Bellecourt, Vernon, 504
Bentley, Elizabeth, 381
Benton, Thomas Hart, 343
Berlin blockade, 361–362, 365, 381
Berlin Wall, 433
Berrigan, Daniel, 490, 528–529
Berrigan, Philip, 490, 528–529
Bestor, Arthur E., 337
Biddle, Francis, 298, 310

Blackmun, Harry, 522
Black Muslims, 492, 494
Black Panthers, 493, 494–495, 497, 501, 527–529, 534
Blacks
   and Afro-American culture, 491–495, 534
   and civil rights, 1945–1960, 347, 366–367, 387, 413–414
   and civil rights in 1960s, 456, 458, 460–461, 491–495
   and civil rights in 1970s, 527–529, 533, 548–549
   in Korean War, 366
   and labor unions, 330
   and racial discrimination, 1945–1960, 322, 331–332
   and racial discrimination after 1960, 442–446, 456, 460–461, 476, 521–522
   and sports, 339
   voting behavior of, 364, 420–442, 480, 533, 542
   and World War Two, 291, 300–301
   see also Race riots
Bloch, Emanuel, 381
Blough, Roger, 440
Bogart, Humphrey, 296
Bogota Treaty, 363
Bohlen, Charles E., 399–400
Bond, Julian, 493
Boorstin, Daniel, 402
Bouton, Jim, 489
Bowles, Chester, 318
Bradley, Omar, 477
Brannon, Charles, 325
Brannon Plan, 325
Brezhnev, Leonid, 523
Bricker, John, 392
Bricker Amendment, 392, 406
Brooke, Edward, 461
Brown, Edmund G., Jr., 535, 545
Brown, H. "Rap," 462
Brown, Norman O., 489
Brown Berets, 501
Brown v. *Board of Education,* 338, 398
Bruce, Lenny, 340–341, 415
Bruner, Jerome, 292
Bryant, Anita, 510
Bundy, McGeorge, 455
Bureau of Indian Affairs (BIA), 323, 502

Burger, Warren E., 521–522
Byrd, Harry F., 364, 422
Byrnes, James F., 289, 297, 348, 351, 353

Cahill, William, 498
Calley, William L., 472, 529
Cambodia, 524, 528, 537, 542
Campus protest, 485–487, 489–490, 510, 533
   and Vietnam war, 475, 476, 490, 495, 526–527
Capra, Fritjof, 514
Carmichael, Stokely, 462, 491
Carson, Rachel, 451
Carswell, Harold, 522
Carter, Jimmy, 535, 542–545
Castaneda, Carlos, 504
Castro, Fidel, 416, 426–428, 452, 465
Catholics
   and Chicano culture, 502
   and John Kennedy, 419–422, 483–484
   after 1960, 479–480, 511, 536
   and Spanish Civil War, 277
   and Vietnam war, 490
   and World War Two, 296
Central Intelligence Agency (CIA), 360, 394–
     395, 490, 537, 542
   and Africa, 425, 465, 542
   and Chile, 465, 530
   and Cuba, 416, 427–428, 436, 474
   domestic spying of, 473, 527, 530, 542, 548–
     549
   and Guatemala, 395–396
   and Indochina, 430, 465–466, 470, 472, 477
   and Watergate, 532, 537, 539, 548–550
Chaffee, Roger B., 506
Chainstores, 321
Chamberlain, Neville, 279
Chambers, Whittaker, 365, 369, 381
Chavez, Cesar, 474, 501
Checker, Chubby, 336, 485
Chiang K'ai-shek, 274, 282, 362–363, 369, 405–
     406
Chicago Eight, 527–528
Chicanos, see Mexican-Americans
Chile, 465, 530
China lobby, 362, 369
Chinese-Americans, 332
Chou En-lai, 523
Churchill, Winston, 404
   and Cold War, 352, 407, 416

and World War Two, 280, 282, 285–287, 304,
   350
Cities
   aid to, 460–461, 473, 518, 536, 540
   decay of, 321–322, 461
   and ethnics, 534–535
   and suburbs, 320–321
Civil Defense Administration, 389
Civil Rights, see Blacks, and civil rights
Civil Rights Act(s)
   of 1957, 414, 442
   of 1960, 442
   of 1964, 456–457, 476, 507
   of 1968, 478, 527
Civil Rights Commission, 322, 365, 414, 444
Civil Rights League, 499
Clark, Tom, 359
Clay, Lucius, 361
Cleaver, Eldridge, 492, 494–495
Clifford, Clark, 353, 360–361, 363, 465, 477–
   478
Coffin, Rev. William Sloane, 527
Cohn, Roy, 382, 400
Cold War
   and atom bomb, 351–353, 368, 381
   and economy, 326–327
   and education, 337–338
   in Eisenhower administration, 389–396, 404–
     410, 416–418
   and FDR, 349–350
   in Kennedy administration, 425, 427, 432–437
   legacy of, 548–500
   and Stalin, 349–351, 362, 391, 407
   in Truman administration, 349–363, 368–369,
     373–377
   and United Nations, 352–353
Colson, Charles, 531
Cominform, 358
Comintern, 358
Commission on Equal Employment Opportunity
   (CEEO), 442
Committee to Re-Elect the President (CRP),
   532–533
Commoner, Barry, 505
Communist party, 359, 365, 380
Congress of Industrial Organizations (CIO), 329–
   331, 367
   see also American Federation of Labor-Congress
    of Industrial Organizations (AFL-CIO)

Congress of Racial Equality (CORE), 443, 491
Connor, Bull, 444
Conscientious objection, 298–299
Conservation, *see* Environment
Consumers, 327–328, 473, 475
Containment, 355–359, 369, 385
Coover, Robert, 384
Corso, Gregory, 343
Cost of Living Council, 519
Coughlin, Father Charles, 298, 301
Council of Economic Advisers, 329
Country music, 513
Cox, Archibald, 495, 538–539
Crime, 334–335, 476, 522, 534
    and prison protests, 497–498
    and World War Two, 302
Crime Control and Safe Street Act, 476
Cuba, 416, 427–428, 436, 474
    Bay of Pigs, 427–428, 452
    missile crisis, 434–436

Daley, Richard, 462, 478–479, 496, 533
Daniels, Jonathan, 303
Davis, Angela, 497
Davis, Ben, 445
Davis, Bette, 294
Dean, John W., 533, 537–538, 540
Defense Intelligence Agency (DIA), 427, 470
DeGaulle, Charles, 436
De Kooning, Wilhelm, 343
DeLoria, Vine, Jr., 505
Demonstration Cities and Metropolitan Develop-
        ment Act, 460–461
    see also Model Cities program
Desegregation, 338, 413–414
    and Nixon, 520–522
    Plessy v. Ferguson, 322, 388
Détente, 435–437, 522–523, 541, 544
Dewey, John, 337
Dewey, Thomas E., 297, 363–365, 371, 385
DeWitt, John, 299
Diem, Ngo Dinh, 404–405, 429–431
Dillon, Douglas, 423, 477
Dirksen, Everett, 370, 456
Dixiecrats, 364–365
Doctorow, E. L., 384
Doenitz, Karl, 310
Dohrn, Bernadine, 496
Dole, Robert, 542

Domestic Council (DC), 517–518
Douglas, Helen Gahagan, 370
Douglas, Paul, 402, 410
Douglas, William O., 383
Dreiser, Theodore, 400
DuBois, W. E. B., 300
Dulles, Allen, 394, 423, 427
Dulles, John Foster, 353, 388
    as secretary of state, 390, 393–394, 396, 399,
        403–409, 415
Dumbarton Oaks Conference, 287

Eagleton, Thomas, 536
Ecology, *see* Environment
Economic Opportunity Act, 456
Education
    and Cold War, 337–338
    Headstart program, 456, 518
    between 1945 and 1960, 314, 336–339
    after 1960, 456–457, 459–460, 473, 476, 484–
        488, 536–537
    and Vietnam war, 489–490
Egypt, 541, 544
Ehrlich, Paul, 505
Ehrlichman, John, 517–518, 531–532, 538, 540
Eichelberger, Clark, 280
Einstein, Albert, 304
Eisenhower, Dwight D.,
    and desegregation, 338, 413–414
    domestic policies of, 396–403, 410–415
    and education, 337
    and election of 1948, 364
    and election of 1952, 386–389
    and election of 1956, 410–421
    farewell address of, 327, 423
    foreign policy of, 389–396, 403–410, 415–418,
        506, 549–550
    and labor unions, 329
    and Rosenberg case, 379
Eisenhower Doctrine, 409
Elderly, 331, 457, 460–461
Election(s)
    of 1940, 273, 281
    of 1944, 297
    of 1948, 363–365
    of 1952, 328, 385–389
    of 1956, 411–412
    of 1960, 327, 415, 419–422
    of 1964, 457–459

of 1968, 474–480
of 1972, 531–533, 536
of 1976, 535, 542–543
Ellsberg, Daniel, 531, 537
Employment Act (1946), 329, 345
Endo case, 300
Energy crisis, 519–520, 541, 545
Energy Policy and Conservation Act, 541
Energy Policy Office, 519
Environment
    and the automobile, 315–316
    and ecological balance, 451, 505–506, 545
    and energy crisis, 519–520
    pollution of, 321, 324, 451
    and scientific technology, 315–317
Environmental Protection Agency (EPA), 520
Equal Employment Opportunity Commission
    (EEOC), 507
Equal Rights Amendment (ERA), 507, 511
Ervin, Sam, 522, 538
Espionage Act (1917), 298
European Defense Community (EDC), 376, 393–
    394
Export-Import Bank, 464

Fair Deal, 366–367
Fair Employment Practices Commission (FEPC),
    291, 300, 345, 363–364, 366, 387
Family
    and crisis of adolescence, 484–489
    between 1945 and 1960, 313, 319, 334–335
    in World War Two, 302–303
Family Assistance Plan (FAP), 518
Farmer, James, 443
Farming, *see* Agriculture
Faubus, Orval, 414
Federal Bureau of Investigation (FBI)
    and counterintelligence program, 472–473,
        493, 504
    domestic spying of, 458, 530, 549
    and Watergate, 532–533, 539
Federal Employee Loyalty program, 359
Federal Energy Administration, 519–520
Federal Housing Authority (FHA), 318
    and segregation, 322, 366
Federally Employed Women (FEW), 507
Feminism, *see* Women
Finletter, Thomas, 360
Flanders, Ralph, 401

Food, *see* Agriculture
Food for Peace, 425
Ford, Gerald, 539–543
Foreign Assistance Act, 426
Foreign Ministers conference (1945), 351
Formosa Resolution, 406–407, 409, 468
Franco, Francisco, 277, 377
Frankfurter, Felix, 384
Free Speech Movement (FSM), 489–490
Friedan, Betty, 438, 439, 507
Fuchs, Klaus, 381–382
Fulbright, J. William, 409, 469, 478
Fundamentalism, 497, 510–511

Gaines, Ernest J., 499
Gaither, Rowan, 414–415
Galbraith, John Kenneth, 331
Gallup, George, 365
Gavin, James A., 469
Gay Activists Alliance, 509
Geneva Accords
    1954, 404–405, 466
    1962, 465
Geneva conference, 407
Georgescu-Roegen, Nicholas, 505
GI Bill of Rights, 297, 313–314
Gillespie, Dizzy, 343
Ginsberg, Allen, 343, 506
Glenn, John, 451
Gold, Harry, 382–383
Goldwater, Barry, 447, 451, 456–459, 549
Gomulka, Wladyslaw, 408
Gonzales, Rudolpho "Corky," 502
Goodman, Paul, 489
Graham, Billy, 342–343
Gray Panthers, 499
Great Society, 456, 459–461, 473, 475–476, 520
Green Berets, 465
Greenglass, David, 382–383
Grissom, Virgil L., 506
Gruening, Ernest, 468
Guatemala, 395–396
Guevara, Ché, 465
Gunther, John, 321, 329, 339
Gutierrez, José Angel, 502

Hagan, Rober, 450
Halberstam, David, 431
Haldeman, H. R., 532–533, 538, 540

Hanrahan, Edward V., 493
Hargis, Billy James, 511
Harriman, Averill, 386, 411
Harris, Frank, 488
Hartz, Louis, 402
Hatch Act, 298
Hayden, Tom, 446
Hayek, Friedrich A., 343
Haynsworth, Clement, 522
Headstart, 456, 518
Health insurance, 460, 545
Hearst, Patricia, 498
Heilbrun, Carolyn, 508
Heller, Joseph, 504
Heller, Walter, 440, 455
Herberg, Will, 343
Hershey, Lewis B., 298, 300
Hickel, Walter, 526
Hickenlooper Amendment, 426
Higher Education Act, 460
Hiss, Alger, 365, 369, 381
Hitler, Adolph, 275–277, 279–283, 309–310
Ho Chi Minh, 350–351, 376, 403–404
Hoffa, Jimmy, 340
Hoffman, Abbie, 527–528
Hoffman, Julius, 527–528
Hofstadter, Richard, 402
Hollywood
    and anti-communism, 359–360
    and blacks, 301
    and Cold War, 295
    between 1945 and 1960, 319, 341–342
    after 1960, 505, 513
    and science fiction, 315, 389
    and World War Two, 288–289, 294–296
    and youth, 321, 335–336, 487
Homosexuals, 399, 533
    and gay liberation, 509–510
Hoover, Herbert C., 274–275
Hoover, J. Edgar, 359, 423, 472–473, 495, 530
House Un-American Activities Committee
    (HUAC), 359, 370
Housing
    and consumers, 326, 519
    federal aid to, 336, 410, 456, 460–461, 473,
        536
    segregation of, 322–323, 366, 442, 475–476,
        478
    and suburbs, 320–321

Hull, Cordell, 282, 308
Humphrey, George, 396, 412
Humphrey, Hubert H., 364
    and election of 1964, 458–459
    and election of 1968, 479–480
    and election of 1972, 533
    as senator, 401, 410, 419–420, 425
Hungary, uprising in, 409, 412
Hunt, E. Howard, 537
Huston, Tom, 530
Huston Plan, 530
Hutton, Bobby, 493, 495
Hydrogen bomb, 315, 368

Immigrants, 461
Immigration restriction, 461
Indian Claims Commission Act, 323
Indians, see Native Americans
Indochina, 368, 544
    and CIA, 430, 465–466, 470, 472, 477
    and Eisenhower, 403–405
    and Kennedy, 428–431
    and Korean War, 375–376
    and Truman, 350–351, 403–405
    and World War Two, 282–283, 350–351
    see also Cambodia; Laos; Vietnam war
Integration, racial, see Desegregation
Intelligence Evaluation Committee, 527, 530
International Military Tribunal,
    see Nuremberg trials
International Monetary Fund, 348
International Telephone and Telegraph (ITT),
    531–532
Iran, 352, 395, 544–545
Irish-Americans, 474, 534, 536
Isolationism, 275–279
Israel, 479, 511, 518, 541, 544
Italian Americans, 296, 534–536
Italo-Ethiopian War, 275–276

Jackson, George, 497
Jackson, Jesse, 511
Jackson, Robert H., 309
Jackson State, 527
Janeway, Elizabeth, 508
Japanese-Americans, 313–314, 332
    and World War Two, 299–300
Jaworski, Leon, 538
Jazz, in postwar era, 343

Jehovah's Witnesses, 299
Jenkins, Walter, 509
Jenner, Arthur, 397
Jewish Defense League (JDL), 499
Jews
    and election of 1968, 480
    and Israel, 511, 541
    and Rosenberg case, 382
    social conservatism of, 511–512
    and World War Two, 301
Job Corps, 456, 518, 536
John Birch Society, 399, 447, 457
Johnson, Lyndon Baines
    and civil rights, 456, 458–460, 475, 478
    domestic policy of, 455–457, 459–463, 472–473, 475–476
    and election of 1960, 420, 422
    and election of 1964, 457–459, 549
    and election of 1968, 478–480, 549
    and Latin America, 464–465
    and New Left, 472–473
    as senator, 392, 396–397, 401–402, 404, 409, 414
    as vice-president, 430, 433, 439, 442, 447
    and Vietnam war, 458–459, 466, 468–470, 477–480, 525–526, 548–549
Johnson Doctrine, 464–465
Jones, LeRoi, see Baraka, Imamu
Joplin, Janis, 487
Juvenile delinquency, see Youth

Kaufman, Irving, 379, 382–384
Keating, Kenneth, 434
Keats, John, 343
Kefauver, Estes, 386, 411
Kellogg-Briand Pact, 274
Kennan, George F., 351–352, 355, 399, 469
Kennedy, Edward M., 479, 526, 530, 544–545
Kennedy, John F.
    assassination of, 449–455
    and civil rights, 442–446
    and election of 1960, 327, 415, 419–422, 442
    foreign policy of, 425–437, 466, 549–550
    legacy of, 455–456, 512
    and New Frontier, 423–425, 437–445, 451, 483, 498, 506, 549
Kennedy, Robert F.
    assassination of, 474–475, 479, 496

as attorney general, 423, 435, 440, 442–444, 458, 473, 549
    and election of 1968, 474–475, 477–479
    as senator, 474
Kennedy, Robert Woods, 315
Kent State, 526
Kerner, Otto, 462
Kerner Commission, see National Advisory Commission on Civil Disorders
Kerouac, Jack, 343
Kerr bill, 397
Kerry, John, 497
Kesey, Ken, 487
Keyserling, Leon, 316
Khomeini, Ayatollah Ruhollah, 545
Khrushchev, Nikita, 407–409, 416–418
    and Kennedy administration, 428, 432–437
Killens, John Oliver, 498
Kim Il Sung, 373
King, Martin Luther, Jr.
    assassination of, 453, 475, 478–479, 496
    and civil rights movement, 413–414, 443–445, 460, 462, 475, 491, 501
    and FBI, 458, 473, 549
    and John Kennedy, 420, 443–445
    and Vietnam war, 493
Kinsey, Alfred C., 315, 335, 342, 399
Kissinger, Henry, 525, 527, 531, 541
Klein, Herbert, 529
Kleindienst, Richard, 529, 532, 538
Knowland, William, 393
Knox, Frank, 280
Knudsen, William, 290
Korean war, 371–376, 382
    blacks in, 366
    and economy, 326
    and election of 1952, 386, 388–389
    peace treaty of, 392–393
    and racism, 375
    and United Nations, 373–375
Korematsu case, 300
Kosygin, Alexei, 523
Krupp industries, 311
Ky, Nguyen Lao, 469

Labor unions, 519
    and blacks, 330
    and Cold War, 330
    and Communist party, 365

Labor Unions (*cont.*)
 and Eisenhower, 329
 between 1945 and 1960, 329–331, 346–347, 365
 and Truman, 329, 346–347, 365
 and Vietnam war, 496–497
 and women, 332–334
 and World War Two, 292–293
Landrum-Griffin Act, 331
Lane, Mark, 452–453
Lansdale, Edward G., 404
Laos, 428, 524
La Raza Unida, 502
Larson, Arthur, 402
Latin America, and LBJ, 464–465
Lawrence, D. H., 488
League of Nations, 274–276
League of United Latin Citizens (LULAC), 500
Leary, Timothy, 487
Lebanon, invasion of, 409–410
Le May, Curtis, 476–477
Lend-Lease Act, 281, 290, 348, 356, 362
Leonard, George, 514
Levitt, Arthur, 320
Levy, Howard, 490
Lewis, John, 445
Lewis, John L., 292–293, 346
Liebman, Joshua Loth, 342
Lindbergh, Charles, 280–281
Lippmann, Walter, 287, 299
Lodge, Henry Cabot, Jr., 420, 466
Lombardi, Vincent, 483, 512
London Naval Conference, 275
Louis, Joe, 339
Love, John, 519
Loyalty
 in Eisenhower administration, 397–402
 in Nixon administration, 512–513
 in Truman administration, 347, 359, 370–371, 397
 and World War Two, 298, 347
Lucas, Scott, 370
Ludlow, Louis, 279

MacArthur, Douglas, 373–375, 388
McCarran Internal Security Act, 370
McCarthy, Eugene, 477–479
McCarthy, Joseph R., 347, 382, 388–389, 509

and anti-communism, 370–371, 381, 385, 397, 400–402
McClellan, James L., 331
McCloskey, Paul, 531
McCloy, John, 477
McCone, John, 427
McCord, James, 537–538
McGovern, George
 and election of 1968, 479
 and election of 1972, 532–533, 536
McIntire, Carl, 511
MacLeish, Archibald, 400
McLeod, Scott, 397
McNamara, Robert
 in Johnson administration, 455, 468, 470, 477, 531
 in Kennedy administration, 423, 427, 431, 435, 440
McNaughton, John, 468
Maddox, Lester, 476
Mailer, Norman, 303, 342
Malcolm X, 445, 453, 492, 494
Malenkov, Georgi, 393
Manhattan Project, 304. *See also* Atom bomb
Mann, Thomas C., 464
Manson, Charles, 487
Mao Tse-tung, 362–363, 369, 376
Marcuse, Herbert, 343, 489
Marshall, George, 357–358, 388
Marshall, Thurgood, 338, 461
Marshall Plan, 326, 357–359, 361–362
Mayaguez incident, 542
Means, Russell, 504
Meany, George, 330, 496
Medicare, 459–460
Meeropol, Michael, 384
Meeropol, Robert, 384
Meredith, James, 444
Metallious, Grace, 342
Mexican-Americans, 332
 and Chicano culture, 499–502
 and election of 1976, 542
 and World War Two, 301–302
Mikulski, Barbara, 535
Miller, Arthur, 400
Miller, Walt, 415
Miller, William, 457, 459
Millis, Walter, 276
Mills, C. Wright, 343

Miranda v. *Arizona,* 476
Mississippi Freedom Democratic party, 458
Mitchell, John N., 522, 526, 532, 537, 540
Mitford, Jessica, 450
Model Cities program, 460–461, 518, 536
Molotov, Vyacheslav, 303, 358
Mondale, Walter, 542
Monroe, Marilyn, 342
Montoya, Malaguios, 501
Moon, Sun Myung, 514
Morgenthau, Henry, 308
Morrison, Jim, 487
Morse, Wayne, 397, 468
Moses, Grandma, 343
Mossadegh, Mohammed, 395
Movies, *see* Hollywood
Moynihan, Daniel P., 518, 520
Multinational corporations, 464, 518–519
Mundt, Karl, 370, 381
Munich conference, 279, 361
Murphy, Audie, 288–289
Muskie, Edmund, 480, 530–533
Mussolini, Benito, 275–277, 285, 309
My Lai massacre, 472, 529
Myrdal, Gunnar, 300–301

Nader, Ralph, 463
Nagy, Imre, 408
Namath, Joe, 488
Nasser, Gamal Abdul, 408–409
National Advisory Commission on Civil Disorders, 462–463
National Aeronautics and Space Administration (NASA), 415, 506
National Association for the Advancement of Colored People (NAACP), 300, 322, 330, 338
in 1960s, 491, 500–501, 521
National Committee for a Sane Nuclear Policy (SANE), 433
National Congress of American Indians (NCAI), 502
National Defense Education Act, 337
National Defense Research Committee, 304
National Indian Youth Council, 503
National Liberation Front (NLF), Vietnam, 430, 466–472, 478–479, 525, 527
National Organization for Women (NOW), 439, 507

National Security Act, 360
National Security Agency (NSA), 530
National Security Council (NSC), 360, 517, 548–549
National Women's Political Caucus, 439
Native Americans
and ecology, 504–505
between 1945 and 1960, 323, 332
and red power, 503–504
NATO, *see* North Atlantic Treaty Organization
Naturalization Act (1924), 299
Nelson, Donald, 289–290, 318
Neutrality Act(s)
1935, 276
1937, 277, 279
1939, 280, 282
New Frontier, 419–425, 439–442, 451, 475, 483, 506, 520
New Left, 445–446, 480, 489, 497–498, 508, 512, 533
and Johnson administration, 472–473
and Nixon administration, 527–530, 548
Newton, Huey P., 493
Niebuhr, Reinhold, 354, 367
Nimitz, Chester, 310, 371
Nine-Power Treaty, 274
Nixon, Richard M., 347, 370, 506, 530
and détente, 522–523
domestic policy of, 510–511, 517–520, 527–530, 536–537
and election of 1952, 386, 388
and election of 1960, 420–422
and election of 1968, 480
and election of 1972, 536
and New Left, 527–530, 548
and racial integration, 520–522
as vice-president, 401–402, 411–412, 416
and Vietnam war, 523–527, 529–530, 533, 536–537, 548
and Watergate, 531–533, 537–540, 549–550
Nixon Doctrine, 524
North Atlantic Treaty Organization (NATO), 357, 368, 376, 393–394, 436, 441
North Vietnam, *see* Vietnam war
Novak, Michael, 513
Nuclear power, 545. *See also* Atom bomb; Hydrogen bomb
Nuremberg trials, 307–312
Nye, Gerald P., 276

O'Brien, Larry, 531–532
Office of Economic Opportunity (OEO), 456, 461, 473, 518, 536, 540
Office of Management and Budget (OMB), 517
Office of Price Administration (OPA), 289, 293, 318–319
Office of Production Management (OPM), 289
Office of Strategic Services (OSS), 347, 350
Office of War Information (OWI), 298, 380
Office of War Mobilization (OWM), 289
Open Door Policy
    and Cold War, 348–350, 362
    and origins of World War Two, 274–275, 279, 283
    in World War Two, 285–286
Operation Phoenix, 472
Oppenheimer, J. Robert, 314–315, 400
Organization of American States (OAS), 363
Ornstein, Robert, 514
Orwell, George, 359
Osborn, Fairfield, 316
Oswald, Lee Harvey, 449, 452

"Pachucos," 301–302
Packard, Vance, 328
Pahlavi, Shah Mohammed Reza, 545
Palestinians, 479, 544
Panama Canal, 543
Panama Canal Treaty (1978), 543
Parker, Charlie, 343
Parks, Rosa, 413
Parsons, Talcott, 302
Peace Corps, 425
Peace and Freedom party, 495
Peale, Norman Vincent, 342
Pearl Harbor, 273, 282–283, 287, 289
Pentagon Papers, 470, 531
Pepper, Claude, 370
Perry, Ralph Barton, 312
Phillips, Kevin, 536
Plath, Sylvia, 336
Plessy v. Ferguson, 322, 338
Point Four program, 369
Polish-Americans, 534
Political Action Committee (PAC), 297
Political Association of Spanish-Speaking Organizations (PASO), 501
Pollock, Jackson, 343
Ponce, Miguel, 501

Pornography, 342, 510
Port Huron Statement, 446, 451
Potsdam conference, 303–304, 308, 351
Powers, Francis Gary, 417
Presley, Elvis, 336, 485
Progressive Citizens of America (PCA), 354
Progressive party (1948), 361, 364–365, 367
Project Independence, 520
Puerto Ricans, 323, 332
Pusey, Nathan, 491
Pyle, Ernie, 303

Race riots
    in 1960s, 461–462, 476, 478, 492, 520
    in World War Two, 301–302
Racial integration, see Desegregation
Radford, Arthur W., 403
Radio Free Europe (RFE), 391, 408
Randolph, A. Phillip, 291, 300
Rankin, Jeannette, 283
Rayburn, Sam, 397, 402, 439
Reagan, Ronald, 495, 542
Redl, Fritz, 302
Redstockings, 508
Reisman, David, 336, 343
Revenue Act (1942), 293
Rhee, Syngman, 373, 393
Rhodes, James, 526
Ribicoff, Abraham, 479
Richardson, Eliot, 538
Rickover, Hyman, 337
Ridgway, Matthew, 403–404, 477
Rio Pact, 363
Rivera, Tomás, 501
Rizzo, Frank, 534–535
Robbins, Tom, 514
Robinson, Jackie, 301, 339
Rockefeller, Nelson D., 420, 457, 497, 540
Rockwell, George Lincoln, 453
Rolling Stones, 487
Roosevelt, Franklin D., 547–548
    and home front, World War Two, 287–292, 298–299, 318
    and origins of Cold War, 349–350
    and origins of World War Two, 273–285
    and wartime diplomacy, 285–287, 301, 304, 350
    and wartime politics, 273, 296–297
Rosenberg, Ethel, 379–384, 400

Rosenberg, Julius, 379–384, 400
Rossi, Alice, 508
Rostow, Walt W., 430
Rothko, Mark, 343
Roybal, Edward, 501
Rubin, Jerry, 527–528
Ruby, Jack, 449–450, 452
Ruckleshaus, William, 538
Rudd, Mark, 496
Rusk, Dean, 423, 427, 455, 466
Russell, Richard, 364, 386, 404
Russo, Anthony, 531

Sadat, Anwar, 544
Sahl, Mort, 415
Salk vaccine, 410
SALT, see Strategic Arms Limitation Treaty
Savio, Mario, 490
Saypol, Irving, 382
Schafly, Phyllis, 511
Schine, G. David, 400
Schlesinger, Arthur M., Jr., 367, 400, 445
Science
    and Cold War, 327, 380–381
    between 1945 and 1960, 315, 343
    in World War Two, 314
Science fiction, in postwar society, 315
Scott, Hugh, 539
Seale, Bobby, 493, 527–529
Seeger, Pete, 445
Segregation, 322, 366
    of housing, 322–323, 366, 442, 475–476, 478
    see also Desegregation
Selective Service Act, 298
Senate Select Committee on Intelligence Activities, 542
Senior Informal Advisory Group, 477
Shaw, Anna Howard, 68, 143
Sheen, Fulton J., 342
Shelley v. Kraemer, 322
Shepard, Alan, 451
Shriver, R. Sargent, 456, 536
Shute, Nevil, 415
Simon, William E., 519
Sirhan, Sirhan, 479
Sirica, John, 538
Smith-Connally Labor Act, 292
Snyder, Gary, 343, 506

Sobell, Morton, 382–383
Soil Bank Act, 325
Sorensen, Theodore, 428
Southeast Asia, see Indochina; Vietnam war
Southeast Asia Treaty Organization (SEATO), 405–406
Southern Christian Leadership Conference (SCLC), 414, 444, 501
South Vietnam, see Vietnam war
Spanish Civil War, 277, 377
Sparkman, John, 386, 400
Special Investigations Unit (Plumbers, Watergate), 531
Spillane, Mickey, 371
Spock, Benjamin, 335, 527
Sports, 339, 483–484, 488–489
Stalin, Josef
    and Cold War, 349–351, 362, 391, 407
    and World War Two, 279, 282, 285–287, 303–304, 310
Standing Bear, Luther, 505
Stans, Maurice, 532
States Rights party, 364–365
Steinem, Gloria, 508
Stennis, John, 538
Stettinius, Edward, 287, 290
Stevenson, Adlai, 410, 416, 418, 420, 423, 434, 447
    and election of 1952, 386–389, 399
    and election of 1956, 411–412, 416
Stimson Doctrine, 275
Stimson, Henry L.
    and Cold War, 314, 351
    and World War Two, 275, 280, 290, 308
Strategic Arms Limitation Treaty (SALT) I, 523
Strategic Arms Limitation Agreement (SALT) II, 544
Strauss, Lewis, 400, 415
Streicher, Julius, 311
Student Non-Violent Coordinating Committee (SNCC), 445, 458, 462, 491, 493
Student Peace Union (SPU), 433
Students for a Democratic Society (SDS), 446, 489
Suburbs, see Cities, and suburbs
Subversive Activities Control Board, 370
Supply Priorities and Allocations Board (SPAB), 289
Symbionese Liberation Army (SLA), 498

Taft, Robert, 321, 353, 355, 357, 370, 391, 393, 400
  and election of 1948, 361, 363
  and election of 1952, 385–387
Taft-Hartley Act, 329–330, 347, 365–366, 387
Tate, Sharon, 487
Taylor, Glen, 364
Taylor, Maxwell, 430, 434, 469
Teamsters Union, 519
Teheran conference, 286
Television, 339, 341, 505
  and family, 334–335
Temporary Commission on Employee Loyalty, 347
Test Ban treaty, 436–437
Tet offensive, 471–472, 477
Thieu, Nguyen Van, 469
Thompson, William Irwin, 514
Thurmond, Strom, 364–365
Tidelands Oil Act, 397
Tijerina, Reies Lopez, 501–502
Tonkin Gulf Resolution, 466, 468
Truman, Harry S.
  and atom bomb, 314, 389
  domestic policy of, 321, 345, 359–360, 366–367, 370–371, 396–397, 460
  and economy, 319, 346–347
  foreign policy of, 348–363, 368–369, 371–377, 548
  and Indochina, 350–351, 403–405
  and labor unions, 329, 346–347, 365
  and race relations, 322, 347, 366–367
  and Rosenberg case, 380
  as senator, 281, 297
  and World War Two, 303–304
Truman Doctrine, 354–359, 361–362, 369
Twining, Nathan, 403
Tydings, Millard, 370

U-2 crisis, 417–418
Unions, see Labor unions
United Nations
  and Cold War, 352–353
  and Korean War, 373–375
  origins of, 286–287, 303, 350
Universal Military Training (UMT), 360
Urban Affairs Council, 518

Vance, Cyrus, 477
Vandenburg, Arthur, 353, 355–357
Vandenburg resolution, 368
Vargas, Roberto, 501
Vasquez, Richard, 501
Vesco, Robert, 532
Veterans Administration (VA), 318
Viet Cong, see National Liberation Front
Vietnamization, 524
Vietnam Moratorium Day, 526, 529
Vietnam Veterans Against the War (VVAW), 497, 537
Vietnam war
  antiwar protest against, 468–469, 474–479, 489–490, 520, 524–530, 533, 537, 548–549
  and Cambodian invasion, 528
  conclusion of, 541–542
  and education, 489–490
  and Eisenhower administration, 403–405
  and election of 1964, 457–459
  and election of 1972, 533
  and Johnson administration, 458–459, 466–472, 477–478, 480, 525–526, 548–549
  and labor, 496–497
  and Nixon administration, 523–527, 529–530, 533, 536–537, 548
Villa, Esteban, 501
Villa, Francisco, 131
Villarreal, José Antonio, 501
Vinson, Fred, 383
VISTA, see Volunteers in Service to America
Vogt, William, 316
Volunteers in Service to America (VISTA), 456
Voting Rights Act, 459–461

Wallace, George C., 510, 520, 536
  and election of 1964, 458
  and election of 1968, 475–477, 480
  and election of 1972, 533
  and primary of 1970, 532
Wallace, Henry A., 297, 353–355, 360–361, 363–365, 367
War Manpower Commission, 290–291
War on Poverty, see Office of Economic Opportunity
War Powers Act, 537
War Production Board (WPB), 289–290, 294, 318–319
War Relocation Authority, 300

Warren, Earl, 299, 338, 398–399, 452, 522
Warren Commission, 452
War Resources Board, 289
Warsaw Pact, 394
Washington Armaments Conference, 274–275
Watergate
    and campaign activities, 531–532
    and CIA, 532, 537, 539, 548–550
    cover-up of, 532–533, 537–540, 549
Watts, Alan, 343
Watts (Los Angeles) rebellion, 462, 473
Watzlawick, Paul, 514
Weathermen, the, 496
Weaver, Robert C., 322, 461
Webb, James E., 506
Welch, Robert, 447
Welles, Sumner, 287
Westmoreland, William, 470, 477
White, Edward H., 506
White, Walter, 366
White, William Allen, 280
Whyte, William H., 327, 343, 403
Williams, John, 499
Willkie, Wendell, 281, 297, 301
Wilson, Charles E., 318, 327
Women
    and election of 1972, 533
    and family, 334–335
    and labor, 332–334
    and women's liberation, 438–439, 506–508
    and World War Two, 291–292, 302–303
Women's Equity Action League (WEAL), 507
Wood, Grant, 343
Woodstock festival, 487
World Bank, 348, 470
World Disarmament Conference, 275
World War Two
    and blacks, 291, 300–301

    conclusion of, 303–304, 308, 351
    and conscientious objectors, 298–299
    diplomacy of, 285–287
    and family, 302–303
    and Hollywood, 288–289, 294–296
    and home front, 287–296, 298–303
    and Hoover, 274–275
    and labor, 255–256, 292–293
    loyalty issue, 298, 347
    and Open Door policy, 274–275, 279, 283,
        285–286
    origins of, 273–285
    postwar period, 348–359, 362
    and Stalin, 279, 282, 285–287, 303–304, 310
    and Stimson, 275, 280, 290, 308
    and women, 291–292, 302–303

Yalta conference, 286–287, 303, 350–351, 391
Yates case, 398
Yglesias, Helen, 384
Young, Andrew, 544
Youth
    and advertising, 485
    and blue-collar morality, 476, 511–512
    and crisis of adolescence, 335–336, 457, 484–
        488
    and election of 1972, 533
    and Hollywood, 321, 335–336, 487
    and juvenile delinquency, 321, 335
    radicalism of, 446, 476, 479, 520
    and World War Two, 301–302
Youth International party (Yippies), 527–528

Zero Population Growth (ZPG), 505
Ziegler, Ronald L., 532, 538
Zoot suit riots, 301–302
Zwicker, Ralph, 401

Student Evaluation of
TWENTIETH CENTURY LIMITED
(Noble/Horowitz/Carroll)

Your comments on this book will help us in developing other new textbooks and future editions of this book. Please answer the following questions and mail this page to:

College Marketing Services
Houghton Mifflin Company
One Beacon Street
Boston, MA 02107

1. What was your overall impression of the text? _____

_____

2. Did you find the book easy to read and understand?   ☐ Yes   ☐ No
If not, what problems did you have? _____

3. Did the illustrations clarify the text in a useful way? _____

_____

4. How would you rate the following features of the text?

	Excellent	Very good	Good	Fair	Poor
Biographical sketches	☐	☐	☐	☐	☐
Spotlights	☐	☐	☐	☐	☐
Photographs	☐	☐	☐	☐	☐
Writing style	☐	☐	☐	☐	☐
Interest level	☐	☐	☐	☐	☐
Treatment of minority groups	☐	☐	☐	☐	☐
Descriptions of historical events	☐	☐	☐	☐	☐
Completeness of coverage	☐	☐	☐	☐	☐

Feel free to comment on any of the above items. _____
_____

5. Which chapters were required reading for your class? _____
_____

6. Did you read any chapters on your own that were not required reading?
_____

7. Did your instructor assign any additional books for this course?
☐ Yes   ☐ No   If so, what were they? _____
_____

8. Did you find the book stimulating? Did you find yourself strongly agreeing or disagreeing with what you read?
_____

9. Did you feel that the book gave you a good grasp of American history in this century?
_____

10. Did you find the bibliographies useful for further reading and research?
_____

11. Do you have any suggestions that might help make this a better textbook?
_____

Name of your school: _____
Prerequisites for this course: _____
Number of students in the class: _____
Your age: _____
Your major: _____